THE FUTURE OF BUSINESS AND HUMAN RIGHTS

AF776782

THE FUTURE OF BUSINESS AND HUMAN RIGHTS

Theoretical and Practical Considerations for a UN Treaty

Edited by
Jernej Letnar Černič
Nicolás Carrillo-Santarelli

intersentia
Cambridge – Antwerp – Portland

Intersentia Ltd
Sheraton House | Castle Park
Cambridge | CB3 0AX | United Kingdom
Tel.: +44 1223 370 170 | Fax: +44 1223 370 169
Email: mail@intersentia.co.uk
www.intersentia.com | www.intersentia.co.uk

Distribution for the UK and Ireland:
NBN International
Airport Business Centre, 10 Thornbury Road
Plymouth, PL6 7PP
United Kingdom
Tel.: +44 1752 202 301 | Fax: +44 1752 202 331
Email: orders@nbninternational.com

Distribution for Europe and all other countries:
Intersentia Publishing nv
Groenstraat 31
2640 Mortsel
Belgium
Tel.: +32 3 680 15 50 | Fax: +32 3 658 71 21
Email: mail@intersentia.be

Distribution for the USA and Canada:
International Specialized Book Services
920 NE 58th Ave. Suite 300
Portland, OR 97213
USA
Tel.: +1 800 944 6190 (toll free) | Fax: +1 503 280 8832
Email: info@isbs.com

The Future of Business and Human Rights. Theoretical and Practical Considerations for a UN Treaty
© The editors and contributors severally 2018

The editors and contributors have asserted the right under the Copyright, Designs and Patents Act 1988, to be identified as authors of this work.

No part of this book may be reproduced, stored in a retrieval system, or transmitted, in any form, or by any means, without prior written permission from Intersentia, or as expressly permitted by law or under the terms agreed with the appropriate reprographic rights organisation. Enquiries concerning reproduction which may not be covered by the above should be addressed to Intersentia at the address above.

Image on cover © Jernej Letnar Černič, Sangat Ampil, Cambodia, January 2017

ISBN 978-1-78068-491-8
D/2018/7849/7
NUR 828

British Library Cataloguing in Publication Data. A catalogue record for this book is available from the British Library.

To Miren, my *bihotz*.
JLČ

To Carol, Mateo and Valeria, my joy and my Triforce of Wisdom
NCS

ACKNOWLEDGEMENTS

We would like to thank the contributors to this volume for their debates, original arguments, hard work and patience. We would also like to thank the Autónoma de Madrid University for providing the venue for the workshop on which this volume is based. We would like to give special thanks to Professor Carlos Esposito Massicci for his support and to Ann-Christin Maak-Scherpe of Intersentia for her invaluable help, comments and assistance.

CONTENTS

PART III. REGIONAL APPROACHES

ABOUT THE CONTRIBUTORS

Jernej Letnar Černič is Associate Professor of Human Rights Law at the Graduate School of Government and European Studies in Kranj (Slovenia) and Senior Research Fellow at the University Institute of European Studies – IUSE (Turin, Italy). He also holds a Diploma in Human Rights Law from the European University Institute and Diplome de droit international et de droit comparé des droits de l'homme (merit) from René Cassin Institut International des droits de l'homme. He completed his PhD in Human Rights Law in 2009 at the University of Aberdeen. He has published articles in Slovenian, English, Spanish, Italian, Romanian and Swedish, and his works have been cited in reports by the United Nations, European Union institutions and the Council of Europe and in academic studies from around the world.

Nicolás Carrillo-Santarelli is Associate Professor of International Law at the La Sabana University in Chía (Colombia) and a member of the International Law Association and its Study Group on Business and Human Rights. He holds a European PhD degree in International Law and International Relations from the Autónoma de Madrid University, and an LLM. in the protection of human rights from Alcalá University. He has published books and articles on the international legal responsibility of non-state actors and other international legal issues in English and Spanish.

Humberto Cantú Rivera is Professor in the School of Law of the University of Monterrey (Mexico). He is a member of the Research Centre on Human Rights and Humanitarian Law (CRDH) of Panthéon-Assas Paris II University (France), an expert advisor to the government of Mexico, before the Open-Ended Intergovernmental Working Group on human rights and transnational corporations and other business enterprises, and in the development of Mexico's National Action Plan on business and human rights, and is a member of the International Law Association's Study Group on Business and Human Rights. He is on the editorial board of the *Business and Human Rights Journal* and is editor of *Derechos humanos y empresas: reflexiones desde América Latina* (Inter-American Institute of Human Rights, 2017), the first book in Spanish on this topic with a regional perspective.

Larry Catá Backer is the W Richard and Mary Eshelman Faculty Scholar and Professor of Law & International Affairs at Pennsylvania State University. His research focuses on governance-related issues of globalisation and the constitutional theories of public and private governance, with a focus on institutional frameworks for public-private law governance systems. Current research includes corporate social responsibility, business and human rights, and the regulation of global production chains. His publications include *Lawyers Making Meaning* (2013) and *Signs in Law* (2014) (both with Jan Broekman), casebooks, *Elements of Law and the US Legal System* (2017), *Comparative Corporate Law* (2002), *Harmonizing Law in an Era of Globalization* (editor, 2007), and a number of articles and contributions to published collections of essays. Shorter essays on various aspects of globalisation and governance appear on his essay site, 'Law at the End of the Day', http://lcbackerblog.blogspot.com. He sits on the editorial/advisory boards of the *Business and Human Rights Journal* (CUP), International Private Law Book Series (Eurilink University Press), and *Iuris Dictio* (Universidad de San Francisco de Quito, Ecuador).

Surya Deva is an Associate Professor at the School of Law of City University of Hong Kong and a Member of the UN Working Group on Business and Human Rights. His primary research interests lie in business and human rights, India-China constitutional law, and sustainable development. He has published extensively in these areas, and has advised UN bodies, states, multinational corporations and civil society organisations on issues concerning business and human rights. His books include *Socio-Economic Rights in Emerging Free Markets: Comparative Insights from India and China* (editor) (2015); *Human Rights Obligations of Business: Beyond the Corporate Responsibility to Respect?* (co-editor with David Bilchitz) (2013); and *Regulating Corporate Human Rights Violations: Humanizing Business* (2012). He is one of the founding editors-in-chief of the *Business and Human Rights Journal* (CUP) and sits on the editorial/advisory board of the *Netherlands Quarterly of Human Rights*, and the *Vienna Journal on International Constitutional Law*. In 2014 Deva was elected a member of the Executive Committee of the International Association of Constitutional Law.

Daniel Fyfe has been working as Research and Advocacy Officer for FIAN International at their Geneva office before the UN Human Rights system since 2015. He holds a BSc in Political Science from the University of Geneva and a MSc in Human Rights from the London School of Economics and Political Science. He has been participating in the negotiations at the UN Human Rights Council on an international legally binding instrument on human rights and transnational corporations and other business enterprises, and supporting the activities of the Treaty Alliance. He additionally works towards mainstreaming States' extraterritorial obligations within UN Human Rights bodies and supports civil society advocacy work with the UN Treaty Bodies and Human Rights Council. He has undertaken research analysing the discourse within the United Nations on business and human rights issues, on the human rights impact of land grabbing by European corporate and financial entities in third countries and is currently researching the causes and human rights impacts of the transformation of peasant seed systems in West Africa. He has previously worked for human rights and trade union organisations.

Dan Kuwali is an Extraordinary Professor of International Law at the Centre for Human Rights, Faculty of Law, University of Pretoria; a Fellow of the Carr Center for Human Rights Policy, Harvard Kennedy School of Government; and a Distinguished Professor of Law and International Affairs, University of Lilongwe. He serves in the Malawi Defence Force where he heads the Directorate of Legal Services with the rank of Brigadier General. He is a Senior Fellow, R2P Scholars Network at the Canadian Centre for the Responsibility to Protect (Canada); correspondent, since 2007, of the *Year Book of International Humanitarian Law;* an editor of the *African Yearbook of International Humanitarian Law*; and an Associate Member of the Institute of International Humanitarian Law (IIHL), Sanremo (Italy). He is a former Research Fellow at the Danish Institute of International Legal Studies in Copenhagen; Marie Curie Researcher at the Grotius Centre, Leiden University (The Hague); Guest Researcher at the Nordic African Institute, Upscale (Sweden); and until recently, Senior Researcher at the Centre for Conflict Resolution, University of Cape Town. He worked as a Division Legal Advisor at the then United Nations (UN) Mission in the Democratic Republic of the Congo (MONUC). He is also the author of *Responsibility to Protect: Implementation of Article 4(h) Intervention* (2011); *Africa and the Responsibility to Protect* (2014), and *By All Means Necessary: Protecting Civilians and Preventing Mass Atrocities in Africa* (2017).

Chiara Macchi is a Postdoctoral Research Fellow at the Sant'Anna School of Advanced Studies (Pisa, Italy). She completed her PhD in 2015 with a thesis on corporate accountability for human rights abuses occurring in transnational supply chains. She teaches courses in business and human rights, and international human rights law. As an associate member of the Essex Business and Human Rights Project, she takes part in consultancy projects for governmental and non-governmental organisations on the human rights impacts of extractive and garment industries. In 2013 she was a consultant for the Italian Ministry for Economic Development and the Italian OECD National Contact Point producing a report on the business and human rights legal and policy framework in Italy. Her current research focuses on the right to water, corporate accountability for human rights violations, and conflict minerals policies.

Sara L Seck (LLB, Toronto; PhD, Osgoode Hall) is an Associate Professor with tenure in the Schulich School of Law at Dalhousie University (Nova Scotia, Canada), where she is a member of the Marine and Environmental Law Institute. Previously, she was a member of the Faculty of Law, Western University in Ontario (Canada). In September 2015 she received the Emerging Scholarship Award from the Academy of Environmental Law of the IUCN

(World Conservation Union) in recognition of her research contributions on sustainable mining and international environmental law. She is a Senior Fellow with CIGI's International Law Research Program, where her research examines business responsibilities for human rights affected by climate change. Seck is a member of the editorial board of the new *Business and Human Rights Journal* (CUP), a member of the International Law Association's Business and Human Rights study group, and a member of the governance committee of Columbia University's Teaching Business and Human Rights Forum.

Ago Shin-Ichi is a Professor of Law at Ritsumeikan University in Kyoto (Japan). Before joining Ritsumeikan University, he was Professor of Law at Kyushu and legal officer at the International Labour Organization (ILO). He received both his LLB. and LLM. from Tokyo University and obtained his Doctorat en Sciences Politiques from the University of Geneva. He worked with the ILO from 1980 to 1993 in its International Labour Standards Department before returning to academia. He has been a judge at the Asian Development Bank Administrative Tribunal since 2013 and a member of the ILO's Committee of Experts on the Application of Conventions and Recommendations since 2015. His latest publication (in English) is *Non-Economic Criteria in the Formulation of the World Trade Regime: From Social Clause to CSR*, (2012).

Manoj Kumar Sinha is Director of the Indian Law Institute. He obtained his doctorate in International Law from Jawaharlal Nehru University, and LLM. from the University of Nottingham and LLB. from the University of Delhi. In 1998 he attended the 29th session of the International Institute of Human Rights in Strasbourg (France). His areas of specialisation are human rights, constitutional law, international humanitarian and refugee law, international criminal law, international law and international institutions. He has published extensively in national and international law journals in the field of international law, international relations, constitutional law, international human rights, humanitarian and refugee laws. He is a member of the editorial boards of various well-known national and international journals.

Ana María Suárez Franco is currently the Permanent Representative of FIAN International before the UN Human Rights system in Geneva, as well as coordinator of the accountability work of the organisation. She holds degrees in law from the Universidad Javeriana (Bogotá), as well as in public policies from the Universidad de los Andes (Bogotá). She has received the titles LLM. from the University of Heidelberg and Doctor Juris from the University of Mannheim. Her main topics of research have been the Justiciability of Economic, Social and Cultural Rights and the monitoring of public policies related to the Human Right to Food. In this practice she has committed her work mainly to case advocacy, public policy monitoring, the gender dimension of the right to food and nutrition and extraterritorial obligations of human rights. She has participated in the process towards the adoption of the Maastricht Principles on the Extraterritorial Obligations of States, the process towards the adoption of an International Declaration on the Rights of Peasants, the discussions on human rights and transnational companies and has been supporting civil society work with the CESCR and CEDAW. She has been working closely with diverse communities affected by right to food and nutrition violations in diverse regions supporting them with case advocacy and co-construction of knowledge.

Tara L Van Ho is an Assistant Professor of Law at Aarhus University (Denmark). In addition to her BA in English, she holds a JD (Cincinnati, USA) and an LLM. in international human rights law and a PhD in law (both from Essex, UK). She has advised governments, intergovernmental organisations, and non-governmental organisations through her work with the Essex Business and Human Rights Project. She researches, writes and teaches on the intersection of human rights, humanitarian law, transitional justice, investment law, and business and human rights. Funding for her research came from the INTRALaw Centre in the Department of Law, Aarhus University.

INTRODUCTION

Jernej LETNAR ČERNIČ and Nicolás CARRILLO-SANTARELLI

What is the future of business and human rights? Would a treaty on business and human rights bring added value to the victims of corporate human rights abuses? The idea that it is important to adopt a treaty on business and human rights has been discussed in civil society and academic circles for quite some time. For instance, several years ago, two human rights law professors suggested that the proposed World Court of Human Rights had jurisdiction over corporations.[1] Aspirations on the codification and development of business and human rights standards came closer to become a legal reality after the formal proposal for the negotiation of a treaty on business and human rights was presented by the delegations of Ecuador and South Africa in the September 2013 session of the Human Rights Council, when they submitted a statement aimed at the adoption of 'an international legally binding instrument, concluded within the UN system, which would clarify the obligations of transnational corporations in the field of human rights, as well as of corporations in relation to States'.[2] Almost, a year later, on 26 June 2014, the UN Human Rights Council adopted, with a majority vote, a resolution establishing 'an open-ended intergovernmental working group on a legally binding instrument on transnational corporations and other business enterprises with respect to human rights; whose mandate shall be to elaborate an international legally binding instrument to regulate, in international human rights law, the activities of Transnational Corporations and Other Business Enterprises'.[3]

Yet, unlike other experiences that were propelled by civil society, such as the ones leading to the adoption of the Rome Statute of the International Criminal

---

1 J KOZMA, M NOWAK and M SCHEININ, *A World Court of Human Rights – Consolidated Statute and Commentary* (Vienna: Wissenschaftlicher Verlag, 2010).

2 Statement on behalf of a Group of Countries at the 24th Session of the Human Rights Council (September 2013). Available at: <https://business-humanrights.org/sites/default/files/media/documents/statement-unhrc-legally-binding.pdf >.

3 UN Human Rights Council, *Resolution on Elaboration of an international legally binding instrument on Transnational Corporations and Other Business Enterprises with respect to human rights* (Bolivia (Plurinational State of), Cuba, Ecuador, South Africa, Venezuela (Bolivarian Republic of)): draft resolution, A/HRC/26/L.22/Rev.1, 25.06.2014, para.1.

Court, the Convention on the Rights of the Child, or the Ottawa Convention on the Prohibition of the Use, Stockpiling, Production and Transfer of Anti-personnel Mines and on their Destruction, the project of a business and human rights treaty has neither been successful yet nor without controversy, even among its supporters. For starters, not everyone is convinced that the treaty should regulate direct corporate obligations, with some considering that it is preferable to focus on States to avoid what they perceive as risks emerging from an alternative approach. Others initially proposed to focus on transnational corporations and leave the responses to local businesses' negative impacts on human rights to domestic procedures, an idea that has been challenged by others on the basis that every corporation has the potential to affect human rights and thus deserves the same basic legal regulation.

These disagreements explain why, besides some general consideration, the proponents of a binding treaty on business and human rights have not fully agreed on what exactly the content of the proposed treaty should include, and why related questions are still being discussed by the aforementioned working group and those delegations and organisations that present observations to it.

Given the persistence of such debates, some consider that the time is not yet ripe for a treaty on business and human rights. Yet others argue that it is high time to clarify the issues and dispel doubts, especially given the potential benefits the treaty could provide: filling protection gaps, getting rid of the idea that some have that corporate responsibility is mostly or exclusively a social responsibility issue; strengthening legal actions based on hard law; and generating symbolic and expressive effects that reinforce the idea that corporate abuses are unacceptable, thus signalling to human rights defenders and authorities that direct protection can and must take place against them everywhere. Indeed, the adoption of a UN treaty on business and human rights would diminish debates on whether corporations have binding human rights obligations – something that is still questioned by some. That being said, some fear that adopting a treaty could forestall developing trends – yet adopting international instruments by no means implies foreclosing the evolution of international law.

This book is an edited volume in which different authors, both younger and established scholars, address the foregoing questions from the perspective of the potential adoption of a treaty on business and human rights, first proposed by Ecuador and South Africa. They engage them from different perspectives, including the following: is it convenient to adopt a treaty on business and human rights? If so, what should its content be like? Should it regulate direct corporate obligations? How should the issue of extraterritorial obligations be addressed? And how can the experiences of other international legal regimes and the developments in regional systems inform or contribute to the global debate on business and human rights? This is an important topic that merits legal analysis because it is undeniable that addressing corporate abuses is necessary insofar as the current approach has proven to have limits when it comes to protecting victims of corporate abuses and also because the transnational activities of businesses sometimes enable them to circumvent State controls. That being said, there are serious debates as to whether it is convenient to develop the normative protection from State abuses via treaty law or, alternatively, through customary law or exclusively in domestic law; and how to do so. The chapters in this volume reflect different positions on the debates about these questions, which in our opinion is an approach that is helpful for readers. In this regard, the editors encouraged the inclusion of contrasting opinions and analysis of the treaty question from the point of view of different dimensions.

The volume explores two overarching themes, the first one being whether a treaty on business and human rights, like the one proposed by Ecuador and South Africa, or alternative instruments that complement the Guiding Principles on Business and Human Rights, should be adopted, or whether, conversely, such adoption is unnecessary or inconvenient. A second general question is related to what specific normative aspects legal developments on the business and human rights field should deal with and how, including aspects on extraterritorial State obligations; the problems posed by the corporate veil in multinational groups; and whether direct corporate obligations ought to be regulated. Some chapters explore how regional systems, such as the Inter-American one, can contribute to paving the way for developments in the field; others examine how the lessons from other regimes of international law, such as international labour law or international environmental law, can shed light on convenient ways to deal with corporate threats to the enjoyment of human rights; and others examine the legal issues from a universal perspective, taking into account theoretical or civil society considerations, among others. Most of the authors of the chapters have been discussing these issues with each other since 26 June 2015, when a workshop organised by the editors of the volume took place at the Autónoma de Madrid University.[4]

Given the novelty of the topic, not much has been written about it in book form, although it is true that some journals and authors in peer-reviewed articles have explored the issues discussed in the volume. However, this edited volume, in which contrasting and differing opinions are discussed, and in which different dimensions of a potential treaty are explored, is an important contribution given the state of the discussions. This makes it useful for readers to have one volume in which they can find all of these studies. Concretely, while much has been

4 See Workshop on the potential Business and Human Rights Treaty, Autónoma de Madrid University, 26.06.2015 <https://business-humanrights.org/en/workshop-on-a-treaty-on-business-human-rights>, accessed 20.05.2017.

written in recent years on business and human rights,[5] none of the research agendas, apart from some recent articles,[6] has so far critically engaged with the proposal for the UN treaty on business and human rights. While there are books on non-State actors and human rights, and others specifically dealing with corporations, a book addressing the treaty debates is necessary. It critically assesses the proposal and focuses on its potential advantages and disadvantages. For this reason, the edited volume adopts a holistic approach when assessing *pro et contra* arguments for a binding UN treaty on business and human rights.

The volume itself is divided into four parts. Part I is devoted to the convenience and possibility of adopting a treaty on business and human rights.

The first chapter, written by Surya Deva, entitled 'Alternative Paths to a Business and Human Rights Treaty', examines the fact that in June 2014 the Human Rights Council adopted Resolution 26/9 to establish an open-ended intergovernmental working group (OEIWG) with a mandate 'to elaborate an international legally binding instrument to regulate, in international human rights law, the activities of transnational corporations and other business enterprises'. According to the author, this is the international-level attempt to regulate a legally binding instrument that may regulate human rights obligations of (transnational) corporations – the earlier two attempts being the 1990 UN Code of Conduct on Transnational Corporations and the 2003 Norms on the Responsibilities of Transnational Corporations and Other Business Enterprises with Regard to Human Rights. Repeated attempts to negotiate a legally binding international instrument should show that the other existing regulatory initiatives – including the Guiding Principles on Business and Human Rights – do not offer effective 'preventive' and/or 'redressive' remedies to the victims of corporate human rights abuses and that there is some merit in taking a stroll along the treaty road. Against this background, Deva advances two claims: first, the idea that a legally binding international treaty should not

5 SR Ratner 'Corporations and Human Rights: A Theory of Legal Responsibility' (2001) 111 *Yale Law Journal* 443–545. N Jägers, *Corporate Human Rights Obligations: In Search of Accountability* 75–95 (Antwerp: Intersentia, 2002); D Kinley, J Tadaki; 'From Talk to Walk: The Emergence of Human Rights Responsibilities for Corporations at International Law' (2004) 44 *Virginia Journal of International Law* 931, 961–93; N Stinnet, 'Regulating the Privatization of War: How to Stop Private Military Firms from Committing Human Rights Abuses' (2005) 28 *Boston College International & Comparative Law Review* 211, 217–18; D Weissbrodt, M Kruger, 'Current Development: Norms on the Responsibilities of Transnational Corporations and Other Business Enterprises with Regard to Human Rights' (2003) 97 *American Journal of International Law* 901, 919–20. L Van den Herik, J Letnar Černič, 'Regulating Corporations under International Law: from Human Rights to International Criminal Law and Back Again' (2010) 8 *Journal of International Criminal Justice* 725. For a contrary view, see JE Alvarez, 'Are Corporations "Subjects" of International Law?' (2011) 9(1) *Santa Clara Journal of International Law* 1.

6 OD Schutter, 'Towards a New Treaty on Business and Human Rights' (2016) 1(1) *Business and Human Rights Journal* 41–67; D Bilchitz, 'The Necessity for a Business and Human Rights Treaty' (2016) 1(2) *Business and Human Rights Journal* 203–27.

be seen in isolation or in competition with other regulatory tools, but rather as an additional tool, it being possible to consider the proposed treaty as a 'logical extension' of the Guiding Principles. Secondly, he argues in favour of the value of adopting a Declaration or another instrument as alternatives to a treaty if the latter is not adopted, since this can, among other things, reiterate the normative hierarchy of human rights and facilitate a 'continuous upward-downward' cycle of norm creation. Even if no treaty is finally adopted, the process of negotiating a treaty or adopting a Declaration may help to clarify some unresolved legal issues and make companies realise that human rights are no longer optional or negotiable rules of the game for doing business.

Thereafter, Nicolás Carrillo-Santarelli, in his chapter entitled 'A Defence of Direct International Human Rights Obligations of (All) Corporations', explores whether, as some authors and practitioners that oppose the regulation of direct corporate obligations under international human rights law argue, the adoption of such obligations is either unnecessary or problematic, in the sense that it could weaken or disrupt the existing human rights edifice. This is pertinent in the study of the proposed treaty on business and human rights insofar as even NGOs and others that favour its adoption debate whether the future treaty, if ever adopted, should regulate corporate obligations or merely focus on State responsibilities. To address this, the chapter explores whether it makes sense to hold corporations directly accountable, proposing that it does, given the fact that businesses can violate human rights. Responding to this, it asks whether expressive and implementation effects of a treaty or other hard law sources could contribute to changing corporate culture and increase the likelihood of protecting victims and responding to corporate abuses by means of creating lowest common denominators that prevent evasion of legal controls. The chapter also explores why neither symbolic nor practical reasons make direct corporate obligations inadvisable, because States will retain their responsibilities and they may actually be further clarified through the regulation of corporate responsibilities, thus even reinforcing protection from State omissions. Finally, the chapter argues that, in any case, corporate obligations currently exist in an implied way and in relation to peremptory norms, and that complementary obligations may fill gaps or further clarify the scope of corporate obligations.

Subsequently, Chiara Macchi's chapter critically reviews the main arguments put forward by the opponents of an international treaty on business and human rights, which generally relate to the possible scope of the instrument; to the political controversies it may raise; and to its potential ineffectiveness in advancing corporate accountability. The chapter starts by focusing on what could be the *ratione personae* and *ratione materiae* scope of the proposed treaty, responding to the critical stance adopted, among others, by the former United Nations Special Representative of the Secretary-General on the issue of human rights and transnational corporations and other business enterprises, John Ruggie. It then addresses the argument that dismisses the treaty route as impracticable based on the difficulties of engaging in a complex negotiation process. Then, the chapter responds to the genuine concern that the new instrument might prove to be ineffective without a credible enforcement and monitoring mechanism. The chapter concludes with a summary of the author's position, highlighting the potential added value of a binding treaty.

Part II of the volume is dedicated to critical analyses of a treaty on business and human rights.

Larry Catá Backer's chapter on 'Considering a Treaty on Corporations and Human Rights' considers what the process of negotiating the proposed instrument may reveal about the state of structuring governance frameworks for business and human rights, either through a treaty framework or under the UN Guiding Principles. For the author, that process reveals substantial normative and conceptual failures, and suggests some not inconsiderable successes. After setting the context of the debate around the treaty project, Section 2 of the chapter considers the normative and structural difficulties of the move toward a comprehensive business and human rights treaty. Section 3 then considers its benefits, both for the process of developing structures of governance for business and human rights, and its substance. Taken together, the author argues that even were the move towards a treaty to end in failure, the movement towards more robust governance of the human rights effects of economic activity will emerge more strongly.

Next, Tara L Van Ho presents a chapter in which she cautions against expanding international responsibility for human rights from States to corporations. Worried that direct obligations on businesses could undermine efforts at securing adequate and effective remedies, Van Ho invokes two UN treaties, those on corruption and against torture, to suggest that a better way forward may be to expand obligations to home States. The chapter reviews the process of getting to the treaty before considering how the current State-centric approach to human rights addresses the impacts of businesses. She then examines how the treaties on corruption and torture have expanded State responsibility beyond the territory State. She concludes that a traditional State-centric approach might do more for victims than expanding direct obligations to corporations.

Ana María Suárez Franco and Daniel Fyfe argue that calls for international regulation of the activities of transnational corporations (TNCs) are not recent. The systematic impunity resulting from corporate human rights abuses and the predominance of voluntary and inadequate standards as a response to this situation have led a large alliance of civil society organisations, social movements and campaign groups to join forces in calling for an international legally binding instrument. The Treaty Alliance was determinant in the adoption by the Human Rights Council in June 2014 of Resolution 26/9 establishing an OEIWG whose mandate is to elaborate an international human rights treaty to regulate the activities of TNCs and other business enterprises. Despite some

States hindering the process, the first two sessions of the OEIWG witnessed constructive deliberations on the content, scope, nature and form of the future treaty. The process has enabled Treaty Alliance members to articulate a wide array of positions regarding the treaty and has most importantly provided a vital international space for affected people and communities to voice their concerns and demonstrate the insufficiency of existing international standards. The chapter presents the reasons behind the demands from civil society for a binding instrument to regulate TNCs, the history of the Treaty Alliance, the adoption of Human Rights Council Resolution 26/9, the deliberations during the first two sessions of the OEIWG and the added values of the process perceived by the authors.

Part III of the volume is dedicated to regional and local experiences and demands in the light of business and human rights initiatives.

First, Humberto Cantú Rivera's chapter on 'Business and Human Rights in the Americas: Defining a Latin American Route to Corporate Responsibility' analyses the different developments taking place in the Americas from both a political and legal perspective in relation to the issue of business and human rights. First of all, the issue of the voting pattern during the adoption of Resolution 26/9 by Latin American States is discussed, followed by an analysis of the participation of Latin American and Caribbean (GRULAC) States in the first two sessions of the business and human rights treaty process. A second section analyses institutional developments taking place in the region, notably regarding the work undertaken in the Organization of American States, before addressing the work undertaken in the Inter-American Human Rights System to contribute indirectly to the crystallisation of regional business and human rights standards.

Manoj Kumar Sinha's chapter on 'The Applicability of Human Rights Treaties to Business Enterprises: A Case Study of India' examines the impact of globalisation on human rights in India. He argues that States have a duty to ensure that private corporations respect human rights. They must create the legal and institutional framework to enforce this obligation. The treaty bodies are the main international accountability and monitoring mechanism for the implementation of the treaties. He makes an attempt to see whether the government of India has taken adequate steps to implement the UN Guiding Principles on Business and Human Rights. This chapter will also analyse some of the important decisions delivered by the Supreme Court and various High Courts of India and how these judgments have ensured that the rights of vulnerable sections of society should not be violated by TNCs.

Dan Kuwali's chapter on 'Reckless Business: Afropolitan Views on Corporate Accountability for Atrocities', focuses on specific challenges faced by victims in Africa and explores whether the proposed international legally binding instrument on corporate human rights responsibility is necessary; and if so, how it can strengthen corporate accountability for violations of human rights.

The global nature of multinational companies, and their political and financial power, pose challenges for prevention of violations, protection of human rights and provision of reparations. Current law and policy does not adequately address these particular obstacles. The point made in this chapter is that since many States do not have the capacity to censure influential corporations and that governments and businesses alike have failed to make the Guiding Principles effective, accountability should be mandated by an international legal regime as opposed to self-regulatory mechanisms. The proposed treaty should therefore reinforce existing mechanisms and require States to enact legislation to encourage responsible business practices that respect human rights and prevent violations, provide adequate safeguards to protect against business-related rights abuses, and ensure victims seek effective redress.

Jernej Letnar Černič's chapter studies and analyses European approaches to business and human rights, including European perspectives on the proposed UN treaty on business and human rights. His chapter first outlines and analyses the European approach to the UN Guiding Principles on Business and Human Rights and to the Treaty Initiative. It thereafter analyses the European approach, from the position of both the European Union and the Council of Europe concerning the perspective of global divisions in business and human rights, trying to draw out lessons concerning the understanding of current developments in Europe. Equipped with this knowledge, his chapter goes on to examine how to move forward in business and human rights and argues that there exist strong legal and moral grounds for European support of the Business and Human Rights Treaty Initiative.

Finally, Part IV explores elements from different branches of international law and the positions of States that can inspire treaty initiative efforts.

The opening chapter of this part is written by Ago Shin-Ichi, and is entitled 'A Convention or a Recommendation? The Experience of International Labour Legislation'. In it he argues that we may learn a lesson from the International Labour Organization's (ILO) experience when we examine the question of whether or not to adopt a binding instrument for the legal regulation of business and human rights. After recapitulating the historical background for the ILO to adopt both Conventions and Recommendations, recognising the difficulties faced by the ILO Tripartite Declaration on Multinational Enterprises, and observing the practice of the ILO in the supervision of its standards in general, the chapter concludes that a well-functioning follow-up mechanism is most important to make the original instrument viable, regardless of whether the original one is legally binding or not.

The purpose of the final chapter of the volume, written by Sara L Seck, is to illuminate the environmental dimensions of the business and human rights treaty debate. First, drawing upon case studies presented in a 2014 Amnesty International report on corporate abuse and the right to remedy, it will be illustrated that each Amnesty case study can be characterised as an example of transnational environmental harm in which corporate power based in a rich State externalises environmental harms onto a poor country and its people. This is done either through the transfer of potentially hazardous industrial technologies through foreign direct investment, or through the actual movement of hazardous waste. Second, the chapter examines the work of the International Law Commission (ILC) on transboundary harm and hazardous activities, which resulted in draft prevention Articles in 2001, and draft loss allocation Principles in 2006. This body of ILC work provides insights into what may be required for an effective regime to prevent and remedy the kinds of problems identified in the Amnesty case studies.

PART I

THE CONVENIENCE AND POSSIBILITY OF ADOPTING A TREATY ON BUSINESS AND HUMAN RIGHTS

ALTERNATIVE PATHS TO A BUSINESS AND HUMAN RIGHTS TREATY

Surya DEVA

1. INTRODUCTION

Despite significant opposition from developed countries,[1] the United Nations (UN) Human Rights Council in June 2014 adopted Resolution 26/9 to establish an open-ended intergovernmental working group (OEIGWG) with a mandate 'to elaborate an international legally binding instrument to regulate, in international human rights law, the activities of transnational corporations and other business enterprises'.[2] The mandate of the OEIGWG 'shall be to elaborate an international legally binding instrument to regulate, in international human

[1] The following 14 countries voted against the resolution: Austria, Czech Republic, Estonia, France, Germany, Ireland, Italy, Japan, Montenegro, Republic of Korea, Romania, Republic of Macedonia, UK, and USA.

[2] Human Rights Council, 'Elaboration of an international legally binding instrument on transnational corporations and other business enterprises with respect to human rights', A/HRC/RES/26/9 (26.06.2014), para. 1, <http://ap.ohchr.org/documents/dpage_e.aspx?si=A/HRC/RES/26/9> (accessed 10.10.2017).

rights law, the activities of transnational corporations and other business enterprises'.[3] The first two sessions of the OEIGWG were to be 'dedicated to conducting constructive deliberations on the content, scope, nature and form of the future international instrument'.[4] The OEIGWG held its first session in July 2015 in Geneva,[5] and the second session in October 2016.[6]

Out of several themes that emerged from the first session of the OEIGWG,[7] the one thing which stood out was that developed countries – where most of the transnational corporations (TNCs) have been incorporated historically[8] – did not want to see any binding international rules in the business and human rights (BHR) field,[9] despite their full support for the corporate responsibility to respect human rights under the Guiding Principles on Business and Human Rights (GPs). Most of these countries did not participate in the first session or boycotted it after the first day.[10] The developed countries' non-participation in the first sessions, as well as their general opposition to the current treaty process, embodies several strands: that the 'footnote' of Resolution 26/9 arbitrarily excludes local/domestic companies from the purview of the treaty; that a discussion about the treaty will break the consensus built by the adoption of the GPs; and that the treaty discussion will divert attention from implementing the GPs through national action plans or otherwise.

The European Union and some other developed countries participated in the second session of the OEIGWG held in October 2016 only after a 'footnote' in the programme of work provided that the discussions in the session 'can include

---

3 Ibid.

4 Ibid, para. 2.

5 Human Rights Council, 'First session of the open-ended intergovernmental working group on transnational corporations and other business enterprises with respect to human rights', <http://www.ohchr.org/EN/HRBodies/HRC/WGTransCorp/Pages/Session1.aspx> (accessed 13.03.2017).

6 Human Rights Council, 'Second session of the open-ended intergovernmental working group on transnational corporations and other business enterprises with respect to human rights', <http://www.ohchr.org/EN/HRBodies/HRC/WGTransCorp/Pages/Session2.aspx>. See C Lopez, 'Struggling to Take Off?: The Second Session of Intergovernmental Negotiations on a Treaty on Business and Human Rights' (2017) 2(2) *Business and Human Rights Journal* 365. The third session is scheduled to take place on 23–27 October 2017.

7 For instance, the number of civil society organisations (CSOs) in the room was more than the number of state representatives: this was reflective of the increasingly important role of non-state actors in creating international norms. The need for establishing a normative hierarchy of human rights over international trade/investment law and improving access to effective remedies were the other two noticeable themes at the first session held in July 2015.

8 This dynamic has been changing slightly in recent years with the emergence of TNCs from the Global South on the world stage.

9 The author, who was invited by the OEIGWG as an independent expert to speak at the first session, can say this based on his observation of the proceedings as well as his conversations with various stakeholders. See also C Lopez and B Shea, 'Negotiating a Treaty on Business and Human Rights: A Review of the First Intergovernmental Session' (2015) 1 *Business and Human Rights Journal* 111.

10 Some such countries though kept a close eye on the treaty discussion.

TNCs as well as all other business enterprises'.[11] This participation was, however, mostly symbolic and superficial, rather than the sign of a deep engagement with, or support for, the current treaty process.

Considering the continued and consistent resistance of developed countries to developing legally binding international rules and their disengagement with the current treaty process, it is uncertain whether the OEIGWG will be able to come up with an agreeable draft of the BHR treaty or whether such a draft would get the support of a reasonable number of states (including from the Global North). In such a scenario, should the idea of negotiating a BHR treaty be discarded as a far-fetched dream, or should other alternative paths for creating international norms be considered? This chapter can be seen as an attempt to explore such alternative paths as Plan B, if the current roadblock continues amidst developed countries' opposition to the proposed treaty. These alternative paths are different from the range of conventional alternatives canvassed by scholars for a potential BHR treaty.[12]

The chapter begins in Section 2 by offering a brief analysis of the UN engagement with the treaty process so far. Drawing an analogy with the phenomenon of tidal cycles, I propose that there have been at least three high tides (including the current treaty process) pushing for some kind of binding international norms for TNCs. While the triggering event, nature and focus of these high tides have been different, I point out why the current high tide has somewhat better chances of success in adopting a binding international instrument as compared to the previous two attempts.

Section 3 then outlines two alternative paths towards an international instrument on the human rights obligations of business. The first path is informed by the evolution of the International Bill of Rights: the adoption of the Universal Declaration of Human Rights (UDHR) was followed by two binding instruments, the International Covenant on Civil and Political Rights (ICCPR) and the International Covenant on Economic, Social and Cultural Rights (ICESCR). Therefore, in the BHR field too, we may start by drafting a UDHR-like Declaration on the Human Rights Obligations of Business (BHR Declaration).[13] Subsequently, an attempt should be made to negotiate a number

---

11 Human Rights Council, 'Second session of the open-ended intergovernmental working group on transnational corporations and other business enterprises with respect to human rights', <http://www.ohchr.org/EN/HRBodies/HRC/WGTransCorp/Session2/Pages/Session2.aspx> (accessed 13.03.2017).

12 See, for example, O De Schutter, 'Towards a New Treaty on Business and Human Rights' (2015) 1 *Business and Human Rights Journal* 41; D Cassel and A Ramasastry, *White Paper: Options for a Treaty on Business and Human Rights* (May 2015), <https://business-humanrights.org/sites/default/files/documents/whitepaperfinal%20ABA%20LS%206%2022%2015.pdf> (accessed 13 March 2017).

13 It is also possible to conceive this Declaration as applying to all non-state actors, not merely companies.

of treaties covering specific sets of rights and/or targeting specific sets of rights holders (e.g., women, children, indigenous peoples, migrant workers).

The second path, which will operate outside the UN process, will be to form a 'coalition of the willing' multi-stakeholders such as states, civil society organisations (CSOs), academics, lawyers, policy makers and business leaders and then draft an international instrument articulating the human rights obligations of business enterprises. This proposal is rooted in the idea of the 'bottom-up' creation of international norms by forging a partnership among the relevant and willing multi-stakeholders.

The chapter ends with some concluding observations in Section 4 about the current regulatory trajectory in the BHR field. In particular, I will suggest that the current cleavage between the GPs and the proposed treaty is reflective of a false dichotomy between voluntary and binding regulations. Both voluntary and binding initiatives are required at national as well as international levels, and national action plans to implement the GPs, *if* drawn up properly, could help in bridging this unfortunate divide.

This chapter does not go into questions about whether a BHR treaty is needed or whether it will serve any useful purpose – rather, it takes the need as well as the usefulness of such an instrument as a starting point. The repeated demands and attempts at the UN level for a binding international instrument to impose human rights obligations on TNCs also point towards some value in agreeing on some legally binding rules of the game for business at the international level. Moreover, academics have not only proposed ways to overcome theoretical, practical or structural difficulties highlighted in negotiating the BHR treaty,[14] but have also made a positive case for why such a treaty is needed.[15]

One more terminological clarification before I proceed further: it is crucial that we understand the term 'human rights' in relation to corporate obligations in a wide sense so as to encompass not only human rights, but also labour rights and environmental rights. A reference to human rights should also include a reference to instruments that elaborate on the human rights of specific vulnerable groups such as children, women, indigenous peoples, minorities, people with disabilities, migrant workers and refugees.

---

14 See, for example, J Ruggie, 'A UN Business and Human Rights Treaty? An Issue Brief' (28.01.2014), <http://business-humanrights.org/media/documents/ruggie-on-un-business-human-rights-treaty-jan-2014.pdf> (accessed 10.02.2014); P Muchlinski, 'Beyond the Guiding Principles? Examining New Calls for a Legally Binding Instrument on Business and Human Rights' (15.10.2013), <http://www.ihrb.org/commentary/guest/beyond-the-guiding-principles.html> (accessed 20.02.2014).

15 See, eg, D Bilchitz, 'The Necessity for a Business and Human Rights Treaty' (2016) 1 *Business and Human Rights Journal* 203; S Deva, 'The Human Rights Obligations of Business: Reimagining the Treaty Business', <https://business-humanrights.org/sites/default/files/media/documents/reimagine_int_law_for_bhr.pdf> (accessed 10.07.2016). See also S Deva and D Bilchitz (eds), *Building a Business and Human Rights Treaty: Context and Contours* (Cambridge: Cambridge University Press, 2017).

2. STATE OF THE ART: BINDING CORPORATE OBLIGATIONS AND THE 'THREE HIGH TIDES'

The relevance and the exact role of international law in regulating human rights abuses by TNCs has been on the discussion table at the UN (and other fora) since the early 1970s.[16] The debate on this issue, which remains far from settled, could be compared to tides, with the momentum of negotiating a binding international instrument going up and down. At least three high tides are discernible during this period. The three high tides differ from each other in terms of the driving force, the focal point and the key participating actors.

2.1. FIRST HIGH TIDE

The first high tide was represented by the 1990 draft of the United Nations Code of Conduct on Transnational Corporations (Code).[17] However, the momentum for this tide began in the early 1970s when the UN's Economic and Social Council requested the Secretary General to constitute a Group of Eminent Persons to study the impact of TNCs on the development process (especially in developing countries) and international relations.[18] The Group recommended that the UN established a Commission on TNCs, which, among other things, should formulate a code of conduct for them.[19] This recommendation led to the establishment of the Commission on Transnational Corporations and the United Nations Centre on Transnational Corporations (UNCTC) in 1974. The quest to establish an agreeable code under the aegis of these UN bodies continued for more than a decade, but the 1990 Draft Code could not be adopted due to significant differences between developed and developing countries.[20] Soon after, the negotiations on the Code were suspended, and the Commission

---

16 See T Sagafi-Nejad and J Dunning, *The UN and Transnational Corporations: From Code of Conduct to Global Compact* (Bloomington, IN: Indiana University Press, 2008); D Bilchitz and S Deva, 'The Human Rights Obligations of Business: A Critical Framework for the Future' in D Bilchitz and S Deva (eds), *Human Rights Obligations of Business: Beyond the Corporate Responsibility to Respect?* (Cambridge: Cambridge University Press, 2013) 1; K Hamdani and L Ruffing, *United Nations Centre on Transnational Corporations: Corporate Conduct and the Public Interest* (London: Routledge, 2015).

17 'Draft Code on Transnational Corporations' in UNCTC, *Transnational Corporations, Services and the Uruguay Round*, Annex IV, p 231 (1990).

18 P Muchlinski, *Multinational Enterprises and the Law* (Oxford: Blackwell Publishing, 1999) 593.

19 Ibid.

20 Ibid, 593–97.

and the UNCTC were dismantled.[21] Thus, the first high tide started receding around 1992–93.

During the first phase, the proposed code sought to deal with *both* responsibilities (linked to TNCs' activities) and rights (linked to TNCs' treatment by host states). In fact, there was an apparent clash between the push for recognising the 'rights' and 'responsibilities' of TNCs. For obvious reasons, whereas developing countries were more interested in solidifying their right to regulate TNCs and outlining the responsibilities of TNCs, developed countries were keener to secure a level playing field for their TNCs operating in emerging markets. Consistent with the then prevailing view of international law, states were the principal actors which pushed for such a binding code and negotiated its content.

It is worth noting that human rights were not the primary concern of the 1990 Draft Code. This perhaps contributed to the former Special Representative of the Secretary General on human rights and transnational corporations and other business enterprises (SRSG) asserting that '[h]uman rights did not feature' in the code formulation initiative of this phase.[22] This assertion does not seem to be entirely correct though, because paragraph 14 of the Draft Code had stated that TNCs '*shall respect human rights* and fundamental rights and fundamental freedoms in the countries in which they operate' (emphasis added).[23] However, the main regulatory focus of binding instruments was set to change during the next two tides. As we will see, there has been almost no discussion about the rights of TNCs in such binding instruments: this was perhaps not needed because TNCs were able to secure their rights through bilateral investment treaties (BITs), which have mushroomed since the mid-1990s.[24]

2.2. SECOND HIGH TIDE

The second high tide was reflected in the approval of the Norms on the Responsibilities of Transnational Corporations and Other Business Enterprises with Regard to Human Rights (Draft Norms)[25] by the Sub-Commission on the

---

21 Economic and Social Council, 'Integration of the Commission on Transnational Corporations into the Institutional Machinery of the United Nations Conference on Trade and Development', Resolution 1994/1 (14.07.1994).

22 J Ruggie, 'Business and Human Rights: The Evolving International Agenda' (2007) 101 *American Journal of International Law* 819.

23 'Draft Code on Transnational Corporations' in UNCTC, *Transnational Corporations, Services and the Uruguay Round* (1990), Annex IV, p 231 at 234, para. 14. See also paras 25, 37 and 41–43.

24 See D Bishop, J Crawford and M Reisman, *Foreign Investment Disputes: Cases, Materials and Commentary* (The Hague: Kluwer Law International, 2005) 1–10.

25 Sub-Commission on the Promotion and Protection of Human Rights, Norms on the Responsibilities of Transnational Corporations and Other Business Enterprises with Regard to Human Rights, UN Doc E/CN.4/Sub.2/2003/12/Rev.2 (13.08.2003).

Promotion and Protection of Human Rights in 2003.[26] This tide, too, retracted quickly because the Human Rights Commission did not approve the Norms and then the SRSG decided to discard the Norms altogether.

The roots of the second tide could be traced to August 1998 when the Human Rights Commission's Sub-Commission on the Promotion and Protection of Human Rights decided to establish a five-member Working Group on the Working Methods and Activities of Transnational Corporations.[27] While the Working Group was still mapping its future course, on 31 January 1999 the then UN Secretary General Kofi Annan at the World Economic Forum in Davos proposed the idea of a Global Compact, originally consisting of nine principles in the areas of human rights, labour and the environment.[28] This was a clear attempt on the part of the UN to re-engage with non-state actors and push for a 'public-private' partnership to make globalisation more inclusive and equitable.[29] The Global Compact, which was officially launched in 2000 and became popular with corporations, received significant criticism from human rights advocates for being too vague and providing nothing more than voluntary moral guidance to companies.[30]

Against the backdrop of these criticisms, the Working Group drafted detailed substantive provisions as to the human rights responsibilities of TNCs and other business enterprises and also incorporated provisions for the implementation of these responsibilities.[31] In mid-2003 it presented to the Sub-Commission the final draft of the Norms.[32] The Draft Norms unsurprisingly attracted criticism from several leading TNCs and business organisations. The Commission on Human Rights in its 2004 session resolved, much to the satisfaction of the business community, that the Draft Norms had 'no legal standing'.[33] The Commission then, in its 2005 session, requested the UN Secretary General to appoint an SRSG,[34] who felt the need to discard the Draft Norms for their conceptual flaws

---

26 Sub-Commission on the Promotion and Protection of Human Rights, Resolution 2003/16 (13.08.2003), E/CN.4/Sub.2/2003/L.11, 52–55.

27 D Weissbrodt and M Kruger, 'Norms of the Responsibilities of Transnational Corporations and Other Business Enterprises with Regard to Human Rights' (2003) 97 *American Journal of International Law* 901, 903–04.

28 The tenth principle (anti-corruption) was added to the Global Compact in 2004.

29 S Deva, 'Global Compact: A Critique of the UN's "Public-Private" Partnership for Promoting Corporate Citizenship' (2006) 34 *Syracuse Journal of International Law and Commerce* 107.

30 J Nolan, 'The United Nations' Compact with Business: Hindering or Helping the Protection of Human Rights?' (2005) 24 *University of Queensland Law Journal* 445; Deva, n 29.

31 See Weissbrodt and Kruger, n 27, 903–07.

32 Sub-Commission on the Promotion and Protection of Human Rights, Norms on the Responsibilities of Transnational Corporations and Other Business Enterprises with Regard to Human Rights, UN Doc E/CN.4/Sub.2/2003/12/Rev.2 (13.08.2003).

33 Commission on Human Rights, Agenda Item 16, E/CN.4/2004/L.73/Rev.1 (16.04.2004), para. (c).

34 Commission on Human Rights, 'Promotion and Protection of Human Rights', E/CN.4/2005/L.87 (15.04.2005).

and divisive nature and build a new framework underpinned by 'principled pragmatism'.[35] Therefore, the second high tide also receded without fulfilling the promise of delivering a human rights instrument that imposes binding obligations on TNCs.

In comparison with the first high tide, the primary focus of the second high tide – which lasted for a much shorter period than the first one – was on cataloguing the human rights responsibilities of TNCs and other business enterprises. As noted above, the omission of TNCs' rights from the drafting debate during this period could be explained by the proliferation of BITs and the establishment of the World Trade Organization (WTO) in 1995. These two developments allowed TNCs to demand – directly or through their home states – fair and equal treatment from host states as well protection of their investment under the WTO or investor–state dispute settlement mechanism. It did not, therefore, remain equally critical to catalogue the rights of TNCs. As compared to the first high tide, the second high tide also provided good evidence of the emerging importance of non-state actors in moulding the contours of international law: TNCs, business organisations and NGOs played an active role in mobilising opinion for or against the Draft Norms (as well as in informing the content of the SRSG's framework). In a way, this is consistent with a future role of non-state actors in creating international law from the 'bottom up',[36] one of the alternative approaches articulated later in this chapter.

2.3. THIRD HIGH TIDE

The third ongoing high tide began in September 2013 when the Republic of Ecuador made a statement at the 24th Session of the Human Rights Council stressing the importance of a legally binding international framework.[37] Apart from the support of at least 85 states, this Ecuadorian initiative is supported

35 Commission on Human Rights, 'Interim report of the Special Representative of the Secretary-General on the issue of human rights and transnational corporations and other business enterprises', E/CN.4/2006/97 (22.02.2006), paras 55–69 and 81. 'Principled pragmatism' means 'an unflinching commitment to the principle of strengthening the promotion and protection of human rights as it relates to business, coupled with a pragmatic attachment to what works best in creating change where it matters most – in the daily lives of people'. Ibid, para. 81.

36 See S Deva, 'Multinationals, Human Rights and International Law: Time to Move beyond the "State-Centric" Conception?' in J Letnar Černič and T Van Ho (eds), *Human Rights and Business: Direct Corporate Accountability for Human Rights* (The Hague: Wolf Legal Publishers, 2015) 27.

37 Republic of Ecuador, 'Statement on behalf of a Group of Countries at the 24th Session of the Human Rights Council' (September 2013), <http://business-humanrights.org/media/documents/statement-unhrc-legally-binding.pdf> (accessed 02.02.2014).

by hundreds of CSOs[38] which have since then formed a Treaty Alliance.[39] This resurgence in the demand for an international binding instrument came quite soon after the unanimous endorsement of the GPs by the Human Rights Council in June 2011 and the subsequent wide uptake of the GPs by states, international institutions, businesses and CSOs alike.[40] In fact, the fear that an attempt to negotiate a treaty will fracture the highly prized 'consensus' built around the GPs is one of the arguments raised against the utility of the current treaty process.[41]

It is difficult to predict at this stage how long this tide will last and what (if anything) it might deliver. However, looking at the developments so far – including the stand taken by states during the first two sessions of the OEIGWG held in July 2015 and October 2016 – it appears that the divisions that were visible between developed and developing countries during the first high tide are resurfacing again. All the developed countries (invariably from the Global North) voted against Resolution 26/9, while all of its supporters were developing countries from the Global South. Even after the resolution was passed, hardly any countries from the Global North participated in the OEIGWG's first session.[42] While the purported exclusion of local business enterprises from the scope of the treaty was the main projected reason for such disengagement (the 'footnote hurdle'), in reality the opposition to any binding international instrument runs deeper. The opposition seemingly goes to the very appropriateness of international law in imposing binding human rights obligations on all types of business enterprises.

One reason for the divide among states is that their political positions in the 21st century are still being informed by the economic conditions that prevailed in the second half of the 20th century. Developed countries did not favour a binding international instrument at a time when the flow of foreign direct

38 'Call for an International Legally Binding Instrument on Human Rights, Transnational Corporations and Other Business Enterprises', <http://www.business-humanrights.org/media/call-for-binding-instrument.pdf> (accessed 02.02.2014). See also '100+ groups publicly call on United Nations to develop new binding instrument to address corporate human rights abuses', <https://www.escr-net.org/news/2013/100-groups-publicly-call-united-nations-develop-new-binding-instrument-address-corporate> and 'Statement to the Human Rights Council in Support of the Initiative of a Group of States for a Legally Binding Instrument on Transnational Corporations', <http://www.stopcorporateimpunity.org/?p=3830> (accessed 02.02.2014).

39 The information about the Treaty Alliance and its statements on the issue are available at <http://www.treatymovement.com/> (accessed 13.03.2017).

40 J Ruggie, 'Life in the Global Public Domain: Response to Commentaries' (05.02.2015), <http://jamesgstewart.com/author/john-g-ruggie/> (accessed 13.03.2017).

41 For a critique of this 'consensus' narrative, see S Deva, 'Treating Human Rights Lightly: A Critique of the Consensus Rhetoric and the Language Employed by the Guiding Principles' in D Bilchitz and S Deva (eds), *Human Rights Obligations of Business: Beyond the Corporate Responsibility to Respect?* (Cambridge: Cambridge University Press, 2013) 78, 81–91.

42 See Lopez and Shea, n 9.

investment (FDI) was almost one-directional (from developed to developing countries) because of a perception that such a regulatory tool would harm their economic interests or the business interests of TNCs based therein. However, this landscape has undergone significant changes over the years, as TNCs from developing countries are emerging on the global stage. For example, in the 2016 Fortune Global 500 list, there are 134 companies from the US and 52 from Japan, as compared to 103 from China and seven each from India and Brazil.[43] This scenario is very different from what the world had experienced during most of the 20th century, when almost 90 per cent of the TNCs were based in the US, Europe and Japan. Moreover, the outflow of FDI from developed economies has been generally declining from a 'one-way' position of dominance, while the outflow from developing and transition economies is on the rise. The World Investment Report 2013 indicated that the FDI outflow from developed countries fell from 88 per cent in 2000 to 65 per cent in 2012 – during the same period, there has been an almost threefold increase in the FDI outflow from developing and transition economies.[44] The FDI outflow from developed countries was 61 per cent in 2014 and 72 per cent in 2015.[45] Despite these fluctuations, it is clear that FDI is no longer one-directional.

2.4. THIRD HIGH TIDE VERSUS PREVIOUS TWO HIGH TIDES

I have already alluded to some differences in the nature of the three high tides. I will suggest that because of these differences, the current high tide offers better chances of getting us closer to a BHR treaty if creative diplomacy is shown by the treaty proponents. At least three such differences are noteworthy.

First, unlike the previous two tides, the third high tide has the 'springboard' of the GPs. Considering that there is a broad consensus about the GPs, the proposed treaty drafted by the OEIGWG should build on useful elements of the GPs to gain political support. In fact, it is highly unlikely that any treaty will not include provisions about the state duty to protect human rights violations by business enterprises (Pillar 1) and enhancing access to effective remedies for

---

43 'Fortune Global 500', <http://beta.fortune.com/global500/list/> (accessed 16.08.2016). In fact, one can notice a gradual decline in the number of TNCs based in developed countries and a corresponding increase in the number of companies from developing countries, especially China. For instance, in the 2005 Fortune Global 500 list, there were 176 US companies (as compared to 134 in 2016) and 81 Japanese companies (as compared to 52 in 2016). On the other hand, the number of Chinese companies went up from 16 in 2005 to 103 in 2016, while the rise was less dramatic for Indian companies during the same period (from 5 in 2005 to 7 in 2016).

44 UNCTAD, *World Investment Report 2013: Global Value Chains: Investment and Trade for Development*, 4.

45 UNCTAD, *World Investment Report 2016 – Investor Nationality: Policy Challenges*, 5–7.

the affected rights holders (Pillar 3). The concept of human rights due diligence under Pillar 2 of the GPs will also be relevant for the proposed treaty, irrespective of whether it imposes 'direct' obligations on TNCs or not. Therefore, if the GPs are used as a springboard to build the treaty provisions, states supportive of the GPs would find it quite difficult to oppose the treaty, especially if the treaty-sponsoring states show sincerity in implementing the GPs within their respective domestic jurisdictions.

Second, the current high tide for a binding international instrument has been supported by the Treaty Alliance's unprecedented global campaign for corporate accountability. This campaign – which also seeks to fight 'corporate capture' and 'dismantle corporate power'[46] – is exposing the limitations of the existing regulatory initiatives by focusing on the victims' struggle for holding corporations accountable for human rights violations, thus countering the state-centric narrative against the need for a binding treaty. More importantly, the Treaty Alliance campaign has put developed states opposing the treaty process in a very uncomfortable situation: how to reconcile their position as the torchbearers of human rights and the key funders of CSOs with the opposition to developing binding human rights norms for TNCs. In other words, the civil society advocacy for a binding treaty might help in softening the opposition of certain states in the Global North.

Third, many states (including developed countries) have started experiencing the side-effects of arbitration triggered by TNCs under BITs:[47] for example, 60 per cent of the investor–state disputes in 2015 were decided on the merits in favour of investors.[48] Thus, asymmetries between 'rights' and 'obligations' of TNCs are no longer a matter of academic argument or mere speculation as TNCs have even challenged legislative reforms in some investment disputes. Moreover, it is quite possible that in the future TNCs from the Global South may turn the tables on developed countries by taking them before arbitration tribunals under BITs. These possibilities may encourage even treaty-sceptic states to claw back the pendulum a little bit towards human rights. And the proposed BHR treaty may offer such an opportunity.

3. EXPLORING ALTERNATIVE PATHS

Despite the third high tide offering some potential, the difficulties in successfully negotiating a binding treaty cannot be underestimated. This section therefore

---

46 See 'Dismantle Corporate Power', <http://www.stopcorporateimpunity.org/> (accessed 13.03.2017).

47 'Prior to 2013, fewer cases were brought against developed countries.' But now about 40 per cent of cases have been brought against them. UNCTAD, *World Investment Report 2016*, n 45, 104–05.

48 Ibid, 107.

explores two alternative paths of a Plan B, which may become relevant if developed countries continue to scuttle attempts to negotiate a binding BHR instrument.

I should note at the outset a few regulatory ideas that underpin both these proposals. Binding regulatory initiatives strengthen the overall regulatory efficacy because even voluntary initiatives work better under the shadow of obligatory regimes.[49] It is telling that all major corporate settlements related to human rights abuses or environmental pollution have been offshoots of litigation against TNCs.[50] It is therefore critical to have binding international instruments regulating corporate behaviour. However, one should not overemphasise the value of a legally binding instrument. Something which is 'binding on paper' may be 'soft in practice' or vice versa. This is more so in cases of international human rights law as compared to domestic human rights laws. Moreover, as the 'bindingness' in the international arena is likely to come with a price (e.g., narrow scope of the treaty), other important considerations should not be ignored. A soft but normatively sound international instrument might prove more useful in practice as compared to a hard but narrow or normatively deficient treaty.

The Plan B alternative paths articulated in this section also recognise the role that non-state actors (e.g., academics, lawyers, CSOs and business enterprises) do and should play in creating as well as enforcing international human rights norms. Finally, I consider that there is a dynamic relationship between the evolution of norms at different levels: the proposed international instrument should therefore be seen as part of a 'continuous upward-downward cycle' of norm creation.[51]

3.1. START WITH A 'DECLARATION ON THE HUMAN RIGHTS OBLIGATIONS OF BUSINESS'

If an optimum level of consensus could not be built for a legally binding international instrument or the negotiation process is likely to take a long time because of complexities involved, one option may be to start with drafting an overarching soft but more ambitious instrument: a BHR Declaration along the lines of the UDHR. As compared to negotiating a treaty, states should be more open to adopting such a Declaration. The proposed Declaration should have

---

49 See S Deva, 'Corporate Human Rights Abuses and International Law: Brief Comments' (28 January 2015), <http://jamesgstewart.com/corporate-human-rights-abuses-and-international-law-brief-comments/> (accessed 13.03.2017).

50 S Deva, 'Bhopal: The Saga Continues 31 Years On' in D Baumann-Pauly and J Nolan (eds), *Business and Human Rights: From Principles to Practice* (London: Routledge, 2016) 22.

51 S Deva, *Regulating Corporate Human Rights Violations: Humanizing Business* (London: Routledge, 2012) 202.

a wide ambit as to whom it applies and what types of human rights it covers. In terms of regulatory targets, it should apply to states as well as all types of business entities and not just TNCs, because the form of a business is hardly relevant from the perspective of the victims of corporate human rights abuses. Similarly, the BHR Declaration should have a wider scope in relation to its subject matter: it should cover all indivisible, interdependent and interrelated human rights, because calls for negotiating a narrow treaty that deals with only egregious abuses is likely to be applicable only to a handful of cases and thus will merely serve a symbolic purpose.

The proposed BHR Declaration should do the following:

- Provide a sound normative basis for why business enterprises have human rights obligations. The application of human rights to companies should not be dependent on the presence of a 'business case' for human rights. Nor should their obligations be determined by what is acceptable to business. Rather, compliance with human rights should be regarded as a non-negotiable pre-condition for having the privilege to conduct business in society.
- Proclaim that human rights applicable to businesses are not limited only to those mentioned in the International Bill of Rights but rather extend to all human rights elaborated in all human rights instruments adopted by the UN.
- Outline the principles governing the extent of corporate obligations in relation to the violation of these rights by oneself as well as one's subsidiaries and suppliers.
- Envisage a number of state-focal and non-state-centric mechanisms to implement and enforce human rights obligations against business enterprises.
- Suggest concrete ways to remove substantive, conceptual, procedural and practical obstacles experienced by victims in holding companies accountable for human rights violations.

Once such a BHR Declaration is in place, simultaneous and/or sequential efforts should be made to concretise the human rights obligations of companies in different areas and also clarify the obligations (including extraterritorial ones) of states in regulating corporate behaviour. This will entail negotiating and adopting in due course a number of binding international instruments which could be specific to a sector, theme or group of rights holders. Such a process will of course take some time, but that itself should not be a ground to delay initiating the process. History tells us that this sequential order – adopting a BHR Declaration followed by treaties – can work in practice. Moreover, it will be normatively sounder than adopting, for instance, a narrow treaty for egregious violations, which will amount to putting the cart before the horse for pragmatic reasons.

Making companies comply with human rights norms and holding them accountable for their failure to do so will require introducing some 'fundamental' changes to the relevant laws and policies that concern the origin and the business operations of companies.[52] These changes should be rooted in the normative assumption that even if companies are specialised social organs, they ought to be subjected to non-negotiable human rights norms. In order to assist states in realising the goal of 'vertical' as well as 'horizontal' coherence under the GPs,[53] it would be desirable to draft several Model Laws on specific areas to provide states with *concrete* guidance as to what legislative reforms and policy adjustments they should make to deal with the privatisation of human rights when acting at domestic, bilateral, regional and international levels.

Such reforms will be especially critical to overcome current barriers faced by victims in access to effective remedies.[54] To illustrate, allocation of liability within a corporate group is an area which requires reform because companies use the principles of separate corporate personality and limited liability to delay and/or deny their liability.[55] The same could be said about the application of the doctrine of *forum non conveniens* outside the European Union and the principles that govern the attribution of criminal liability to corporate officials and companies. The absence of human rights from BITs and consequently from arbitration awards also raises significant challenges, which must be addressed.[56]

The Accountability and Remedy Project of the Office of United Nations High Commissioner for Human Rights (OHCHR) has resulted in some useful recommendations for states to enhance corporate accountability by improving access to judicial remedy for business-related human rights abuses.[57] The idea of Model Laws could build on these recommendations and provide more specific and concrete guidance to states, as done by UNCITRAL Model Laws in commercial areas.

Keeping in mind the fractured nature of international law, it will be crucial for the BHR Declaration to assert the normative hierarchy of human rights and human rights instruments in relation to other areas and their relevant

---

52 This proposal goes beyond what the GPs contemplate, for instance, in Principle 3.

53 Principles 8–10.

54 Zerk notes that 'the present system of domestic law remedies is patchy, unpredictable, often ineffective and fragile. It is failing victims who are unable in many cases to access effective remedies for the abuses they have suffered.' J Zerk, 'Corporate Liability for Gross Human Rights Abuses: Towards a Fairer and More Effective System of Domestic Law Remedies', a report prepared for the Office of the UN High Commissioner for Human Rights (2014) 7.

55 See Amnesty International, *Injustice Incorporated: Corporate Abuses and the Human Rights to Remedy* (London: Amnesty International, 2014); G Skinner, R McCorquodale and O De Schutter, *The Third Pillar: Access to Judicial Remedies for Human Rights Violations by Transnational Business* (ICAR, CORE and ECCJ, 2013).

56 See M Krajewski, 'Ensuring the Primacy of Human Rights in Trade and Investment Policies: Model Clauses for a UN Treaty on Transnational Corporations, Other Businesses and Human Rights' (March 2017), <http://www.cidse.org/publications/business-and-human-rights/business-and-human-rights-frameworks/ensuring-the-primacy-of-human-rights-in-trade-and-investment-policies.html> (accessed 13.03.2017).

57 OHCHR, 'Improving Accountability and Access to Remedy for Victims of Business-Related Human Rights Abuse', A/HRC/32/19 (10.05.2016).

instruments. The Declaration should inform the mandate of not only the UN but also other international agencies such as the International Labour Organization (ILO), the International Monetary Fund, the WTO and the World Bank. The arbitration tribunals operating under BITs should also take on board the BHR Declaration's implications for their work.

The BHR Declaration (and subsequent treaties) should conceive a range of enforcement mechanisms – both state-based and non-state-based – at municipal and international levels to ensure that the companies that do not comply with the agreed obligations could be held accountable in an efficient and speedy manner. The current institutional practice of the UN to deal with BHR issues in an ad hoc way should give way to the establishment of a permanent body within the OHCHR (or a treaty body under the BHR treaty). While it might not be feasible for such a body to monitor or investigate all allegations of corporate human rights abuses, it should use selected representative cases to issue authoritative interpretation of human rights norms applicable to business.

More critically, the BHR Declaration should contemplate institutionalising the role of CSOs in enforcing and implementing human rights norms against business enterprises.[58] For example, a committee of CSOs in each state could be allowed to receive and deal with complaints of human rights abuses by business in a transparent manner. Although such Committees might not have formal enforcement and compliance powers, their determinations could be posted on a designated website to be used in dynamic ways by diverse stakeholders.

In addition to recognising the role of traditional civil, criminal and administrative sanctions in ensuring corporate compliance, the BHR Declaration should acknowledge the importance of informal means and social (dis)incentives in enforcing human rights norms. These tools will be especially crucial for victims in those situations where there is no clear business case for human rights and states are unwilling or unable to act robustly against companies for diverse reasons.

At least two objections may be raised against the idea of 'Declaration first, then Treaties' mooted in this chapter. First, considering the time taken by the international community in moving from the UDHR to the ICCPR/ICESCR, this approach would also take a similarly long time. While this is a valid concern, a key difference should be noted: unlike the process of getting to an International Bill of Rights, there is no need to start from scratch and reinvent the wheel – rather, we just need to identify obligations of business enterprises with reference to already agreed state-centric human rights instruments. Doing so should not

---

58 Building on 'new governance' literature, Melish and Meidinger contend that CSOs could play a critical role in building an effective human rights governance system. T Melish and E Meidinger, 'Protect, Respect, Remedy and Participate: "New Governance" Lessons for the Ruggie Framework' in R Mares (ed), *The UN Guiding Principles on Business and Human Rights: Foundations and Implementation* (Leiden: Martinus Nijhoff Publishers, 2012) 303.

take too long, provided of course there is the requisite political will on the part of states to walk the talk on the importance of human rights.

Second, considering that we already have the GPs, what extra advantages will the BHR Declaration bring? As I have argued elsewhere, the GPs make several compromises and bypass complex/controversial issues in order to achieve consensus.[59] The BHR Declaration should build on the GPs but at the same plug their gaps. Let me offer a concrete illustration. The GPs define 'internationally recognised human rights' as the rights 'expressed in the International Bill of Human Rights and the principles concerning fundamental rights set out in the International Labour Organization's Declaration on Fundamental Principles and Rights at Work'.[60] Consequently, several other *core* international conventions – such as the Convention on the Elimination of All Forms of Racial Discrimination (CERD), the Convention on the Elimination of All Forms of Discrimination Against Women (CEDAW), the Convention on the Rights of the Child (CRC) and the Convention of the Rights of Persons with Disabilities (CRPD)[61] – do not form part of this 'minimum' list; rather they may become relevant as 'additional standards' depending on circumstances.[62] Nor do the GPs expressly refer to any international instruments related to environmental rights or the rights of indigenous people. Therefore, it will be critical for the proposed BHR Declaration to bring within its ambit all human rights recognised by the UN, because corporations can and do violate all human rights.

3.2. DRAFTING A 'MULTI-STAKEHOLDER BOTTOM-UP INSTRUMENT'

Another potential Plan B path may be to assemble a 'coalition of the willing' multi-stakeholders such as states, CSOs, academics, lawyers, policy makers, trade unions, associations of consumers and investors, and business organisations to draft an international instrument articulating the human rights obligations of business enterprises. This plan will unfold outside the formal UN system as part of what is described by scholars as developing international norms from the 'bottom up'.[63] Treaties are only one of the multiple sources of

---

59 S Deva, 'Treating Human Rights Lightly', n 41.

60 Principle 12.

61 It is pertinent to note that CERD (175), CEDAW (187) and CRC (193) have been ratified by more states than the ICCPR (167) and the ICESCR (160).

62 Commentary on Principle 12.

63 For the 'bottom-up' making of international law, see B Rajagopal, *International Law from Below: Development, Social Movements and Third World Resistance* (Cambridge: Cambridge University Press, 2003); J Koven, 'A Bottom-Up Approach to International Lawmaking: The Tale of Three Trade Finance Instruments' (2005) 30 *Yale Journal of International Law* 125; J Koven Levit, 'Bottom-Up International Lawmaking: Reflections on the New Haven School of International Law' (2007) 32 *Yale Journal of International Law* 393.

international law.[64] The unique nature of international law in which norms could evolve in diverse ways and from diverse sources should be utilised as an advantage rather than taken as a limitation.[65]

There are several examples where non-state actors – acting alone or in collaboration with states – have created international law norms in the area of BHR or human rights generally. Some of these initiatives took place within the aegis of international organisations, eg, the Global Compact and the ILO Tripartite Declaration of Principle concerning Multinational Enterprises.[66] However, there are also examples of how diverse actors can join hands outside formal institutional mechanisms to contribute to the concretisation and/or evolution of international norms. The 2010 International Code of Conduct for Private Security Providers, the 2011 Maastricht Principles on Extraterritorial Obligations of States in the Area of Economic, Social and Cultural Rights, and the 2012 Children's Rights and Business Principles are examples of such dynamics. The civil society campaign to draft an International Peoples Treaty on the Control of Transnational Corporations is another case in point.[67]

While drafting such an instrument, the multi-stakeholder coalition can, in part, rely on existing soft law instruments and voluntary codes of conduct adopted by companies and business associations to codify human rights obligations of business enterprises. Since corporate codes hook themselves to the International Bill of Rights in many instances,[68] this linkage can be used as evidence of emerging (customary) business practice to respect universal human rights norms. The wide uptake of the GPs by business should also provide strong evidence of such practice.

One may wonder what useful purpose such a soft instrument with no institutional endorsement will serve. I will suggest that even soft instruments could contribute to the evolution of (hard) international law norms if they deal with important pressing issues which could not be recognised in other peer instruments because of lack of political consensus or some other reasons. For example, the Maastricht Principles have proved influential in developing

---

64 Statute of the International Court of Justice, Article 38.

65 See generally J Pauwelyn, RA Wessel and J Wouters, 'When Structures Become Shackles: Stagnation and Dynamics in International Lawmaking' (2014) 25(3) *European Journal of International Law* 733.

66 See Deva, n 29.

67 Global Campaign to Dismantle Corporate Power and Stop Immunity, 'International Peoples Treaty on the Control of Transnational Corporations', <http://www.stopcorporateimpunity.org/?page_id=5534> (accessed 16.08.2016).

68 Business and Human Rights Centre, 'Company Policy Statement on Human Rights', <https://business-humanrights.org/en/company-policy-statements-on-human-rights> (accessed 16.08.2016).

states' extraterritorial obligations,[69] an area in which other international BHR instruments (including the GPs) seem to have fallen short of both what the international law *is* and *ought to be*.[70] Therefore, if a multi-stakeholder instrument proposed here is able to provide useful guidance on BHR issues which lack clarity or are underdeveloped, it should be able to influence law-cum-policy making and in turn strengthen corporate accountability for human rights violations.

4. CONCLUSION

The quest to negotiate a legally binding international instrument to regulate business operations of TNCs has been continuing for over four decades. There have been at least three attempts (labelled as 'high tides' in this chapter) at the UN level, the most recent being in pursuance of the Human Rights Council Resolution 26/9 of June 2014.

Some stakeholders are worried about the impact of exploring and/or taking the treaty route on the GPs. These worries are underpinned, among others, by the 'either or' mindset, a debate which in the past used to be framed as 'voluntary vs. obligatory' regulation. In my view, we need both sets of regulatory tools, not either one of them. Rather than undermining the GPs, the proposed binding international instrument could complement them in several ways.[71] In turn, the availability of the 'springboard' of the GPs means that the third high tide has higher chances of success in comparison to the previous two attempts.

Nevertheless, considering the history of failed attempts as well as developed countries' opposition to the current treaty process, there is a legitimate scepticism about the success of the treaty project led by the OEIGWG. What should the international community do if the 'roadblock' continues? This chapter explored two alternative paths to achieving an international instrument in the worst-case scenario. The first path entails adopting a BHR Declaration first and then negotiating human rights treaties specific to a business sector, theme or group of rights holders. On the other hand, the second path involves a 'coalition of the willing' multi-stakeholders drafting an international instrument about the

---

69 See F Coomans and R Künnemann, *Cases and Concepts on Extraterritorial Obligations in the Area of Economic, Social and Cultural Rights* (Antwerp: Intersentia, 2012); materials available at ETO Consortium website: <http://www.etoconsortium.org/en/> (accessed 13.03.2017).

70 De Schutter, n 12, 45–47.

71 See S Deva, 'Moving Forward in the Implementation of the UN Guiding Principles on Business and Human Rights' (27 October 2016), <http://www.ohchr.org/Documents/HRBodies/HRCouncil/WGTransCorp/Session2/PanelVSubtheme1/SuryDeva.pdf> (accessed 13.03.2017).

human rights obligations of business enterprises. This will be an expression of the 'bottom-up' creation of international law norms.

While the initial documents generated under both these paths will be soft, I have argued that we should not over-stress the importance of a 'binding' international instrument: in certain circumstances, a soft but normatively sound instrument could do a better job of humanising business than a hard but deficient instrument. Moreover, *bindingness on paper* may not translate into *bindingness in practice* under international human rights law and vice versa. What is critical, therefore, is that the flexibility of international law is used to craft creative regulatory solutions – eg, employing one set of non-state actors (CSOs) to monitor the conduct of another set of non-state actors (TNCs) – to the challenges posed in regulating business enterprises which operate transnationally and through complex supply chains. This chapter is part of such an exploratory journey.

A DEFENCE OF DIRECT INTERNATIONAL HUMAN RIGHTS OBLIGATIONS OF (ALL) CORPORATIONS

Nicolás Carrillo-Santarelli

1. INTRODUCTION

One of the most challenged and discussed ideas in the evolving field of business and human rights, which has been particularly challenged in debates about a treaty on that issue, is the one that espouses that corporations must have direct international human rights obligations.[1] That is to say, that international law ought to directly regulate human rights obligations of their own.

Challenges to this notion rest, at first glance, on theoretical, policy and legal arguments. The former rest, for instance, in the belief that it is States who are properly addressees of human rights obligations, and that imposing burdens on corporations could wreck the human rights edifice. Policy considerations point out things such as the difficulty of coming up with an adequate international system of supervision of corporate conduct or that the time is not yet ripe for

1 See Human Rights Council, *Report on the first session of the open-ended intergovernmental working group on transnational corporations and other business enterprises with respect to human rights, with the mandate of elaborating an international legally binding instrument, Chair-Rapporteur: María Fernanda Espinosa*, A/HRC/31/50, 05.02.2016, paras 47, 83.

imposing duties on corporations, given their reluctance and the opposition of developed States, the reason why insisting on the creation of those obligations could undermine efforts to come up with clarifications and developments about crucial aspects, such as extraterritorial State obligations, which are not dependent on the existence of direct corporate obligations. Finally, some challenge the legality of those obligations based on notions of subjectivity, which is apparently lacked by corporations under contemporary international rules.

In light of those objections, voiced even by some NGOs, the purpose of this chapter is threefold: first, to demonstrate that the challenges are, ultimately, not about insurmountable theoretical, policy or legal obstacles to direct corporate human rights duties but rather – perhaps unconsciously so – due to fear, selfishness or a lack of imagination; secondly, to argue that corporate duties already exist to some degree, and that complementary standards need to be enacted for individuals to be fully and effectively protected from corporate abuses; and finally, to draw attention to the fact that direct obligations may be a necessary dimension – not the only one – to tackle a problem that has to be addressed: that corporations can and do participate in human rights violations.

The latter should actually be treated as the starting point and the underlying problem, given the legal and ethical implications and demands, both in the sense that victims be protected and abusers held accountable.

To explore these aspects, I will first examine what the real implications of corporate abuses are, and whether a system without direct corporate obligations can sufficiently tackle the problems they pose. Afterwards, I will rebut the objections to the creation of direct corporate duties, indicating what the potential consequences of their denial can be and what are the positive expressive, procedural and substantive effects that the presence of direct duties can generate. Finally, I intend to defend the idea that international law already envisages some direct human rights obligations of businesses, the reason why the human rights framework would not be drastically altered by the recognition and creation of additional obligations.

2. THE CENTRALITY OF VICTIMS AND THE EXISTENCE OF CORPORATE *VIOLATIONS*: KEY ISSUES FREQUENTLY IGNORED

Language and the expressions we use can have an impact on the way in which we perceive reality and its problems, and so can make us more or less prone to do something about it. For too long, the international legal community has been presented with euphemistic expressions that may divert attention away from the full extent of the implications of corporate participation in violations of human rights. Those expressions are *abuse* or *destruction* of human rights.

Sometimes, academics, practitioners and agents have resorted to their use when describing corporate misdeeds in order – consciously or not – to avoid saying that businesses or other non-state actors *violate* or have violated human rights in a given case.[2]

Perhaps, sometimes it is feared that States could take advantage of the recognition of non-state violations to attempt to either avoid their obligations to secure, ensure, protect or fulfil[3] the enjoyment of human rights or to impose arbitrary and abusive restrictions on those rights. And maybe at other times the refusal to acknowledge corporate and other non-state violations is strategic, seeking to prevent the blaming of actors that a given State or entity sympathises with – for financial or ideological reasons.

Whatever the case, it cannot be denied that, from a factual point of view, corporations have the capacity to directly cause or contribute to the lack of enjoyment of human rights and fundamental liberties. This may be triggered by different causes, such as a disordered desire for profit, but that corporations can negatively affect the enjoyment of human rights cannot be denied. John Ruggie himself acknowledged so when admitting that corporations can potentially participate in the denial or violation of any human right.[4] The full implications of this acknowledgement must be considered.

Who can deny that corporations can and have sometimes financially contributed to authoritarian and dictatorial regimes, perhaps contributing to their persistence? Or that businesses can illicitly ask for the assistance of non-state armed groups to 'deal with' protesters who object to a given project? That they can contribute to erecting hurdles against those who desire to elect a given candidate? That often the effectiveness and enjoyment of the right to work is made dependent on corporate action? That negligent provisions of services can have a negative impact on the rights to water and food? Or even that abusive exercises of rights of foreign investors can have a dramatic outcome on the capacity of States to secure economic, social and cultural rights? These are but

---

2 See A Clapham, 'Human Rights Obligations for Non-State-Actors: Where Are We Now?' in F Lafontaine and F Larocque (eds), *Doing Peace the Rights Way: Essays in International Law and Relations in Honour of Louise Arbour*, Intersentia, Cambridge, forthcoming; I Bantekas and S Nash, *International Criminal Law*, Cavendish Publishing Limited, London 2003, p 14; A Clapham, *Human Rights Obligations of Non-State Actors*, Oxford University Press, Oxford 2006, p 49.

3 Committee on Economic, Social and Cultural Rights, General Comment 12, The right to adequate food (art 11), E/C.12/1999/5, 12 May 1999, para 15; articles 1 of the European Convention on Human Rights and 2 of the International Covenant on Civil and Political Rights.

4 Human Rights Council, *Protect, Respect and Remedy: A Framework for Business and Human Rights*, Report of the Special Representative of the Secretary-General on the issue of human rights and transnational corporations and other business enterprises, John Ruggie, A/HRC/8/5, 07.04.2008, para 52.

some examples of how corporations can deny or contribute to the denial of the enjoyment of human rights.

This demands that law properly responds to the need for protection. After all, one of the things that legal systems are expected to do is to properly respond to the realities and challenges present in their societies.[5] Some people consider that, precisely because of this, direct human rights obligations of corporations are allegedly unnecessary and undesirable due to some supposed negative implications that their creation can have. According to them, this is due to the fact that domestic legal systems exist and are the ones in charge of protecting individuals from corporate abuses.

Indeed, States are meant and required by international law to protect individuals and their human rights from private threats – corporate ones included – by preventing and responding to them. Accordingly, they are under an obligation to adjust their domestic legal systems and practice so as to prohibit and protect victims from corporate and other abuses.[6] It is important to consider that those State duties will not simply 'vanish' if corporate human rights obligations are regulated,[7] and that multiple participants in a wrongful act may have simultaneous coexistent responsibilities – each responding for its own conduct in relation to a given violation.[8] As a result, the existing human rights edifice will not be weakened if corporate duties are included in it. Thus, the question that follows is not whether corporate obligations will

5 A Remiro-Brotóns, R Riquelme-Cortado, J Díez-Hochleitner, E Orihuela-Calatayud, L Pérez-Prat-Durbán, *Derecho Internacional*, Tirant Lo Blanch, Valencia 2007, p 46.

6 I/A Court H.R., *Case of Velásquez Rodríguez v. Honduras*. Merits. Judgment of 29.07.1988. Series C No. 4, paras 172–77, 187–88; *Mastromatteo v Italy*, no 37703/94, ECHR 2002-VIII, paras 67–68; I/A Court H.R., *Case of González et al. ('Cotton Field') v. Mexico*. Preliminary Objection, Merits, Reparations and Costs. Judgment of 16.11.2009. Series C No. 205, paras 243, 246, 252; I/A Court H.R., Juridical Condition and Rights of the Undocumented Migrants. Advisory Opinion OC-18/03 of 17.09.2003. Series A No. 18, paras 73–74, 77–81, 140–53; I/A Court H.R., *Case of 'The Last Temptation of Christ' (Olmedo-Bustos et al.) v. Chile*. Merits, Reparations and Costs. Judgment of 05.02.2001. Series C No. 73, para 87; article 2 of the American Convention on Human Rights; A Reinisch, 'The Changing International Legal Framework for Dealing with Non-State Actors' in P Alston (ed), *Non-State Actors and Human Rights*, Oxford University Press, Oxford 2005, pp 78–82.

7 A Reinisch, above n 6, pp 81–82; *Norms on the Responsibilities of Transnational Corporations and Other Business Enterprises with Regard to Human Rights*, U.N. Doc. E/CN.4/Sub.2/2003/12/Rev.2 (2003), para 1 and its commentary.

8 I/A Court H.R., International Responsibility for the Promulgation and Enforcement of Laws in Violation of the Convention (arts 1 and 2 of the American Convention on Human Rights). Advisory Opinion OC-14/94 of 09.12.1994. Series A No. 14, para 56; Application of the Convention on the Prevention and Punishment of the Crime of Genocide (*Bosnia and Herzegovina v. Serbia and Montenegro*), Judgment, I.C.J. Reports 2007, p 43, paras 419–20; B Cheng, *General Principles of Law as Applied by International Courts and Tribunals*, Cambridge University Press, Cambridge 2006, pp 208–10.

wreck international human rights law, but rather whether their introduction is necessary. This leads us to the question of whether domestic protection from potential corporate abuses is sufficient *for victims*. As to voluntary initiatives, the fact that save for indirect effects based on good faith they are not binding, makes clear, to my mind, that they provide no strong protection and thus their existence alone fills no gaps of required guarantees.

In that regard, it is useful to consider that current discussions acknowledge that for human rights to be fully and effectively protected one cannot conceive such a protection in a compartmentalised manner. Accordingly, it is said that such protection must be based on a multi-level scheme, to which agents and norms of different legal systems and authorities, not only domestic ones, contribute.[9] In fact, the very existence of State human rights obligations is based on the acknowledgement that protection from State abuses by means of domestic legal systems may not always be expected or relied upon.[10] That being said, should one have doubts about States protecting individuals from corporate abuses, especially considering that if States are negligent or unwilling to provide such protection they will be held responsible, and individuals will have remedies against those States?

That is all well and good, but that argument actually fails to convince as regards the supposed needlessness of direct corporate obligations. This is because just as protection from State abuses if necessary given the possibility of failures in domestic protection from them, the State may equally fail to protect from actors different from its own agents. This possibility includes scenarios of failure of domestic protection *in spite* of (due) diligent State efforts. To avoid impunity and the absence of protection and reparations of victims of corporate abuses, other levels of governance, the international legal level included, are called upon to provide complementary protection. This is consistent with the logic of subsidiarity and complementarity and with the goal that international justice offers hope when none is found locally.[11] Indeed, a framework of protection

---

9 *Statement issued by the President of the European Court of Human Rights (Jean-Paul Costa) concerning Requests for Interim Measures (Rule 39 of the Rules of Court)*, p 2 <http://www.strasbourgconsortium.org/content/blurb/files/20110211_ART_39_Statement_EN.pdf> accessed 08.04.2016; A Peters, 'Humanity as the A and Ω of Sovereignty' (2009) 20 *European Journal of Human Rights* 513, 535–36, 544.

10 F Gómez-Isa, 'International Protection of Human Rights' in F Gómez-Isa and K de Feyter (eds), *International Protection of Human Rights: Achievements and Challenges*, Universidad de Deusto, Deusto 2006, pp 19, 26.

11 Concurring Opinion of Judge AA Cançado Trindade to: I/A Court H.R., *Case of Castillo Petruzzi et al v. Peru*. Preliminary Objections. Judgment of 04.09.1998. Series C No. 41, para 35; Preamble and articles 1 and 17 of the Rome Statute of the International Criminal Court; I/A Court H. R., *Case of Duque v. Colombia*. Preliminary Objections, Merits, Reparations and Costs. Judgment of 26.02.2016. Series C No. 310, para 128.

from corporate violations that is based on State obligations may be insufficient for several reasons.

In the first place, State duties to protect from corporate abuses are obligations *of means*.[12] This implies that States are not always and automatically responsible for violations perpetrated by private actors as businesses or in which such actors participate. This is not only what positive law says, but also something that to my mind is fair: it would be too burdensome and artificial to hold States accountable for every single violation committed by non-state actors. After all, the law of responsibility requires a nexus of attribution of a breach of an obligation,[13] and if States diligently try to prevent or adequately respond to corporate abuses there is no justification for holding them accountable.

In many of those events, without State accountability, individuals may have no effective remedy against corporate abuses. Why so? Because if they institute proceedings in the State in whose territory a corporation perpetrated or was complicit in an abuse, and despite the fact that the State diligently conducts those proceedings, perhaps the corporation will get away with its violation. And States can choose, but will not be obliged, to provide reparations in those cases.[14] Several legal and social factors make this scenario of impunity more likely in some cases.

Among those factors is the separate legal personality of corporations in a multinational group. Perhaps the one operating in a territory is dissolved, or 'jumps' to another jurisdiction,[15] and the parent company is not held responsible under a given jurisdiction.

In those cases, the importance of counting on other authorities to defend victims is important, and direct corporate obligations can provide the missing key. This is because if there is a substantive international legal basis for going after corporate abusers, then other States acting on behalf of international law and

---

12 I/A Court H.R., *Case of Velásquez Rodríguez v. Honduras*. Merits. Judgment of 29.07.1988. Series C No. 4, paras 172, 174; I/A Court H.R., *Case of González et al. ('Cotton Field') v. Mexico*. Preliminary Objection, Merits, Reparations and Costs. Judgment of 16.11.2009. Series C No. 205, para 252; *Mastromatteo v Italy*, no 37703/94, ECHR 2002-VIII, para 68; I/A Court H.R., *Case of the Pueblo Bello Massacre v. Colombia*. Merits, Reparations and Costs. Judgment of 31.01.2006. Series C No. 140, paras 123, 126.

13 See articles 2 of the articles on Responsibility of States for Internationally Wrongful Acts and 4 of the Draft Articles on Responsibility of International Organizations (2011 version), both drafted by the International Law Commission.

14 Basic Principles and Guidelines on the Right to a Remedy and Reparation for Victims of Gross Violations of International Human Rights Law and Serious Violations of International Humanitarian Law, para 15; Declaration of Basic Principles of Justice for Victims of Crime and Abuse of Power, para 12.

15 Human Rights Council, *Report on the first session of the open-ended intergovernmental working group on transnational corporations and other business enterprises with respect to human rights, with the mandate of elaborating an international legally binding instrument, Chair-Rapporteur: María Fernanda Espinosa*, A/HRC/31/50, 05.02.2016, para 50.

legal interests can act on the basis of universal jurisdiction or norms permitting transnational litigation.[16] But international bodies and agents can have a say too: regional and universal bodies entrusted with the promotion of human rights may publicly denounce corporate abuses in their general comments, advisory opinions, reports and press releases, even if they lack the competence and jurisdiction to condemn them in contentious procedures.[17] This may happen, for instance, with the Inter-American Commission on Human Rights or United Nations working groups and rapporteurs, among others.

Therefore, imposing obligations on corporations does not necessarily signify overburdening international authorities with an impossible workload. After all, in international law frequently there is a dissociation between the substantive and the procedural dimensions, with the latter not always being present to provide enforcement or supervision of the former.[18] Moreover, it has been accepted that it is possible for international law to respond to non-state threats not only by regulating State duties of protection, but also by either imposing obligations on non-state actors or by coming up with bodies and mechanisms that can supervise non-state compliance with duties of their own.[19] This confirms that the imposition of obligations on businesses does not automatically translate into a greater workload for existing bodies, although they can sometimes reasonably deal with corporate abuses with promotion functions and new bodies could be created.

On the other hand, regarding fears of congestion by making international authorities examine complaints in which businesses are involved, we must ask ourselves whether there are not double standards. After all, are corporations not allowed to present cases under regimes for the protection of foreign investors? Why should we favour them as applicants and dismiss them as defendants? Difficulties demand imagination, not denial of protection, and the current system is unbalanced, favouring applications made by investors while doing nothing about the many hurdles faced by victims of foreign investors and the

---

16 A Cassese, 'Remarks on Scelle's Theory of "Role Splitting", (*dédoublement fonctionnel*) in International Law' (1990) 1 *European Journal of International Law* 210, 226–31.

17 Inter-American Commission on Human Rights, *Report on Terrorism and Human Rights*, OEA/Ser.L/V/II.116, Doc. 5 rev. 1 corr., 22.10.2002, para 48; N Carrillo-Santarelli, 'La protección y promoción de los derechos humanos frente a violaciones no estatales por los órganos internacionales' (2013) 26 *Revista Electrónica de Estudios Internacionales* 1, 12–13, 14, 17–19, 21.

18 A Clapham, 'The Role of the Individual in International Law' (2010) 21 *European Journal of International Law* 25, 29; H Lauterpacht, *International Law and Human Rights*, Steven & Sons Limited, London 1950, pp 27, 34; Clapham, *Human Rights Obligations of Non-State Actors*, above n 2, 74.

19 JH Knox, 'Horizontal Human Rights Law' (2008) 102 *American Journal of International Law* 1, 20–31.

lack of clarity about corporate responsibilities.[20] This sends a not-so-subtle message that money matters more than the protection of dignity to many law makers.

Granted, there may be cases in which States and businesses collude in abuses, or in which States are unwilling to prosecute or try corporations for reasons that may include the fear that investments go elsewhere. In such cases, the respective States will be held responsible. Some could argue that in those cases direct obligations of the businesses add nothing insofar as international protection against the State and reparations can be claimed. However, this is too narrow a point of view. This is because violations affect multiple human dimensions, psychological and symbolic ones included, and are often complex operations. Thus, if one focuses not on the responsible party but rather on the individual, the victim, the one that *should be* the protagonist, interesting things arise. For instance, concerning the right to reparations – which include satisfaction, compensation and restitution–, is it not insufficient if only the State apologises and provides guarantees of non-repetition but the corporate participant in the violation is not required to repair? Reparations will then not be complete and full, and victims have a *right* to *full* reparations, which will not be satisfied. Precisely because of this, international standards and scholars recognise the need to make non-state actors make reparations to their victims.[21] Furthermore, when different actors participate in a violation, all of them can be responsible.[22]

The centrality of victims is the starting point that ought to guide every analysis of business and human rights. It is a travesty to make corporations and their interests the central point of analysis. International law *must* answer to that demand for protection either when domestic law and institutions cannot protect

---

20 Inter-American Commission on Human Rights, *Indigenous Peoples, Afro-Descendent Communities, and Natural Resources: Human Rights Protection in the Context of Extraction, Exploitation, and Development Activities*, OEA/Ser.L/V/II, Doc. 47/15, 31.12.2015, paras 74, 81, 141–48; Human Rights Council, *Report on the first session of the open-ended intergovernmental working group on transnational corporations and other business enterprises with respect to human rights, with the mandate of elaborating an international legally binding instrument, Chair-Rapporteur: María Fernanda Espinosa*, A/HRC/31/50, 05.02.2016, para 30.

21 T Van Boven, 'The United Nations Basic Principles and Guidelines on the Right to a Remedy and Reparation for Victims of Gross Violations of International Human Rights Law and Serious Violations of International Humanitarian Law', *United Nations Audiovisual Library of International Law* 1, p 3 <http://legal.un.org/avl/pdf/ha/ga_60-147/ga_60-147_e.pdf> accessed 26.04.2016; I/A Court H. R., *Case of the Kaliña and Lokono Peoples v. Suriname.* Merits, Reparations and Costs. Judgment of 25.11.2015. Series C No. 309, para 221; Basic Principles and Guidelines on the Right to a Remedy and Reparation for Victims of Gross Violations of International Human Rights Law and Serious Violations of International Humanitarian Law, para 15; Declaration of Basic Principles of Justice for Victims of Crime and Abuse of Power, paras 8, 12.

22 I/A Court H.R., International Responsibility for the Promulgation and Enforcement of Laws in Violation of the Convention (arts. 1 and 2 of the American Convention on Human Rights). Advisory Opinion OC-14/94 of 09.12.1994. Series A No. 14, para 56.

individuals from corporate abuses or when systems based on State obligations do not *fully* provide that protection. And in order to provide that protection there is an undeniable reality: corporations (and other non-state actors) *violate* human rights.[23] This recognition is actually what explains and justifies positive State duties of prevention, response and protection against corporate misdeeds.

Thus, without resorting to euphemisms of non-state 'abuse' of rights that fail to fully acknowledge, in symbolic and legal terms, the reality that non-state actors do violate human rights and prevent their enjoyment, it is necessary that there is corporate conduct (either through action or inaction) that is contrary to liberties and fundamental entitlements based on human dignity. Accordingly, we are called to come up with the design of how other levels of governance and legal systems can make up for the shortcomings of domestic guarantees and State obligations. Part of that complementarity rests in corporate obligations, which are the basis for holding corporations legally accountable. Such accountability not only empowers different authorities, foreign and international, to provide protection (and requires them to do so when they are under extraterritorial obligations) by authorising the enforcement of those obligations and the related responsibilities, but can also trigger changes in non-State culture and attitudes. Those changes can be brought about out of the fear of potential sanctions, reactions (boycotts, among others) and trials (which are costly both in time, money and reputation terms), or due to conviction or the desire to achieve recognition, reputation, and market or consumer support.[24]

Apart from the previous ideas, one may wonder whether it is not sufficient to impose obligations on States to criminalise or outlaw certain corporate conduct in their *domestic* legislations, as happens with some norms on protection from terrorism and transnational organised crime. After all, international law may address non-state abuses *indirectly*, by obliging States to respond to or prevent them in their domestic sphere, or *directly*, by directly regulating duties of non-state actors and even by supervising compliance with them, as has been argued by John H Knox.[25] In regard to that question, it is my humble argument that the indirect approach is insufficient, for two reasons: States may fail to comply

---

23 I/A Court H. R., *Case of the Kaliña and Lokono Peoples v. Suriname*. Merits, Reparations and Costs. Judgment of 25.11.2015. Series C No. 309, paras 220–25; I/A Court H.R., *Case of Velásquez Rodríguez v. Honduras*. Merits. Judgment of 29.07.1988. Series C No. 4, paras 166, 172–77, 187–88; A Clapham, 'Human Rights Obligations for Non-State-Actors: Where Are We Now?', above n 2.

24 On stimuli for compliance and obedience, and the impact of reputation for businesses regarding legal and non-legal human rights standards, see HH Koh, 'Review Essay: Why Do Nations Obey International Law?' (1997) 106 *The Yale Law Journal* 2599, 2600–01; A Clapham and S Jerbi, 'Categories of Corporate Complicity in Human Rights Abuses' (2001) 24 *Hastings International and Comparative Law Review* 339, 340, 347–48.

25 Knox, above n 19; article 5 of the United Nations Convention against Transnational Organized Crime.

with their duties, and while they may have responsibility engaged as a result, especially when such failure leads to the impunity of corporate abuses, the fact that the respective corporate abuser is not made responsible will be translated into a lack of full reparations, because, for instance, for victims it is important to receive satisfaction and guarantees of non-repetition from *all* participants in a violation. Furthermore, directly regulating corporate duties under international law will reduce the possibilities for corporate abusers to elude controls because wherever they are found they will have violated international law and so will have committed a wrongful act, regardless of whether this is also recognised in a domestic forum or not. This may also empower States acting under transnational litigation, universal jurisdiction or other norms permitting the exercise of extraterritorial jurisdiction to hold the respective actor accountable and demand the protection and reparations of victims – or even to order precautionary measures on their behalf, among other possibilities available to creative authorities while respecting the rule of law and due process.

I stress how obligations are but part of the different pieces of the puzzle required to provide robust protection from corporate abuses. Certainly, other aspects, like extraterritorial obligations, are important as well, insofar as exclusively voluntary extraterritorial protection, which is suggested in the Guiding Principles,[26] is already outdated given the many problems faced by financially or otherwise weak States when trying to prevent or respond to certain corporate abuses. This is the reason why it is unjust for countries that economically benefit from companies with their nationality or that are otherwise closely related to them simply do nothing, especially if they knew about risks of violations and vulnerability of victims. Thus, efforts such as those made by the drafters of the Maastricht Principles or by Human Rights Committees who call for extraterritorial responsibility of States[27] are to be applauded.

Likewise, if direct corporate obligations are but *one* dimension required for better and fully protecting victims, fears about undermining processes such as those leading to voluntary principles, the Guiding Principles included, can be allayed. There is consensus that hard law and soft law approaches are

---

26 Office of the United Nations High Commissioner for Human Rights, *Guiding Principles on Business and Human Rights: Implementing the United Nations 'Protect, Respect and Remedy' Framework*, United Nations, 2011, commentary to Principle 2, 3–4.

27 Maastricht Principles on Extraterritorial Obligations of States in the Area of Economic, Social and Cultural Rights; Committee on the Elimination of Discrimination against Women, *General recommendation No. 34 on the rights of rural women*, CEDAW/C/GC/34, 04.03.2016, para 13; Committee on Economic, Social and Cultural Rights, *General comment No. 22 (2016) on the right to sexual and reproductive health (article 12 of the International Covenant on Economic, Social and Cultural Rights)*, E/C.12/GC/22, 02.05.2016, para 60; Committee on Economic, Social and Cultural Rights, *General Comment No. 23 (2016) on the Right to just and favourable conditions of work (article 7 of the International Covenant on Economic, Social and Cultural Rights)*, E/C.12/GC/23, 08.03.2016, paras 69–70.

complementary and by no means mutually exclusive insofar as strategies based on the Guiding Principles are helpful and compatible with others.[28] Indeed, codes of conduct, social labels[29] and the Principles themselves can pave the way for changes in practice and corporate culture (which is essential for improving the situation).[30] However, the failure to observe voluntary standards carries no legal consequence and generates no responsibility; and strategies such as shaming and boycotts have proven to have quite limited – even negligible – effects in some cases.[31] Furthermore, empirical research suggests that corporate social responsibility and voluntary initiatives have not had sufficient positive impact and cannot replace binding law.[32] Therefore, voluntary strategies are not always enough to protect victims and to properly deal with the violations that businesses can and do commit. Among other things, they cannot be successfully invoked as solid arguments in courts (save for exceptional cases, in which they have some indirect legal relevance due to the principle of good faith).[33] Direct obligations can help to fill gaps and permit protection where none can be offered

---

28 Holy See, XXVI Ordinary Session of the Human Rights Council, Statement of Archbishop Silvano M. TOMASI Permanent Observer of the Holy See to the United Nations and Specialized Agencies in Geneva, Guiding Principles on Business and Human Rights, 'Protect, Respect and Remedy', Geneva, 11.06.2014 <http://www.vatican.va/roman_curia/secretariat_state/2014/documents/rc-seg-st-20140611_tomasi-diritti-umani_en.html> accessed 10.05.2016; 'Response of Surya Deva and David Bilchitz to Comments of Professor John Ruggie on "Human Rights Obligations of Business: Beyond the Corporate Responsibility to Respect?" (Cambridge University Press, 2013)' <http://business-humanrights.org/sites/default/files/media/documents/surya-deva-david-bilchitz-re-ruggie-15-01-14.pdf> accessed 10.05.2016.

29 A Gatto, 'Corporate Social Responsibility in the External Relations of the EU' (2005) 24 *Yearbook of European Law* 423, 429–32.

30 Human Rights Council, *Report on the first session of the open-ended intergovernmental working group on transnational corporations and other business enterprises with respect to human rights, with the mandate of elaborating an international legally binding instrument, Chair-Rapporteur: María Fernanda Espinosa*, A/HRC/31/50, 05.02.2016, para 88; Human Rights Council, *Protect, Respect and Remedy: A Framework for Business and Human Rights*, Report of the Special Representative of the Secretary-General on the issue of human rights and transnational corporations and other business enterprises, John Ruggie, A/HRC/8/5, 07.04.2008, paras 27, 29–32, 83, 105; F Halliday, 'The Romance of Non-state Actors' in D Josselin and W Wallace (eds), *Non-state Actors in World Politics*, Palgrave, New York 2001, p 35.

31 M Hobbes, 'The Untouchables: Why It's Getting Harder to Stop Multinational Corporations' (*Foreign Policy*, 11.04.2016) <https://foreignpolicy.com/2016/04/11/the-untouchables-zimbabwe-green-fuel-multinational-corporations/> accessed 26.04.2016; MT Kamminga, 'The Next Frontier: Prosecution of Extraterritorial Corporate Misconduct before Non-US Courts' in WJM Van Genugten, Michael P Scharf and Sasha E Radin (eds), *Criminal Jurisdiction 100 Years after the 1907 Hague Peace Conference*, T.M.C. Asser Press, The Hague 2009, p 186.

32 D Sogge, 'The Corporate Wax Nose', *tni*, 17.11.2016 <https://www.tni.org/en/article/the-corporate-wax-nose> accessed 02.12.2016.

33 International Law Association, Non-State Actors Committee, 'Preliminary issues for the ILA Conference in Rio de Janeiro' (2008) p 3.

by voluntary standards. As a result, those obligations *must* be enacted. That being said, can they really be created under international law? Do they already exist? Such questions will be addressed in the next sections.

On the other hand, it is important to stress that I do not argue that the pillar or principle of corporate respect is the only relevant one: the other two are as important. The point is, precisely, that the principle of respect is currently conceived by many in a way that is too weak, as supposedly being mostly voluntary or based on social responsibility rather than legal responsibility,[34] rendering it ineffective in too many cases. If this is so, saying that obligations of State protection already exist, and that it is difficult to think of an effective system of supervision of corporate obligations under international law, amounts to invoking technicalities that condemn victims to suffer and reward abusers with impunity, especially because then in many cases businesses could violate human rights but would not face the consequences they should face, and victims who had suffered would be unprotected (fully or to some extent, which is always unacceptable). The very existence of substantive obligations creates new perceptions and opportunities for protection, and raises awareness, and creativity is required – as has been the case throughout history.

3. REBUTTING THE OBJECTIONS TO DIRECT INTERNATIONAL HUMAN RIGHTS OBLIGATIONS OF *ALL* CORPORATIONS, AND AFFIRMING THE BENEFITS OF THOSE DUTIES

Two issues that have been widely debated in the human rights and business field (human rights', being the most important element, should precede 'business' indeed) are whether corporations can and should have international obligations, and if all types of businesses should be addressed by international norms – either indirectly, by means of regulating State duties and remedies concerning them, or directly.

As to the first question, several types of objections have been raised. Some are based on pragmatic arguments, and include, among others, the following ideas: that regulation of direct corporate obligations could be exploited by abusive States in order to divert attention away from their own responsibilities or impose abusive restrictions on human rights; that the aforementioned regulation could somehow weaken the human rights field and undermine its progress; or that such regulation is unfeasible insofar as it would require supervision of the conduct of

---

34 On non-legal responsibilities and their differences from legal responsibility, see Cheng, above n 8, pp 163–64, 167, 169–70.

the myriad corporations present in the world, which is allegedly impossible and would clog the international system.

Other objections have a more legal nuance, and frequently put forward the idea that corporations are not subjects of international (human rights) law – not mentioning that, even if this were true, they could still become such subjects. Finally, there are challenges based on theoretical or philosophical ideas about the nature of human rights. They often espouse the argument that human rights emerged and exist to protect individuals from States, the former being the weak parties and the latter the powerful ones prone to abuse. Such arguments, however, force us to look at two issues: what is the rationale and the foundation of human rights? And are States always the most powerful parties in the equation? What about situations in which corporate actors have dramatically much more economic power and leverage than the territorial State?

Granted, there are more challenges, but I will focus on the ones mentioned herein. Moreover, as pointed out above, I think that these objections can be summarised as answering to fear, preconceptions or bias. Let me expound this.

Some challenges are explained by the fear that regulating international human rights obligations of corporations could create problems in the human rights field: either because they could be used as excuses for abuses and unaccountability or because they could make the universal and regional human rights regimes less effective. Other arguments against corporate obligations can be synthesized as reflections of the prejudice and repetition of State-centred conceptions of international law concerning its intended addressees. Quite frankly, to my mind these conceptions are outdated, especially considering that human rights are – fortunately – clearly protected under international law and so if they are violated by businesses and their protection cannot be universal and effective without changing the paradigm then we are called to change it and accept the only sensible thing: protecting human beings when a system based on State duties cannot. Finally, there may be some bias or selfishness: I have the inkling that, perhaps, some States and corporations are adamantly opposed to corporate human rights duties because of fear of litigation or the desire to do business unhindered, maximising profit without really being concerned about those who suffer. By erecting money as the supreme value (making it a deity, mammon), they distort things.

This is acutely revealed when they have no qualms about demanding international protection of corporations – even under human rights law, which could be detrimental for human rights law[35] – such as under foreign investment

[35] I/A Court H. R. Request of Advisory Opinion submitted by the State of Panama before the Inter-American Court of Human Rights, 28.04.2014; JE Alvarez, 'Are Corporations "Subjects" of International Law?' (2011) 9 *Santa Clara Journal of International Law* 1, 27–30, 34–35.

norms, but have sometimes fiercely opposed any sort of responsibility of corporations, as industrialised nations have done, for instance when voting on the resolution proposing a treaty on business and human rights.[36] Perhaps some have a realist[37] perception that makes them reject necessary standards due to attaching more priority to economic interests? Their priorities are clear. Such context further illustrates one of the aspects that make the recognition and regulation of corporate human rights obligations so important: they serve to protect rights that are central and, meta-legally speaking, much more important than economic interests, and address the fact that since corporations have increasingly been granted international entitlements, they should accept responsibilities as well, lest there is an imbalance regarding the international entitlements and legal burdens of corporations.[38] Moreover, due to the teleological and systemic interpretation of international law,[39] regulating corporate duties also serves to prevent abuse of rights[40] in legal regimes such as that of foreign investment, because just as human rights and human rights duties of States can and must be considered when interpreting and implementing foreign investment standards and evaluating State police powers – as was recently shown in the *Philip Morris v Uruguay* case[41] – so can human rights obligations of non-state actors. Finally, progress towards the developments of an instrument on business and human rights ends up being an unavoidable fact

---

36 See 'UN Human Rights Council 26th Session (Geneva, 10–27 Jun 2014)' in Business & Human Rights Resource Centre, 'UN Human Rights Council Sessions' <http://business-humanrights.org/en/binding-treaty/un-human-rights-council-sessions> accessed 04.05.2016. There it is mentioned that regarding a resolution drafted by Ecuador and South Africa on the 'Elaboration of an international legally binding instrument on transnational corporations and other business enterprises with respect to human rights' and the establishment of an 'open-ended intergovernmental working group' on such instrument, on 26.06.2014 the resolution was adopted with the following votes: '*20 in favour* (Algeria, Benin, Burkina Faso, China, Congo, Côte d'Ivoire, Cuba, Ethiopia, India, Indonesia, Kazakhstan, Kenya, Morocco, Namibia, Pakistan, Philippines, Russia, South Africa, Venezuela, Vietnam), *14 against* (Austria, Czech Republic, Estonia, France, Germany, Ireland, Italy, Japan, Montenegro, South Korea, Romania, Macedonia, UK, USA) and *13 abstentions* (Argentina, Botswana, Brazil, Chile, Costa Rica, Gabon, Kuwait, Maldives, Mexico, Peru, Saudi Arabia, Sierra Leone, UAE).'

37 MS McDougal, 'The Realist Theory in Pyrrhic Victory' (1955) 49 *American Journal of International Law* 376; Koh, above n 24, 2600.

38 *Draft report on the second session of the open-ended intergovernmental working group on transnational corporations and other business enterprises with respect to human rights* (version of 28.10.2016 – corrected by Secretariat), p 5.

39 International Law Commission, *Fragmentation of International Law: Difficulties Arising from the Diversification and Expansion of International Law. Report of the Study Group of the International Law Commission, Finalized by Martti Koskenniemi*, A/CN.4/L.682, 13.04.2006, paras 35–43, 130.

40 On the institution of abuse of rights, see: M Byers, 'Abuse of Rights: An Old Principle, A New Age' (2002) 47 *McGill Law Journal*, 397–404.

41 ICSID Case No. ARB/10/7, Award, 08.07.2016, paras 291, 300, 304, 306.

and may persuade those initially opposed to it that it is either unavoidable or that it is politically costly to ignore it, which may explain why some of those States that voted against the resolution on the 'Elaboration of an international legally binding instrument on transnational corporations and other business enterprises with respect to human rights' and the establishment of an 'open-ended intergovernmental working group' drafted by Ecuador and South Africa ended up attending meetings of the working group.[42] Let us look now at the objections and how I would respond to them.

Regarding those objections that warn about potential undesirable outcomes of regulating corporate obligations, I have many things to say. First, that temptations already exist. Let us look, in analogy, at international criminal law. States may be persuaded to try to come up with abusive restrictions or to highlight the crimes committed by rebel groups in some places. However, should this be a reason to forbid restrictions or to campaign for the elimination of the international criminal responsibility of individuals? Not at all. Rather, what is required is that there are checks and guarantees, and in fact there are: restrictions must be proportionate, necessary and lawful, among other requirements and limitations.[43] But since it is human beings who perpetrate abuses heinous to the international community and conscience, as the International Military Tribunal put it, then it is imperative to hold those individuals accountable,[44] lest repetition of misdeeds is encouraged and impunity is fostered.

Likewise, making corporations bound by norms that dictate how they must behave themselves lest they disrespect human rights or contribute to their lack of enjoyment is something to be welcomed. First, the absence of such norms could send the wrong message, and corporate entities and their agents could (wrongly) feel that human rights has nothing to do with them or that human rights standards are mere suggestions, at the most. Secondly, the fact that non-state actors have obligations does not diminish or eliminate State obligations at all: actually, human rights bodies have stressed that the vicarious responsibility of States and their positive obligations remain even in cases of delegation and

42 *Draft report on the second session of the open-ended intergovernmental working group on transnational corporations and other business enterprises with respect to human rights* (version of 28.10.2016 – corrected by Secretariat), p 3.

43 I/A Court H.R., Compulsory Membership in an Association Prescribed by Law for the Practice of Journalism (arts. 13 and 29 American Convention on Human Rights). Advisory Opinion OC-5/85 of 13.11.1985. Series A No. 5, paras 30, 35–52; I/A Court H.R., The Word 'Laws' in Article 30 of the American Convention on Human Rights. Advisory Opinion OC-6/86 of 09.05.1986. Series A No. 6, paras 14, 28–37; *Sunday Times v UK*, no 6538/74, ECHR 1979, paras 47–49, 59, 62, 67; Human Rights Committee, *General Comment No. 29, States of Emergency (Article 4)*, CCPR/C/21/Rev.1/Add.11, 31.08.2001, paras 3–9, 11–12.

44 'Principles of International Law recognized in the Charter of the Nürnberg Tribunal and in the Judgment of the Tribunal, with commentaries', *Yearbook of the International Law Commission, 1950*, vol. II, 1950, commentary to Principle I, para 99.

privatisation; and that States must strive to diligently prevent and respond to abusive actors.[45] Actually, the (defunct) Draft Norms on the Responsibilities of Transnational Corporations and Other Business Enterprises with Regard to Human Rights mentioned at the very beginning how 'States have the primary responsibility to promote, secure the fulfilment of, respect, ensure respect of, and protect human rights recognised in international as well as national law, including assuring that transnational corporations and other business enterprises respect human rights'.

Therefore, States will retain their obligations and will have no legal grounds to ignore them by invoking corporate duties or identifying non-state abuses. In other words, they are unable to lawfully avoid their responsibilities by saying that a corporate actor has committed or participated in a violation. If States are diligent they will not be responsible, but this already happens and makes sense, as discussed in the previous section. In fact, regulating obligations of businesses has several advantages over the contrary scenario. As indicated above, it can have an expressive and symbolic impact,[46] with the potential to change corporate culture and the attitudes of both (international and local) authorities and victims and their defenders. All of them will be made aware of the presence of *legal* obligations. Furthermore, the stigma attached to human rights – given the legitimacy they provide[47] – can be quite important, by conferring greater strength to discourses and campaigns against corporate abuses; and the existence of obligations may inspire or help to trigger processes of internalisation, socialisation and acculturation.[48] But apart from this, the very legal nature of the standards would expose corporations to judicial action in domestic fora where transnational or universal jurisdiction is permitted, thus diminishing the risks of 'forum shopping' or evasion of jurisdiction of the places where abuses are committed. Additionally, this would generate momentum and put greater pressure on States linked with corporations acting abroad in an unlawful way to monitor and act against their abuses.

---

45 Reinisch, above n 6, pp 80–82; I/A Court H.R., *Case of Ximenes Lopes v. Brazil.* Merits, Reparations and Costs. Judgment of 04.07.2006. Series C No. 149, paras 96–99, 102.

46 R Goodman and D Jinks, 'Incomplete Internalization and Compliance with Human Rights Law' (2008) 19 *European Journal of International Law* 725, 735; M García-Villegas, 'De qué manera se puede decir que la Constitución es importante' in A Jaramillo (ed), *Doce ensayos sobre la nueva Constitución*, Diké, Medellín 1991, p 40.

47 SR Ratner, *The Thin Justice of International Law: A Moral Reckoning of the Law of Nations* (Oxford University Press, Oxford 2015) pp 65, 73, 90–94.

48 Koh, above n 24; Goodman and Jinks, above n 46, pp 728, 730–43; D Capie, 'Influencing Armed Groups: Are there Lessons to Be Drawn from Socialization Literature?' in G Call (ed), *Exploring Criteria & Conditions for Engaging Armed Non-State Actors to Respect Humanitarian Law & Human Rights Law, Conference Report – Geneva, 4–5 June 2007* (2008) pp 87–90.

Altogether, we can say that rather than being inimical, the scenario in which corporate obligations are present is much stronger in terms of the protection of human rights than the alternative. Furthermore, the so-called risks are not exclusively dependent on their existence, but refer to temptations States can already have. This does not imply that risks do not exist, but they are already here and make it necessary that State obligations and supervision of State conduct remain in place.

Additionally, apart from their immediate impact, recognition of corporate obligations may strengthen other pillars (State duties and remedies). For instance, they may highlight the importance of developing stronger extraterritorial State obligations in light of the goal of reducing spaces of impunity and lack of protection. After all, the protection of human rights is meant to be universal,[49] but universality must not only be conceived in territorial terms, but also in *ratione personae* terms, that is to say against every possible offender. This is especially acute considering that human rights are founded on human dignity, which being non-conditional[50] cannot be made dependent on any factor different from the human identity of those who are entitled to those rights. This includes the (corporate or other) nature of the offender, which then cannot be a factor to deny protection to some victims lest they are discriminated against,[51] especially because such discrimination would be contrary to *jus cogens*.[52]

As to the fear of overburdening international bodies, some of which already have heavy workloads and backlogs, I wish to begin by recalling the distinction between substantive and procedural responses in international law, referred to in Section 1. Imposing and regulating human rights obligations of businesses does not necessarily entail coming up with new or old bodies with competence and jurisdiction over corporations. Actually, the mere regulation of their duties facilitates the work of international authorities already tasked with supervising positive State duties, since they could more easily identify conduct that States

---

49 Vienna Declaration and Programme of Action, Adopted by the World Conference on Human Rights in Vienna on 25.06.1993, paras I.1, I.5, I.8.

50 O Sensen, 'Human Dignity in Historical Perspective: The Contemporary and Traditional Paradigms' (2011) 10 *European Journal of Political Theory* 71; C Villán-Durán, *Curso de Derecho Internacional de los Derechos Humanos*, Trotta, Madrid 2006, pp 63, 92; O Schachter, 'Human Dignity as a Normative Concept' (1983) 77 *American Journal of International Law* 848, 853; R Andorno, 'Human Dignity and Human Rights as a Common Ground for a Global Bioethics' (2009) 34 *Journal of Medicine and Philosophy* 223; Resolution 41/120 of the United Nations General Assembly; Helsinki Final Act, 01.08.1975, Conference on Security and Co-Operation in Europe; J Donnelly, 'Human Rights and Human Dignity: An Analytic Critique of Non-Western Conceptions of Human Rights' (1982) 76 *The American Political Science Review* 303.

51 J Almqvist, 'Facing the Victims in the Global Fight against Terrorism' (2006) 18 *FRIDE Working Paper* 1, 8–17.

52 I/A Court H.R., Juridical Condition and Rights of the Undocumented Migrants. Advisory Opinion OC-18/03 of 17.09.2003. Series A No. 18, paras 100–01, 110–11.

must prevent and respond to. Likewise, the clarification of when corporations commit abuses would inform States clearly about what conduct they must deal with, and so it would be harder for them to say that they did not respond to such conduct because they did not know about its illegal character. Their diligence would be measured in light of, among other things, the clarifications and developments.

That being said, why can there not be direct pronouncements against serious abuses? Reports can serve to highlight and condemn them, giving some satisfaction to victims (the declaration and publication of wrongful acts is regarded as a form of satisfaction).[53] And if corporations benefit from procedural venues to protect some of their rights, e.g. as investors, why can they not be held accountable for egregious abuses? Difficulties demand imagination, not surrender.

Moving on to the challenges about the (alleged lack of) subjectivity of businesses, let me express that I agree with those who consider that the notion of subjectivity is frequently used to curtail or exclude new frontiers of international law, thus operating as a mental prison.[54] In this regard, international law has already demonstrated that it can and does regulate obligations of non-state actors, as happens in the fields of international humanitarian law or international criminal law, among others. In fact, international human rights law already envisages the possibility of regulating *and* supervising obligations of non-state actors such as the European Union and other international organisations, as the Convention on the Rights of Persons with Disabilities or the European Convention on Human Rights demonstrate.[55] But apart from this empirical demonstration, being a subject or a legal person simply amounts to being an addressee of international law, even in a limited way – different addressees may have different capacities and duties to different degrees.[56] In the case under examination, and for the purposes of this discussion, the human rights subjectivity of businesses requires the creation and regulation of obligation(s) by a source

---

53 *Application of the Convention on the Prevention and Punishment of the Crime of Genocide (Bosnia and Herzegovina v. Serbia and Montenegro), Judgment, I.C.J. Reports 2007*, p 43, paras 463–64; International Law Commission, 'Draft articles on Responsibility of States for Internationally Wrongful Acts, with commentaries, 2001' in *Yearbook of the International Law Commission, 2001, vol. II, Part Two*, paras 5–6 of the commentary to article 37, 106–07.

54 JM Cortés-Martín, *Las Organizaciones Internacionales: Codificación y Desarrollo Progresivo de su Responsabilidad Internacional*, Instituto Andaluz de Administración Pública, Seville 2008, pp 109–11; Clapham, *Human Rights Obligations of Non-State Actors*, above n 2, pp 62–63; R Higgins, *Problems and Process: International Law and How We Use It*, Oxford University Press, Oxford 2004, p 49.

55 Articles 59 of the European Convention on Human Rights, 43 and 44 of the Convention on the Rights of Persons with Disabilities, and 11 and 12 of the Optional Protocol to the Convention on the Rights of Persons with Disabilities.

56 Clapham, *Human Rights Obligations of Non-State Actors*, above n 2, pp 71–73.

of international law (including customary law); complying with the principle of legality, along with its components of foreseeability and accessibility;[57] and the absence of logical or normative impediments,[58] which are not present in our case.

The previous consideration does highlight an interesting aspect: the regulation of corporate obligations does not necessarily have to be made by treaty law. In fact, I contend that peremptory norms created by customary law already do envisage some implied obligations. However, the benefits of taking advantage of the opportunity to adopt treaty norms about them are twofold: first, treaty norms provide greater clarity on what is expected but do not terminate customary regulation;[59] and second, they can facilitate progressive development after discussions on issues as the necessity of forbidding some corporate conduct in spite of it not being criminal or contrary to peremptory law, as happens with certain violations of economic, social and cultural rights, which must nonetheless be addressed urgently.

Regarding the challenges based on the presumptive objective of human rights law to deal with and protect from State abuses exclusively, a couple of things can be said. First of all, we must look at their purpose, as the very general rule of interpretation demands.[60] If those fundamental rights and freedoms exist to protect human dignity, among other things, and such dignity can be ignored by corporations, and additionally a framework exclusively based on State responsibility is insufficient to cope with those violations, then the very idea of human rights *demands* doing something else, completing the protection. Solidarity[61] with those who suffer at the hands of businesses requires this. And if contemporary international law does not afford that protection yet in a full way, then it must evolve to offer it. The Appeals Court in the *Kiobel* case, which opposed the recognition of current corporate responsibilities (in a mistaken way, to my mind and that of others),[62] acknowledged that if corporations do not have international human rights obligations, those obligations can still be created in

57 *Sunday Times v UK*, no 6538/74, ECHR 1979, para 49; *Kononov v Latvia*, no 36376/04, ECHR 2010-IV, paras 185, 236; article 22 of the Rome Statute of the International Criminal Court.

58 G Pentassuglia, 'Review of: Meijknecht, Anna. *Towards International Personality: The Position of Minorities and Indigenous Peoples in International Law*' (2003) 14 *European Journal of International Law* 390, 391.

59 *Military and Paramilitary Activities in and against Nicaragua (Nicaragua v. United States of America), Jurisdiction and Admissibility, Judgment, I.C.J. Reports 1984*, p 392, para 73; JP Trachtman, 'Reports of the Death of Treaty Are Premature, but Customary International Law May Have Outlived Its Usefulness [Agora: The End of Treaties?]' (*AJIL Unbound*, 29.04.2014) <https://www.asil.org/blogs/reports-death-treaty-are-premature-customary-international-law-may-have-outlived> accessed 04.05.2016.

60 Article 31 of the Vienna Convention on the Law of Treaties.

61 A Clapham, *Human Rights: A Very Short Introduction*, Oxford University Press, Oxford 2015, pp xiii, 22, 24, 165.

62 United States Court of Appeals, Seventh Circuit, *Boimah FLOMO*, et al., *Plaintiffs-Appellants, v. Firestone Natural Rubber Co., LLC, Defendant-Appellee*, No. 10-3675, decided 11.07.2011.

the future.[63] To some extent they exist already, as discussed in Section 3, but there are still some gaps that call for additional regulation of duties.

Furthermore, authors in the Enlightenment who provided precedents and a background for the emergence of human rights[64] based many of their theories, among others, on the need for States to *protect from* private abuses;[65] and not only on protection from State abuses, which is telling. This supports the idea that in a multi-level system, if the State level is unable to provide protection in spite of diligent efforts, then complementary levels must come into play. This is especially so because just as international human rights law emerged as a reaction to the fact that protection from State abuses at the domestic level proved to be insufficient, so there must be a proper response to the fact that, as has been argued in this chapter, a system that relies only on State responsibility to protect from corporate abuses is limited and insufficient too. Moreover, as Alexandra Gatto and others have explained, nowadays many corporations are much more powerful than States,[66] and so if the rationale is protecting individuals from the powerful parties, then corporations must certainly be included in the equation. In fact, in the working group on transnational corporations and other business enterprises with respect to human rights, it has been discussed how powerful corporations may attempt to exert their influence to 'block binding regulation'.[67]

This leads us to another question, namely which corporations are to have direct international human rights obligations. Only the richest ones? Only transnational ones? This has proven to be a hotly contested topic in debates.[68]

---

63 United States Court of Appeals for the Second Circuit, *Esther Kiobel et al. Plaintiffs-Appellants-Cross-Appellees, v. Royal Dutch Petroleum Co., Shell Transport and Trading Company PLC*, Docket Nos. 06-4800-cv, 06-4876 cv, decided 17.09.2010 (at 49).

64 D Boucher, *The Limits of Ethics in International Relations: Natural Law, Natural Rights, and Human Rights in Transition*, Oxford University Press, Oxford 2011, p 3; Sensen, above n 50.

65 J Locke, *Second Treatise of Government and A Letter Concerning Toleration*, Oxford University Press, Oxford 2016; Clapham, *Human Rights: A Very Short Introduction*, above n 61, 9, 27; I Kant, *Perpetual Peace*, Cosimo, New York 2005, p 13.

66 Gatto, above n 29, 423; Human Rights Council, *Report on the first session of the open-ended intergovernmental working group on transnational corporations and other business enterprises with respect to human rights, with the mandate of elaborating an international legally binding instrument, Chair-Rapporteur: María Fernanda Espinosa*, A/HRC/31/50, 05.02.2016, para 55.

67 *Draft report on the second session of the open-ended intergovernmental working group on transnational corporations and other business enterprises with respect to human rights* (version of 28.10.2016 – corrected by Secretariat), p 22.

68 Human Rights Council, *Report on the first session of the open-ended intergovernmental working group on transnational corporations and other business enterprises with respect to human rights, with the mandate of elaborating an international legally binding instrument, Chair-Rapporteur: María Fernanda Espinosa*, A/HRC/31/50, 05.02.2016, paras 13, 16, 25, 44, 58–61; International Justice Resource Center, 'In Controversial Landmark Resolution, Human Rights Council takes First Step toward Treaty on Transnational Corporations' Human Rights Obligations', 15.07.2014 <http://www.ijrcenter.org/2014/07/15/in-controversial-landmark-resolution-human-rights-council-takes-first-step-toward-treaty-on-transnational-corporations-human-rights-obligations/> accessed 04.05.2016.

To address it, I return to the central point: the existence of victims and of corporate violations. As empirical and theoretical studies demonstrate, *any* corporation, not only transnational ones, can perpetrate abuses,[69] and in fact sometimes local or small corporations elude some strategies, such as those based on shaming or boycotts, more easily.[70] If this is so, does it make sense to say that only transnational corporations are to be under duties to respect human rights? That would be inconsistent and run against what has been argued thus far. All corporations must be placed under obligations not to participate in human rights abuses. An entirely different thing is what must and can be done concerning some challenges particularly posed by transnational businesses, such as issues of extraterritorial jurisdiction or evasion of responsibility by parent companies based on the corporate veil, among others. They do require specific treatment, but it can be done without excluding the regulation of obligations of all corporations, especially given how nowadays all of them can potentially act transnationally.[71] After all, there may be actors that are local in origin but still can operate in a transnational or even in an international way or space.[72]

Having defended the idea that we are better with than without corporate obligations, and that there are no real impediments to them or risks uniquely dependent on their presence, I will now explore why there are implied obligations of all non-state actors – businesses included – to not participate in international crimes (not only as perpetrators) and to not act against the supreme effects of peremptory norms; and then I will argue why, in addition to this, express obligations that clarify or complement those implied duties are important.

69 Human Rights Council, *Report on the first session of the open-ended intergovernmental working group on transnational corporations and other business enterprises with respect to human rights, with the mandate of elaborating an international legally binding instrument, Chair-Rapporteur: María Fernanda Espinosa*, A/HRC/31/50, 05.02.2016, para 61; International Justice Resource Center, above n 68; Office of the United Nations High Commissioner for Human Rights, *Guiding Principles on Business and Human Rights: Implementing the United Nations 'Protect, Respect and Remedy' Framework*, United Nations, 2011, Principle 14 and its commentary.

70 Hobbes, above n 31.

71 Human Rights Council, *Report on the first session of the open-ended intergovernmental working group on transnational corporations and other business enterprises with respect to human rights, with the mandate of elaborating an international legally binding instrument, Chair-Rapporteur: María Fernanda Espinosa*, A/HRC/31/50, 05.02.2016, paras 57–58. Moreover, article 3.2 of the United Nations Convention against Transnational Organized Crime can serve as analogy or inspiration when identifying transnational operations of businesses.

72 B Reinalda, 'Private in Form, Public in Purpose: NGOs in International Relations Theory' in B Arts, M Noortmann, B Reinalda (eds), *Non-State Actors in International Relations*, Ashgate, New York 2001, pp 12–14.

4. THE EXISTENCE OF IMPLIED GENERAL DUTIES AND THE RELEVANCE OF COMPLEMENTARY EXPRESS OBLIGATIONS

A discussion on whether businesses can and should have direct international human rights obligations should not ignore the question of whether they already have (some) obligations in that regard, and if so whether they are sufficient for the protection of human rights to be robust.

As to the current existence of corporate obligations, it is my belief that all corporations are under an obligation to not participate in violations of peremptory law – criminal or not. This is interesting because international criminal norms can be considered as having a *jus cogens* nature[73] and so the duty to not participate in conduct contrary to them would be *one* of the implicit obligations. But in addition to it, there is a duty to respect non-criminal but peremptory human rights norms. After all, currently not every human rights norm has a *jus cogens* character.[74]

John Ruggie himself has said that those who argue that corporate responsibilities to respect are merely social or outside the realm of hard law are mistaken, insofar as the legal dimension of corporate duties of respect is not excluded and may exist in criminal matters (international and domestic).[75] Moreover, as Roland Portmann indicates, some case law and practice, apart from logical arguments, seem to support the idea that private actors are constrained by a legal duty to not act contrary to peremptory law, lest their legal responsibility is engaged.[76] To my mind, ethical and logical arguments support the existence of those duties as well: the effective protection of human dignity and the prevention of impunity in relation to peremptory norms demand them, considering the reality of corporate abuses. Moreover, the recognition of victimisation by businesses also serves as the basis of direct remedies against them, which in turn can permit full reparations. Overall, it is important to recognise the illegality of – at the very least – serious corporate abuses everywhere, regardless of domestic legislation.

---

73 A Gómez-Robledo, *El ius cogens internacional: Estudio histórico-crítico*, Universidad Nacional Autónoma de México, Mexico City 2003, pp 169–70.

74 Ibid, pp 166–70; Human Rights Committee, *General Comment No. 29, States of Emergency (Article 4)*, above n 43, para 11; S Kirchner, 'Relative Normativity and the Constitutional Dimension of International Law: A Place for Values in the International Legal System?' (2004) 5 *German Law Journal* 47, 59–60.

75 Concerning the fact that the Framework and the Guiding Principles do not exclude the possibility of corporate (international or domestic) legal responsibility, see JG Ruggie, 'Kiobel and Corporate Social Responsibility', *Issues Brief*, 04.09.2012, pp 3–4.

76 R Portmann, *Legal Personality in International Law* (Cambridge University Press, Cambridge 2010) pp 166–67, 273–74, 280.

Given the discussions on the importance or inconvenience of enacting *express* human rights obligations of businesses, which often reveals the lack of clarity about whether they exist or not, it can be said that the duty to not infringe peremptory human rights is an *implied* obligation. This means that even absent an *express* norm addressing those actors and obliging them to do or refrain from doing something, they are under an international legal obligation. Authors such as Jordan J Paust and José E Alvarez, and bodies such as the European Court of Human Rights, have either affirmed or hinted that non-state actors can have implicit international duties, for instance concerning peremptory law.[77] Naturally, such obligations must come from a source of international law, such as custom. In this regard, it is important to recall that human rights bodies have held that the principle of legality is upheld and not affected when non-state actors are made responsible on the basis of the breach of customary law obligations – or those originating in any source of international law.[78]

Having said this, what is the legal basis of implied obligations? In my opinion, it would be the necessity of permitting the achievement of the goal of protecting human dignity from corporate abuses, considering that in international law implied capacities have been recognised when they are functionally necessary to accomplish certain legal objectives. If the implied capacities that international organisations have are based on the importance and necessity of permitting them to carry out their functions and achieve their objectives, according to the ICJ,[79] is it then not logical to come up with a normative framework that requires everyone to refrain from preventing the accomplishment of the respect and integrity of the most fundamental goals of international law, which are those enshrined in the hierarchically superior norms that admit no exception whatsoever and have an aspiration of utter effectiveness, namely *jus cogens*?[80] The *effet utile* and

77 Alvarez, above n 35, 32; JJ Paust, 'The Other Side of Right: Private Duties Under Human Rights Law' (1992) 5 *Harvard Human Rights Journal* 51, 52, 54–55, 59, 62; JJ Paust, 'The Reality of Private Rights, Duties, and Participation in the International Legal Process' (2004) 25 *Michigan Journal of International Law* 1229, 1242–43; JJ Paust, 'Human Rights Responsibilities of Private Corporations' (2002) 35 *Vanderbilt Journal of Transnational Law* 801, 810–17, 824; *Kononov v Latvia*, no 36376/04, ECHR 2010-IV, para 236.

78 *Kononov v Latvia*, no 36376/04, ECHR 2010-IV, paras 118–22, 185–86, 199, 207–08, 211–13, 227, 236, 243; articles 7 of the European Convention on Human Rights and 15 of the International Covenant on Civil and Political Rights Human Rights; Principles of International Law recognised in the Charter of the Nürnberg Tribunal and in the Judgment of the Tribunal, with commentaries, *Yearbook of the International Law Commission, 1950, vol. II*, 1950, Principles I and II, with their respective commentaries.

79 *Reparation for injuries suffered in the service of the United Nations, Advisory Opinion: I.C.J. Reports 1949, p. 174*, pp 10–12.

80 N Carrillo-Santarelli, 'La inevitable supremacía del *ius cogens* frente a la inmunidad jurisdiccional de los Estados' (2008) 18 *RJUAM* 55, 58–63.

pro personae principles[81] lend support to this conception. Especially considering that saying that businesses are not bound by or constrained by a duty to refrain from participating in or contributing to conduct such as genocide, torture (which, among other abuses, can certainly be perpetrated by non-state actors),[82] crimes against humanity and war crimes, among others, would imply that there would be no consequences for such conduct. This would deprive victims of direct remedies against corporate participants in those misdeeds, generating impunity. This, in turn, would compromise the effectiveness of the norms in question, insofar as the lack of proper responses to violations begets or encourages repetition, as the Inter-American Court of Human Rights has stated – and that would be unacceptable.[83] Moreover, the fight against impunity is a demand of both international criminal law and human rights law.[84] Altogether, implied *capacities* include not only rights, but also duties, and both are two sides of the protection of important international legal interests, among which peremptory ones reign supreme.

As to the legal basis and explanation of the implicit corporate duties to not violate human rights *jus cogens* norms, I will add the following. Every potential offender or participant in violation of peremptory law is bound by a duty to abstain from doing so, lest the supreme and absolute effectiveness of peremptory law, which admits no exception whatsoever and excludes all

---

81 M Pinto, 'El principio *pro homine*. Criterios de hermenéutica y pautas para la regulación de los derechos humanos' in M Abregú and C Courtis (eds), *La aplicación de los tratados sobre derechos humanos por los tribunales locales*, Centro de Estudios Legales y Sociales, Buenos Aires 1997; M Fitzmaurice, 'Interpretation of Human Rights Treaties' in D Shelton (ed), *The Oxford Handbook of International Human Rights Law*, Oxford University Press, Oxford 2013, pp 755–56; HV Condé, *A Handbook of International Human Rights Terminology*, 2nd edn, University of Nebraska Press, Lincoln, NE 2004, pp 207–08; José P Aguirre-Arango, 'La interpretación de la Convención Americana sobre Derechos Humanos', pp 80–81 <http://www.corteidh.or.cr/tablas/R22853.pdf> accessed 05.05.2016; Separate Opinion of Judge AA Cançado Trindade in I/A Court H.R., *Case of the Pueblo Bello Massacre v. Colombia.* Merits, Reparations and Costs. Judgment of 31.01.2006. Series C No. 140, paras 33, 50; I/A Court H.R., *Case of the Constitutional Court v. Peru.* Competence. Judgment of 24.09.1999. Series C No. 55, para 36.

82 Committee against Torture, *Sadiq Shek Elmi v. Australia*, Communication N° 120/1998, Date of adoption of Views: 14.05.1999, paras 4.5, 5.2, 6.4–6.9; Redress, *Not only the State: Torture by Non-State Actors: Towards Enhanced Protection, Accountability and Effective Remedies*, The Redress Trust, 2006.

83 Preamble to the Rome Statute of the International Criminal Court; I/A Court H.R., *Case of González et al. ('Cotton Field') v. Mexico.* Preliminary Objection, Merits, Reparations and Costs. Judgment of 16.11.2009. Series C No. 205, paras 158, 163, 289, 377–78, 388, 400, 453–54, 460.

84 Ibid.; I/A Court H.R., *Case of Almonacid Arellano et al. v. Chile.* Preliminary Objections, Merits, Reparations and Costs. Judgment of 26.09.2006. Series C No. 154, paras 106–07, 110–11, 119.

contrary manifestations,[85] is compromised. This, naturally, includes the idea that no actor, corporations included, can perpetrate or participate in violations of *jus cogens* with impunity and no adverse legal consequences. The absolute nature of peremptory law and the exclusion of any detrimental or contrary manifestation (normative or of conduct) is confirmed by two sources: first, by the idea that no circumstance precludes the wrongfulness of violations of peremptory law;[86] and secondly that, as considered by the International Criminal Tribunal for the former Yugoslavia, if such violations are committed by non-state actors (individuals and corporations are non-state actors, and the latter *can* also be made responsible for participating in the perpetration of crimes),[87] then any actor – with competence on the basis of international law – can try and persecute them on the basis of the protection of international law.[88]

Needless to say, it cannot be denied that corporations *can* violate all human rights,[89] some of which are peremptory. Interestingly, in its Advisory Opinion 18 the Inter-American Court of Human Rights, after declaring that the principle of non-discrimination is peremptory, went on to say that even private employers are bound to respect the rights of migrant workers, who cannot be discriminated against.[90] This logic echoes and endorses the theory I present.

---

85 Articles 53 and 64 of the Vienna Convention on the Law of Treaties; CARRILLO-SANTARELLI, 'La inevitable supremacía del *ius cogens* frente a la inmunidad jurisdiccional de los Estados', above n 80; International Law Commission, 'Draft articles on Responsibility of States for Internationally Wrongful Acts, with commentaries, 2001' in *Yearbook of the International Law Commission, 2001, vol. II, Part Two*, paras 2 and 3 of the commentary to article 26, pp 84–85.

86 International Law Commission, 'Draft articles on Responsibility of States for Internationally Wrongful Acts, with commentaries, 2001' in: *Yearbook of the International Law Commission, 2001, vol. II, Part Two*, articles 26 and 50 and paras 4 and 6 of the commentary to article 26, pp 84–85, 131.

87 Office of the United Nations High Commissioner for Human Rights, *Guiding Principles on Business and Human Rights: Implementing the United Nations 'Protect, Respect and Remedy' Framework*, United Nations, 2011, commentary to Principle 23, 25–26; Commission on Human Rights, *Working paper on human rights and non-State actors submitted by Gáspár Biró and Antoanella-Iulia Motoc*, E/CN.4/Sub.2/2005/40, 11.07.2005, paras 4, 25, 34, 46; H VAN DER WILT, 'Corporate Criminal Responsibility for International Crimes: Exploring the Possibilities' (2013) 12 *Chinese Journal of International Law* 43, 43–49, 72–77; Human Rights Council, *Protect, Respect and Remedy: a Framework for Business and Human Rights*, Report of the Special Representative of the Secretary-General on the issue of human rights and transnational corporations and other business enterprises, John Ruggie, A/HRC/8/5, 07.04.2008, paras 31, 74, 83.

88 International Criminal Tribunal for the former Yugoslavia, Trial Chamber, *Prosecutor v. Anto Furundžija*, Judgment, 10.12.1998, paras 154–57.

89 Office of the United Nations High Commissioner for Human Rights, *Guiding Principles on Business and Human Rights: Implementing the United Nations 'Protect, Respect and Remedy' Framework*, United Nations, 2011, commentary to Principle 12.

90 I/A Court H.R., Juridical Condition and Rights of the Undocumented Migrants. Advisory Opinion OC-18/03 of 17.09.2003. Series A No. 18, paras 101, 146.

While they are important, implied peremptory obligations are not enough for the human rights and business framework to be robust. After all, corporations can and do participate in violations of rights not covered by peremptory norms, and if those violations are not fully addressed (which, as argued above, requires regulating duties of abstention) there will be gaps that need to be filled. For this reason, I think that it is convenient to create additional obligations that are express and specialised.

In this sense, it is useful to bear in mind that human rights law has undergone a process of specialisation to deal in a detailed manner with specific worrying abuses or to protect vulnerable persons. Corporations, in turn, pose problems that merit special attention and regulation; and certain corporate conduct may be more adequately dealt with by specialised norms that focus on some of their abuses, victims (e.g. indigenous peoples)[91] and rights they affect; or on the specific challenges posed by certain businesses. Some authors precisely suggest a specialised approach to human rights and business.[92] While I understand the merits of such points of view and agree that special attention must be paid to some victims or situations, it is important not to exclude general standards of protection, lest the protection is not universal, impunity and repetition are encouraged and victims are undefended in cases not covered by specialised norms, given the shortcomings of domestic strategies. The specialised and general (implied) approaches are complementary. Furthermore, express obligations may not only complement the implied peremptory ones, but also codify them, dispelling doubts about their existence and providing greater clarity about their content, perhaps even generating or progressively contributing to potential future developments that reinforce those and other duties.

One interesting question that ensues is whether corporate obligations – be they express or perhaps even implied ones – are necessarily obligations of respect, i.e. obligations of abstention.[93] Those obligations demand that businesses refrain or abstain from perpetrating, being complicit in or else participating in human rights violations. They are necessary and indeed seek to tackle the fact that corporations contribute or cause the disrespect of human rights. That being said, it must be noted that human rights may be affected not only by action, but

91 Office of the United Nations High Commissioner for Human Rights, *Guiding Principles on Business and Human Rights: Implementing the United Nations 'Protect, Respect and Remedy' Framework*, United Nations, 2011, commentary to article 12, p 14.

92 On this discussion see, for instance: JG Ruggie, 'A UN Business and Human Rights Treaty?: An Issues Brief by John G. Ruggie', Harvard John F. Kennedy School of Government, 2014, pp 3–4.

93 I/A Court H.R., *Case of Velásquez Rodríguez v. Honduras*. Merits. Judgment of 29.07.1988. Series C No. 4, paras 164–65; I/A Court H.R., Juridical Condition and Rights of the Undocumented Migrants. Advisory Opinion OC-18/03 of 17.09.2003. Series A No. 18, paras 102–03, 143; Office of the United Nations High Commissioner for Human Rights, *Guiding Principles on Business and Human Rights: Implementing the United Nations 'Protect, Respect and Remedy' Framework*, United Nations, 2011, Principles 11–13 and their commentaries.

also by inaction, especially when given their functions (such as the provision of safe water)[94] there are expectations on human rights enjoyment with a direct dependence on or nexus of causality with the proper and proactive conduct of a corporation. From the point of view of the general regime of responsibility, it is clear that primary norms can demand abstention or action; and in philosophical discussions it has been considered that human dignity may sometimes demand the performance of certain actions to ensure the enjoyment of human rights.[95]

Logically, great care must be taken when considering the adoption and regulation of positive duties, since clearly corporations are not States, which should not have the same functions as them. Yet, it should not be ignored either that there is sometimes indeed a direct impact of the proper conduct of corporations that have certain roles and functions on the actual enjoyment of some human rights in certain situations. Thus, neither rushed, expansive regulation of positive duties nor absence of the respective standards are advisable. Those duties, if ever adopted, must preferably be based on the standard of due diligence and be obligations of means rather than duties of result, following this wise criterion endorsed by the Guiding Principles on Business and Human Rights in relation to the pillar of corporate respect[96] (which in those Principles is not only or necessarily based on legal obligations)[97] and also by the commentary on the Norms on the Responsibilities of Transnational Corporations and Other Business Enterprises with Regard to Human Rights. According to the latter, businesses must use 'due diligence in ensuring that their activities do not contribute directly or indirectly to human abuses, and that they do not directly or indirectly benefit from abuses of which they were aware or ought to have been aware'.[98]

5. CONCLUSIONS

State obligations to protect individuals from human rights abuses in which corporations participate, and the provision of domestic remedies against them, are useful and indeed necessary. They contribute to offering protection in cases

---

94 Human Rights Council, *Report of the independent expert on the issue of human rights obligations related to access to safe drinking water and sanitation, Catarina de Albuquerque*, A/HRC/15/31, 29.06.2010, paras 26–28.

95 Clapham, *Human Rights Obligations of Non-State Actors*, above n 2, pp 546–47.

96 Office of the United Nations High Commissioner for Human Rights, *Guiding Principles on Business and Human Rights: Implementing the United Nations 'Protect, Respect and Remedy' Framework*, United Nations, 2011, Principle 15.

97 Ibid, commentary to Principle 12, p 14.

98 Commentary on the Norms on the Responsibilities of Transnational Corporations and Other Business Enterprises with Regard to Human Rights, U.N. Doc. E/CN.4/Sub.2/2003/38/Rev.2 (2003), commentary to para 1.

in which it may not exist otherwise, and they make sure that States are obliged to be diligent and cannot simply ignore corporate abuses, folding their arms and blaming corporations alone. Their legitimacy rests in the fulfilment, among other things, of such protection.[99]

That being said, the reach and effectiveness of domestic legal systems and State obligations to protect from corporate abuses are limited, among other things because the latter are based on a logic of primary norms that impose duties of means. Blaming States for every single corporate abuse when the business eludes or circumvents domestic controls is not legally sound and would not be fair. Many States earnestly strive but fail to tackle those abuses.

It has been argued that the emergence of direct obligations that impose burdens of respect (and eventually positive duties) on corporations is not only legally feasible but also crucial for human rights to be universally protected in a *ratione personae* sense, given how those obligations can fill some gaps in the human rights and business field. For instance, international condemnation of a given abuse ensures that corporate abusers are regarded as *legally* responsible anywhere, even if they try to flee to other jurisdictions. And such regulation of duties also empowers and calls for different authorities, foreign and international, to contribute with their reactions and preventive measures, such as by condemning or even trying corporate abusers. Conversely, corporations are not 'legitimized' or empowered if given international legal obligations.[100]

In sum, corporate duties can create a level playing field and constitute some lowest common denominators applicable everywhere, for instance regarding gross abuses, that is to say level playing fields in regulatory terms, which, by making certain standards binding in respect of businesses everywhere, help to prevent a race to the bottom, labour dumping and normative competition (e.g. by economically weak States which do not want to miss out on investment) and so can also counter forum shopping and jurisdiction 'jumps' by companies, since some core norms bind them in every country and in respect to every individual.

In this regard, the working group on transnational corporations and other business enterprises with respect to human rights has mentioned how a binding treaty may offset dynamics of deregulation or unwillingness to domestically regulate corporate conduct.[101] The required international norms can perfectly

---

99 Concurring Opinion of Judge AA Cançado Trindade in I/A Court H.R., Juridical Condition and Human Rights of the Child. Advisory Opinion OC-17/02 of 28.08.2002. Series A No. 17, para 19.

100 See, in comparison: common article 3 to the Geneva Conventions of 1949; Inter-American Commission on Human Rights, *Third Report on the Human Rights Situation in Colombia*, OEA/Ser.L/V/II.102, Doc. 9 rev. 1, 26.02.1999, para 18 of Chapter IV; Clapham, *Human Rights Obligations of Non-State Actors*, above n 2, pp 51–53, 58.

101 *Draft report on the second session of the open-ended intergovernmental working group on transnational corporations and other business enterprises with respect to human rights* (version of 28.10.2016 – corrected by Secretariat) p 10.

have businesses as addressees. Corporations already benefit from legal protection of their economic interests, and human rights should be regarded as having priority over them, due to their being directly founded – as they must be – on the human dignity of every single human being. That dignity and the protection it demands do not depend on who the offender is. Moreover, corporations have undeniable power nowadays and rule-of-law considerations call for holding every actor that contravenes essential interests of the international society, or has the potential to do so, accountable.[102]

Given the importance of peremptory law, which protects community dimensions, the legal system of that community already binds corporate actors that infringe *jus cogens* human rights norms in a legal – albeit implied – and not merely in a social way. However, – implied – peremptory obligations of businesses do not cover all the range of potential corporate abuses, potentially leaving protection gaps and victims unprotected when the pertinent domestic norms are not operative. Therefore, alongside norms that clarify the content of implicit obligations, complementary specific obligations are necessary for the system to be robust and more complete, and the adoption of such additional express duties may contribute to truly creating a lowest common denominator of protection everywhere from corporate abuses. Such additional obligations may be envisaged in the potential treaty on business and human rights proposed by Ecuador and South Africa, especially since, as mentioned in Section 2, while they can – and should – also be created by other sources, regulating them in a treaty provides certain advantages of clarity and foreseeability. Moreover, such a treaty may crystallise or pave the way for future obligations, even customary ones, with which treaty norms can coexist.[103]

Granted, the legal dimension is not the only relevant or present one in human rights terms,[104] but out of the three main principles or pillars of the human rights and business field, namely (State) protection, remedies and corporate responsibility, the latter is the one that requires greater theoretical development and acceptance about its much needed (legal) strengthening, since a merely social responsibility is too weak and does a disservice to victims, who should be and are the protagonists in these discussions. Granted, remedies must be developed as well, given shortcomings in access by victims; and the serious discussion and acceptance of extraterritorial State obligations is pending. Human beings deserve all of this.

---

102 JE Nijman, 'Non-state Actors and the International Rule of Law: Revisiting the 'Realist Theory' of International Legal Personality' (2010) *Amsterdam Center for International Law Research Paper Series* 1, 7–19, 40.

103 Militarv and Paramilitary Activities in and against Nicaragua *(Nicaragua v. United States of America).* Merits, Judgment. I.C.J. Reports 1986, p 14, paras 175, 177–79.

104 A Sen, 'Elements of a Theory of Human Rights' (2004) 32 *Philosophy and Public Affairs* 315, 323–28; Knox, above n 19, 44.

A TREATY ON BUSINESS AND HUMAN RIGHTS: PROBLEMS AND PROSPECTS

Chiara MACCHI

1. INTRODUCTION: MOVING THE BUSINESS AND HUMAN RIGHTS AGENDA FORWARD

The dismissal of the UN Norms in 2003 and the subsequent adoption of the UN Guiding Principles on Business and Human Rights (hereinafter, GPs) did not end calls for an international binding instrument in the area of business and human rights. Quite the contrary, the revival of the international debate on business and human rights, spurred by the successful mandate of the Special Representative of the Secretary-General on human rights and transnational corporations and other business enterprises (hereinafter, SRSG), constituted a springboard for those sectors of international civil society and of the community of States advocating for legally binding solutions.[1]

Thus, in 2014, three years after having adopted the GPs, the Human Rights Council was faced with the initiative, led by the government of Ecuador, to promote the adoption of an international treaty. The process started with

1 L CATÁ BACKER, 'The Guiding Principles of Business and Human Rights at a Crossroads: the State, the Enterprise, and the Spectre of a Treaty to Bind Them All' (Working Paper no. 7(1), Coalition for Peace and Ethics, July 2014) 42.

a 2013 declaration in which Ecuador, speaking for a number of countries that had rallied around the proposal,[2] put forward the idea to the UN Human Rights Council (HRC) that the UN should start working on the drafting of a binding instrument.[3] The declaration made clear that for the proposing States, while the GPs were a welcome progress, they were nothing more than a 'first' step, incapable of triggering concrete changes in the absence of a binding instrument clarifying 'the obligations of transnational corporations' and providing 'for the establishment of effective remedies for victims in cases where domestic jurisdiction is clearly unable to prosecute effectively those companies'.[4] This joint position was translated into a formal proposal at the 26th session of the HRC through a resolution drafted by Ecuador and South Africa and signed by Bolivia, Cuba and Venezuela,[5] which was finally adopted on 26 June 2014. In the resolution it was decided:

> … to establish an open-ended intergovernmental working group on a legally binding instrument on transnational corporations and other business enterprises with respect to human rights, the mandate of which shall be to elaborate an international legally binding instrument to regulate, in international human rights law, the activities of transnational corporations and other business enterprises.[6]

The content, scope, nature and form of the future international instrument were left to be discussed at the first two sessions of the new working group.[7] The resolution was adopted with 22 votes in favour, 14 against and 13 abstentions,[8] but evinced a sharp division between developing and emerging countries, on one side, and developed countries, none of which voted in favour of the resolution, on the other.[9] At the same session, the HRC adopted a second resolution,

2 Namely, the African Group, the Arab Group, Pakistan, Sri Lanka, Kyrgyzstan, Cuba, Nicaragua, Bolivia, Venezuela, Peru and Ecuador.

3 Republic of Ecuador, 'Statement on behalf of a Group of Countries at the 24th Session of the Human Rights Council General Debate – Item 3 "Transnational Corporations and Human Rights"' September 2013 <http://business-humanrights.org/sites/default/files/media/documents/statement-unhrc-legally-binding.pdf> accessed 01.12.2015.

4 Ibid.

5 Human Rights Council, 'Elaboration of an international legally binding instrument on transnational corporations and other business enterprises with respect to human rights' 25.06.2014, UN Doc. A/HRC/26/L.22/Rev.1 (hereinafter, 'Ecuador Resolution').

6 Ibid., para 1.

7 Ibid., para 2.

8 BHRRC, 'UN Human Rights Council sessions' <http://business-humanrights.org/en/binding-treaty/un-human-rights-council-sessions> accessed 01.12.2015.

9 Algeria, Benin, Burkina Faso, China, Congo, Côte d'Ivoire, Cuba, Ethiopia, India, Indonesia, Kazakhstan, Kenya, Morocco, Namibia, Pakistan, Philippines, Russia, South Africa, Venezuela and Vietnam voted in favour. Austria, Czech Republic, Estonia, France, Germany, Ireland, Italy (also speaking on behalf of the EU), Japan, Montenegro, South Korea, Romania, the Former Yugoslavia, UK and US voted against. Abstentions: Argentina, Botswana, Brazil, Chile, Costa Rica, Gabon, Kuwait, Maldives, Mexico, Peru, Saudi Arabia, Sierra Leone, UAE (ibid.).

sponsored by Norway, which called on the UN Working Group on Business and Human Rights, among other things, to investigate 'the benefits and limitations of a legally binding instrument, and to prepare a report thereon'.[10] This second resolution, supported by 22 countries from all regions of the world,[11] is more inscribed within the path indicated by the SRSG: instead of considering the GPs as a mere transitional step in a process inevitably leading to the adoption of a more effective (legally binding) instrument, it reaffirms the importance of implementing the GPs in the domestic legal orders of States and encourages collaboration and exchange of best practices, particularly as concerns improved access to remedy.[12]

As noted by Backer, the Norway Resolution, which also extended the mandate of the UN Working Group, 'sought to contextualise treaty making within the greater project of developing the GPs'.[13] However, the renewed calls for a legally binding solution stemmed largely from the perceived inadequacy of the GPs' 'soft law' character and their slow implementation process, which relies on the commitment of States to operationalise the Principles through their domestic policies and regulations.[14]

Civil society organisations have pointed out that the adoption of National Action Plans (NAPs) for the implementation of the GPs, strongly encouraged by the UN Working Group,[15] has been too slow[16] and has usually failed to give rise to 'concrete actions'.[17] Already at the time of their adoption (2011), a group of

---

10 Human Rights Council, 'Human rights and transnational corporations and other business enterprises' (23.06.2014) UN Doc. A/HRC/26/L.1, para 8 (hereinafter the Norway Resolution).

11 The resolution was signed by Andorra, Argentina, Australia, Austria, Bulgaria, Colombia, France, Georgia, Ghana, Greece, Guatemala, Iceland, India, Lebanon, Liechtenstein, Mexico, New Zealand, Norway, Russia, Serbia, the former Yugoslavia, Turkey.

12 Human Rights Council, above n 10, paras 6–13.

13 Backer, above n 1, p 53.

14 R Dumbuya, 'Corporate responsibility to respect human rights: Is the UN Guiding Principles on Business and Human Rights up to the task or is there a need for a Treaty on Business and Human rights?' 10.09.2014, p 5 <http://papers.ssrn.com/sol3/papers.cfm?abstract_id=2541420> accessed 02.12.2015; C Pitts, 'The world needs a treaty on business and human rights' 26.05.2014 *OpenDemocracy* <https://www.opendemocracy.net/openglobalrights-blog/chip-pitts/world-needs-treaty-on-business-and-human-rights> accessed 02.12.2015.

15 UN Working Group on Business and Human Rights, 'Guidance on National Action Plans on Business and Human Rights' December 2014 <http://www.ohchr.org/Documents/Issues/Business/UNWG_%20NAP Guidance.pdf> accessed 01.12.2015.

16 To date, countries that have finalised their NAPs are: UK, the Netherlands, Italy, Denmark, Spain, Finland, Lithuania, Sweden, Norway and Colombia. At the time of writing, the drafting process is ongoing in 19 more countries, and still at the starting blocks in 7 others. See: OHCHR, 'State National Action Plans' <http://www.ohchr.org/EN/Issues/Business/Pages/NationalActionPlans.aspx> accessed 01.12.2015.

17 CIDSE, 'UN Business & Human Rights Framework: More action required at national and international level to stop human rights abuses by business' December 2014, Briefing paper <https://business-humanrights.org/sites/default/files/documents/CIDSE%20-%20BHR%20Framework_More%20action_%20EN.pdf> accessed 02.12.2015.

influential NGOs had identified some crucial weaknesses of the GPs, such as the vagueness of the human rights responsibilities of businesses and the fact that they allegedly took an excessively conservative approach to the extraterritorial human rights obligations of States.[18] By 2013, civil society organisations advocating for a binding instrument rallied around the 'Treaty Alliance', which presently counts more than 600 members.[19] In its first Joint Statement the Treaty Alliance requested, among other things, the affirmation of the applicability of human rights obligations to corporations; the imposition on States of an obligation to monitor and regulate the operation of businesses domiciled in their jurisdiction, regardless of where they operate; and the drafting of an international treaty under the aegis of the UN.[20]

In July 2015, the first session of the 'Open-ended intergovernmental working group on transnational corporations and other business enterprises with respect to human rights' (hereinafter, IGWG) marked the first concrete step towards the elaboration of a binding international instrument and opened the way to a complex debate concerning the nature and content of the proposed treaty and its political feasibility. This first session witnessed the participation of around 60 States (including eight EU Member States),[21] of various intergovernmental organisations (among others: the EU, the International Labour Organization and the Organisation for Economic Co-operation and Development) and of many civil society organisations, many of which have been animating the treaty debate since its dawning. While fraught with challenges, the beginning of the treaty negotiations marked a step that seemed unthinkable until a few years ago.

18 'Joint Civil Society Statement on the draft Guiding Principles on Business and Human Rights' January 2011 <https://www.fidh.org/IMG/pdf/Joint_CSO_Statement_on_GPs.pdf> accessed 03.12.2015 (signatories were: Amnesty International, CIDSE, ESCR-Net, FIDH, Human Rights Watch, International Commission of Jurists, RAID).

19 At the 2013 ESCR-Net Peoples Forum on Human Rights & Business (Thailand), participants formulated a Joint Statement calling for States to develop a treaty to address corporate human rights violations. Initially spurred by organisations like CETIM, Dismantle Corporate Power Campaign, ESCR-Net, FIAN, FIDH, Franciscans International, Friends of the Earth International and Transnational Institute, support for the treaty movement rapidly expanded (See: Treaty Alliance <http://treatymovement.com/> accessed 01.12.2015).

20 Treaty Alliance, 'Joint Statement: Call for an international legally binding instrument on human rights, transnational corporations and other business enterprises' 2013 <http://treatymovement.com/> accessed 01.12.2015.

21 Algeria, Argentine Austria, Bangladesh, Plurinational State of Bolivia, Brazil, Bulgaria, Chile, People's Republic of China, Colombia, Costa Rica, Cuba, Dominican Republic, Ecuador, Egypt, El Salvador, Ethiopia, France, Ghana, Guatemala, Republic of Haiti, Greece, Republic of Honduras, India, Indonesia, Islamic Republic of Iran, Iraq, Italy, Kenya, Republic of Korea, Kuwait, Latvia, State of Libya, Liechtenstein, Luxembourg, Malaysia, Republic of Moldova, Morocco, Myanmar, Nicaragua, Namibia, Netherlands, Pakistan, Peru, Philippines, Qatar, Russian Federation, Singapore, South Africa, Switzerland, Syrian Arab Republic, Thailand, Trinidad and Tobago, Tunisia, Ukraine, Mexico, Uruguay, Bolivarian Republic of Venezuela, Vietnam.

The session constituted the first occasion to launch a structured discussion on issues such as the *ratione materiae* and *ratione personae* scope of the treaty, the obligations of States in relation to Transnational corporations' (TNCs) extraterritorial activities, the opportunity to include standards for corporate legal liability in the new treaty and the creation of an international mechanism to remedy violations.[22] All of these issues, at the heart of a lively international debate concerning the desirability and feasibility of a legally binding instrument on business and human rights, were addressed again at the second session of the IGWG, which took place in October 2016.[23]

While Ecuador's proposal has gained ample support from civil society organisations,[24] the treaty option continues to be met with diffidence or overt hostility by sections of the community of States and by part of the business sector. As is widely known, one of its main critics is the former SRSG John Ruggie, whose scepticism towards a hard-law solution at the international level long predates the Ecuador resolution and can, in fact, be traced back to his critique of the Draft Norms on the Responsibilities of Transnational Corporations and Other Business Enterprises with Regard to Human Rights. The main arguments raised by Ruggie and by other detractors of the treaty option can be grouped under the following categories: arguments linked to the scope and nature of the proposed treaty; the political argument, i.e. the possible political drawbacks of embarking on the long process of negotiation of a new international instrument; and the 'enforcement' argument, meaning the difficulties of monitoring and enforcing a treaty on business and human rights. The present chapter will examine those arguments and respond to them, making reference to the most recent developments in the treaty negotiation process initiated in July 2015. Sections 2 and 3 will focus respectively on the possible *ratione personae* and *ratione materiae* scope of the proposed treaty, critically reviewing the trends emerging from the debate taking place within the IGWG, as well as the opinion expressed on the matter by the former SRSG John Ruggie. Section 4 will address the critique which dismisses the treaty route as impracticable based on the difficulties of

22 Human Rights Council, 'Report of the open-ended intergovernmental working group on transnational corporations and other business enterprises with respect to human rights' 10.07.2015 Draft report <http://www.ohchr.org/Documents/HRBodies/HRCouncil/WGTransCorp/Session1/Draftreport.pdf> accessed 07.01.2016.

23 Human Rights Council, 'Second session of the open-ended intergovernmental working group on transnational corporations and other business enterprises with respect to human rights' 2016 <http://www.ohchr.org/EN/HRBodies/HRC/WGTransCorp/Session2/Pages/Session2.aspx> accessed 29.11.2016.

24 See, for example: Dismantle Corporate Power, 'Statement to the Human Rights Council in support of the initiative by a group of States for a legally binding instrument on transnational corporations' 13.09.2013 Press release <http://www.stopcorporateimpunity.org/?p=3830> accessed 01.12.2015.

engaging in a long and complex negotiation process at the international level. Section 5 will deal with the necessity to make sure that the new instrument is sustained by a credible and effective enforcement and monitoring mechanism. The chapter will conclude with a summary of the author's position on the possible added value of a binding treaty.

2. THE *RATIONE PERSONAE* SCOPE OF THE PROPOSED TREATY

A controversial aspect of the proposed treaty, as matters stand, lies in its *ratione personae* scope. The think tank Human Rights Watch has expressed the view that the treaty process is flawed by its narrow focus on TNCs.[25] ESCR-Net, a member of the Treaty Alliance, expressed a similar concern.[26] In fact, a footnote in the Ecuador Resolution explains that the expression 'other business enterprises' in the title solely refers to those enterprises that have a 'transnational character in their operational activities', explicitly excluding 'local businesses registered in terms of relevant domestic law'.[27] This narrows down the scope of a future binding instrument, leaving out of it all those local companies that constitute the segments of global supply chains, and yet it appears that precisely this limitation convinced countries like India to vote in favour of the resolution.[28] This aspect constitutes one of the central themes discussed during the first two sessions of the IGWG, with several voices arguing for the need to include provisions addressed at all businesses, but others firmly supporting the limitation to TNCs.[29] While many delegations agreed on the need to primarily tackle the challenges posed by TNCs,[30] civil society organisations warn against the risk of giving too rigid a definition of what constitutes a 'TNC', as they may exclude complex supply chain

25 A Ganesan, 'Dispatches: A Treaty to End Corporate Abuses?' 01.07.2014 *Human Rights Watch Dispatches* <http://www.hrw.org/news/2014/07/01/dispatches-treaty-end-corporate-abuses> accessed 01.12.2015.

26 ESCR-Net, 'Statement of the ESCR-Net Corporate Accountability Working Group (CAWG)' 30.06.2014 <http://goo.gl/rJrK3r> accessed 03.12.2015.

27 Ecuador Resolution, above n 5, fn. 1.

28 S Chakravarti, 'Business as usual on human rights?' 15.05.2015 *Live Mint* <http://www.livemint.com/Opinion/l9sdg79DAY6GXPVO0684dK/Business-as-usual-on-human-rights.html> accessed 01.12.2015.

29 European Coalition for Corporate Justice, 'UN Treaty on Business & Human Rights Negotiations Day 2 – EU disengagement & Lack of consensus on scope' 08.07.2015 *ECCJ* <http://corporatejustice.org/news/174-un-treaty-on-business-human-rights-negotiations-day-2-eu-disengagement-lack-of-consensus-on-scope> accessed 07.08.2017; Human Rights Council, above n 23, Panel IV.

30 Human Rights Council, above n 23, Panel IV.

relationships from the scope of the treaty.[31] Some countries – e.g. South Africa, India, Pakistan, China, Cuba and Venezuela – remained of the firm opinion that the footnote should be applied literally, whereas the EU, supported by some of its Member States, proposed a divisive amendment aimed at including all kinds of corporations in the IGWG mandate.[32] Whether the *ratione personae* scope of Resolution 26/9 will be interpreted expansively is an issue to be discussed in the future steps of the negotiation, and Ecuador itself has expressed a certain degree of openness in this sense.[33] Interestingly, the country's position might have shifted towards a more inclusive approach during the second session of the IGWG, when it stressed that the name of the IGWG itself (working group on 'transnational corporations and other business enterprises') provides guidance as to the scope of the future instrument.[34]

It suffices for now to note that, if the future treaty will be conceived as a treaty 'of states for states'[35] – aimed at reaching agreed solutions on issues such as States' extraterritorial human rights obligations (ETOs), the exercise of prescriptive and adjudicative extraterritorial jurisdiction (ETJ), and parent-based regulations (e.g. extraterritorial monitoring obligations; parent liability within complex corporate groups) – the peculiar problems posed by TNCs will constitute the natural focus of the new instrument. But even so, it is difficult to see such an instrument working effectively without a strong focus on international cooperation[36] between home States of TNCs and host States

---

31 CNR-IRISS, 'IRISS-CNR Written Statement to Open-ended Intergovernmental Working Group on Transnational Corporations and other Business Enterprises' August 2016, para 2 <https://www.iriss.cnr.it/irisswp/wp-content/uploads/2016/09/IRISS-Written-Statement-to-IGWG-2016.pdf> accessed 22.11.2016; European Coalition for Corporate Justice, above n 29; SOMO, 'Oral statement joint submission in Panel II on scope' 07.07.2015 <http://www.babymilkaction.org/wp-content/uploads/2015/07/SOMO-oral-statement-joint-submission-in-Panel-II-on-scope_final.pdf> accessed 07.08.2017.

32 Ibid.; R Bucherer, 'IGWG on TNCs and other Businesses: No agreement reached, consultations are continuing' 06.07.2015 *RIDH* <http://ridh.org/igwg-on-tncs-and-other-businesses-no-agreement-reached-consultations-are-continuing/> accessed 07.01.2016; Treaty Alliance, 'Discussions on scope of the treaty on day four of the intergovernmental working group session in Geneva' 28.10.2016 <http://www.treatymovement.com/news/4ec8df00-6690-4dc2-8178-aca3be143e31> accessed 09.11.2016.

33 European Coalition for Corporate Justice, above n 29, 2015; Ecuador oral statement during the 2015 UN Forum on Business and Human Rights, November 2015 <http://www.ohchr.org/Documents/HRBodies/HRCouncil/WGTransCorp/Session1/Panel4/States/Ecuador.pdf> accessed 07.08.2017.

34 Treaty Alliance, above n 32.

35 Backer, above n 1, p 52.

36 De Schutter has stressed the 'increasing recognition of the duty of the home State to cooperate with the host State to ensure that victims' of corporate abuses 'have access to effective remedies' (O De Schutter, 'Regulating Transnational Corporations: A Duty under International Human Rights Law' March 2014 Conference paper <http://www.ohchr.org/Documents/Issues/Food/EcuadorMtgBusinessAndHR.pdf> accessed 01.12.2015). See also: O De Schutter, 'La responsabilité des Etats dans le contrôle des sociétés transnationales: vers une convention internationale sur la lutte contre les atteintes aux droits de l'homme

(where subsidiaries and suppliers – i.e. local companies – are located). It would be restrictive – and inconsistent both with the GPs and with international law[37] – not to reaffirm that the host State has a duty to protect human rights from private companies operating under its jurisdiction, whether or not they have a transnational character.[38] The narrow focus on TNCs, whereas possibly justified by the complexity of legal and practical problems that transnational corporate groups raise, may actually reinforce Backer's concern that the resolution's stated aim to regulate corporate activities in 'international human rights law' might ultimately conceal a strategic shift from a concrete commitment by adhering States to eradicate corporate abuses domestically, to a symbolic gesture that will have little domestic effect.[39] The unconvincing position, expressed by some delegations during the second session of the IGWG, that companies with a domestic dimension 'do not have any possibility to evade their responsibilities' under national legal frameworks[40] is contradicted by abundant evidence that serious human rights violations in global supply chains are often linked to governance gaps (or even complicity, in the worst cases) in host countries that allow local companies to act in contravention of local laws and/or international standards.[41] The NGO SOMO, on behalf of a group of civil society organisations, has proposed a 'hybrid' option according to which the treaty should focus on

commises par les sociétés transnationales', in E Decaux (ed), *La responsabilité des entreprises multinationales en matière de droits de l'homme* (Collection Droit et Justice 89), Bruylant & Nemesis, Brussels, 2010, pp 20–100, at pp 41–42, <http://papers.ssrn.com/sol3/papers.cfm?abstract_id=2446911> accessed 05.05.2017.

37 It can also be noted that the CRC, as well, in its General Comment 16 on States' obligations regarding the impact of business on children's rights, also refers to all business enterprises, whether transnational or national (CRC, General Comment 16 (2013) CRC/C/GC/16, para 3).

38 S Deva, 'The Human Rights Obligations of Business: Reimagining the Treaty Business' March 2014 Conference paper, p 7 <http://www.etoconsortium.org/nc/en/library/documents/?tx_drblob_pi1%5Bdownl oadUid%5D=106> accessed 03.12.2015 ('[t]he proposed instrument should apply to all types of business entities and not just MNCs, despite the fact that the operations of MNCs do pose more significant regulatory challenges. This non-differentiation is quite critical because the form of the business should not matter when it comes to protecting victims against human rights abuses'); Ganesan, above n 25.

39 Backer, above n 1, pp 50–51. Backer contends: '[the Ecuadorian Resolution] rejects the central premises of the GPs, but offers nothing more substantive than the promise of an international instrument that will be used by its adherents and ignored by the rest of the states. It will then produce large margins of appreciation in standards for governing human rights related to business that will in turn contribute to a widening incoherence in those human rights standards that the GP project was itself meant to narrow' (ibid., p 51).

40 Human Rights Council, above n 23, Panel IV.

41 To quote but some examples: Anti-Slavery, 'Background: Forced labour in the Uzbek cotton industry' <http://www.antislavery.org/english/campaigns/cottoncrimes/forced_labour_in_uzbekistan_background.aspx> accessed 02.02.2017; BHRRC, 'KiK lawsuit (re Pakistan)' <https://business-humanrights.org/en/kik-lawsuit-re-pakistan> accessed 02.02.2017; J Kasperkevic, 'Rana Plaza collapse: workplace dangers persist three years later, reports find' 31.05.2016 *The Guardian* <https://www.theguardian.com/business/2016/may/31/rana-plaza-bangladesh-collapse-fashion-working-conditions> accessed 07.08.2017.

the obligation of States 'to regulate the extraterritorial activities of business, and to provide mutual assistance between states in investigating violations and in enforcing judgements'.[42] This would constitute a way to maintain the problems posed by TNCs' transnational operations as the main target of the binding instrument without, however, formally excluding any type of business from its scope.[43]

3. THE NATURE OF THE PROPOSED TREATY AND ITS *RATIONE MATERIAE* SCOPE

The former SRSG John Ruggie has held that it is illusionary to seek 'to subject the entire bundle of business and human rights issues to some overarching binding international legal instrument', and has rejected the idea of a 'silver bullet' solution, which he defines as 'some idealized global command-and-control regulatory regime'.[44] His contention is, in substance, that 'the category of business and human rights is not so discrete an issue-area as to lend itself to a single set of detailed treaty obligations'.[45] He only accepts a role for binding instruments as far as they are 'carefully constructed precision tools', addressed to specific governance gaps.[46] There is, as yet, no certainty as to the exact features of the instrument that may arise from the process initiated by the Ecuador Resolution. One of the questions dominating the debate is the choice between an instrument imposing directly binding international obligations on corporations – therefore re-writing in hard-law terms the concept of corporate Responsibility to Respect – and one focusing, instead, on the State Duty to Protect. The first approach would undeniably have a strong expressive value, sanctioning private corporations as bearers of human rights obligations in international law. In this way, the treaty would at least partly compensate for the inability or unwillingness of some States to hold corporations accountable for human rights violations in their national legal systems. One of the most interesting implications is the potential influence that this type of treaty could have on investment law and trade law, areas in which the internationally sanctioned rights of corporations are rarely balanced by explicit international obligations safeguarding the human rights of the subjects potentially affected by business activities. However, this option would

---

42 SOMO, above n 31.

43 Ibid.

44 JG Ruggie, 'Progress in Corporate Accountability' 04.02.2013 Institute for Human Rights and Business <http://www.ihrb.org/commentary/progress-in-corporate-accountability.html> accessed 04.12.2015.

45 JG Ruggie, 'A UN Business and Human Rights Treaty?' 28.01.2014 Issues Brief, Harvard University, p 3 <http://business-humanrights.org/en/pdf-a-un-business-and-human-rights-treaty-an-issues-brief-by-john-g-ruggie> accessed 04.12.2015.

46 Ibid., p 5.

also be faced with a number of serious challenges, as it would uphold a principle which is not consolidated under current international law and that is strongly opposed by key States. Moreover, codifying direct human rights obligations of corporations would not *per se* resolve the crucial issue of enforcement, which would require the establishment of a strong mechanism at the international level or the strengthening of existing ones, and would largely continue to depend, in any case, on the States Parties' willingness to cooperate.

Although several delegations at the second session of the IGWG supported the idea of setting out direct obligations for legal persons in the treaty,[47] it must be pointed out that it would be misplaced to think that the 'command-and-control' solution described above is generally preferred by the human rights groups taking part in the treaty debate.[48] In fact, not only is there no precedent for such a kind of international treaty, but the civil society organisations more deeply involved in the debate are not advocating for it, preferring an approach that focuses on States' duties.[49] While the option is not off the table yet, advocates of the treaty solution are aware that it entails risks.[50] The above-mentioned Treaty Alliance makes it clear that the proposed treaty should require *States* to adopt legislation and other measures to regulate the conduct of TNCs and to hold them accountable for failure to comply; as well as allow people with a claim access to judicial remedies 'not only in their own home States, but in all other States that have jurisdiction over the concerned business enterprise'.[51] The proposed treaty, therefore, should focus primarily on the States' duty to protect and to

47 Human Rights Council, above n 23, Panel III.

48 T Melish, 'Putting "Human Rights" Back into the UN Guiding Principles on Business and Human Rights: Shifting Frames and Embedding Participation Rights' 2014 *Buffalo Legal Studies Research Paper Series* 2014-032, p 17, <http://papers.ssrn.com/sol3/papers.cfm?abstract_id=2475629> accessed 01.12.2015. Contrast with: JG Ruggie, *Just Business – Multinational Corporations and Human Rights*, WW Norton & Company, New York, NY and London, 2013, p xxii.

49 Melish, above n 48, p 17; People's Forum on Human Rights and Business, 'Call for an international legally binding instrument on human rights, transnational corporations and other business enterprises' November 2013 <http://www.fian.org/fileadmin/media/publications/Joint_Statement_PeoplesForumBangkok_Binding_Instrument_Nov2013.pdf> accessed 01.12.2015; CM Vásquez, 'Human Rights Obligations of Corporations Under International Law' 10.01.2004 Conference paper, UC Berkeley, pp 16–17, <http://escholarship.org/uc/item/7631r5tn> accessed 01.12.2015.

50 R Hertanti, 'Oral Statement of FIAN International to the First Session of the open-ended intergovernmental working group on transnational corporations and other business enterprises with respect to human rights' 07.07.2015, Panel III <http://www.ohchr.org/Documents/HRBodies/HRCouncil/WGTransCorp/Session1/Panel3/Others/FoodFirst_InformationandActionNetworkFIAN.pdf> accessed 07.11.2016; SOMO et al., 'UN Treaty on transnational corporations, other business enterprises & human rights: Options for justice' 30–31 May 2016 Legal Seminar Report <https://www.somo.nl/wp-content/uploads/2016/09/UN_Treaty-Legal_Seminar_Report.pdf> accessed 07.11.2016.

51 Treaty Alliance, 'Enhance the International Legal Framework to Protect Human Rights from Corporate Abuse' <http://www.treatymovement.com/statement/> accessed 06.12.2015.

act collaboratively to improve the victims' access to judicial remedies.[52] Such an instrument, according to the Treaty Alliance, should then also clarify the kind of company conduct that will give rise to legal liability and the 'modalities in which TNCs and other business enterprises participate in the commission of human rights abuses', including corporate complicity and parent company liability. Finally, an international monitoring and accountability mechanism (e.g. a dedicated unit within the UN) should be provided. The idea promoted by the biggest civil society network involved in the debate is, therefore, that of a treaty directly binding on States, not on corporations.[53] This is also the approach favoured by several academic commentators[54] and reaffirmed by many civil society organisations in their oral statements during the first IGWG meeting.[55]

Going back to Ruggie's critique, it is here contended that an international treaty on business and human rights is not necessarily in contrast with the former SRSG's idea of a 'precision tool' aimed at bridging governance gaps that are not adequately addressed by existing instruments. Quite the contrary, it is precisely the purpose of specialised human rights treaties not to create new rights but to clarify 'the scope and specialized content of more generally articulated rights and duties'.[56] Depending on what future negotiations will produce, this may well be the case for a specialised treaty articulating and specifying States' human rights obligations (already established in other human rights treaties and in international customary law) in relation to the complex realm of business and human rights, with particular attention to the challenges posed by extraterritoriality.[57] For instance, the existence and scope of ETOs constitutes one of the controversial issues that the treaty could contribute to settling, taking stock of the most recent trends in the case-law of international courts and treaty bodies.[58] Whereas the existence of ETOs is clearly established

---

52 'Provisions for international legal and judicial cooperation among countries should facilitate the investigation and trial of cases of transnational nature' (ibid.).

53 Backer, above n 1, p 52 ('the problem is not the transnational corporation and its abuses, it is the state and its failures. It is to the overcoming of those failures that treaty making ought to be directed *by states for states*').

54 Ibid; S Deva, *Regulating Corporate Human Rights Violations: Humanizing Business*, Routledge, London, 2012, pp 238–40; O De Schutter, 'Sovereignty-plus in the Era of Interdependence: Toward an International Convention on Combating Human Rights Violations by Transnational Corporations', in PHF Bekker, R Dolzer and M Waibel (eds), *Making Transnational Law Work in the Global Economy: Essays in Honour of Detlev Vagts*, Cambridge University Press, Cambridge, 2010, pp 245–84, at p 283.

55 Human Rights Council, above n 22.

56 Melish, above n 48, p 19.

57 Ibid.; De Schutter, above n 54, pp 247 *et seq.*

58 An option that, however, that was regarded with concern by Russia and China at the first session of the IGWG (J Martens and K Seitz, 'The Struggle for a UN Treaty. Towards global regulation on human rights and business' August 2016 ETO Consortium, p 20 <http://www.etoconsortium.org/nc/en/main-navigation/our-work/what-are-etos/?tx_drblob_pi1%5BdownloadUid%5D=192> accessed 07.08.2017).

under international human rights law only in very narrow situations, there are increasing indications that international treaty bodies expect States to take steps to prevent corporations from infringing human rights in the foreign countries where they operate, as part of those States' duty to protect human rights.[59] In light of this trend, the GPs are often criticised for their overly prudent approach to the extraterritorial scope of States' human rights obligations.[60] A binding treaty may be crucial in defining the conditions under which States are required to regulate the extraterritorial activities of businesses they are in a position to influence.[61]

The form that the new treaty may take is still open to debate.[62] De Schutter contends that an option for the IGWG would be, for instance, to negotiate a treaty focusing on States' mutual legal assistance to ensure access to effective remedies for victims harmed by transnational operations of corporations. Such an instrument would not only respond to a very specific challenge posed by the transnational nature of some business operations, but would also allow the 'unworkable' Ecuador Resolution's footnote limiting the treaty's *ratione personae* scope to be overcome (see previous section).[63] A possible alternative could be to

---

59 To quote but a few examples: CERD, Concluding observations: United Kingdom of Great Britain and Northern Ireland (14.09.2011) UN Doc. CERD/C/GBR/CO/18–20; CESCR, Concluding Observations: Austria (13.12.2013) UN Doc. E/C.12/AUT/CO/4; CESCR, Concluding Observations: China (13.06.2014) UN Doc. E/C.12/CHN/CO/2; CRC, Concluding Observations: Germany (25.02.2014) CRC/C/DEU/CO/3–4; Human Rights Committee, Concluding Observations: Canada (2015) UN Doc CCPR/C/CAN/CO/6; Human Rights Committee, Concluding Observations: Germany (2012) CCPR/C/DEU/CO/6.

60 D Augenstein and D Kinley, 'When Human Rights "Responsibilities" Become "Duties": The Extra-territorial Obligations of States that Bind Corporations', in S Deva and D Bilchitz (eds), *Human Rights Obligations of Business – Beyond the Corporate Responsibility to Respect?*, Cambridge University Press, Cambridge, 2013, pp 271–94, at p 294; O De Schutter, 'Towards a New Treaty on Business and Human Rights' (2016) 1 *Business and Human Rights Journal* 41, 45 *et seq*; N Jägers, 'UN Guiding Principles on Business and Human Rights: Making Headway Towards Real Corporate Accountability?' (2011) 29(2) *Netherlands Quarterly of Human Rights* 159, 162.

61 De Schutter, above n 60, pp 45 *et seq.*; Geneva Infant Feeding Association (IBFAN-GIFA), Bread for the World, Friends of the Earth Europe, SOMO, CIDSE, Global Policy Forum, International Baby Food Action Network (IBFAN), 'Contributions to the legal building blocks of the Treaty regarding the scope, the state duty to protect and direct obligations for corporations' July 2015 <http://www.cidse.org/publications/business-and-human-rights/business-and-human-rights-frameworks/cidse-s-contribution-to-the-un-intergovernmental-working-group-on-transnational-corporations-and-other-business-enterprises-with-respect-to-human-rights.html> accessed 07.08.2017; D Cassel and A Ramasastry, 'Options for a treaty on business and human rights' May 2015 White paper, p 43 <http://business-humanrights.org/sites/default/files/documents/whitepaperfinal%20ABA%20LS%206%2022%2015.pdf> accessed 08.01.2016; Human Rights Council, above n 22, Panel V – Obligations of States to guarantee the Respect of Human Rights by TNCs and other business enterprises, including extraterritorial obligation.

62 Human Rights Council, above n 23, Panel IV.

63 De Schutter, above n 60, p 41.

develop a framework convention on business and human rights setting general obligations of results and leaving the means and timing of their realisation to the discretion of States, under the monitoring of a treaty body.[64] In any case, the idea of an instrument imposing direct wide-ranging international obligations on corporations and overstretching the current boundaries of international law appears to have been, at the very least, marginalised in the ongoing treaty debate. It is the opinion of the author that this trend is to be welcomed, as the legal and political controversies that would derive from such an approach would probably have the effect of derailing the negotiations, whereas imposing direct international human rights obligations on companies would not necessarily result in increased accountability, especially in the absence of a strong commitment to cooperate on the part of States. A treaty focusing on the State Duty to Protect, on the contrary, might trigger the gradual harmonisation of rules concerning key aspects such as the exercise of ETJ or the allocation of responsibility within complex corporate groups, something that is not new to the community of States, as similar steps have been taken in the realm of anti-corruption and anti-trust legislation.

A few words must be devoted, however, to an alternative option put forward by Ruggie. The former SRSG, being concerned that a business and human rights treaty would have too ample a *ratione materiae* scope, holds that a more feasible option could be to focus only on the most heinous categories of human rights violations, i.e. international crimes.[65] This restrictive solution, however, has crucial drawbacks, as it leaves out most corporate-related human rights abuses and may distract from the goal of elaborating more effective mechanisms to prevent and redress wrongful conducts that do not amount to international crimes.[66] In addition, as noted by Bilchitz, the necessity for embarking on negotiations for such an instrument is questionable, in light of the fact that corporate accountability for international crimes could be addressed by amending the Rome Statute of the International Criminal Court to allow prosecutions against corporations.[67] It is commendable that, during the first session of the IGWG, which devoted a specific panel to discussing the material

64 Ibid., pp 55–56.

65 JG Ruggie, 'The Past as Prologue? A Moment of Truth for UN Business and Human Rights Treaty' 8 July 2014 Institute for Human Rights and Business, p 5, <http://www.ihrb.org/commentary/past-as-prologue.html> accessed 06.12.2015.

66 Deva, above n 38, p 8. Melish stresses that a solution focusing solely on egregious violations would be 'so politicized, distracting, and selectively deployed (given the global North's power and structural interest in protecting its own) – and so dominated by the usual narrow band of ICL suspects – as to be non-relevant to local struggles and actors on the ground' (Melish, above n 48, p 12).

67 D Bilchitz, 'The Necessity for a Business and Human Rights Treaty' November 2014 *SSRN*, p 27, <http://ssrn.com/abstract=2562760> accessed 05.12.2015.

scope, the possibility of limiting the treaty to only a sub-set of rights was generally rejected,[68] and this position does not seem to have shifted during the second session.[69] As rightly recognised by many delegations, participants and panellists, the added value of the new treaty should rather be to close the legal and practical gaps that make it extremely difficult nowadays to hold corporations liable for violations with a transnational dimension, for instance by operationalising States' extraterritorial obligations and encouraging interstate cooperation.[70] At the same time, ruling out a narrow focus on international crimes should not overshadow the important contribution that a new binding instrument can bring to a more precise definition of corporate criminal liability.[71] In fact, States now have the possibility to recognise in a binding international treaty the principle of corporate criminal liability for international crimes, closing a debate that the Rome Statute negotiations in the 1990s could not settle,[72] and establishing clear standards for complicity and conspiracy.[73]

4. THE LONG AND WINDING ROAD TOWARDS AN INTERNATIONAL TREATY

A crucial argument raised by Ruggie and other commentators points to the difficulties of embarking on the lengthy process of negotiation of an international treaty, a process that could take 'a decade or more'.[74] If the length and complexity of treaty making were sufficient reasons to dismiss the treaty route as impracticable, we would not have most of the human rights instruments that exist today, including the International Covenant on Economic, Social and Cultural Rights (ICESCR) and the International Covenant on Civil and Political Rights (ICCPR). While the complexity of the process does not suffice to dismiss the idea of a treaty, there are problematic aspects that must be addressed, in order not to dissipate the political achievements of the SRSG's mandate. First

68 Human Rights Council, above n 22.

69 Human Rights Council, above n 23, Panel IV.

70 Human Rights Council, above n 22.

71 Human Rights Council, above n 23, Panel III, Subtheme 2.

72 N Bernaz, 'Including Corporate Criminal Liability for International Crimes in the Business and Human Rights Treaty: Necessary but Insufficient' 2015 *BHRRC* <http://business-humanrights.org/en/including-corporate-criminal-liability-for-international-crimes-in-the-business-and-human-rights-treaty-necessary-but-insufficient> accessed 08.01.2016.

73 Human Rights Council, above n 22, para 77; Human Rights Council, above n 23, Panel III, Subtheme 2.

74 Ruggie, above n 48, pp xxii–xxiii; Ruggie, above n 65. See also: S Tripathi, 'A Business and Human Rights Treaty? More Immediate Actions Would Make a Bigger Difference' 26.06.2014 Institute for Human Rights and Business <http://www.ihrb.org/commentary/business-and-human-rights-treaty-more-immediate-actions-required.html> accessed 04.12.2015.

of all, in the indefinite period of time that might be necessary for the drafting of an international instrument, it is crucially important not to put the business and human rights agenda 'on hold' and to continue promoting the implementation of the GPs in domestic policies and regulations, as well as in the operations of businesses.[75] Ruggie's concern is that civil society and governmental supporters of a treaty solution, especially when overtly critical of the 'soft law' character of the GPs, may not be motivated to take this commitment further in a meaningful way.[76] The former SRSG's view on this point, however, appears overly pessimistic. It must be noted that even some of the most forthright critics of the GPs, instead of flatly rejecting them as an instrument, are referring to them in their business and human rights advocacy work, contributing to the identification of their flaws and potential, as well as suggesting future courses of action to the UN Working Group.[77] It would be illogical of civil society organisations to give up this advocacy role precisely when it is most needed: lobbying States into undertaking meaningful implementation of the GPs is all the more important in view of the possible adoption of a binding treaty. Whether a State has supported the Ecuador Resolution or the Norway Resolution at the HRC, civil society organisations can leverage the argument of political coherence in asking to show genuine commitment to the business and human rights agenda, including

75 PJ Selvanathan, 'The Business and Human Rights Treaty Debate: Is Now the Time?' 26.11.2014 Working paper, Kenan Institute for Ethics, p 3, <http://business-humanrights.org/sites/default/files/documents/IsNowtheTime_TreatyDebate.pdf> accessed 04.12.2015.

76 Ruggie, above n 65.

77 See, for example: Amnesty International, 'Business and Human Rights: Ensuring the United Nations effectively addresses key challenges around corporate accountability' 04.06.2012 Public statement <https://www.amnesty.org/en/documents/ior40/013/2012/en/> accessed 05.12.2015 ('The effectiveness of the Guiding Principles and the UN "Protect, Respect and Remedy" Framework need to be tested in practice. They need to be further developed or strengthened where effectiveness is lacking'); ESCR-Net, Intervention at the CSO meeting prior to the UN Regional Forum on Business & Human Rights, August 2013 <https://business-humanrights.org/sites/default/files/media/documents/escr-net-statement-aug-2013.pdf> accessed 08.08.2017; FIDH, 'UN Human Rights Council adopts Guiding Principles on business conduct, yet victims still waiting for effective remedies' 17.06.2011 <http://www.fidh.org/en/globalisation-human-rights/business-and-human-rights/UN-Human-Rights-Council-adopts> accessed 04.12.2015 ('FIDH welcomes the creation of a working group ... but regrets that it fails to sufficiently address victims dire need to access effective remedies ... Situations of corporate abuses should always be analysed in light of the [Protect, Respect, Remedy] Framework and applicable international human rights standards'); FIDH, SOMO, ESCR-Net, 'Joint Submission to the OHCHR's consultation on "Exploring the feasibility of establishing a global fund to support capacity building on business and human rights"' 31.01.2014 <http://goo.gl/XZrLGc> accessed 06.12.2015 ('FIDH, SOMO and the ESCR-Net Corporate Accountability Working Group ... welcome the initiative taken by the OHCHR to explore the feasibility of establishing a global fund to enhance the capacity of stakeholders to implement the Guiding Principles on Business and Human Rights, and appreciates the opportunity to share its view').

through the adoption, as recommended by the working group, of NAPs. As Selvanathan puts it, '[a]ll stakeholders, business in particular, should be assured that actioning the GPs now is the most ready one could be for any hard-law', a prospect that 'should catalyse the uptake of the GPs'.[78] Although the opposition of corporations and business organisations to a hard-law solution is unlikely to fade away,[79] the treaty process may still benefit from a participatory approach, drawing on the inputs of all categories of stakeholders.[80] Clearly, though, one crucial feature of the treaty route is that it provides for a regulatory instrument that, unlike voluntary initiatives, does not depend on the existence of a 'business case' for complying with human rights and brings back States as authors of the process.[81]

In this perspective, the most problematic aspect of the current treaty debate is arguably the sharp divide that emerged at the 26th session of the HRC – almost along Cold War lines[82] – between developing and emerging countries on one side, and developed countries on the other. As noted by one commentator, the debate at the 26th session of the HRC 'seemed a political replay of a time in the 1970s when the UN began negotiating a Code of Conduct for Transnational Corporations and the proposal met the opposition of Western countries as well as the business community'.[83] There is clearly a 'disparity in needs and preferences'

---

78 Selvanathan, above n 75, p 3.

79 See, for instance: International Organisation of Employers, 'Consensus on business and human rights is broken with the adoption of the Ecuador initiative' 26 June 2014, Press release <http://www.ioe-emp.org/index.php?id=1238> accessed 06.12.2015.

80 Selvanathan, above n 75, p 2. As Buhmann noted concerning the SRSG's mandate, '[a]lthough unusual for international human rights law-making, the SRSG process involved economic non-state actors as prospective duty-bearers … This does not mean that international law-making to curtail adverse business impact on society should be subjected to the whims of business. What it does suggest is that engaging with and appealing to the interests of key stakeholders offer a way towards the effective adoption of international policy and law on issues that require a multi-stakeholder approach for their solution' (K Buhmann, 'Navigating from "Train Wreck" to being "Welcomed": Negotiation Strategies and Argumentative Patterns in the Development of the UN Framework', in Deva and Bilchitz (eds), above n 60, pp 29–57, at p 55).

81 Deva, above n 38, p 3 ('[w]e … need an international instrument which is not rooted in the business case for human rights. Rather it should be underpinned by the normative hierarchy of human rights norms over business, trade and investment norms'). It has also been argued that a company which has committed to voluntary standards (or to soft law instruments such as the GPs) has nothing to lose from an international treaty, 'unless it misinterprets voluntariness as opportunism, that is, as the possibility to opt out of its obligations whenever this might yield an economic advantage' (F Wettstein, *Multinational Corporations and Global Justice – Human Rights Obligations of a Quasi-Governmental Institution*, Stanford University Press, Stanford, 2009, p 346).

82 Backer, above n 1, p 47.

83 I Pietropaoli, 'High tide in Lake Geneva. Business and human rights events at the 26th session of the UN Human Rights Council' 27.06.2014 Commentary, p 2, <http://business-humanrights.org/sites/default/files/media/high_tide_in_lake_geneva.pdf> accessed 06.12.2015.

among States[84] but there might also be a different ideological paradigm, with the key supporters of the Ecuador Resolution promoting a model that subjects the private sector 'to the command of the state and its direction'.[85] The Treaty Alliance has reported vehement US lobbying of representatives of developing countries, while the EU, which had initially announced its Member States would not take part in the treaty-drafting process, attended the first session only in part.[86] With such a political divide, and keeping in mind that some of the States supporting the treaty have among the worst labour rights records in the world,[87] a legitimate concern is the risk that treaty negotiations end up settling for the lowest common denominator.[88]

However, a few observations are needed. First of all, some of the countries supporting the Ecuador-South Africa Resolution are among those that have been most affected by the commercial and political power of foreign TNCs, which have rarely paid the price for their wrongful conduct (these include, for instance, countries in the Africa group and Ecuador itself).[89] Therefore, dismissing their position as instrumentally 'anti-Western' or ideologically motivated is probably simplistic. Moreover, while the opposition of States which are currently home to the largest number of major TNCs is undoubtedly worrying,[90] if it is true that, by 2025, nearly half of the Global Fortune 500 firms will be domiciled

---

84 JG Ruggie, 'A Business and Human Rights Treaty? International legalisation as precision tools' 13.06.2014 Institute for Human Rights and Business <http://www.ihrb.org/commentary/business-and-human-rights-treaty-international-legislation-as-precision-tools.html> accessed 06.12.2015.

85 Backer, above n 1, p 49. Backer underlines that Ecuador, Cuba, Venezuela, and Bolivia are all core members of the ALBA trade group, which he defines as 'the command economy alternative to the free trade model of globalization' (L Catá Backer and A Molina, 'Cuba and the Construction of Alternative Global Trade Systems: ALBA and Free Trade in the Americas' (2010) 31(3) *Journal of International Law* 679 <https://www.law.upenn.edu/journals/jil/articles/volume31/issue3/Backer31U.Pa.J.Int'lL.679(2010).pdf> accessed 20.11.2015).

86 N Mardirossian, 'US & EU Oppose Stronger Regulation of Corporations at HRC Despite Compatibility with Guiding Principles' 22.06.2014 Network for Justice in Global Investment <http://justinvestment.org/2014/06/us-eu-oppose-stronger-regulation-of-corporations-at-hrc-despite-compatibility-with-guiding-principles/> accessed 11.01.2016.

87 A Rhodes, 'The False Promise of an International Business and Human Rights Treaty', 07.10.2014 *The Huffington Post* <http://www.huffingtonpost.com/aaron-rhodes/the-false-promise-of-an-i_b_5575236.html> accessed 03.12.2015.

88 JG Ruggie, 'Business and Human Rights – Treaty Road Not Travelled', 06.05.2008 *Ethical Corporation* <http://www.ethicalcorp.com/content/john-ruggie-business-and-human-rights-treaty-road-not-travelled> accessed 08.08.2017; Ruggie, above n 48, p 64; Ruggie, above n 65.

89 J Kyriakakis, 'The Debate about having a debate about a business and human rights treaty' 17.02.2015 Castan Center for Human Rights Law – Official Blog <http://castancentre.com/2015/02/17/debateaboutbusinessandhumanrights/> accessed 11.01.2016.

90 Ganesan, above n 25.

in emerging market countries,[91] and by then the proposed treaty will hardly only concern 'Western' TNCs. One may also wonder to what extent it would be possible or convenient, for instance, for European countries to disregard the new international regime, should that become the standard for their global competitors (e.g. China and India) and for the countries that are recipients of their investments (e.g. African countries). Secondly, treaty negotiations are likely to further revive national debates about business and human rights in countries that have not supported the Ecuador Resolution. For instance, Brazil, one of the abstaining countries, decided to engage with the IGWG and initiated a dialogue with civil society organisations about the position that the government would take during the first IGWG meeting in July 2015.[92] The European Parliament, while remarking on the importance of implementing the GPs, has invited Member States 'to engage in the emerging debate on a legally binding international instrument on business and human rights',[93] an engagement that even the former SRSG deems likely, despite the EU countries' opposition to the Ecuador Resolution.[94] Undoubtedly, EU Member States' involvement in the first session of the IGWG has not been uncontroversial, with some civil society organisations criticising their insufficient participation in some crucial panel discussions, including the one regarding the *ratione personae* scope of Resolution 26/9, whose enlargement the EU itself had strongly advocated.[95] Despite this, the EU, under pressure from civil society and in spite of its persistent opposition to a binding instrument, took part more consistently in the second session of the IGWG.[96] The fact that some European countries are open to at least discussing the pros and cons of a binding instrument – as also testified by the adoption of the Norwegian Resolution – should be looked at positively as the possibility to engage reluctant countries

---

91 JG Ruggie, 'Life in the global public domain: responding to commentaries', 05.02.2015 *James G Stuart* <http://jamesgstewart.com/life-in-the-global-public-domain-response-to-commentaries/> accessed 11.01.2016.

92 Friends of the Earth International, 'Brazil will engage with group to establish treaty on businesses and human rights', 03.06.2015 <http://www.foei.org/news/brazil-will-engage-group-establish-treaty-businesses-human-rights> accessed 03.12.2015. In spite of this revived dialogue, Brazilian civil society organisations point out that the Brazilian government is still not fully engaged in the treaty debate, nor in the implementation of the GPs, for which no NAP has been adopted, yet (E Cardoso, I Miola, 'The Treaty on Transnational Corporations and Human Rights', 02.2016, p 40 <http://csnbricsam.org/wp-content/uploads/2013/08/The-Treaty-on-Transnational-Corporations-and-Human-Rights.pdf> accessed 08.08.2017).

93 European Parliament, 'Resolution of 12 March 2015 on the EU's priorities for the UN Human Rights Council in 2015' (2015) 2015/2572(RSP), paras 29–32.

94 Ruggie, above n 91.

95 No agreement reached; European Coalition for Corporate Justice, above n 29.

96 FIDH, 'A step further towards an international treaty on human rights and business enterprises' 31.10.2016 <https://www.fidh.org/en/issues/globalisation-human-rights/business-and-human-rights/a-step-further-towards-an-international-treaty-on-human-rights-and> accessed 13.11.2016.

in the debate. More generally, different national agendas, pressure by lobbying groups and ideological differences have characterised most major processes of adoption of international binding instruments – see, for instance, the ICCPR, the ICESCR or the birth of the International Criminal Court[97] – and fear of these dynamics is not a sufficient reason to freeze a debate that can help catalyse a change of pace also in the uptake of the GPs by national governments.

5. MONITORING THE TREATY: WHAT ROLE FOR A BUSINESS AND HUMAN RIGHTS TREATY BODY?

The proposed business and human rights treaty (not unlike other human rights treaties) will inevitably face enforcement and monitoring issues.[98] The possibility of establishing a treaty monitoring body through an optional protocol was raised during the July 2015 negotiations,[99] although it will need to be more specifically discussed in the near future. Ruggie, in the course of his mandate, has advanced one more critical argument against the treaty option by calling attention to the practical difficulties that a treaty body would incur when trying to handle the monitoring of 'millions of companies'.[100] He has argued that existing treaty bodies already struggle to keep up with the monitoring of 192 States (at most).[101] Ruggie's concern is not without merit, including because there is currently no clarity about the type of monitoring/enforcement mechanism that would be created alongside the new treaty. While some NGOs put forward the idea of a 'tribunal' or 'court' able to issue binding judgments and fill the gap in access to remedies,[102] the issue is still open to discussion, including because it is strictly related to the unsettled questions regarding the nature and scope of the treaty.

However, if we consider what currently appears to be the most likely scenario, i.e. the States as direct duty-bearers under the new instrument, a treaty body might be tasked with scrutinising State conduct with respect to the regulation, monitoring and sanction of their corporate citizens' conduct. It seems unlikely that such a treaty body could be mandated to act as an 'inspector' of the daily activities of millions of businesses. The treaty body would, instead, most probably

97 Bilchitz, above n 67, pp 25–26.
98 Ruggie, above n 88.
99 Human Rights Council, above n 22, paras 41, 88.
100 Ibid.
101 Ibid.
102 Human Rights Council, above n 23, Panel II, Panel III. See, for instance: Global Campaign to Reclaim Peoples Sovereignty, 'Building a UN treaty on Human Rights and TNCs. A way forward to stop corporate impunity' October 2016, p 11 *et seq.* <https://www.tni.org/files/publication-downloads/six-points_eng.pdf> accessed 13.11.2016.

carry out, scale up and systematise in light of the new treaty's provisions what other human rights treaty bodies are, in part, already doing, i.e. dealing with cases of corporate human rights abuses as part of their monitoring compliance with the State Duty to Protect. This trend in the UN treaty bodies' case-law has gained momentum with the adoption of the GPs, and has increasingly focused on the extraterritorial dimension of the States' duty to protect. A specialised treaty body could more effectively identify specific governance gaps (e.g. in national legislative frameworks or available judicial remedies) and formulate targeted recommendations, also fulfilling the fundamental function of interpreting and developing the treaty norms.[103] As Cassel and Ramasastry suggest, this could be usefully combined with a treaty provision requiring that States create and implement NAPs, and it would also allow civil society organisations to contribute to the monitoring process by exposing critical aspects of the conduct of both companies and States.[104]

6. CONCLUSION: THE ADDED VALUE OF A TREATY ON BUSINESS AND HUMAN RIGHTS

The road towards the adoption of an international binding instrument on business and human rights is undoubtedly fraught with concrete challenges, starting from the need to rally a genuine political commitment of the community of States around this process. Once adopted, the extent to which the new treaty will be concretely implemented will continue to depend – not unlike the effectiveness of the GPs – on the political willingness of adhering States. Ruggie raises a real problem in noting that States already have a treaty-based and customary-law obligation to protect human rights from the activities of business actors, and that 'if they are unwilling to discharge it, an additional treaty is unlikely to help'.[105] However, this and other legitimate concerns should not translate into a defeatist dismissal of a renewed treaty debate,[106] which has at least three important merits. First of all, it brings back States as the central actors of a process that, after the abandonment of the project for a draft UN code of conduct in the 1990s,[107] has been mostly left to the work of experts. This should

103 Bilchitz, above n 67, p 23.
104 Cassel and Ramasastry, above n 61, p 27.
105 Ruggie, above n 88.
106 The author of the present contribution agrees with Kyriakakis that 'fear of conversations should always be viewed with scepticism' (Kyriakakis, above n 89).
107 The reference here is to the attempted elaboration of a binding code by the Commission on transnational corporations, established by the ECOSOC in 1974 and composed of 48 member States. The code was never adopted.

help defuse fears – by States and businesses alike – that human rights protection will be 'privatized'[108] and the role of sovereign States sidelined.[109]

Secondly, the process is rooted in international human rights law, and the resulting instrument can have an expressive value and contribute to the development of international customary law, as well as influence developments at the national level.[110] An international treaty on business and human rights would fulfil the need to anchor more firmly in international human rights law the so-called corporate 'Responsibility to Respect',[111] which Ruggie grounded in an unstable and largely uncharted concept of 'social expectations', arguably leaving the existence of corporate human rights responsibilities hostage of the changing sentiment of the 'global society'.[112] This task demands affirmation and clarification of the human rights obligations of companies, going beyond the GPs' differentiation between State 'duties' and corporate 'responsibilities'.[113] As Deva notes, 'it would be naïve to think that the existing state-focal human rights instruments could be taken off the shelf and applied to business actors', which is why human rights duties should be 'reoriented' according to the

---

108 IOE, ICC, 'Joint views of the IOE and ICC on the draft "Norms on the responsibilities of transnational corporations and other business enterprises with regard to human rights"' March 2004 <http://business-humanrights.org/en/joint-views-of-the-ioe-icc-onthe-un-human-rights-norms-for-business> accessed 19.11.2015.

109 Kyriakakis, above n 89.

110 Bilchitz, above n 67, pp 6, 25.

111 The term 'responsibility' was chosen by Ruggie instead of 'duty' in order to indicate that companies, unlike States, are not directly bound by international human rights law. He claimed that the RtR is a widely recognised principle in the international society, as testified by the numerous international soft law and CSR instruments upholding it. Ruggie defines the RtR as a baseline responsibility that exists independently of States' duties and that is part of a company's 'social license' to operate. The basis of this responsibility, in his paradigm, is defined by social expectations (Ruggie, 'Protect, Respect and Remedy: A Framework for Business and Human Rights' 07.04.2008b, UN Doc. A/HRC/8/5, paras 54–55). The normative foundations of that choice have been authoritatively criticised by Bilchitz: D Bilchitz, 'A Chasm between "Is" and "Ought"? A Critique of the Normative Foundations of the SRSG's Framework and the Guiding Principles', in Deva and Bilchitz (eds), above n 60, pp 107–37.

112 It might be observed that the content of international human rights norms is also evolving over time and is affected by a certain degree of indeterminacy. However, the international community has developed mechanisms for the interpretation of those norms and the evolution of human rights law is sanctioned by either its conventional nature (treaty law) or its emergence as customary law or *jus cogens*. The evolution of social expectations, on the contrary, is a largely unexplored process that may affect not just the content of the RtR, but also its very existence. While the study of the emergence and evolution of those expectations can be extremely interesting, their inclusion as foundational principles in a 'regulatory dynamic' aimed at advancing the protection of human rights ultimately weakens the whole framework (ibid).

113 Deva, above n 38, p 2; A Teitelbaum, 'New initiative to end multinational companies impunity' 29.05.2014 Commentary <http://business-humanrights.org/en/binding-treaty/statements-initiatives-commentaries> accessed 02.12.2015; Treaty Alliance, above n 20.

specific role that these non-State actors play in society.[114] As explained earlier, this does not necessarily mean upholding the idea of a command-and-control treaty imposing direct international human rights obligations on private companies, nor equating their role and responsibilities to those pertaining to sovereign States. It does require, however, recognising that the corporate 'duty' to respect human rights derives from internationally sanctioned human rights norms, and reaffirming that its effective enforcement is an essential part of the State Duty to Protect. Shifting from a blurred notion of 'responsibility' to one of (internationally sanctioned) 'duty' is not a merely symbolic step, but also a way to balance the extensive rights that private companies enjoy under several branches of international law – e.g. investment law, trade law and human rights law itself.

A third and related added value of adopting an international treaty consists in the clarification of the duties of States, especially as concerns the existence of extraterritorial human rights obligations and the exercise of ETJ in respect of overseas business activities.[115] Through the codification of home States' obligations and common rules for liability allocation within complex corporate groups, a treaty is potentially a powerful instrument to improve access to remedies for victims of human rights abuses, even when the host State is unable or unwilling to provide avenues for redress.[116] At present, avenues for transnational litigation in the realm of business and human rights remain scarce, notwithstanding encouraging signs from a number of jurisdictions.[117]

---

114 Deva, above n 38, p 5. Deva proposes an *interim* step entailing the adoption of a Declaration on the Human Rights Obligations of Business (Declaration) along the lines of the UDHR, which, by clarifying this important aspect, would pave the way to the subsequent development of one or more binding instruments (ibid., pp 5, 8 *et seq.*). Deva generally favours the hypothesis of imposing such obligations on companies through States (Deva, above n 54, pp 238–40).

115 Backer, above n 1, p 54; N Bernaz, 'Enhancing Corporate Accountability for Human Rights Violations: Is Extraterritoriality the Magic Potion?' (2013) 117 *Journal of Business Ethics* 493, 507–08; De Schutter, above n 36; C Lopez, 'Paving the Way for a Legally Binding Instrument' March 2014 Conference paper <http://businesshumanrights.org/sites/default/files/media/documents/clopez_statement_side_event_march2014.pdf> accessed 01.12.2015; Melish, above n 48, p 17; Vásquez, above n 49, p 17.

116 Deva, above n 38, pp 2–3; Lopez, above n 114, pp 4–5; Teitelbaum, above n 112. Patiño, the Ecuadorian Minister of Foreign Affairs, points to the need to counterbalance the strong legal protection and recourse mechanisms (e.g. international arbitration) that investors can benefit from, in contrast with insufficient access to remedies for victims of corporate abuses (R Patiño, 'Transnational Misconduct Must End' *The Huffington Post* (24.10.2014) <http://www.huffingtonpost.co.uk/ricardo-patino/ecuador-ricardo-patino_b_6040920.html> accessed 04.12.2015).

117 BHRRC, 'Hudbay Minerals lawsuits (re Guatemala)' <https://business-humanrights.org/en/hudbay-minerals-lawsuits-re-guatemala-0> accessed 19.11.2016; BHRRC, 'NGOs sue cement manufacturer Lafarge in France for financing ISIS & complicity in war crimes in Syria' <https://business-humanrights.org/en/ngos-sue-cement-manufacturer-lafarge-in-france-for-financing-isis-complicity-in-war-crimes-in-syria#c147205> accessed 08.08.2017; BHRRC,

The extraterritorial dimension of the US Alien Tort Claims Act (ATCA) is going to be increasingly challenged after the *Kiobel* Supreme Court ruling, and developments in other countries will take time. In this context, an important merit of the treaty process could be to explore and translate in legal terms the feasible ways in which States could cooperate to improve chances of redress for victims of human rights abuses. The occasion should also be seized to include in the new instrument the principle of corporate criminal liability for international crimes, urging States Parties to implement it within their national legal systems.

Finally, the 'business case' for a treaty must be highlighted, considering that, as in the domain of anti-corruption legislation, an international treaty, if widely ratified, may create a level playing field, i.e. avert the risk that more responsible companies, or companies subjected to stronger social and environmental requirements, suffer a competitive disadvantage in the global market.[118] Selvanathan, a former member of the UN Working Group on Business and Human Rights (speaking in his personal capacity), has held that if 'laggards' are not compelled to observe certain binding standards against which all companies are measured, the competitive disadvantage may erode the responsible companies' willingness to observe higher standards.[119]

One of the main challenges that the treaty process faces is the political divide that still characterises the community of States concerning the desirability of pursuing the hard-law approach at the international level in the realm of business and human rights. The reflexive approach proposed by the Norway Resolution and fully situated within the GPs' implementation process, however, is by no means incompatible with negotiations for a binding treaty. The more credibility its promoters are able to confer on the proposed instrument, the easier it will be to take on board some of the currently reluctant States in the negotiations. What is to be hoped, in any case, is that the two parallel processes do not happen disjointedly or in mutual conflict, but that they create a synergic dynamic whereby one is able to feed into the other, safeguarding, as far as possible, the political consensus which has rallied around the SRSG's mandate.

'Shell lawsuit (re oil pollution in Nigeria)' <https://business-humanrights.org/en/shell-lawsuit-re-oil-pollution-in-nigeria> accessed 19.11.2016; *Chandler v Cape plc*, [2012] EWCA Civ 525, 25.04.2012.

118 CIDSE, above n 17; Deva, above n 38, 6; Lopez, above n 114, 3; Pitts, above n 14; P Sutherland, '"Responsibility and Complicity" from the Perspective of Business', in M Shinn (ed), *The 2005 Business and Human Rights Seminar Report – Exploring responsibility and complicity*, Report, 08.12.2005, pp 4–9, pp 6–7 <http://www.scu.edu.tw/hrp/Teng/TengText3.pdf> accessed 05.12.2015; Wettstein, above n 81, p 346.

119 Selvanathan, above n 75, p 2.

PART II

CRITICAL ANALYSES OF A TREATY ON BUSINESS AND HUMAN RIGHTS

CONSIDERING A TREATY ON CORPORATIONS AND HUMAN RIGHTS: MOSTLY FAILURES BUT WITH A GLIMMER OF SUCCESS

Larry Catá BACKER*

1. INTRODUCTION

Is it necessary or advisable to draft a treaty on corporations and human rights? What ought to be the content of that treaty? What ought to be the objectives and implications of such a treaty for enterprises, non-governmental organisations (NGOs), individuals and states? These questions, emerging simultaneously with and in part propelled by the complex transformations that produced

* My thanks to Angelo Mancini (Penn State JD expected 2018) for excellent research assistance.

economic globalisation, were at the foundation of a decades-long and fruitless effort through the United Nations that started in the 1970s with the unsuccessful quest to produce a Code of Conduct for Transnational Corporations[1] and ended with the failure of the draft UN Norms on the Responsibilities of Transnational Corporations and Other Business Enterprises with Regard to Human Rights in the first years of the 21st century.[2] By 2011, these questions appeared to have been answered as the United Nations Human Rights Council unanimously endorsed what from that time became the UN Guiding Principles for Business and Human Rights (UNGP).[3]

But the UNGP did not prove to be a sufficiently authoritative or comprehensive answer for all stakeholders, key elements of which were not thrilled by events that led to the adoption of the UNGP, and less by the UNGP itself.[4] That discontent was at first internal to the UNGP discussion and discrete, taking definitive form on the eve of the adoption of the UNGP.[5] It became more open and vocal after 2011,[6] and led to substantial mobilisation of political power in the years thereafter as both civil society actors and small and developing states began considering alternatives or supplements to the UNGP and the means to achieve their adoption.[7]

Ironically, the post-endorsement architecture created by the UN Human Rights Council provided a site for advancing and consolidating discontent. The post-UNGP endorsement mechanism is centred on a Working Group.[8]

---

1 T Sagafi-nejad and J H Dunning, *The UN and Transnational Corporations* (Indiana University Press, 2008) pp 89–123.

2 See D Weissbrodt and M Kruger, 'Norms on the Responsibilities of Transnational Corporations and Other Business Enterprises with Regard to Human Rights' (2003) 97(4) *American Journal of International Law* 901.

3 Office of the High Commissioner for Human Rights, *Guiding Principles on Business and Human Rights: Implementing the United Nations 'Protect, Respect and Remedy' Framework* (United Nations, New York and Geneva, 2011).

4 'Critiques of Guiding Principles by Amnesty Intl., Human Rights Watch, FIDH, others – debate with Ruggie, Business and Human Rights Resource Centre' (*Business & Human Rights Resource Centre*) <http://business-humanrights.org/en/critiques-of-guiding-principles-by-amnesty-intl-human-rights-watch-fidh-others-debate-with-ruggie> accessed 12.12.2016.

5 Amnesty International and others, 'Joint Civil Society Statement on the draft Guiding Principles on Business and Human Rights' (*FIDH*, 14.01.2011) <https://www.fidh.org/IMG/pdf/Joint_CSO_Statement_on_GPs.pdf> accessed 12.12.2016.

6 Human Rights Watch, 'UN Human Rights Council: Weak Stance on Business Standards: Global Rules Needed, Not Just Guidance', Human Rights Watch News (16.06.2011) <https://www.hrw.org/news/2011/06/16/un-human-rights-council-weak-stance-business-standards> accessed 05.12.2017.

7 J G Ruggie, 'The Past as Prologue? A Moment of Truth for UN Business and Human Rights Treaty', *Institute for Human Rights and Business* (08.07.2014) <http://www.ihrb.org/commentary/past-as-prologue.html> accessed 12.12.2016.

8 The 'Working Group on the issue of human rights and transnational corporations and other business enterprises' was established by the UN Human Rights Council at its 17th Session, UN Human Rights Council, Resolution, *Human rights and transnational corporations and other business enterprises*, A/HRC/17/4 (06.07.2011) <https://documents-dds-ny.un.org/doc/RESOLUTION/GEN/G11/144/71/PDF/G1114471.pdf?OpenElement> accessed 05.05.2017.

The Working Group is charged, among other things, with bringing states, enterprises, NGOs (and a motley crew of others) together to meet a number of objectives to move the UNGP project forward. But it also became a site for growing criticism of and eventually opposition to the UNGP themselves as the way forward.[9] Within that space, discontent evolved to mobilisation and eventually to the invocation of institutional mechanisms to challenge the primacy of the UNGP as the central element of managing the human rights impacts of economic activity.

Led initially by the members of the UN delegation from Ecuador, and allied eventually with a large collective of NGOs,[10] and states,[11] a movement grew, the purpose of which was to replace the UNGP with a traditional and conventionally drafted multilateral treaty to bind states to a regime of human rights obligations for business enterprises, and through them, to bind such enterprises themselves. By June 2014, three years after it endorsed the UNGP, the UN Human Rights Council moved to establish an open-ended Intergovernmental Working Group (IGWG) to elaborate an international legally binding instrument to regulate, in international human rights law, the activities of transnational corporations and other business enterprises.[12] Simultaneously, the Human Rights Council indicated its continuing support for the UNGP.[13]

These actions brought into the open long-festering tensions among stakeholders involved in developing governance frameworks to manage the human rights behaviours of enterprises. Its formal manifestation produced a duelling set of resolutions, the first already mentioned proposed by Ecuador and its allies, the other, a resolution drafted by Norway and its allies, supportive of the UNGP and of the role of the Working Group for its embedding within

9 The tone was set from the first Business and Human Rights Forum. 'The United Nations Forum on Business and Human Rights is a space for representatives and practitioners from civil society, business, government, international organizations and affected stakeholders to take stock of challenges and discuss ways to move forward on putting into practice the Guiding Principles on Business and Human Rights.' See 'Working Group on the issue of human rights and transnational corporations and other business enterprises', *The 4th Annual United Nations Forum on Business and Human Rights: About the Forum*, <http://www.ohchr.org/EN/Issues/Business/Forum/Pages/2015ForumBHR.aspx> accessed 04.05.2017.

10 Ruggie, 'The Past as Prologue?', above n 7.

11 The draft that emerged was developed by Ecuador and South Africa and signed also by Bolivia, Cuba and Venezuela. See, Human Rights Council, 'Elaboration of an international legally binding instrument on transnational corporations and other business enterprises with respect to human rights, Human Rights Council', A/HRC/26/L.22/Rev.1 <https://documents-dds-ny.un.org/doc/UNDOC/LTD/G14/064/48/PDF/G1406448.pdf?OpenElement> accessed 20.05.2017.

12 Ibid.

13 Discussed in L C Backer, 'Moving Forward the UN Guiding Principles for Business and Human Rights: Between Enterprise Social Norm, State Domestic Legal Orders, and the Treaty Law that Might Bind Them All' (2015) 38(2) *Fordham International Law Journal* 457.

states and business enterprises.[14] But these tensions, lurking from the time of the abandonment of the *Norms* project, were not merely a repetition;[15] they represented the transformation of those perspectives, now layered atop changing power dynamics brought on by globalisation.[16] The substantive positions of most stakeholders are now quite clear and well developed, and are quite sharply drawn.[17] To some extent, they appear perhaps irreconcilable and touch on now ancient divisions in global political discourse about the nature of law, the role of the state, the character of non-state actors, the fundamental nature of human rights, and the possibility of an ordering or hierarchy among them.[18] These are important debates, though the essential shape of these debates were well established by the fourth quarter of the last century.[19] There has been little real movement in the debate since, and even less possibility of consensus.

Rather than adding to that discourse, this chapter will consider what the *process* of negotiating the contemplated treaty may reveal about the state of structuring governance frameworks for business and human rights either within the anticipated treaty framework or under the UNGP. For that purpose, I assume that the move towards treaty negotiation is inevitable in some form. I assume further that this move ought to be welcomed, even by those who, like me, view the undertaking as ill conceived, misdirected and doomed to

---

14 Human Rights Council, Resolution 26/22, para 10–11, 27.06.2014 <https://documents-dds-ny.un.org/doc/UNDOC/LTD/G14/062/40/PDF/G1406240.pdf?OpenElement> accessed 30.05.2017.

15 Sub-Commission on the Promotion and Protection of Human Rights, Norms on the Responsibilities of Transnational Corporations and Other Business Enterprises with Regard to Human Rights, UN Doc. E/CN.4/Sub.2/2003/12/Rev.2 (2003), available at http://www.unhchr.ch/html/menu2/2/55sub/55sub.htm; D Weissbrodt and M Kruger, above note 2. For a sense of the evolution of the critique, see essays in S Deva and D Bilchitz (eds), *Human Rights Obligations of Business: Beyond the Corporate Responsibility to Respect?*, Cambridge University Press, 2013.

16 L C Backer, 'Economic Globalization Ascendant and the Crisis of the State: Four Perspective on the Emerging Ideology of the State in the New Global Order' (2006) 17 *La Raza Law Journal* 141 <http://scholarship.law.berkeley.edu/blrlj/vol17/iss1/8> accessed 12.12.2016.

17 J Chaplier, 'EU engagement critical for adoption of strong business & human rights treaty, says NGO', *Business and Human Rights Resource Centre*, 03.09.2015 <http://business-humanrights.org/en/eu-engagement-critical-for-adoption-of-strong-business-human-rights-treaty-says-ngo> accessed 12.12.2016; Joint Civil Society, 'Joint Civil Society Statement on the draft Guiding Principles on Business and Human Rights' (*FIDH*, 2011) <https://www.fidh.org/IMG/pdf/Joint_CSO_Statement_on_GPs.pdf> accessed 11.09.2015.

18 J P Doh and T R Guay, 'Corporate Social Responsibility, Public Policy, and NGO Activism in Europe and the United States: An Institutional-Stakeholder Perspective' (2006) 43(1) *Journal of Management Studies* 47.

19 Discussed in L C Backer, 'Multinational Corporations, Transnational Law: The United Nation's Norms on the Responsibilities of Transnational Corporations as a Harbinger of Corporate Social Responsibility as International Law' (2006) 37 *Columbia Human Rights Law Review* 287.

fail, at least in relation to the purpose for which it was created.[20] What such analysis may reveal is that while the move towards the negotiation of a treaty may show substantial normative and conceptual failures, it also suggests some not inconsiderable successes. The process of treaty negotiation is necessary and advisable, not because it will succeed but precisely because, in its failure, it will move the project of creating a coherent structure for business and human rights governance one step closer to reality. This pattern is becoming visible through the very work of the IGWG. Its first two sessions, 'dedicated to conducting constructive deliberations on the content, scope, nature and form of the future international instrument', may lay the foundation going forward.[21]

The object of this chapter, then, is to consider what the process of treaty negotiation reveals about the state of structuring governance frameworks for business and human rights. It undertakes this examination within the context of the questions posed since the 1970s and described at the beginning of this introduction – is a treaty necessary, is it advisable, what ought to be included in such a treaty, and what are the implications of that effort? Section 2 considers the normative and structural difficulties of the move towards a comprehensive business and human rights treaty, the reasons why necessity, advisability, content and implications will produce failure. Section 3 then considers the reasons why the process of getting to failure is so necessary and advisable, both for the process of developing structures of governance for business and human rights, and its substance. Taken together, what may become clear is that even were the move towards a treaty to end in failure, the movement towards more robust governance of the human rights effects of economic activity will emerge stronger.

2. THE FAILURES THAT THE TREATY PROCESS REVEALS

One starts an analysis of this kind in the shadow of the fundamental contradictions on which the treaty negotiation project is built. The first touches on the unresolved conceptual issue of the relation between state, law and

20 See Backer, 'Moving Forward the UN Guiding Principles For Business And Human Rights' above n 13.

21 'Elaboration of an international legally binding instrument on transnational corporations and other business enterprises with respect to human rights', above n 11. The first session was described in 'Report on the first session of the open-ended intergovernmental working group on transnational corporations and other business enterprises with respect to human rights, with the mandate of elaborating an international legally binding instrument', A/HRC/31/50, 05.02.2016. The second session was reported in 'Report on the second session of the open-ended intergovernmental working group on transnational corporations and other business enterprises with respect to human rights', A/HRC/34/47, 04.01.2017.

enterprise. The second touches on the unresolved conceptual issue of the nature and hierarchy of human rights embedded in the domestic legal orders of states.

I have spoken to the *conceptual* substantive failures of this return to a treaty model for managing the human rights effects of enterprises.[22] I have also spoken to the roots of these conceptual weaknesses *embedded in historical context* – the still unresolved controversy about the scope of human rights, and precedence of certain human rights over others.[23] With respect to the first, one enters the nebulous realm of controversy over the consequences of the legal personality of non-state actors in public law.[24] With respect to the second, one relives the schismatic battles that tore asunder the Universal Declaration of Human Rights, splitting it irrevocably into a civil and political rights camp and an economic, social and cultural rights camp.[25] Little has changed on that score since the 1970s.[26] The treaty process will not heal this rupture. These two foundational realities will doom the treaty process precisely because they define the gulf that exists not merely between critical stakeholders in the treaty debate, but more importantly because they divide, as strongly as they did after 1945, those states on whose goodwill and good faith the success of the treaty process depends.[27]

The contradictions add an important layer of challenge to any treaty-making enterprise. In this light, questions – whether it is necessary or advisable to draft a treaty on corporations and human rights; what the content of that treaty and its implications could or should be; and related aspects – acquire a more interesting dimension when considered in the process dimensions of the treaty-making enterprise. Necessity, advisability, content and implications – these are the stuff of the fundamental failure of the treaty movement in this emerging age of globalisation, of global governance, and of the creation of world power systems in which the grand principles of state primacy and the horizontal equivalence of states has become largely a formal construct belied by the functional realities of

---

22 See Backer, 'Moving Forward the UN Guiding Principles For Business And Human Rights' above n 13.

23 L C Backer, 'On the Evolution of the United Nations' "Protect-Respect-Remedy" Project: The State, the Corporation and Human Rights in a Global Governance Context' (2011) 9 *Santa Clara Journal of International Law* 37.

24 On the issue of the legal personality of non-state actors, see, e.g., A Clapham, *Human Rights Obligations of Non-State Actors*, Oxford University Press, 2006.

25 For a discussion of the history of the evolution of the two international covenants, see, e.g., D Okeowo, 'Economic, Social and Cultural Rights: Rights or Privileges?' (2008) <http://dx.doi.org/10.2139/ssrn.1320204> accessed 11.09.2015; M J Perry, 'The Morality of Human Rights: A Nonreligious Ground?' (2005) 54 *Emory Law Journal* 97.

26 Discussed in L C Backer, 'Realizing Socio-Economic Rights Under Emerging Global Regulatory Frameworks: The Potential Impact of Privatization and the Role of Companies in China and India' (2013) 45(4) *The George Washington International Law Review* 615.

27 Backer, 'Moving Forward The UN Guiding Principles for Business and Human Rights' above n 13.

complex multi-systemic and anarchic global governance systems that mark the current global order.

2.1. LET US SPEAK FIRST TO NECESSITY

Much of the discussion about the necessity of the treaty (and certainly its process) focuses on the need to create a legal basis for whatever substantive provisions are eventually adopted and more generally as a necessary step in creating a legal basis for the governance of multinational or transnational enterprises (however defined). Yet necessity is better understood in a different way. The treaty process is necessary as a crucial means by which small and developing states may have their voices heard, may preserve even a semblance of their sovereignty. Small and less developed states have had their sovereignty eroded over the last half century.[28] They find themselves less able to engage in the most basic decisions that affect their internal macro-economic, social, political and cultural policies. These are increasingly in the hands of international organisations, including international financial institutions and unofficial collectives of the most powerful states. International financial institutions have come to manage developing states through the increasingly controversial conditions attached to loans.[29] The larger states have managed similar effects through trade and related agreements.[30] The largest multinational non-governmental actors have also become increasingly important stakeholders in the development of social norms that constitute the foundations of customs and traditions on which behaviours on the ground are practised and disciplined in society and through markets.[31]

That combination of developments has effectively shut small states out of governance.[32] The treaty process is crucial to ensure that small and developing

---

28 Backer, 'Economic Globalization Ascendant and the Crisis of the State' above n 16; N Villaroman, 'The Loss of Sovereignty: How International Debt Relief Mechanisms Undermine Economic Self-Determination' (2009) 2(4) *Journal of Law and Politics* 3; W E Murray and J Overton, 'The Inverse Sovereignty Effect: Aid, Scale and Neostructuralism in Oceania' (2011) 52(3) *Asia Pacific Viewpoint* 272.

29 G Bird and D Rowlands, 'The Catalytic Effect of Lending by the International Financial Institutions' (2002) 20(7) *The World Economy* 967.

30 D W Drezner, 'The Power and Peril of International Regime Complexity' (2009) 7(1) *Perspectives on Politics* 65.

31 G Teubner, 'Self-Constitutionalizing TNCs?: On the Linkage of "Private" and "Public" Corporate Codes of Conduct' (2011) 18 *Indiana Journal of Global Legal Studies* 617; N-L Sum, 'Wal-Martization and CSR-ization in Developing Countries' in J C Marques and P Utting (eds), *Corporate Social Responsibility and Regulatory Governance*, Palgrave Macmillan, 2010 pp 50–76; cf. S Bottomly, *The Constitutional Corporation: Rethinking Corporate Governance*, Ashgate, 2007.

32 On the effects of unequal power in the development of international norms, see, e.g., N Krisch, 'International Law in Times of Hegemony: Unequal Power and the Shaping of the International Legal Order' (2005) 16(3) *European Journal of International Law* 369.

states are not swallowed up by powerful enterprises, developed states and even the largest NGOs, all of which dwarf many of the smaller and less developed states in power and influence in the public sector and within the halls of international organisations. That is what appears from the realities of the treaty process thus far. It is not for nothing that it was a group of developed states, led in part by Ecuador and South Africa, that spearheaded this effort.[33] It is not for nothing that the vote for the resolution to create the open-ended IGWG on transnational corporations and other business enterprises with respect to human rights[34] divided developed from small and developing states.[35] It is not for nothing that a coalition of influential NGOs was necessary to put the finishing touches on the effort to secure an international imprimatur on a treaty-making process.

The treaty process, then, serves as an important means of bringing small and less developed states back into global norm-making processes. But those very processes will end in failure – crushed under the weight of the *substantive agendas* of powerful NGO alliances,[36] influential multinational enterprises (MNEs),[37] rich states,[38] and the international organisations that serve them.[39] But even the treaty *process* itself may consume the small and less developed states that are unable individually to devote the resources necessary to engage in the sort of sustained politics essential to the successful negotiation of the treaty. They are unlikely to sustain a unified front, which may be ground under the agendas and authority of larger states and powerful NGOs. That influence was much in evidence during the first session of the IGWG.[40] Indeed, the so-called

---

33 See Business and Human Rights Resource Centre, 'Binding Treaty' <https://business-humanrights.org/en/binding-treaty> accessed 01.06.2017.

34 See above n 11.

35 The Ecuador resolution was supported by developing states and Norway's by developed states. See above n 11 and n 14.

36 For the NGO Alliances supporting the treaty see, e.g., Treaty Alliance, 'Enhance the International Legal Framework to Protect Human Rights from Corporate Abuse' <http://www.treatymovement.com/statement/> accessed 05.09.2015.

37 BIAC and others, 'UN Treaty Process on Business and Human Rights. Initial Observations by the International Business Community on a Way Forward', *United States Council for International Business*, 29.06.2015 <http://www.uscib.org/uscib-content/uploads/2015/07/2015-06-29-Business-observations-on-UN-Treaty-on-Bus-and-Human-Rights.pdf> accessed 11.09.2015.

38 K Lappin, H Pedersen and T Khan, 'Influence of Corporations in Treaty Process Would Undermine Affected Communities' Interests', *Business & Human Rights Resource Centre* <http://business-humanrights.org/en/influence-of-corporations-in-treaty-process-would-undermine-affected-communities%E2%80%99-interests> accessed 09.09.2015.

39 For an example, see, L C Backer, 'Private Actors and Public Governance Beyond the State: The Multinational Corporation, the Financial Stability Board, and the Global Governance Order' (2011) 18 *Indiana Journal of Global Legal Studies* 751.

40 See, 'Report on the first session of the open-ended intergovernmental working group', above n 21.

Treaty Alliance[41] appears to have a legitimacy of state action that may be denied to small and less developed states. There is irony there. Indeed, consider that the imprimatur might not have been necessary had the initiative come from the Organisation for Economic Co-operation and Development states, the G20 or a coalition led by the influential BRICS countries (Brazil, Russia, India, China and South Africa). Yet the very power dynamics that have made the treaty process necessary will also doom it to failure. And failure here is measured both by the inability to produce a treaty and, as likely, the inability of small and less developed states to retain a significant engagement with the treaty-making process.

2.2. LET US THEN SPEAK TO ADVISABILITY

The treaty-making process is advisable not for the sake of the development of governance architectures within the traditional systems of legal standards generated by international public bodies and transposed into the law of adhering states, but because in the absence of such an effort there will be no architecture and no law to speak of.[42] That is to say, the treaty is advisable to create a system, grounded in law, where none (system or law) exists. One has a sense of this context of advisability from the second statement of the so-called Treaty Alliance.[43] This statement nicely made the case for the advisability of an international legal framework to protect human rights against abuse by transnational enterprises. It reflects the strongly held traditional view that posits legitimacy centred on states adhering to democratic values, collaborating through the production of international law, which binds them all.

Yet the legal architecture posited through the treaty itself poses a challenge to the legitimacy of law and the integrity of the state system on which it relies. Indeed, the more the treaty is structured as a set of compulsory obligations (on states and enterprises), the more the treaty will serve as an instrument for the substitution of the legal order inherent in its terms for that of the domestic legal orders of states. Like other comprehensive treaties, the effect is anti-democratic, but for a good cause. In any case in states with working democratically elected governments, the democratic deficit is only indirect; in other states the legal orders constructed by the community of states fills a democratic gap. Still it should trouble that the treaty might be understood to undermine the rationale for its creation – preservation of robust democratic orders based in states. Indeed, the treaty structure might be understood to undermine principles of democratic governance and the integrity of states through ordering premises

41 See above n 36.

42 This is the essence of the critique of the UNGP. See discussion above n 4.

43 See above n 36.

grounded in the compulsion of international law especially where, as here, it is unlikely that any but the most powerful states, or powerful alignments of states, will have a substantial influence on the shape and scope of the treaty's provisions. The advisability of the treaty, then, is a marker for the advisability of the use of the state system to ensure that the substantive objectives of powerful coalitions of states are imposed globally.

That understanding of advisability suggests the alternative justification. A structure grounded in anything but compulsion leaves only an international patchwork that is as easily achieved without the bother of a formal treaty process. Indeed, the case for the advisability of a treaty embodying a specific set of norms that legalises a specific set of ideologies also makes the case for the failure of the treaty process itself. Consider the Treaty Alliance, that has advanced the suggestion that an international legal framework is advisable as a function of its objectives. These include methodological objectives (e.g., to use the power of international organisations to compel states to 'adopt legislation'); substantive objectives (e.g., to determine for all states the scope of company conduct that will result in civil or criminal liability); and process-remedial objectives (e.g., to determine the interlinkages sufficient to convert production chains into liability chains within one or more states; to produce remedial structures that defy borders; and to carve out a special place in law for a class of persons in the performance of their roles as defenders of human rights against enterprises.[44] Beyond the *plausibility* of these objectives, there is no doubt that they are *advisable* (as opposed to alternatives) for anyone seeking to develop a vigorous legally binding instrument that is meant to function as global law, leaving to states only the ministerial function of transposing its provisions into the indigenous forms of national law.[45] But their advisability also undermines the integrity of states and the sovereign capacity of their peoples.

Again, the logic that makes a treaty of this sort advisable, given its objectives, will also doom the project to failure. The Treaty Alliance, much more than the states that supported the Human Rights Council Resolution, understand that the treaty is advisable only if it becomes embedded in a disciplined way across

---

44 Ibid; M Ibrahim, 'Summary of discussions of the Forum on Business and Human Rights, prepared by the Chair, Mo Ibrahim' (2015) *Human Rights Council Forum on Human Rights* <http://www.ohchr.org/Documents/Issues/Business/A-HRC-FBHR-2014-3_en.doc>; B Leather, 'Human Rights Defenders Must Be at Core of Treaty Process and Outcomes', *Business & Human Rights Resource Centre* (2015) <http://business-humanrights.org/en/human-rights-defenders-must-be-at-core-of-treaty-process-and-outcomes> accessed 11.09.2015.

45 D Bilchitz, 'The Moral and Legal Necessity for a Business and Human Rights Treaty', *Business & Human Rights Resource Centre* (2015) <http://business-humanrights.org/sites/default/files/documents/The%20Moral%20and%20Legal%20Necessity%20for%20a%20Business%20and%20Human%20Rights%20Treaty%20February%202015%20FINAL%20FINAL.pdf> accessed 11.09.2015.

national borders – and is enforced.[46] But A/HRC/RES/26/9 (14 July 2014) itself is far less ambitious, calling only for 'an international legally binding instrument to regulate, in international human rights law, the activities of transnational corporations and other business enterprises'. And thus the failure; the objective of the treaty process is itself undermined by the scope of the charge of the Human Rights Council.[47]

What is *possible* is the creation of an internationally legally binding instrument – that is to say, one binding on states through the normal modalities of international relations – but only relating directly to international human rights law, the international human rights law currently in force and to the extent enforced. That would require the acceptance of principled pragmatism into the construction of a treaty framework.[48] What is *advisable* is a comprehensive global legal order in which international legal standards must apply to states the way that regulations apply within the European Union to its Member States. But that itself creates not just failure but contradiction – in order to preserve the traditional international state order, it is necessary to undo it by creating an elaborate framework that essentially tramples state sovereignty, especially that of small and less developed states, now subject to the will of a larger polity. The protection of core human rights principles of democratic government as a core value of human rights in the face of its extinction through this advisable approach to treaty making creates a contradiction that has yet to be discussed to any great extent. The answer – variations of the ends justifying the means is either empty or suggests the very creation of hierarchies of human rights that the treaty is itself supposed to avoid.

2.3. LET US SPEAK TO CONTENT

We have focused on at least one influential approach to the content of the treaty suggested by the Treaty Alliance.[49] There is little point to speaking to context other than to suggest the way that content itself inevitably contributes to failure. These failures are the consequence of the structural framework that will likely inform treaty negotiations. There are three principal structural contributors to content-based failure worth noting.

---

46 See above n 36.

47 Discussed further in L C Backer, 'The Perils and Promise of Drafting a Comprehensive Treaty on Business and Human Rights: Principles, Pragmatism and Principled Pragmatism in Shaping a Global Law for Business Enterprises' (2016) 42(1) *North Carolina Journal of International Law* 417.

48 Consider its deployment in D Renfrey, '"Narrative power" and the UN business and human rights treaty', *Social Watch: poverty eradication and gender justice*, 01.09.2015, <http://www.socialwatch.org/node/17024> accessed 20.05.2017.

49 See above n 36.

First, whatever the content, the treaty elaborated will tend to reflect the ethos of the international lawyer and policy maker; it will reflect the macro-economic predilections of states. But it will be oblivious to, indeed contemptuous of, the cultures, traditions, law and strongly embedded values that underlie business practice across the globe; it will marginalise the ethos of the corporate and securities lawyer. The draft report of the Second Session of the IGWG might be said to reflect these perspectives.[50] This is not a special consequence of a business and human rights treaty effort; globalisation itself has adopted this stance as it has moved towards harmonisation of practices, customs and expectations.[51] This orientation, meant perhaps to counter what was perceived as the unbalanced deference to the business sector, derided by NGOs[52] in John Ruggie's important concept of principled pragmatism for the development of the UNGP,[53] may create two structural consequences.

One touches on the inevitability of challenging the fundamental approach in law, economics and social organisation, of the primacy and characteristics of aggregations of capital now dominant in most states. Whatever one thinks of the development of corporate law, and the practices of business, however one thinks that several generations of large groups of people 'got it wrong' when they developed corporate law, accounting, financial disclosure, and finance markets, one cannot defeat them by ignoring them and seeking to supplant them through international instrument making.[54] And yet, the fundamental objectives of the treaty will not merely require the adoption of human rights standards applicable to transnational enterprises, but will also require many states to substantially alter their approaches to the legal regulation of enterprises themselves – to a fundamental transformation of corporate law.[55] That transformation is an

---

50 See, 'Report on the second session of the open-ended intergovernmental working group', above n 21.

51 On the harmonising effects of globalisation see, e.g., J Wiener, *Globalization and the Harmonization of Law*, Cassell, 1999.

52 On the NGO critique of principled pragmatism, see, e.g., 'NGOs Should Expose the Limitations of Pragmatism', *Conectas*, 02.12.2013 <http://www.conectas.org/en/actions/business-and-human-rights/news/8495-ngos-should-expose-the-limitations-of-pragmatism> accessed 13.09.2015.

53 On John Ruggie and principled pragmatism see, e.g., J G Ruggie, 'Business and Human Rights: The Evolving International Agenda' (2007) 101(4) *American Journal of International Law* 819; J G Ruggie, 'Regulating Multinationals: The UN Guiding Principles, Civil Society, and International Legalization' in C Rodriguez-Garavito (ed), *Business and Human Rights: Beyond the End of the Beginning* Cambridge University Press, 2017.

54 Discussed in Backer, 'Multinational Corporations, Transnational Law' (n 19).

55 On academic and political calls for adoption of a stakeholder welfare maximisation model to replace the shareholder welfare maximisation model at the core of most corporate law, see, e.g., M J P Magill, M Quinzii and J-C Rochet, 'A Critique of Shareholder Value Maximization (2013) *Swiss Finance Institute Research Paper* No. 13-16.

undertaking that contributed to the failure of the Norms project,[56] and one which academics continue to seek to overcome within the current legal framework.[57] Recognition of the power of corporate culture in law and practice underlay John Ruggie's principled pragmatism.[58] Efforts to transform it indirectly through an international instrument focused on human rights behaviours is likely to doom the contemporary treaty project as well.

The other touches on the consequences of developing a legal framework that threatens the operation of modern business, and its practices. To the extent that dissatisfaction with the UNGP derives from a sense of imbalance in favour of business, the solution is not a system that produces imbalance against business. Indeed, that blindness to the realities of a well-established legal and business culture (and its practice), and an unwillingness to engage, will itself produce content, whatever its form, that will encounter substantial and perhaps fatal opposition. I noted over a decade ago that the tragedy of the *business* of managing the human rights responsibilities of economic enterprises was the utter inability of those with a conventional internationalist and human rights law and policy orientation, and those with a domestic corporate and business law and policy orientation, to break out of the normative silos within which each has constructed a comfortable ideological and practical home.[59] The treaty continues that tragedy on a new stage. The problem with a business and human rights treaty will likely centre on the rigidity of efforts to force the logics and practices of economic organisation globally to conform to the expectations of human rights ideology whose characteristics and applications have yet to produce consensus.

Second, the regulatory objects of the treaty are already both obsolete and increasingly less relevant. The treaty exercise is directed towards building a legal regulatory framework for 'transnational corporations and other business enterprises'.[60] That reflects a conception of the way that business operates that might have been plausible up to the later part of the last century, but which increasingly is at variance with the way in which global business is now undertaken. It is no longer clear that the management of global economics

---

56 Backer, 'Multinational Corporations, Transnational Law' above n 19; J G Ruggie and T Nelson, 'Human Rights and the OECD Guidelines for Multinational Enterprises: Normative Innovations and Implementation Challenges' (2015) *Corporate Social Responsibility Initiative Working Paper No. 66* <https://www.hks.harvard.edu/index.php/content/download/76202/1711396/version/1/file/workingpaper66.pdf> accessed 11.09.2015; Ruggie, 'Business and Human Rights' above n 53.

57 S R. Ratner, 'Corporations and Human Rights: A Theory of Legal Responsibility' (2001) 111(3) *Yale Law Journal* 443.

58 Ruggie, 'Regulating Multinationals' above n 53.

59 Discussed in Backer, 'Multinational Corporations, Transnational Law' above n 19.

60 A/HRC/RES/26/9 (14.07.2014), see above.

is grounded in state-based legal frameworks or even in state-based macroeconomic policy. Indeed, the expression of that economics in multinational enterprises might be better conceived as system rather than as entity, and *an effectively targeted treaty might seek to regulate production chains rather than the enterprises that may serve as convenient vessels for its realization.*[61] The thrust of contemporary regulatory efforts appears focused on the supply chain as the basis of governance, rather than the enterprise, or the state.[62] The difference is important for developing a legal framework; yet this difference appears to elude those focused on the treaty making. There are a large number of production chains,[63] to be sure, that continue to operate as vertically integrated simple command structures grounded in corporate chains. But it is as likely that production chains are now characterised by hybridity in organisation – with some corporate chains, some contract chains, some understandings, and increasing amounts of segmentation at all levels of production from raw materials to consumer sales.[64] A treaty limited to corporations misses entirely that enterprises may not operate in corporate form and more importantly, that the object of regulations is increasingly a system (supply or production chains) rather than an enterprise. The model that is the basis of the treaty, building on the conceptual framework of the 1970s and the work of the UN then leading to the Norms is now largely irrelevant. This is a problem unless, of course, the object of the treaty exercise is merely to produce optics – the appearance of action without much effort at creating an identity between problem and solution. Yet so much effort for optics itself suggests failure of the treaty enterprise, and perhaps on a monumental scale – so much effort for so little effect – the definition of bathos.

Third, whatever its content, the efforts towards a viable international instrument will ultimately fail precisely because it focuses on the wrong rule set as its regulatory target. It is not just that the treaty is misdirected by focusing on entities rather than production systems as the object to be regulated. It is that the legalisation project fails to develop a coherent set of global baseline human rights standards on which any project of enterprise regulation building must be built. It is an easy matter to seek to internationalise and legalise what the UNGP organised as the Second Pillar responsibility of enterprises to respect

61 Discussed in L C Backer, 'Regulating Multinational Corporations – Trends, Challenges and Opportunities' (2015) 22(1) *Brown Journal of World Affairs* 153–73.

62 For example, Organization for Economic Cooperation and Development, *OECD Due Diligence Guidance for Responsible Supply Chains of Minerals from Conflict-Affected and High-Risk Areas*, OECD, Paris, 2016, pp 12–16.

63 On production chains, see E Andriesse and others, 'Business Systems, Value Chains and Inclusive Regional Developments in Southeast Asia' in A H J Helmsing and S Vellema (eds), *Value Chains, Social Inclusion, and Economic Development: Contrasting Theories and Development*, Routledge, 2011, pp 151–77.

64 Ibid.

human rights.[65] Indeed, the object of much of the work of the UNGP Working Group, and the stakeholders active in its field of operations, have focused on methods for 'taming' the Second Pillar by bringing it back within systems of law and resisting efforts to expand the notion of autonomous extra-legal governance regimes. National Action Plans have been particularly well focused on this effort, as have the agendas of many human rights NGOs invested in this enterprise.[66] Yet the strength of the corporate responsibility to respect human rights–derived from the Second Pillar's autonomy from state-based law systems and its coherence within the context of the International Bill of Human Rights– is precisely the reason that, where incorporated within a treaty structure, the effectiveness of such a structure will collapse. To incorporate the Second Pillar within the conventional structures of state obligation under international law is to fracture the governance integrity of the Second Pillar's normative order.

In this light, consider that few states have actually embedded the entirety of the International Bill of Human Rights within their domestic legal orders.[67] And even among those that have there are considerable potential variations in domestic application.[68] States have come no closer to closing the human rights standards gap since the 1970s. Given their constitutional traditions and their national agendas, states have adopted a wide variety of approaches to what constitute human rights enforceable within their borders. The meaning and practice of human rights among states varies even between states whose legal systems and constitutional traditions are quite similar. It is not clear how one can develop a harmonised system of human rights standards for business behaviours when states have stubbornly (though for the best of human rights reasons – that is, for the purpose of giving effect to national sovereign will) refused to align their First Pillar duty to protect human rights in any coherent fashion.[69]

---

65 UNGP, above note 3, at para 11–24. Moreover the Second Pillar standardises applicable baseline substantive provisions; para 12 provides that 'The responsibility of business enterprises to respect human rights refers to internationally recognised human rights – understood, at a minimum, as those expressed in the International Bill of Human Rights and the principles concerning fundamental rights set out in the International Labour Organization's Declaration on fundamental Principles and Rights at Work.'

66 UN Working Group on Business and Human Rights, *Guidance on National Action Plans on Business and Human Rights* (United Nations, 2014). Available at <http://www.ohchr.org/Documents/Issues/Business/UNWG_%20NAPGuidance.pdf>.

67 United Nations, 'Multilateral Treaties Deposited with the Secretary-General, Status as of December 31, 2006' UN Doc. ST/LEG/SER.E/25, U.N. Sales No. E.07.V.3, United Nations, 2007, pp 160–242 <https://treaties.un.org/doc/source/publications/MTDSG/2006-vol.1-english.pdf> accessed 12.12.2016.

68 Ibid.

69 The UNGP recognise wide variation in the extent of a state's duty to protect human rights. See UNGP, above, n 3, at General Principles ('Nothing in these Guiding Principles should be read as creating new international law obligations, or as limiting or undermining any legal obligations a State may have undertaken or be subject to under international law with regard to human rights.').

Again, the result of any treaty will be formal coherence and functional failure in the face of wide variations in state recognition of human rights. Absent coherence in the legal obligations of states to protect human rights, the best one can hope for in the legalisation of enterprise conduct may be disclosure.

2.4. LET US SPEAK TO IMPLICATIONS

The process of treaty making may bring down the UNGP precisely because the success of the treaty process must be based, at least in part, on proof of the failure of the UNGP process itself.[70] The consequence is a perverse effect – the creation of incentives to actively contribute to UNGP failure to prove the necessity of a treaty. Here, the implications of the treaty process again point to failure, but on a more comprehensive level. That failure involves, to some extent, the consequences of signalling. In this case the signalling of A/HRC/RES/26/9 (14 July 2014) suggests a willingness to eviscerate all of the work leading to the UNGP as a failure. That is a conclusion that would be rejected even by treaty defenders who politely suggest that the UNGP were a necessary 'step in the right direction' but fundamentally insufficient.[71] Still that sort of talk does signal both a rejection of the long-term value of the UNGP (indeed that sort of talk implies that the UNGP served its purpose the moment the UNGP was endorsed) and of its substantive elements. And thus the greatest failure of the treaty process will be to produce a failure of development of the UNGP even as its own direct objectives fail for want of coherence and relevance. We could be left with neither treaty nor UNGP.

Therein lies the great tragedy of the treaty process: in the willingness of its proponents to construct from out of the failure of the UNGP the foundation of the rationale for the inevitability of the treaty process itself. The process of business and human rights treaty elaboration itself, then, is usefully understood as a means of using the UNGP as the means of its own undoing. The process is based on framing something that appears to be an internal conversation between the UNGP and what is proposed as its better or idealised version (in the form of the treaty). The object of the dialogue is to substantially question the legitimacy of the UNGP as its structures and premises are juxtaposed against what is put forward as the 'better version of the UNGP' in the form of a proper (and well-constructed) treaty. This strategic use of the UNGP is clever, but perhaps too

---

70 On arguments that the UNGP process has failed or has not progressed fast enough, see, e.g., C Albin-Lackey, 'Without Rules: A Failed Approach to Corporate Accountability' (2013) *Human Rights Watch World Report*.

71 See, e.g., FIDH, 'Business and Human Rights: Enhancing Standards and Ensuring Redress' (2014) *FIDH*, <https://www.fidh.org/IMG/pdf/201403_briefing_paper_enhance_standards_ensure_redress_web_version.pdf> accessed 09.09.2015.

much so. It carries with it the temptation to apply or resist the UNGP project in a way that helps prove that the UNGP fail to meet their objectives. At its limits, this strategic approach may well signal to stakeholders that in order to move forward a treaty project it may be necessary to actively contribute to the failure of the UNGP![72]

3. FROM OUT OF FAILURE … SMALL SUCCESS: WHY THE TREATY PROCESS OUGHT TO EMBRACE ITS DESTINY

Though it is easy enough to describe the weaknesses of the treaty project, as to its substance and its process, it would be misleading to suggest that the process of treaty making is itself something that ought to be abandoned merely because it is likely to fail, and fail quite spectacularly. Indeed, from my perspective, the exercise of treaty making in the context of the human rights obligations of enterprises (and of states) constitutes an important exercise necessary for the development of a vigorous and more coherent set of standards that might produce a common system of custom and expectation that can drive governance and law. Indeed, even were the treaty enterprise to fail, it would, to some extent be a success.

I do not speak to the well-developed argument, raised elsewhere, that suggests that treaty negotiations are welcome to the extent they seek to focus on quite narrow topics on which there is already a move towards consensus. That, though a worthy goal, proffers an alternative to the current treaty project envisioned in A/HRC/RES/26/9 (14 July 2014). Rather I consider the benefits of engaging vigorously in what the Human Rights Council Resolution describes as 'conducting constructive deliberations on the content, scope, nature and form of the future international instrument', even if, as I have suggested, the exercise is doomed to failure. This section suggests briefly why even a project doomed to failure may well succeed in advancing the project of embedding human rights elements in business operations.

3.1. FOR STATES: MOVING TOWARDS COHERENCE IN THE STATE DUTY TO PROTECT HUMAN RIGHTS

Even if the treaty process fails, the process of getting to failure proves valuable in the elaboration of a legal framework within which states will come to

72 Discussed in more detail in Backer, 'The Perils and Promise of Drafting a Comprehensive Treaty on Business and Human Rights', above n 47.

understand the nature of their duty to protect human rights. In particular, treaty negotiation itself may be a useful exercise to the extent that it exposes the limits and regulatory gaps within states. The treaty negotiation process itself may actually serve to produce a series of action plans relating to core consensus issues required to move forward on a treaty – the definition of human rights that must be transposed to national law, the establishment of remedial mechanisms that produce coherence in such mechanisms and the like. The effect of the treaty negotiation process, then, may produce the sort of national action plans for human rights embedding within national law that has proven elusive under the UNGP framework – producing close and critical discussion of the scope of a state's human rights obligation and the extent of remedies available for redress of human rights violations. Indeed, it may be possible that the treaty negotiations may serve as a means of bridging the near half-century divide in approaches to human rights that has stymied the advancement of coherent governance norms in this field except in very narrow areas.

3.2. FOR MARKETS AND CONSUMERS: THE CLOSING OF GOVERNANCE GAPS

But, of course, A/HRC/RES/26/9 (14 July 2014) is supposed to focus on the legalisation of the UNGP's Second Pillar. That focus, even if likely to end in failure relating to a treaty, may produce important successes through the process of treaty negotiation. Principal among them would be advances in the elaboration of coherent glosses on the Second Pillar, from the specification of human rights instruments binding on corporate activity, to the legal effects of human rights due diligence.[73] A move to incorporate human rights due diligence as part of the financial reporting requirements necessary for the public trading of securities would provide a great step forward for the UNGP, even in the face of the failure to successfully negotiate a treaty. Thus, if an important value of comprehensive treaty negotiations is to spotlight the deficiencies of international law in the development of a coherent space within which the state duty to protect human rights must be articulated and applied (the UNGP's First Pillar), then an equally important element of success turns on the ability of negotiating parties to focus on the elaboration of a legal framework for the UNGP's Second Pillar. Even failed treaty negotiations will expose those governance gaps within transnational space

[73] This effort is currently aided through efforts undertaken by the UN Working Group on Business and Human Rights through its National Action Plan project. See Working Group on Business and Human Rights, 'Guidance on National Action Plans on Business and Human Rights', UN Geneva, 2016 <http://www.ohchr.org/Documents/Issues/Business/UNWG_NAPGuidance.pdf> accessed 01.06.2017, pp 1, 12–13.

and make clearer the scope of governance that might require filling by MNEs and transnational civil society within the Second Pillar context.

3.3. FOR NGOs: SOLIDARITY AND GLOBAL MASS DEMOCRACY

Treaty negotiation, and indeed *the failure of treaty negotiation*, will create greater solidarity among human rights NGOs. The process of getting to A/HRC/RES/26/9 (14 July 2014) suggests the power of failure to generate solidarity and to produce the sort of mass democratic mobilisation that might produce effects on the ground. Beyond the positive possibilities of greater solidarity inherent in treaty negotiations (successful or not), negotiation permits such actors to learn to better engage in governance at the highest international levels. Even treaty negotiation failure (and perhaps especially treaty negotiation failures) also may produce the sort of solidarity that would aid local and national NGOs in their efforts to shape the governance of the human rights affecting behaviours of enterprises within states, in the negotiation of bilateral and multilateral trade agreements, and in the shaping of corporate practice. In the process of moving towards failure, the process itself might contribute to making NGOs better advocates within states.

But more importantly, as treaty negotiations progress, the role of NGOs within the architecture of any international instrument will necessarily be far more diminished than under the UNGP's Second Pillar. International instruments, addressed to states and focused on the regulation of economic enterprises, will relegate NGOs to the margin of systems of monitoring and enforcement. NGOs will likely have only the smallest role within remedial frameworks. As a consequence, NGOs will either have to become specialised legal centres – representing individuals and groups with standing to bring action against enterprises within one of the states adhering to any international instrument (and to the extent such an instrument has been transposed into national law), or they will be relegated to the usual peripheral, though important, roles of outside monitoring and accountability functions. Yet a treaty negotiation failure might well provide the impetus necessary for NGOs to begin more aggressively to serve as an important site for Second Pillar governance. Indeed, NGOs might well determine that they play the most important role in the social norm sphere of the Second Pillar, rather than as 'civil society' elements within traditional public law structures.

3.4. FOR SMALL AND LESS DEVELOPED STATES: SOLIDARITY GAINS

Treaty negotiation may produce a similar effect on small and developing states in terms of producing a solidarity that has been absent since the end of the Third World Movement. It might serve as a basis for more effective regionalism grounded in the shared interests of these states against both the largest enterprises and the more developed states. It may provide a nexus point for producing a better engagement of these states with the logic and evolution of global economic activity and provide a basis for engaging an area that A/HRC/RES/26/9 (14 July 2014) avoids – the way that emerging systems of law and governance, sourced in international norms, bilateral and multilateral treaties, the rules of international organisations, and the peculiarities of agreements with specific large firms, have effectively transformed most small and less developed states from a territory marked by a single and coherent set of laws to a nexus point for multiple legal systems that apply to specific segments within the national territory. The treaty negotiation process, in other words, may help states confront the reality of the myth of the legally integrated state and, through that confrontation, determine how states might reacquire a greater measure of control or coherence of law and policy within their territories.[74] For small and developing states there might be an additional gain, an opening to a better approach to regionalism, one with teeth, to replace the tired and ritualised forms of regionalism that currently appear long on rhetoric and ideology and quite short on effective development implementation strategies.

3.5. FOR ENTERPRISES: AFFECTING BUSINESS CULTURE AND STRENGTHENING THE AUTONOMY OF BUSINESS GOVERNANCE

Treaty negotiation, whether or not it succeeds, may finally create a space in which *enterprises begin to understand the language and referents of public law-based human rights structures* and NGOs may begin to understand the singular power of the state-based notions of legal personality of corporations and similar enterprises. The policy discussions that may be produced in the course of treaty negotiations may serve as an important source for the development of social norm standards and governance frameworks that might be elaborated through the Second Pillar. In this respect, the treaty negotiations may be the most important impetus for business and enterprise embrace of the notions of human rights due diligence and of the incorporation of human rights elements in the way in which all enterprises (private and state owned) evaluate and approach business decisions.[75] This is particularly useful because of the narrowness of the

74 Discussed in L C Backer, 'Fractured Territories and Abstracted Terrains: The Problem of Representation and Human Rights Governance Regimes Within and Beyond the State' (2016) 23(1) *Indiana Journal of Global Legal Studies* 61–94.

75 These are efforts that have already acquired a substantial footing within the soft law frameworks of transnational governance, even those overseen by large transnational public actors. See, e.g., D Abrahams and Y Wyss, 'Guide to Human Rights Impact Assessment and

treaty-making focus. While states may focus on transnational enterprises operating in corporate form, business may elaborate governance structures more compatible with the management of production chains within which issues of human rights may be more effectively embedded with targeted and specific effect.

4. CONCLUSION

The chapter ends where it started – in a state of expectation. In her opening statement to the second session of the open-ended IGWG on transnational corporations and other business enterprises with respect to human rights, the Chair-Rapporteur María Fernanda Espinosa noted that:

> The initiative of a binding instrument was based on respect for the principles of fairness, legality and justice, which should prevail for the benefit of all in the international context, and the objective of the process was to fill gaps in the international system of human rights and to provide better elements for access to justice and remedy for victims of human rights abuses related to transnational corporations. That objective was in no way aimed at undermining host States or the business sector, but was intended to level the playing field with respect to human rights.[76]

Yet, the very movement to a treaty has polarised the business and human rights communities. It has brought out into the open a number of tensions that were submerged during the development of what became the UNGP as stakeholders held their fire in the hope of making some progress on advancing the business and human rights agenda. But those tensions – the irrelevance of small and developing states in international discourse and standards development, the frustration of human rights NGOs in the face of the need to compromise, the instrumentalism of business whose commitment to substantial changes in business cultures might be hard to gauge – should not produce reaction but advancement. A treaty is necessary and advisable. But its greatest utility may be only as a step towards the development of a better grounding for the governance of the human rights impacts of business activity – whether by private or public enterprises. That better grounding may well be advanced even in the face of the failure of the treaty process initiated through A/HRC/RES/26/9 (14 July 2014). To that extent, the process of elaborating a treaty might well provide a glimmer of success.

Management (HRIAM)' (2010) *International Business Leaders Forum and the International Finance Corp*, <http://www.ifc.org/wps/wcm/connect/8ecd35004c0cb230884bc9ec6f601fe4/hriam-guide-092011.pdf?MOD=AJPERES> accessed 12.12.2016.

76 'Report on the second session of the open-ended intergovernmental working group', above n 21, para 7.

'BAND-AIDS DON'T FIX BULLET HOLES': IN DEFENCE OF A TRADITIONAL STATE-CENTRIC APPROACH*

Tara L Van Ho[1]

1. INTRODUCTION: 'SO IT'S GONNA BE FOREVER OR IT'S GONNA GO DOWN IN FLAMES'[2]

While international obligations do, and can, exist for non-state actors, international human rights law (IHRL) has traditionally been framed through a state-centred lens, with states as duty-bearers and individuals as rights-holders.[3]

---

* Taylor Swift, et al., 'Bad Blood', on Taylor Swift, *1989* (2014).

1 This chapter benefitted from comments from participants at the Madrid workshop, Anil Yilmaz, Jena Martin, Sheldon Leader, Adrian Traylor, and Timothy Shoffner. Financial support for research on this chapter came from INTRAlaw, University of Aarhus, Department of Law.

2 Taylor Swift, et al., 'Blank Space', on Taylor Swift, *1989* (2014).

3 N Rodley, 'Non-state Actors and Human Rights', in: S Sheeran, N Rodley (eds), *Routledge Handbook of International Human Rights Law* (Routledge 2013), 523 at 523–24, 526. See also, A Clapham, *Human Rights Obligations of Non-State Actors* (Oxford University Press, 2006), 25, 33–35, 39. Clapham criticises this approach – as well as the approach of this book chapter – throughout his piece.

As this chapter explains, this approach requires the state to regulate the relationship between non-state actors and to ensure adequate remediation for victims whose human rights have been impacted by other non-state actors.[4] Some scholars, including others in this volume, argue that this state-centred approach fails victims by expecting weaker states to attempt to regulate corporations that are stronger economically. While a legitimate criticism and concern, the solution may not rest in direct obligations for corporations but instead in retaining the state focus and expanding the jurisdiction states are expected to use when regulating and providing remedies against business for the protection of human rights. In its second meeting, the open-ended intergovernmental working group (IGWG) on transnational corporations and other business enterprises with respect to human rights continued to debate whether to ascribe direct human rights obligations to corporations.[5] Focusing the treaty on direct IHRL obligations for corporations, however, may be providing a solution to the wrong problem.

In this chapter I suggest the issue that needs to be addressed is not who has the obligations but how the obligations are enforced. I further examine how current language from state-centric treaties can be modified to close the gaps in accessible and effective remedies. Readers will note that throughout the piece, I use lyrics from Taylor Swift songs to convey the specific themes of both the chapter as a whole and the particular section in which a lyric is being employed; sometimes the lyrics are explained within the section, while other times I assume the lyric's theme is self-explanatory. This is done with the hope that the lessons of the chapter are easily remembered, and the primary lesson is that of the title of this chapter: 'Band-Aids Don't Fix Bullet Holes', meaning that an easy solution to a complicated issue is perhaps not a solution at all. If the proposed treaty on business and human rights undermines the state-centric approach to IHRL, it may ultimately undermine the means by which victims can force accountability and obtain remedies. Instead, I suggest that the current, state-centric approach to IHRL may best address the needs of victims and weaker states in part because the weaknesses are not the result of a state-centric approach but rather states' unwillingness to grant strong enforcement protections to human rights victims, a reality unlikely to change simply because the defendant does. This means that while a state-centric treaty is unlikely to provide strong remedial mechanisms for human rights victims, a focus on

---

4 Rodley, above n 3, 527.

5 Human Rights Council, 'Draft Report of the Second Session of the Open-Ended intergovernmental working group on transnational corporations and other business enterprises with respect to human rights (version of 28 October 2016)', 7, 16–18, <http://www.ohchr.org/EN/HRBodies/HRC/WGTransCorp/Session2/Pages/Session2.aspx> (accessed January 2017), ('IGWG, Draft Report').

direct obligations for businesses is both unlikely to provide a strong remedial mechanism and likely to undermine the clarity of obligations and authority the current approach provides.

There are a few assumptions underpinning this chapter. The first is that the purpose of the treaty must be aimed at increasing adequate remedies for victims. A treaty that fails to accomplish this has little worth and even less purpose.[6] The international community has documented its awareness of the impact of businesses on human rights since the 1960s.[7] It is no longer sufficient to document, assess, analyse or contemplate how businesses impact human rights; it is time to ensure effective protections for victims. An additional assumption is that the treaty should not be used to create new rights, only to clarify obligations and relationships around fuller protection and enforcement of rights already recognised in IHRL.

The third assumption is that this treaty is a one-shot opportunity; it will, as the title of this section suggests, last or it will go down in flames. Human rights treaties are rarely amended after adoption, in part because doing so effectively requires greater consensus than even an initial treaty negotiation.[8] States can often be pressured and persuaded into acceding to a human rights treaty they had no intention of agreeing to, and still have no intention of fully implementing, if ratification offers economic, diplomatic or other advantages.[9] Altering a treaty so that it applies to all the states parties, however, requires that all existing states parties – including those who acceded only as a result of significant pressure and who have little intention of following through on their commitments – agree to the new provisions.[10] Instead, optional protocols are often developed to address particular needs or failings of a core treaty.[11] Optional protocols adopted through the United Nations (UN) have never reached the same number of ratifications as the original, or core, treaty.[12] The human rights community must therefore be prepared to accept the long-term consequences of the treaty and choose its path cautiously.

---

6 Jeffrey Sachs made a similar point at the second session of the IGWG. See, ibid, 4.

7 See K Buhmann, 'Navigating the "Train Wreck" to Being "Welcomed": Negotiation Strategies and Argumentative Patterns in the Development of the UN Framework', in: S Deva, D Bilchitz (eds), *Beyond the Corporate Responsibility to Respect?* (Cambridge University Press, 2013), 29 at 30.

8 Vienna Convention on the Law of Treaties (1969), 1155 UNTS 331, article 40 ('VCLT').

9 See OA Hathaway, 'Why Do Countries Commit to Human Rights Treaties' (2007) 51 *Journal of Conflict Resolution* 588, 595.

10 VCLT, article 40.

11 See, e.g, Optional Protocol to the International Covenant on Civil and Political Rights (1966), 999 UNTS 171.

12 See Office of the High Commissioner for Human Rights, 'Status of Ratification Interactive Dashboard', <http://indicators.ohchr.org/> (accessed January 2016).

This leads to the final, perhaps the most central, underlying assumption of this chapter: if we are to navigate away from a traditional approach to one that embraces direct human rights obligations on corporations, it should be because both (1) the current state-centric approach to human rights law does not offer the tools necessary for tackling the issue of corporate accountability, and (2) the alternative suggestion *clearly* offers a better course of action. Moving from a known understanding of IHRL to an unknown and less clear approach can be justified, in my opinion, only if these two conditions are met. Otherwise, we are hoping for outcomes rather than planning for them. I suggest through this chapter that the first condition is not met as the current state-centric approach to IHRL offers important tools that can ensure the treaty has an effective impact on combating business impacts on human rights.

The question for this chapter is not whether a treaty *could* assign IHRL obligations to corporations – for me, there is no doubt that is an acceptable legal position[13] – but rather whether doing so is the best approach for victims. In doing so, the chapter suggests the business and human rights community would do well to remember the purpose and the focus of the state-centric approach before discarding it quickly. This chapter focuses on the need of victims to access effective remedies, the barrier to this posed by the doctrine of separate corporate personalities, and the means for addressing victims' needs through the traditional, state-centric approach. I leave the issue of corporate criminal accountability to other authors[14] and focus only on establishing means for civil liability. I suggest that the key to closing the gaps in accountability comes from expanding the jurisdiction of states to provide concurrent jurisdiction in multiple venues. The remainder of the chapter is divided into five sections. In Section 2, I assess the need for a treaty, including the path to the UN Guiding Principles on Business and Human Rights ('Guiding Principles' or 'UNGP'),[15] currently the most authoritative statement on responsibilities in the area of business and human rights,[16] and the potential for the new treaty to provide a robust enforcement mechanism. In Section 3, I examine the current state-centric approach to horizontal human rights impacts and consider how the doctrine of separate corporate personalities can lead to difficulties for victims seeking to enforce their human rights responsibilities. In Section 4, I invoke the

---

13 For more on this issue, see, e.g., Clapham, above n 3; D Murray, *Human Rights Obligations of Non-State Armed Groups* (Hart Publishing, 2016).

14 For a discussion corporate criminal accountability, see N Bernaz, 'Corporate Criminal Liability under International Law: The *New TV S.A.L.* and *Akhbar Beirut S.A.L.* Cases at the Special Tribunal for Lebanon,' (2015), 13 *Journal of International Criminal Justice*, 313.

15 'Guiding Principles on Business and Human Rights: Implementing the United Nations' "Protect, Respect and Remedy" Framework', UN Doc. A/HRC/17/31 (21.03.2011) ('UNGP').

16 See, e.g., A Shemberg, 'New Global Standards for Business and Human Rights' (2012) 13 *Business Law International* 27, 27–28.

UN Conventions against Torture and Corruption to consider how current treaty language can be modified to expand the jurisdictional obligations of states to hear civil claims and provide greater access to remedies. Finally, in Section 5, I conclude that there is little reason to shift away from a traditionalist approach in the business and human rights treaty.

2. THE GUIDING PRINCIPLES AND THE NEED FOR A TREATY: 'YOU GAVE ME EVERYTHING AND NOTHING'[17]

It is worth briefly recalling the path to the treaty and examining why it is needed, which has developed partly in response to what many see as limitations in the UNGP. This section explains that the UNGP have offered little in terms of effective incorporation and implementation of their standards, and that significant issues remain unaddressed (or under-addressed).

2.1. GETTING TO THE UNGP

The impact corporations have on human rights has been debated at the UN since the 1960s.[18] The UN Human Rights Council's 2011 universal endorsement of the UN Guiding Principles seemed to suggest the international community had finally coalesced around an answer: states have an obligation to regulate corporate impacts on their own territory; businesses have a responsibility to respect human rights in their operations; and both are expected to ensure adequate remedies and reparations to victims.[19] Initially, states and businesses agreed with the model, while some civil society organisations and academics expressed doubts about the long-term viability of the proposal.[20] John Ruggie, the UN Special Representative of the Secretary-General on the issue of human rights and transnational corporations and other business enterprises, drafted what many scholars considered to be a minimalist approach.[21] Ruggie retreated from an earlier proposition at the UN that businesses have direct international

17 Taylor Swift, et al., 'I Wish You Would', on Taylor Swift, *1989* (2014).
18 See Buhmann, above n 7, 30.
19 UNGP, 2011.
20 See, e.g., generally S Deva, 'Treating Human Rights Lightly: A Critique of the Consensus Rhetoric and the Language Employed by the Guiding Principles', in: Deva, Bilchitz, above n 7, 78; C López, 'The "Ruggie Process": From Legal Obligations to Corporate Social Responsibility?', in: Deva, Bilchitz, above n 7, 58.
21 See Deva, above n 20, 80.

obligations to respect, protect and fulfil human rights.[22] The proposition was rejected by the Commission on Human Rights (the predecessor to the Human Rights Council),[23] but some criticised Ruggie for following the Commission's lead rather than sticking to the higher standard.[24] Additionally, he eschewed some of the more difficult questions in human rights law, such as whether and to what extent there was an extraterritorial obligation on corporate home states to regulate their nationals' actions abroad.[25] Finally, the Guiding Principles, as a non-binding 'soft law' instrument, lacked any enforcement mechanism or accountability for either states or corporations, suggesting limited practical impact for victims.[26]

Some of the concerns have been borne out as states have done little to further the regulation of corporations for the purpose of human rights. States' national action plans (NAPs) – when they are developed – are supposed to outline concrete steps the state recognises it must take to further compliance with its obligations towards regulation and providing remedies.[27] At the time of editing, there are 12 NAPs in effect following late 2016 releases by Colombia, Switzerland, the United States (US), and Germany's baseline study.[28] With the exception of the US and Colombia, all existing NAPS come from European states,[29] and the NAPs collectively have offered limited reflection on the need for reform.[30] The treatment of remedies in NAPs gives a clear indication of their limitations. In one of the first two NAPs, the UK government would only 'commit[] to keeping the UK provision of remedies under review, but [did] not propose any change

22 See 'Draft Norms on the Responsibilities of Transnational Corporations and Other Business Enterprises with Regard to Human Rights', UN Doc. E/CN.4/Sub.2/2003/12 (2003).

23 UN Doc. E/CN.4/2004/116.

24 See, e.g., D Bilchitz, 'A Chasm between "Is" and "Ought"? A Critique of the Normative Foundations of the SRSG's Framework and the Guiding Principles', in: Deva, Bilchitz, above n 7, 107, 115–18.

25 D Augenstein, D Kinley, 'When Human Rights "Responsibilities" become "Duties": the Extra-territorial Obligations of States that Bind Corporations', in: Deva, Bilchitz, above n 7, 274.

26 See, J Letnar Černič, 'An Elephant in a Room of Porcelain: Establishing Corporate Responsibility for Human Rights', in: J Letnar Černič, TL Van Ho (eds), *Human Rights and Business* (Wolf, 2015), 131 at 155.

27 See, generally D de Felice, A Graf, 'The Potential of National Action Plans to Implement Human Rights Norms: An Early Assessment with Respect to the UN Guiding Principles on Business and Human Rights' (2015) 7 *Journal of Human Rights Practice* 40.

28 Updated lists of the NAPs can be seen at Office of the High Commissioner for Human Rights, 'State National Action Plans', <http://www.ohchr.org/EN/Issues/Business/Pages/NationalActionPlans.aspx> (accessed January 2017); Business & Human Rights Resource Centre, 'National Action Plans', <https://business-humanrights.org/en/un-guiding-principles/implementation-tools-examples/implementation-by-governments/by-type-of-initiative/national-action-plans> (accessed January 2017).

29 Ibid.

30 See de Felice, Graf, above n 27, 58–59.

to existing judicial remedy options'.[31] In the Dutch NAP 'the actions planned' to address the ineffectiveness of the current remedial system 'are minimal', even though there was a detailed analysis of the topic.[32] Newer NAPs do not fare much better. Because they have not yet been published in English and were released after this volume was accepted for publication, I was unable to review the Colombian and German NAPs. Of the other existing NAPs, only those of Lithuania,[33] Switzerland[34] and Italy[35] discuss directly or indirectly the barriers they place to effective remedies. Instead, states often explain how their remedial processes work, but do not reflect seriously on existing structural barriers. The US NAP notes that states are 'responsible' for providing mechanisms for an effective remedy – which under IHRL is an obligation[36] – but rather than focusing on barriers to remedies within the US, the NAP quickly pivots to recognise that 'not all countries have such mechanisms in place'.[37] It commits to using and protecting its own non-judicial remedial processes and to 'seek to strengthen judicial systems in other countries through its foreign assistance programs'.[38] Denmark,[39] Sweden,[40] Finland,[41] and Norway[42] similarly fail to

---

31 Ibid, 60.

32 Ibid, 60.

33 See 'Lithuania's Action Plan on the Implementation of the United Nations Guiding Principles on Business and Human Rights' (2015), 8–11, <http://www.ohchr.org/Documents/Issues/Business/NationalPlans/Lithuania_NationalPlanBHR.pdf> (accessed January 2017).

34 'Rapport sur la stratégie de la Suisse visant à mettre en œuvre les Principes directeurs des Nations Unies relatifs aux enterprises et aux droits de l'homme' (2016), 38–43 (available in French only) <https://www.newsd.admin.ch/newsd/message/attachments/46602.pdf> (accessed January 2017).

35 'Italian National Action Plan on Business and Human Rights, 2016–2021', 26–27, <http://www.cidu.esteri.it/NR/rdonlyres/82FBBD9B-EBA5-4056-A45C-281F0D2C9398/49117/NAPBHRENGFINALEDEC152017.pdf> (accessed January 2017).

36 See, e.g., D Shelton, *Remedies in International Human Rights Law*, 3rd edn (Oxford University Press, 2015), 13.

37 See 'Responsible Business Conduct: First National Action Plan for the United States of America' (16 December 2016), 23, <https://www.state.gov/documents/organization/265918.pdf> (accessed January 2017).

38 Ibid.

39 See 'Danish National Action Plan – Implementation of the UN Guiding Principles on Business and Human Rights' (March 2014), 20–21, <http://www.ohchr.org/Documents/Issues/Business/NationalPlans/Denmark_NationalPlanBHR.pdf> ('Danish NAP') (accessed January 2017).

40 Government Offices of Sweden, 'Action Plan for Business and Human Rights' (2015), 15, <http://www.government.se/4a84f5/contentassets/822dc47952124734b60daf1865e39343/action-plan-for-business-and-human-rights.pdf> (accessed January 2017).

41 Finnish Ministry of Employment and the Economy, 'National Action Plan for the Implementation of the UN Guiding Principles on Business and Human Rights' (2014), 30, <http://tem.fi/documents/1410877/3084000/National%20action%20plan%20for%20the%20implementation%20of%20the%20UN%20guiding%20pronciples%20on%20business%20and%20human%20rights/1bc35feb-d35a-438f-af56-aec16adfcbae> (accessed January 2017).

42 Norwegian Ministry of Foreign Affairs, 'Business and Human Rights: National Action Plan for the Implementation of the UN Guiding Principles', <https://www.regjeringen.no/globalassets/departementene/ud/vedlegg/mr/business_hr_b.pdf>, 40.

identify any internal steps necessary to improve access to judicial remedies. This sits in contradiction to the findings of, at least, the Human Rights Committee, which has identified limitations to effective remedies in each of these states, ranging in severity from limited legal aid making access to effective remedies financially inaccessible, to limited knowledge of human rights by lawyers and the judiciary, to broad grants of immunity that impact the ability to seek civil redress even against private actors, and discrimination that can impact equal access in areas of the judiciary.[43] Increased protection cannot begin if states do not adequately account for any limitations, including difficulty accessing legal counsel or difficulty in obtaining relevant evidence, including information about a corporation's structure.[44]

Businesses have not done much better than the states. While corporate entities have started to use a 'human rights reporting framework', developed and promoted by the organisation Shift, corporate reports still offer little clarity on businesses' actual human rights impacts and the effectiveness of their remedial processes. For example, manufacturing giant Unilever's 2015 human rights report focused on work the company did to ensure women in Indian had jobs with adequate health, safety and wages.[45] The company admitted that '[i]n India, we found incidents of poor health and safety practices and a lack of proper process of wage payment at a salt pan'.[46] It failed, however, to discuss a lawsuit it was still fighting, brought by Indian workers who claimed the company's failure to provide them with adequate protective gear led to mercury poisoning.[47] The company settled that case several months later.[48]

The response to the Guiding Principles by both states and corporations could have remained unchanged but for claims by corporations using international investment arbitration to challenge actions Ecuador and South Africa took in furtherance of human rights.[49] Provisions in South Africa's post-apartheid Black Economic Empowerment Act were challenged by European investors who

---

43 See Concluding Observations: Norway, UN Doc. CCPR/C/NOR/CO/6 (18.11.2011), paras 5–6; Concluding Observations: Finland, UN Doc. CCPR/C/FIN/CO/6 (21.08.2013), para 5; Concluding Observations: United States of America, UN Doc. CCPR/C/USA/CO/4 (22.04.2014), paras 12, 20; Concluding Observations: Sweden, UN Doc. CPR/C/SWE/CO/7 (30.03.2016), at paras 5, 12, 14.

44 See Section 2, below.

45 Unilever, 'Enhancing Livelihoods, Advancing Human Rights: Human Rights Report 2015', 30, <https://www.unilever.com/Images/slp-unilever-human-rights-report-2015_tcm244-437226_1_en.pdf> (accessed January 2017).

46 Ibid, 23, 30.

47 See 'Unilever settles dispute over mercury poisoning in India', *The Guardian* (09.03.2016), available at <http://www.theguardian.com/environment/2016/mar/09/unilever-settles-dispute-over-mercury-poisoning-in-india> (accessed March 2016).

48 Ibid.

49 D Bilchitz, 'The Necessity for a Business and Human Rights Treaty' (2016) 1 *Business and Human Rights Journal* 203, 204.

alleged that the provisions constituted an expropriation of their mining rights.[50] Ecuador is still fighting a complex investment arbitration claim arising from a court order made against oil company Chevron for environmental damage in the Amazon.[51] The two states' woes led to a change in the discourse over the Guiding Principles. Now, the interest of several members of the Global South was in ensuring a hard-law approach to regulating transnational corporations to protect human rights in weaker states. Bolivia, Cuba and Venezuela joined South Africa and Ecuador in proposing the treaty, finding that the Guiding Principles were simply not enough.[52]

The treaty is an effort to close governance gaps and ensure businesses are regulated and victims have access to effective remedies, even in states with weak governance or limited power. Some appear to believe giving businesses direct obligations is a means of securing these two goals. That assumption should be questioned. The next subsection considers how international law provides remedies to IHRL victims and the likelihood of this changing with a treaty focused on business impacts on human rights. This discussion informs the question of whether direct obligations are necessary.

2.2. THE LIKELIHOOD OF IMPROVED REMEDIAL PROCESSES

IHRL has limited enforcement generally. At the UN level, decisions of treaty bodies, even through individual complaints, are non-binding.[53] In the regional human rights systems, compliance with what are supposed to be binding court judgments is limited, even in the oft-touted European system.[54] The weakness in human rights protection stems from the refusal of states to accept effective oversight of human rights by treaty bodies and regional courts. While some might hope for a binding, enforceable and strong judicial mechanism aimed at securing victims' rights against corporations, nothing to date suggests this

50 *Piero Foresti, et al. v. South Africa*, ICSID Case No. ARB(AF)/07/01, Award (2010).

51 See, e.g., *Republic of Ecuador v. Chevon, et al.*, Case No. C/09/477457 / HA ZA 14-1291 (Judgment, 20.01.2016), available at <http://www.italaw.com/sites/default/files/case-documents/italaw7104.pdf> (accessed June 2017).

52 See 'Elaboration of an International Legally Binding Instrument on Transnational Corporations and Other Business Enterprises to Human Rights', UN Doc. A/HRC/26.L/22/Rev.1 (25.06.2014).

53 M Nowak, 'The Need for a World Court of Human Rights' (2007) 7 *Human Rights Law Review* 251, 252. For more problems on the current system, see D Cassell, A Ramasastry, 'White Paper: Options for a Treaty on Business and Human Rights' (2016) *Notre Dame Journal of International & Comparative Law*, Article 4, 30–31, <http://scholarship.law.nd.edu/cgi/viewcontent.cgi?article=1044&context=ndjicl> (accessed January 2016).

54 Shelton, above n 36, 384–85, 387–88; D Hawkins, W Jacoby, 'Partial Compliance: A Comparison of the European and Inter-American Courts of Human Rights' (2010–11) 6 *Journal of International Law and International Relations* 35, 43–44.

is likely to happen. Expanding the remedial system is not the natural result of attaching direct international obligations. Stronger mechanisms have been discussed before the IGWG, but there appears to be greater support for replicating the existing UN treaty bodies.[55]

There are additional reasons to doubt stronger mechanisms would ever be adopted, even with a shift to direct obligations on business. States tend to be particularly protective of their own ability to control economic activity both within, and directly affecting, their territory.[56] Katz Cogan has suggested that 'courts are accorded independence on the condition that there are sufficient effective controls in place'.[57] A strong international human rights tribunal would necessarily limit the controls states can exercise over the tribunal's work and its impact. 'States generally lack the ability to correct interpretive errors made by' international tribunals and 'are unable to direct judges to decide cases in certain ways or otherwise control the substance of judicial decisions'.[58] States therefore seem hesitant about creating, much less subjecting themselves to, any robust IHRL mechanisms. This general scepticism seems likely to increase when the state's economy is subject to review. Scott explains that 'the dominant view [is] that economic policy belongs in some more intrinsic way to the very idea of sovereignty' rather than other areas of IHRL, such as torture.[59] Since decisions relating to the business and human rights treaty are likely to have economic impacts and affect relationships between business and states, it seems highly unlikely that the new business and human rights treaty would provide a stronger mechanism for oversight than that which is currently employed under existing IHRL treaties.

While states may be hesitant to cede control to a robust treaty mechanism, they may be more willing to expand their own jurisdiction so as to ensure authority over their corporate actors when they operate abroad.[60] Before considering how this can be done, it is necessary to consider whether there is a significant benefit to having direct international obligations without a stronger international mechanism. The call for direct obligations without

---

55 See IGWG, Draft Report, 11, 13, 19, 30; but see also ibid, 29.

56 C Scott, 'Translating Torture into Transnational Tort: Conceptual Divides in the Debate on Corporate Accountability for Human Rights Harms', in: C Scott (ed), *Torture as Tort: Comparative Perspectives on the Development of Transnational Human Rights Litigation* (Hart Publishing, 2001) 45, at 53; see also SL Seck, 'Home State Responsibility and Local Communities: The Case of Global Mining' (2008) 11 *Yale Human Rights and Development Journal* 177, 193.

57 JK Cogan, 'Competition and Control in International Adjudication' (2008) 48 *Virginia Journal of International Law* 411, 415.

58 Ibid, 415.

59 Scott, above n 56, 53.

60 Seck argues that the economic factors are still significant in cases where concurrent jurisdiction already exists. Seck, above n 56, 193.

a clear, international means of effectively enforcing those obligations seems justified only when placed in the context of the debate over the US's Alien Tort Statute (ATS), a law that allowed foreigners to institute civil suits for violations of customary international law.[61] Only a few of the cases against corporations have been truly successful, yet the ATS was routinely used for business and human rights claims until a 2013 Supreme Court decision limited the statute's usefulness for overseas victims.[62] Before the Supreme Court's decision, the US Court of Appeals for the Second Circuit concluded that corporations were not subject to suit under the ATS because they did not have direct obligations under IHRL and therefore could not violate customary IHRL.[63] On appeal to the US Supreme Court, defendant Royal Dutch Petroleum (the oil company commonly known as Shell) used this reasoning and pointed to the UNGP to support the position that corporate defendants owed no obligations under IHRL, which applied only to states and in certain circumstances natural persons.[64] Ruggie was shocked at the use of his findings[65] (although more jaded members of the business and human rights community were not). The Supreme Court did not address this argument – constraining jurisdiction under the statute narrowly to cases that 'touch and concern' the US and dismissing the case against Shell for not meeting this standard – but the Second Circuit's reasoning meant the lack of direct international obligations posed a serious threat to one of the few tools being actively used to ensure business and human rights victims had access to remedies.

Transnational litigation has evolved, however, and more cases are being filed against transnational corporations in European home states.[66] ATS claims

61 28 U.S.C. §1350; see also TL Van Ho, 'Transnational Civil and Criminal Litigation', in S Michalowski (ed), *Corporate Accountability in the Context of Transitional Justice* (Routledge, 2013) 52.

62 See, e.g., Letnar Černič, above n 26, 141.

63 *Kiobel v. Royal Dutch Petroleum*, 621 F.3d 111 (2nd Circuit Court of Appeals, 2010). For the background to this argument, see JG Ku, 'The Curious Case of Corporate Liability under the Alien Tort Statute: A Flawed System of Judicial Lawmaking' (2011) 51 *Virginia Journal of International Law* 352.

64 See JG Ruggie, 'Kiobel and Corporate Social Responsibility', Harvard Kennedy School of Government (04.09.2012), <http://business-humanrights.org/sites/default/files/media/documents/ruggie-kiobel-and-corp-social-resonsibility-sep-2012.pdf> (accessed January 2016).

65 See ibid.

66 See, e.g., *Vereniging Milieudefensie, et al., v. Royal Dutch Shell, Plc*, Case No. 330891 / HA ZA 09-579, Judgment in Motion Contesting Jurisdiction of 30 December 2009 (Court of The Hague); European Center for Constitutional and Human Rights, 'Case Report: Pakistan – Cheap Clothes, Perilous Conditions', available at <https://www.ecchr.eu/en/our_work/business-and-human-rights/working-conditions-in-south-asia.html> (accessed January 2017); Sherpa, 'French Company Lafarge Sued for Financing ISIS and Complicity in War Crimes and Crimes Against Humanity' (15.11.2016), <https://www.asso-sherpa.org/french-company-lafarge-sued-for-financing-isis-and-complicity-in-war-crimes-and-

against businesses also continue in the US in jurisdictions other than the Second Circuit.[67] Expanding obligations to new actors makes sense only if it is likely to increase the protection or enforcement of human rights. Without a robust international mechanism, and with some advance in domestic enforcements, the need to prove direct obligations is not as necessary as it once seemed. Asserting direct obligations for the purpose of securing a particular form of remedy in one state, rather than focusing on the obligation of all states to ensure adequate and effective remedies, will not secure the significant or long-term changes necessary for victims. Efforts at expanding domestic enforcement of IHRL may be a more viable, long-term approach.

As explained above, a treaty seems necessary to secure effective enforcement of existing IHRL standards against businesses. Constructing a 'creative' treaty that expands the responsible parties may, however, be unnecessary. The next section considers the current approach to horizontal human rights impacts, suggesting this approach provides a strong foundation for the new treaty. It then explains how the doctrine of separate corporate personalities undermines the strength of the state-centric approach and represents a significant barrier to victims' attempts to secure remedies against corporate actors.

3. HORIZONTAL HUMAN RIGHTS IN A STATE-CENTRIC APPROACH: 'CAUSE WE NEVER GO OUT OF STYLE'[68]

While the UNGP explain the relationship between state duties and business responsibilities in the area of business and human rights, the state's obligations stem not from the Guiding Principles but from existing treaty obligations.[69] The familiar typology that recognises that each human right requires three connected state obligations – respect, protect and fulfil[70] – sets the framework for addressing horizontal human rights impacts. The protect obligation requires states to adopt regulations aimed at likely or known impacts by third-party, non-state actors, and to ensure horizontal impacts are remedied.[71] Notably, the

crimes-against-humanity-in-syria> (accessed January 2017); see also, N Jägers, KD Jesse, JM Verschuuren, 'The Future of Corporate Liability for Extraterritorial Human Rights Abuses: The Dutch Case Against Shell' (2014) *AJIL Unbound: Agora: Reflections on Kiobel* 36, 37.

67 See, e.g., *Al-Zuba'e v. CACI Premier Technology, Inc.*, No. 15-1831 (4th Cir. Ct. of Appeals); *Penaloza v. Drummond Co., Inc.*, No. 16-10921 (11th Cir. Ct. of Appeals).

68 Lyrics from 'Style' by Taylor Swift, on Taylor Swift, *1989* (2014).

69 See Buhmann, above n 7, 52.

70 See F Mégret, 'Nature of Obligations', in: D Moeckli, S Shah, S Sivakumaran (eds), *International Human Rights Law*, 2nd edn (Oxford University Press, 2010), 96 at 101–02.

71 Ibid.

Human Rights Committee, the Committee on Economic, Social and Cultural Rights (CESCR), and every regional system have addressed the state's duty to regulate and to provide adequate remedies in regard to business and human rights claims.[72] An exhaustive discussion of the jurisprudence is unnecessary, but the next subsection outlines how these claims are treated and the question as to whether these obligations exist extraterritorially. It suggests that the foundation of horizontal applications is a significant one that is adaptable to a variety of actors (and in this way need not go out of style).This section then turns to considering how the doctrine of separate corporate personalities creates an impediment to the effective operation of this system.

3.1. ADDRESSING HORIZONTAL IMPACTS

Under this traditional approach, IHRL obligations attach only directly to the state but are passed down to the business through domestic laws and regulations.[73] By viewing horizontal IHRL impacts through the lens of state conduct, there is a centrality of responsibility: the state is accountable for its actions or failure to act, either in advance or after the violation occurs and regardless of how many other actors are involved, their nationality, and their economic or political power. Human rights impacts by non-state actors are not immediately internationally wrongful acts but can be imputed to the state and 'can lead to international responsibility of the State, not because of the act itself, but because of the lack of due diligence to prevent the violation or to respond to it'.[74] Consequently, a traditional approach evaluates business impacts on human rights by asking two distinct questions: first, did the company negatively impact human rights; second, did the state act with due diligence in advance to regulate the corporation's impacts and/or did it respond with due diligence to complaints once they arose? If the state failed to exercise due diligence in

---

72 See, e.g., *Yanomami Community v. Brazil*, Inter-American Commission on Human Rights, Case No. 7615, Resolution No. 12/85; *Case of the Saramaka People v. Suriname*, Inter-American Court of Human Rights, Preliminary Objections, Merits, Reparations, and Costs (28.11.2007); *Lopez Ostra v. Spain*, European Court of Human Rights, Application no. 16798/90 (1994); *Social and Economic Rights Action Center v. Nigeria*, African Commission on Human and Peoples Rights, Communication 155/96, 15th ACHPR AAR Annex V (2000–01); Human Rights Committee, 'General Comment 27', UN Doc. CCPR/C/21/Rev.1/Add.9 (1999), para 7; Committee on Economic, Social, and Cultural Rights, 'General Comment No. 14', UN Doc. E/C.12/2000/4 (2000), para 51.

73 See Rodley, above n 3, 526.

74 *Velasquez Rodrguez v. Honduras (Judgment)*, IACthR Series C No 4 (29.07.1988), at para 172. See also *Lopez Ostra v. Spain*, paras 56–58; *Social and Economic Rights Actions Center v. Nigeria*, Communication, para 8; CESCR, General Comment No. 14, para 51; Human Rights Committee, General Comment 27, para 7.

regulating to prevent a violation, it can incur responsibility. If the state regulates adequately but the company still violates the law, the state incurs international responsibility only if victims are unable to access adequate and effective remedies. This approach currently allows IHRL to address the impact of a variety of 'new' actors by retaining a focus on the state's centrality and responsibility. While the current discussion is on businesses, the broader discussion of power dynamics within the international order has raised questions about the responsibility of other actors.[75] Maintaining a legal order that is sufficiently flexible to address new challenges without requiring the proliferation of new law is an advantage, and one that should be altered with caution.

This is not to suggest the current system is perfect in addressing horizontal impacts. The current approach has benefits and detriments for victims. On the benefit side, victims can easily identify the internationally responsible party (the state); on the detrimental side, the internationally wrongful act is evaluated not in terms of the impact on victims, but in terms of the state's response to that harm. Some might fear that this approach would leave victims vulnerable but the duality of the state's obligations to regulate and remedy make it difficult to imagine a factual scenario in which the state would not be internationally responsible if a business negatively impacted human rights but was able to escape responsibility. Consequently, it is not the construct of the law but the lack of effective and binding international remedies that undermines victims' rights.

Once thought to be only the responsibility of the host state, recent decisions suggest that the obligation to protect is also, concurrently, the responsibility of a corporation's home state. Both the Human Rights Committee's and CESCR's most recent Concluding Observations on Canada expressed concern about the impact of Canadian corporations on human rights abroad.[76] Both Committees recommended the state provide greater oversight of its corporate nationals' human rights impacts abroad, including through the state's remedial systems.[77] CESCR recommended, inter alia, that the state (1) 'strengthen its legislation governing the conduct of' its corporate citizens, 'including by requiring those corporations to conduct human rights impact assessments prior to making investment decisions',[78] and (2) adopt 'effective mechanisms to investigate complaints filed against' its corporate nationals, and 'facilitate access to justice before domestic courts'.[79] CESCR has made similar recommendations in its

---

[75] See, e.g., generally Clapham, above n 3; Willem van Genugten, *The World Bank Group, the IMF, and Human Rights* (Intersentia, 2015).

[76] See Human Rights Committee, Concluding Observations: Canada, UN Doc. CCPR/C/CAN/CO/6 (2015), para 6; CESCR, Concluding Observations: Canada, UN Doc. E/C.12/CAN/CO/6 (23.03.2016), para 16.

[77] See ibid.

[78] CESCR, Concluding Observations: Canada, para 16.

[79] Ibid.

conclusions on China[80] and the UK,[81] and called on France to 'expedite the adoption of a law which would impose a binding obligation on' its corporate nationals 'to fulfill their duty of care' to conduct due diligence throughout their operations.[82] The Human Rights Committee recently praised Germany for undertaking 'to provide remedies against German companies acting abroad allegedly in contravention of relevant human rights standards'.[83] Since 'such remedies may not be sufficient in all cases', the Committee recommended that the state 'set out clearly the expectation that all business enterprises domiciled in its territory and/or its jurisdiction respect human rights standards' and 'take appropriate measures to strengthen the remedies provided' for victims of German entities operating abroad.[84]

While the Committees found the duty to protect has some extraterritorial application, home states themselves have been less accepting of this proposition. In response to the List of Issues by the Human Rights Committee, Canada wrote that it:

> wish[ed] to emphasize the clear territorial and jurisdictional limits to its obligations under the Covenant. As per Article 2(1), Canada's obligations are to ensure the Covenant rights with respect to individuals who are within Canada's territory and subject to its jurisdiction. It must be noted that the individuals who can be affected by the activities of Canadian companies operating abroad are not, generally speaking, within Canada's territory and subject to its jurisdiction.[85]

A dispute therefore exists as to which states owe victims the obligations to protect and to remedy in the context of business and human rights. The treaty provides an opportunity to clarify this relationship, and in doing so to potentially close gaps that allow businesses to escape responsibility.

While states may be hesitant to find an existing obligation to exercise extraterritorial jurisdiction, they may be willing to adopt, through a treaty, expanded jurisdictional obligations. It appears that at least some home states hope the treaty will clarify their obligations. While the Danish NAP failed to discuss domestic limitations to accessible remedies, the NAP did suggest that the issue of access to judicial remedies 'is an extremely difficult issue that is best

---

80 CESCR, Concluding Observations: China, UN Doc. E/C.12/CHN/CO/2 (13.06.2014), para 13.

81 CESCR, Concluding Observations: United Kingdom of Great Britain and Northern Ireland, UN Doc. E/C.12/GBR/CO/6 (24.06.2016), para 11.

82 CESCR, Concluding Observations: France, UN Doc. E/C.12/FRA/CO/4 (13.07.2006), para 13.

83 Human Rights Committee, Concluding Observations: Germany, UN Doc. CCPR/C/DEU/CO6 (2012), para 16.

84 Ibid.

85 Human Rights Committee, 'List of Issues in Relation to the Sixth Periodic Report of Canada', UN Doc. CCPR/C/CAN/Q/6/Add.1, para 14.

handled at an international level'.[86] As Denmark can easily address any domestic failings it has, this position makes sense only if Denmark recognises that there needs to be international clarity and agreement on home state responsibility. As will be discussed in Section 3, below, there is also relevant precedence for expanding a state's jurisdiction through an IHRL treaty. Before turning to that precedence, however, it is important to understand that the need for expanded jurisdiction is, at least in part, the result of complex corporate structures and the doctrine of separate corporate personalities, which collectively can create an effective barrier for victims. The next subsection explains the barriers created, which illustrates the need for clarifying the home state's responsibility to protect.

3.2. THE IMPACT OF SEPARATE CORPORATE PERSONALITIES

Multinational corporations often escape liability precisely because they are powerful enough to ignore the judgments of developing state courts and their corporate structures allow them to evade effective oversight by their home states.[87] The doctrine of separate corporate legal personalities, sometimes called the corporate veil, was designed to encourage economic investment by limiting the liability of owners.[88] Shareholders – including parent corporations – are excused from liability for the actions taken by the corporation or on the corporation's behalf.[89] Multinational corporations routinely incorporate each new venture as a distinct corporation, meaning that each company in the group is generally responsible only for its own actions and conduct and the parent companies do not incur responsibility for the actions or liabilities of the subsidiaries.[90] The doctrine also generally means that victims can only sue each member of the corporate group in those states that have jurisdiction over the company.[91] If a parent and subsidiary are incorporated and operate exclusively in separate jurisdictions, it is likely that neither the home nor

86 Danish NAP, 20.

87 See, e.g., G Skinner, 'Rethinking Limited Liability of Parent Corporations for Foreign Subsidiaries Violations of International Human Rights Law' (2015) 72 *Washington and Lee Law Review* 1769, 1802–05; see also D Cambou, 'The Dutch Shell Case: Foreign Direct Liability Claims as an Avenue for Holding Multinational Corporations Accountable for Human Rights Violations', in: Letnar Černič, Van Ho, above n 26, 347; G Skinner, R McCorquodale, O De Schutter, *The Third Pillar: Access to Judicial Remedies for Human Rights Violations by Transnational Business*, The International Corporate Accountability Roundtable (2013), 21 *et seq.*, available at <http://corporate-responsibility.org/wp-content/uploads/2014/02/The-Third-Pillar-FINAL.pdf> (accessed January 2016).

88 Skinner, McCorquodale, De Schutter, above n 87, 1796.

89 Ibid, 1773.

90 Ibid, 1772.

91 See, e.g., ibid, 1802–05.

host state has jurisdiction that covers both parts of the corporate group.[92] Corporations have often avoided liability for human rights impacts by their overseas subsidiaries by relying on the separate corporate personality to dismiss claims in a parent company's home state for lack of personal jurisdiction over the subsidiary.[93] While there are exceptions to doctrine of separate personalities and means of 'piercing the corporate veil', doing so has proven difficult because of 'vague and oftentimes inconsistent application' of tests states have developed to shield parent corporations from liability.[94]

The Guiding Principles call on corporations to work to 'prevent or mitigate adverse human rights impacts that are directly linked to their operations, products or services by their business relationships, even if they have not contributed to those impacts'.[95] This implies that parent corporations are expected to undertake due diligence and work to mitigate the impact of their subsidiaries such as Shell Petroleum Development Company of Nigeria (SPDC).[96] Yet, the doctrine on separate personalities has been used by multinational corporations to effectively avoid judicial oversight for impacts on victims in developing states.[97] Litigation in the Netherlands against oil giant Royal Dutch Petroleum ('Shell') and its Nigerian subsidiary, SPDC, for environmental and property damage caused by leaking oil pipelines provides a good example of how separate corporate personalities can be used as a barrier to effective remedies for victims.[98] The case was brought by Nigerian claimants and followed a pattern in Nigeria in which SPDC would often spend years vehemently defending claims related to oil spills.[99] Because Shell did not operate on the territory of Nigeria, claimants would have had difficulty establishing jurisdiction over the parent. When SPDC was ordered to pay damages or to undertake clean-up and restoration efforts, the Nigerian government did not take direct action to ensure compliance[100] and SPDC allegedly failed to follow the orders itself or did so in an incomplete

---

92 See *Daimler AG v. Bauman*, 134 S.Ct. 746, 749 (2014) (US Supreme Court).

93 See generally Van Ho, above n 61; see also *Bigio v. Coca-Cola*, 675 F.3d 163, 170–71 (2nd Cir. Ct. of Appeals) (2012); *William v. AES Corp*, 28 F.3d 553, 51–563 (Eastern District of Virginia) (2014).

94 Skinner, McCorquodale, De Schutter, above n 87, 1796.

95 UNGP, Principle 13.

96 N Jägers, 'UN Guiding Principles on Business and Human Rights: Making Headway towards Real Corporate Accountability?' (2011) 29 *Netherlands Quarterly of Human Rights* 159, 162.

97 Skinner, McCorquodale, De Schutter, above n 87, 1777.

98 See *Vereniging Milieudefensie* above n 66, para 2.2.

99 See S Leader, D Ong, T Van Ho, A Yilmaz, S Michalowski, U Neto, R Danesi, B Wlodarczak, 'Corporate Liability in a New Setting: Shell and the Changing Legal Landscape for the Multinational Oil Industry in the Niger Delta', Essex Business and Human Rights Project, 68–70, <http://www.essex.ac.uk/ebhr/documents/niger-delta-report.pdf> (accessed January 2016) ('EBHR').

100 Ibid.

manner.[101] In light of the difficulties with getting SPDC to comply with judgments or to respond quickly to allegations, claimants felt it was necessary to seek judicial protection overseas, notably in dual cases filed in both the UK[102] and the Netherlands.[103]

In the Dutch litigation, SPDC argued that the Court did not have jurisdiction over the claims against it because it was a Nigerian company with operations only in Nigeria.[104] It claimed that the plaintiffs were 'abusing procedural law by initiating claims against RDS on a patently inadequate basis for the sole purpose of creating jurisdiction with regard to SPDC'.[105] The Dutch Civil Code would allow for jurisdiction if the claims against the two corporations were connected.[106] To establish jurisdiction over SPDC, the victims needed to demonstrate that the claims against Shell and SPDC were substantively 'connected to such an extent that reasons of efficiency justify a joint hearing'.[107] This would not 'pierce the veil' – claimants had to attempt to separately prove their claims against both SPDC and Shell – but it would allow the Dutch courts to exceptionally exercise jurisdiction against the Nigerian company despite the fact that it did not operate on the territory of the Netherlands.[108] To do this, the plaintiffs argued that while SPDC was directly responsible for the oil spill, Shell was responsible for failing to take steps necessary to prevent the spill and to ensure its proper clean-up.[109] Shell's 2011 Sustainability Report claimed that

> [i]n the event that a spill occurs, we have in place a number of recovery measures to minimise the impact. Our major installations have plans to respond to a spill. We are able to call upon significant resources such as containment booms, collection vessels and aircraft. We conduct regular response exercises to ensure these plans remain effective.[110]

---

101 See ibid; HO Yusuf, K Omoteso, 'Combating Environmental Irresponsibility of Transnational Corporations in Africa: An Empirical Analysis' (2015) 21 *Local Environment: The International Journal of Justice and Sustainability*, 1372, 1380–82; J Kaufman, 'Stop Oil Companies from Denying, Delaying, and Derailing Local Justice', EarthRights International (13.07.2010), <https://www.earthrights.org/blog/stop-oil-companies-denying-delaying-and-derailing-local-justice> (accessed January 2016).

102 *Bodo Community, et al. v. Shell Petroleum Development Company of Nigeria, Ltd.* [2014] EWHC 1973.

103 *Fidelis Ayoro Oguru*, Subpoena.

104 *Vereniging Milieudefensie*, above n 66, para 2.4.

105 Ibid.

106 Ibid, para 3.4.

107 Ibid.

108 See Jägers, et al., above n 66, 39–40.

109 *Fidelis Ayoro Oguru and Alai Efanga and Royal Dutch Shell plc and Shell Petroleum Development Company of Nigeria, Ltd.*, Subpoena (2009), para 130, <https://milieudefensie.nl/publicaties/bezwaren-uitspraken/subpoena-oruma/> (accessed January 2016).

110 Royal Dutch Shell Plc, 'Annual Report and Form 20-F for the Year Ended December 31 2010', (2011), 51.

The report further claimed that the corporate 'Group strategy is aligned with the interest of the Parent Companies', and that the group 'define[s] who is responsible for applying' environmental and social standards while 'we monitor performance'.[111] Yet, before the Court, the parent company argued that it could not be liable for what occurred in Nigeria or by its Nigerian subsidiary.[112] Shell submitted that it was 'not directly involved in operations of its operating companies' and that it 'could not be expected to interfere in the clean-up and remedial work of the oil spill in dispute' without violating the corporate veil.[113]

Shell also argued that the parent company named in the suit, Royal Dutch Shell, did not exist at the time of the actions.[114] This defence also relates to the doctrine of separate corporate personalities and demonstrates the difficulty victims face in pursuing claims against corporate groups. Shell indicated a corporate restructuring led to the creation of Royal Dutch Shell after the spill occurred replacing as the 'parent' two other, still-existing companies.[115] Neither of the original parent companies was dissolved; they simply fell down the corporate chain.[116] According to Shell, this meant that any responsibility for the original parent companies' actions or inaction during the spill remained with the other corporations, although it did not identify which company would have been the responsible party.[117] As others have pointed out, victims often identify a corporation based on its logo and the common understanding of its identity.[118] In the Netherlands case, Shell used this confusion and uncertainty as the basis of its defence: if the claimants could not identify the 'right' corporate entity, then the claim should be dismissed. When the corporate structure can be used specifically to hide the responsible party's identity then the nature of the separate corporate personality becomes an effective barrier to the protection and remediation of human rights.

While these defences were ultimately unsuccessful – the Court allowed the case to proceed before later finding the plaintiffs did not prove Shell was responsible for the damage,[119] – the defences in the case are emblematic of larger issues in business and human rights. Neither the Dutch nor Nigerian courts could easily and clearly have jurisdiction over both the parent and the company. Shell claimants sought access to remedies against the parent company when the host state (the victim's home state) proved either unwilling and/or unable to both regulate and enforce remediation measures. By creating a legal entity within Nigeria that was subject only to Nigeria's local courts, the group was able to effectively ignore court

---

111 See EBHR, 21.
112 Ibid.
113 Ibid.
114 Ibid, 47.
115 Ibid, 47.
116 Ibid, 48.
117 See ibid, 48, 98.
118 See SKINNER, above n 87, 1802.
119 *Fidelis Ayoro Oguru*, 2013.

orders in the host state. This benefit to SPDC was ultimately passed on to Shell, the parent company.[120] Yet, Shell attempted to avoid any responsibility for what the subsidiary did by using the corporate veil and a complex, non-public corporate structure. Shell's response suggests that by limiting liability of parent corporations, the corporate veil encourages parents to disengage from issues of human rights.

The discussion in this chapter might lead one to believe that the problem is not corporate personality but Shell itself.. That assumption would be inaccurate. While Shell has utilised the corporate veil to its advantage, the law itself allows corporate groups to structure themselves in such a way as to avoid effective regulation, oversight and remedies. Corporations can divide their operations in a way that generally precludes any one state from overseeing the string of decisions and operations that lead to a negative human rights impact. For a treaty on business and human rights to be effective, it needs to ensure effective cooperation between states and expand jurisdiction so that individual states may be able to oversee the totality of a group's operations, which in turn should incentivise parent corporations to intervene when their subsidiaries are failing to address serious human rights claims. As will be demonstrated in the next section, a treaty could accomplish this even while using a state-centric approach.

4. ASSESSING AND MODIFYING THE CURRENT TOOLS: 'ARE WE OUT OF THE WOODS YET?'[121]

A traditionalist state-centric approach can provide clarity and certainty while significantly increasing the protection for human rights. The Convention against Torture and the Convention against Corruption each provide relevant paths for the business and human rights treaty to follow. This section first examines how those treaties responded to issues of impunity and the second section considers how some of the provisions in those treaties can be adopted for the proposed business and human rights treaty.

4.1. EXPANDED JURISDICTION AND COOPERATION IN THE CONVENTIONS AGAINST TORTURE AND CORRUPTION

Both the Convention against Torture (UNCAT)[122] and the Convention against Corruption[123] use the traditionalist state-centric approach but each contains

120 On how this works generally, see Skinner, above n 87, 1775, 1807, et seq.

121 Taylor Swift, Jack Antonoff, 'Out of the Woods', on Taylor Swift, *1989* (2014).

122 Convention against Torture and Other Cruel, Inhuman or Degrading Treatment or Punishment, GA res. 39/46, annex, UN Doc. A/39/51, *entered into force* 26.06.1987 ('UNCAT').

123 Convention against Corruption, GA res. 58/4, UN Doc. A/58/422, *entered into force* 14.12.2015.

specific clauses aimed at providing concurrent and overlapping responsibilities as well as effective cooperation between states.[124] UNCAT provides for an expansion of traditional jurisdictional approaches[125] while the Convention against Corruption includes provisions requiring states to assist one another in gaining relevant information for criminal investigations and in developing procedures to allow other states to initiate civil actions.[126] These provisions could be modified to allow for states to exercise an expanded jurisdiction that could be used to address business impacts on human rights. These provisions are briefly explained in turn.

UNCAT requires states to establish as crimes specific acts related to torture and to establish jurisdiction over them.[127] Article 4 requires states to 'ensure that all acts of torture are offences under its criminal law',[128] while Article 5 provides an obligation to establish jurisdiction over offences committed on their territory (including on ships or aircraft registered in the territory) or by their nationals.[129] States parties are encouraged to establish passive personality jurisdiction, meaning jurisdiction over crimes in which their nationals were the victims.[130] Finally, each state party is also to establish universal jurisdiction, 'tak[ing] such measures as may be necessary to establish its jurisdiction over such offences in cases where the alleged offender is present in any territory under its jurisdiction and it does not extradite him' to another state where he can face prosecution.[131] The extradite or prosecute standard is intended to ensure that those who torture cannot enjoy impunity by creating 'a single conventional mechanism aimed at preventing suspects from escaping the consequences of their criminal responsibility, if proven'.[132] The articles provide potentially overlapping jurisdiction so that multiple states may simultaneously have a responsibility to prosecute.[133]

In *Questions Relating to the Obligation to Prosecute or Extradite*, the International Court of Justice (ICJ) determined that the object and purpose of UNCAT is to 'make more effective the struggle against torture',[134] and that the

124 As Doug Cassell and Anita Ramasastry point out, this is not exclusive to the Convention against Torture and the Convention against Corruption. Cassell, Ramasastry, above n 53, 25–30. These Conventions are used in this chapter as illustrative examples.
125 UNCAT, articles 4–5.
126 E.g., Convention against Corruption, articles 26, 46, 51, 53.
127 UNCAT, articles 4–5.
128 Ibid, article 4.
129 Ibid, article 5(1)(a)–(b).
130 Ibid, article 5(1)(c).
131 Ibid, article 5(2).
132 *Questions Relating to the Obligation to Prosecute or Extradite (Belgium v. Senegal)*, Judgment, ICJ Reports 2012, 422, para 91.
133 UNCAT, article 5(2).
134 *Belgium v. Senegal*, above n 132, para 86.

extradite or prosecute standard is a requirement of both means and outcome.[135] According to the Court, Senegal was required to 'exercise its jurisdiction over any act of torture' by undertaking a serious investigation of the facts and pursuing prosecution where appropriate.[136] States can choose between extradition or prosecution, but the ICJ was clear that this 'does not mean that the two alternatives are to be given the same weight. Extradition is an option offered to the State by the Convention, whereas prosecution is an international obligation under the Convention, the violation of which is a wrongful act.'[137] It follows that the state may extradite to another party when necessary, relying on international cooperation to prevent impunity, but that the obligation to prosecute is the primary obligation.

The Convention against Corruption requires states to establish criminal jurisdiction over corruption-related crimes arising from conduct on their territory or by their nationals.[138] States also must adopt criminal, civil and/or administrative standards to facilitate the liability of legal persons.[139] States parties agree to both regulate for the prevention of corruption and 'where appropriate, provide effective, proportionate and dissuasive civil, administrative or criminal penalties for failure to comply with such measures'.[140]

The Convention also requires states to 'afford one another the widest measure of mutual legal assistance'.[141] In criminal matters, states must assist one another in a variety of ways, including by interviewing witnesses, executing searches and seizures, and providing expert evaluations, evidence and relevant financial, corporate or business documents, all for the benefit of another state's investigation and prosecution.[142] While the strongest measures in the Convention relate to criminal enforcement, states parties agree to take necessary measures to allow 'another State Party to initiate civil action in its courts' in order to recover stolen assets and property.[143] It is also recommended that states do assist one another in civil and administrative proceedings '[w]here appropriate and consistent with their domestic legal system'.[144] Through the expanded and clarified jurisdiction and cooperation provisions, the parties aim to attack the financial benefits that would normally accrue from corruption and make it more difficult for individuals and legal entities to escape liability.

135 Ibid, para 84.
136 Ibid, para 85.
137 Ibid, para 95.
138 Convention against Corruption, articles 46, 51.
139 Ibid, article 26.
140 Ibid, article 12(1).
141 Ibid, articles 46, 51.
142 Ibid, article 46.
143 Ibid, article 53(1).
144 Ibid, article 43.

4.2. ADAPTING LANGUAGE FOR THE BUSINESS AND HUMAN RIGHTS TREATY

Given that the Conventions against Torture and Corruption were designed in a manner so as to facilitate state efforts at combating impunity for unacceptable conduct, it is possible to adapt these provisions to help close the accountability gap that currently exists in business and human rights. This section considers how the treaty language in the Conventions against Torture and Corruption can be modified for the needs of the business and human rights treaty. While the provisions employed often relate to criminal liability, they can also be adapted to ensure that victims have access to effective civil remedies. I propose particular language here, and where necessary use the footnotes to indicate where the original provision comes from.

First, the Convention against Corruption works to establish the liability of legal persons.[145] It does this without excusing the possibility of concurrent responsibility for natural persons.[146] UNCAT, meanwhile, requires states to adopt 'legislative, administrative, judicial or other measures' necessary to effectively prevent torture.[147] Combining aspects of each of these, the business and human rights treaty could reflect concerns about the impact of the doctrine of separate corporate personalities.

1. Each State Party shall take effective legislative, administrative, judicial or other measures to prevent their corporations from having a negative impact on the realisation of human rights throughout their operations.[148]
2. Each State Party shall adopt such measures as may be necessary, consistent with its legal principles, to establish the liability of businesses and other legal persons for impacts on human rights.[149]
3. Subject to the legal principles of the State Party, the liability of businesses will be civil and administrative. [If the state otherwise establishes criminal liability for legal persons, the state shall also provide criminal liability for business entities for criminal violations of human rights.][150]
4. Such liability shall be without prejudice to the criminal liability of the natural persons who have committed the offences.
5. With regard to the obligations in subparagraphs 1, 2 and 3 of this article, where a corporate group exists, the State Party in which the ultimate parent corporation resides or is registered shall, consistent with its legal principles,

145 Ibid, article 26.
146 Ibid, article 26(2).
147 UNCAT, article 2(1).
148 Adapted from UNCAT, article 2(1).
149 Adapted from UNCAT, article 5(2).
150 The language in brackets is simply to demonstrate the potential for including corporate criminal responsibility in the treaty.

> take effective legislative, administrative, judicial or other measures as may be necessary to establish jurisdiction for the entirety of the corporate group based on the presence of the ultimate parent company.

This language would allow for the establishment of group-based liability, meaning that the corporate veil would not act as an effective impediment to adequate and accessible remedies. One issue not addressed by this language, however, is how states should define 'impacts on human rights'. That part of the first paragraph states in the original: 'established in accordance with this Convention'.[151] Replicating that language is unlikely to make sense in the business and human rights treaty.

Second, the Convention against Torture establishes specific jurisdictional bases for prosecuting criminal acts of torture.[152] Modifying that language, while staying focused on civil claims and assuming universal civil jurisdiction is not yet appropriate,[153] could result in the treaty using language such as:

> Each State Party shall take such measures as may be necessary to establish its civil jurisdiction over the corporations accused of human rights impacts in the following cases:
>
> (a) When the impacts occur in the territory under its jurisdiction or on board a ship or aircraft that is registered in that State;
> (b) When the alleged offender or the ultimate parent company is a national of that State; and
> (c) Where the victim is a national of that State if that State considers it appropriate.[154]

Finally, the Shell defence in the Netherlands demonstrates the importance of ensuring victims can access necessary information, including information relating to the relevant corporate entities and their relationships. It is therefore necessary to include specific language about mutual assistance and cooperation in the conduct of activities. The Convention against Corruption includes relevant language that could be easily modified into the following:

> 1. States Parties shall afford one another the widest measure of mutual legal assistance in investigations and judicial proceedings related to the human rights impacts of businesses operating on their territory or incorporated, registered or headquartered in their territory.

---

151 Convention against Corruption, article 26(1).
152 UNCAT, article 5.
153 I realise this is a controversial position, but I have yet to be persuaded that individuals – even legal entities – should be subject to the civil jurisdiction of a state that is neither the state in which they are present or their home state.
154 Adapted from UNCAT, article 5.

2. Mutual legal assistance shall be afforded to the fullest extent possible under relevant laws, treaties, agreements and arrangements of the requested State Party with respect to investigations and judicial proceedings in relation to corporate impacts on human rights for which a legal person may be held liable in the requesting State Party.
3. Mutual legal assistance to be afforded in accordance with this article may be requested for any of the following purposes:
   a. Taking evidence or statements from persons;
   b. Effecting service of judicial documents;
   c. Executing searches and seizures, and attaching or freezing profits or income appropriate for the protection of the right of victims to full reparation;
   d. Examining objects and sites;
   e. Providing information, evidentiary items and expert evaluations;
   f. Providing originals or certified copies of relevant documents and records, including government, bank, financial, corporate or business records;
   g. Identifying or tracing proceeds of crime, property, instrumentalities or other things for evidentiary purposes;
   h. Facilitating the voluntary appearance of persons in the requesting State Party;
   i. Any other type of assistance that is not contrary to the domestic law of the requested State Party.
4. The provisions of this article shall not affect the obligations under any other treaty, bilateral or multilateral, that governs or will govern, in whole or in part, mutual legal assistance.[155]

This language intentionally excludes provisions relevant only to criminal proceedings, solely to demonstrate the potential for using a traditional approach to the treaty to create avenues for victims to pursue full remediation and compensation.

These provisions indicate that a traditional approach to international law can be used in formulating the business and human rights treaty so as to increase protection and victims' access to adequate and effective remedies and remediation. Crafting an effective treaty does not require the alteration of IHRL so as to provide corporations with direct international obligations. In fact, simply attaching direct obligations to corporations does little to alleviate the real issue outlined in Sections 1 and 2 regarding the availability of adequate remedies for victims. As noted in Section 3, states have been reluctant to give international bodies effective control over the enforcement of human rights. Simply changing the duty holder is unlikely to change that. But, as the Conventions against Torture and Corruption indicate, states are willing to increase their own responsibility

[155] Adapted from Convention against Corruption, article 46.

and the jurisdictional reach of their own courts to address serious issues of general control.

5. CONCLUSIONS: 'REMEMBER WHAT WE WERE FIGHTING FOR'[156]

Without a treaty, it appears the international community will make little progress in the protection of human rights from corporate impacts. On this, I agree with the other scholars who have contributed to this volume. Because the purpose of a treaty (what we are fighting for) should be to provide greater protection for victims, this chapter began with the premise that we should abandon the state-centric approach to international law only if we are certain that (1) the current state-centric system will not adequately address victims' needs, *and* (2) the alternative will provide a better solution. This chapter suggests that the first part of that test is not met when it comes to the business and human rights treaty as a traditionalist approach can allow us to increase protection for victims and establish means by which to measure and strengthen a state's human rights compliance. The impediment victims face is not in the design of IHRL as a state-centric approach but rather in securing adequate remedial structures.

While a state-centric approach may be complemented by direct obligations on corporations – a path that seems to emerge at times in the IGWG sessions – human rights scholars and advocates should be concerned with the implications of expanding the law to new actors without further developing the remedial systems. If the law as it exists in a state-centric approach provides a means of adequately addressing the problems caused by business impacts on human rights, then the focus may more appropriately be on ensuring enforcement of that law rather than on changing the nature of the law in a way that may not give greater effect to the needs of victims.

This chapter has argued that by modifying language in existing treaties, a traditionalist approach can provide victims with greater access to effective remedies. As discussed in Section 2, there is a significant need to tackle the impact separate corporate personalities have on the availability of information to victims, and the ability of victims, particularly in developing states, to access a clear means of redress. Using a traditionalist approach can also streamline the process for victims, allowing them to seek the corporate parent rather than to try to find information about the entire corporate group.

The provisions outlined in this chapter are not guaranteed to address all the hurdles victims currently face when trying to access remedies against businesses.

---

156 Swift, Antonoff, 'I Wish You Would', on Taylor Swift, *1989* (2014).

That would require drafting an entire treaty, which is well beyond the scope of a book chapter. But even if one is not convinced by the particulars of the provisions in this chapter, those calling for direct obligations on corporations bear the burden of demonstrating that this approach provides a better avenue for victims than the traditional state-centric one. It is easy to argue that the current system is failing and needs to be replaced with *something* but unless that *something* is actually effective at filling existing gaps, then it will simply be – as the title to this chapter suggests – a band-aid on a bullet hole, a response that might mask the pain while doing little to alleviate it.

VOLUNTARY vs. BINDING: CIVIL SOCIETY'S CLAIM FOR A BINDING INSTRUMENT

Ana María Suárez Franco and Daniel Fyfe

1. INTRODUCTION

The initiative towards a UN 'Binding Instrument on Transnational Corporations [hereinafter TNCs] and other business enterprises with respect to Human Rights'[1] has been strongly driven by civil society organisations worldwide. Although the views and contributions of civil society on the specific content for the proposed treaty are rich and diverse, they share the common claim for a transition from the current voluntarist regulatory trend of the human rights system to an obligatory legal framework. This claim constitutes a unifying and solid pillar in civil society, the same that gave birth to the Treaty Alliance,[2] a coalition of more than 1,000 committed individuals, organisations, networks and campaign groups around the world joining to collectively organise advocacy activities in support of developing a binding instrument to address human rights abuses committed by TNCs and other business enterprises.

1 UNHRC Resolution 26/9, UN Doc A/HRC/RES/26/9, 2014.
2 Treaty Alliance <www.treatymovement.com> accessed 27.01.2016.

Departing from their perspective as civil society actors actively participating in the process, and crossing the borders of academic research, the authors of this chapter will explain the recent historical and political process behind the treaty initiative. Along this historical account, they will introduce some of the main arguments supporting the demands of civil society and the main agreements of the Treaty Alliance regarding the content, nature and form of the future international binding instrument. They will also highlight the benefits that the process has already delivered for those suffering the consequences of businesses activities impairing the enjoyment of their human rights.[3]

2. THE REASONS BEHIND THE DEMAND FOR A BINDING INSTRUMENT TO REGULATE TNCs

Non-governmental organisations (NGOs), civil society organisations (CSOs), and social movements have been denouncing corporate human rights crimes and calling for international regulation of the activities of TNCs and other business enterprises since the 1970s.[4] The increasing size and power of, and complex transnational structures developed by, corporations during the second half of the last century, accompanied by high-profile cases of human rights abuses by TNCs as well as collusion between TNCs and governments, increased public attention on the need to close existing gaps in human rights protection and accountability through binding international law. Notorious cases such as the Bhopal gas tragedy of 1984,[5] the Chiquita case in Colombia in the 1990s,[6] and the more recent 2013 Rana Plaza disaster[7] have shown how TNCs can impair the realisation of a wide spectrum of human rights. Beyond these well-known cases, a large number of other crimes committed by business enterprises are taking place every day, though not receiving the same important visibility as the above-mentioned cases. Grassroots communities have multiplied their denunciations

---

3 The present chapter is the result of the personal analysis of the authors and is not written in the name of the Treaty Alliance. When describing specific positions of the Treaty Alliance, the authors will refer to agreed documents of the Alliance as well as their source.

4 P Feeney, 'Business and Human Rights: The Struggle for Accountability in the UN and the Future Direction of the Advocacy Agenda' (2009) *Revista Internacional de Direitos Humanos* 160.

5 Amnesty International, 'Injustice Incorporated: Corporate Abuses and the Human Right to Remedy: Corporate Abuses and the Right to Remedy', Amnesty International, 2014 <www.amnesty.org/en/documents/POL30/001/2014/en/> accessed 12.01.2017.

6 Business and Human Rights Resource Centre, 'Chiquita lawsuits (re Colombia)' <https://business-humanrights.org/en/chiquita-lawsuits-re-colombia> accessed 28.11.2016.

7 Clean Clothes Campaign, 'Rana Plaza' <https://cleanclothes.org/safety/ranaplaza> accessed 24.01.2017.

of the impact of TNCs and other businesses activities on their livelihoods,[8] and women's rights movements have documented the impact that extractive industries are having on the enjoyment of their rights.[9] It is the systematic character and the impunity resulting from such cases which have driven the demands by NGOs, CSOs and social movements for concerted international efforts in the regulation, monitoring and adjudication of activities of TNCs.

The initial international responses came in the shape of the 1976 Organisation for Economic Co-operation and Development (OECD) Guidelines for Multinational Enterprises and the 1977 International Labour Organization (ILO) Tripartite Declaration of Principles Concerning Multinational Enterprises and Social Policy. Both are non-binding voluntary standards touching upon diverse issues such as industrial relations and environmental and consumer issues. They were seen at the time as a means by industrial countries to accommodate demands for binding regulations.[10]

Despite calls by States from the 'global south' in the 1970s at the UN General Assembly 'to formulate, adopt and implement an international code of conduct for transnational corporations',[11] the UN began taking up the issue seriously only during the late 1990s. In 1998 the then UN Sub-Commission on the Promotion and Protection of Human Rights set up a Working Group on TNCs, which drafted the *Norms on the Responsibilities of Transnational Corporations and Other Business Enterprises with Regard to Human Rights*. The Norms were,

---

8 JC Morales González, 'Declaración oral de FIAN Internacional. Panel I: Impactos sociales, económicos y ambientales sobre los derechos humanos de las poblaciones campesinas relacionados con las empresas transnacionales y otras empresas', Second session of the Intergovernmental Working Group on transnational corporations and other business enterprises with respect to human rights, Geneva 2016 <www.ohchr.org/Documents/HRBodies/HRCouncil/WGTransCorp/Session2/Panel1/FIANInternational_Panel1%20-%20Copy.pdf> accessed 21.11.2016; J Borras, R Herre, P Seufert, S Backes, D Fyfe, L Michele and E Mills, *Land Grabbing and Human Rights: The Involvement of European Corporate and Financial Entities in Land Grabbing outside the European Union*, European Parliament Directorate-General for External Policies, Policy Department, 2016 <www.europarl.europa.eu/RegData/etudes/STUD/2016/578007/EXPO_STU(2016)578007_EN.pdf> accessed 31.01.2017; Global Network for the Right to Food and Nutrition, 'A Life without Dignity – The Price of Your Cup of Tea: Abuses and Violations of Human Rights in Tea Plantations in India', Global Network for the Right to Food and Nutrition, 2016 <www.fian.org/fileadmin/media/publications_2016/FFMReport_June_2016.pdf> accessed 01.09.2016; Amnesty International, 'The Great Palm Oil Scandal: Labour Abuses Behind Big Brand Names', Amnesty International, 2016 <www.amnesty.org/en/documents/asa21/5184/2016/en/> accessed 01.12.2016.

9 Women's International League for Peace & Freedom, 'Life at the Bottom of the Chain: Women in Artisanal Mines in DRC', WILPF 2016 <http://wilpf.org/wp-content/uploads/2016/10/WomenInArtisanalMinesInDRC_web.pdf> accessed 02.12.2016.

10 S Jerbi, 'Business and Human Rights at the UN: What Might Happen Next?' (2009) 31 *Human Rights Quarterly* 299.

11 Programme of Action on the Establishment of a New International Economic Order, UNGA Res S-6/3202, 01.05.1974.

however, rejected by the then UN Commission on Human Rights for having 'no legal standing'.[12] The failure of the Norms prompted the appointment by UN Secretary-General Kofi Annan of Harvard Professor John Ruggie as Special Representative on Human Rights and Transnational Corporations and other business enterprises. In 2011 Ruggie's *UN Guiding Principles on Business and Human Rights* were adopted by the UN Human Rights Council.[13]

In the midst of this, during the 1999 World Economic Forum, the UN Secretary-General called for a 'global compact of shared values and principles'.[14] This call led in 2000 to the launch of the UN Global Compact, a purely voluntary initiative committing companies to help achieve UN goals and uphold 10 principles which derive from international treaties in the domain of human rights, labour, the environment and anti-corruption. Conceived as a set of principles to be integrated into corporations' codes of conduct, the UN Global Compact lacks any monitoring and accountability mechanism. Companies are solely required to communicate with their stakeholders on their progress in implementing the 10 principles. If they fail to do so over time, companies 'may be removed from the initiative'.[15] The Global Compact has been heavily criticised by CSOs for being a 'bluewashing' tool for corporations to enhance their reputation without changing their behaviour, as there are no accountability or sanction mechanisms whatsoever.[16]

A common feature of all these initiatives (except for the failed Norms) is their voluntary nature and lack of any form of legal accountability of human rights perpetrators and, as a consequence, their failure to guarantee access to remedy for affected people and communities. While the 'legal conception of human rights presupposes and demands accountability',[17] and although these initiatives claim to deal with human rights, the absence of accountability mechanisms suggests they should rather be understood as Corporate Social Responsibility (CSR) tools, reduced to mere moral duties without legal enforceability.

---

12 UNCHR Res 2004/116 (2004) UN Doc E/CN.4/DEC/2004/116; See also: J Martens and K Seitz, *The Struggle for a UN Treaty: Towards Global Regulation on Human Rights and Business*, Global Policy Forum and Rosa Luxemburg Stiftung, 2016.

13 UNHRC Res 32/10 (2016) UN Doc A/HRC/32/10.

14 'Secretary-General Proposes Global Compact on Human Rights, Labour, Environment, in address to World Economic Forum in Davos', Press Release SG/SM/6881, United Nations, 1999. <www.un.org/press/en/1999/19990201.sgsm6881.html> accessed 01.12.2016.

15 United Nations Global Compact, 'About the UN Global Compact: Frequently Asked Questions', United Nations Global Compact <www.unglobalcompact.org/about/faq> accessed 28.11.2016.

16 Friends of the Earth International, 'Reclaim the UN from corporate capture', Friends of the Earth International, 2012 <www.foei.org/wp-content/uploads/2013/12/Reclaim-the-UN.pdf> accessed 02.12.2016.

17 UNHRC 'Report of the Special Rapporteur on extreme poverty and human rights' (2016) UN Doc A/HRC/32/31.

As an example, the OECD Guidelines on Multinational Enterprises have not proven to be an effective system 'fit for purpose' for CSOs bringing complaints to the guidelines' National Contact Points (NCP).[18] This was the conclusion of a report from Amnesty International,[19] which furthermore describes the NCPs' treatment of complaints as 'inconsistent, unreliable and biased towards businesses'.[20] The statistics gathered by OECD Watch, an international network of CSOs promoting corporate accountability and testing the effectiveness of the Guidelines, clearly illustrate this reality. Between 2001 and 2015, 43 per cent of cases were rejected by NCPs.[21] A study by OECD Watch analysing 250 complaints to NCPs since 2000 found that a mere 1 per cent of cases led to an actual improvement in the conditions of the affected individuals and communities.[22]

The fact that these different instruments share a non-binding form can most probably be attributed to the similar political processes they underwent. The regulation of TNCs at the international level has from its inception received strong opposition from industrial States, many of which are home to TNCs. The polarisation of debates around this issue has led many of these initiatives to be driven by 'independent experts' receiving inputs from 'multistakeholders', including from the corporate sector, as opposed to State-led multilateral discussions. This is most notably the case with the UN Global Compact and the UN Guiding Principles on Business and Human Rights, whose elaboration was led by John Ruggie after consultations with States, some civil society groups and the business sector.[23]

Beyond their form and process, the NGOs, CSOs and social movements campaigning against impunity resulting from corporate human rights crimes and abuses have not found the content of current instruments and initiatives satisfactory. None of the above-mentioned instruments effectively provides for a legal obligation for States to adopt binding regulatory measures to prevent corporate human rights abuses. Moreover, they do not deal in a clear way with

---

18 Amnesty International, *Obstacle Course: How the UK's National Contact Point handles human rights complaints under the OECD Guidelines for Multinational Enterprises* (Amnesty International UK 2016) <www.amnesty.org.uk/sites/default/files/uk_ncp_complaints_handling_full_report_lores_0.pdf> accessed 05.12.2016.

19 ibid.

20 OECD Watch, 'Amnesty International exposes the OECD Guidelines as a system not fit for purpose', OECD Watch <www.oecdwatch.org/news-en/amnesty-international-exposes-the-oecd-guidelines-as-a-system-not-fit-for-purpose> accessed 05.12.2016.

21 OECD Watch, 'Case Statistics (June 2015)', OECD Watch <www.oecdwatch.org/cases/statistics> accessed 05.12.2016.

22 C Daniel, J Wilde-Ramsing, K Genovese and V Sandjojo, *Remedy Remains Rare: An analysis of 15 years of NCP cases and their contribution to improve access to remedy for victims of corporate misconduct*, OECD Watch, 2015 <www.oecdwatch.org/publications-en/Publication_4201> accessed 05.12.2016.

23 UNGA, 'Report of the Special Representative of the Secretary-General on the issue of human rights and transnational corporations and other business enterprises, Addendum, Summary of five multi-stakeholder consultations', UN Doc A/HRC/8/5/Add.1, 2008.

States' extraterritorial obligations to respect, protect and fulfil human rights, including provisions for State cooperation and mutual assistance in order to adjudicate and enforce legal decisions.[24] Finally, they do not provide any accountability mechanisms to enable affected individuals and communities to hold States and TNCs accountable, but rather focus on company-level grievance mechanisms, which have been shown to be used by enterprises to hinder affected individuals' and communities' access to impartial State-based judicial remedy mechanisms.[25]

These initiatives have not provided adequate responses to closing existing human rights protection and accountability gaps for abuses committed by TNCs and other business enterprises. In the current context of globalisation, liberalisation and voluntary regulations, impunity for corporate human rights abuses has become widespread and even systematic. While human rights suffer from inadequate protection from corporate abuses and crimes, corporations and investors benefit from robust binding trade and investment agreements, which reflects the existing asymmetry in protection existing between these two types of law.

Forty years after the first international instrument aimed at regulating the activities of TNCs (OECD Guidelines for Multinational Enterprises), civil society is calling attention to many unresolved issues:

a) At the national level, many States do not have criminal, civil and administrative mechanisms in place to hold national companies and TNCs accountable as legal persons.
b) The multinational nature and strategies TNCs use in order to escape liability across borders require States to cooperate jointly at the international level to regulate, monitor, adjudicate and enforce judicial decisions to ensure the liability of the companies involved in abuses and remedy for affected individuals and communities. Such international cooperation is currently lacking and depends on the goodwill of States.
c) States systematically fail to comply with their extraterritorial obligations to respect, protect and fulfil human rights,[26] and binding regulations clarifying what such obligations imply for States regarding TNC regulation is currently lacking.

---

24 Maastricht Principles on Extraterritorial Obligations of States in the Area of Economic, Social and Cultural Rights 2011, Principle 27.

25 Rights and Accountability in Development, 'Principles without Justice: The corporate takeover of human rights', Rights and Accountability in Development, 2016 <www.raid-uk.org/sites/default/files/principles_without_justice.pdf> accessed 23.11.2016.

26 Above n 24; The Commentary to the Maastricht Principles on Extraterritorial Obligations of States clearly presents the legal bases for these obligations: O De Schutter, A Eide, A Khalfan, M Orellana, M Salomon and I Seidermann, 'Commentary to the Maastricht Principles on Extraterritorial Obligations of States in the Area of Economic, Social and Cultural Rights' (2012) 34 *HRQ* 1084. The jurisprudence of the UN Treaty Bodies has reaffirmed these obligations e.g. UN Committee for the Elimination of All Forms of Discrimination

d) Remedy mechanisms available to affected individuals and communities in order to hold the home States of TNCs accountable for their failure to comply with their extraterritorial obligations to protect human rights beyond their borders are non-existent in many countries or have been weakened.[27]
e) There is a clear asymmetry between binding trade and investment law protecting corporate interests on the one side, and weak enforcement of human rights law on the other side.[28]
f) Arbitration tribunals or Investor–State Dispute Settlement (ISDS) mechanisms included in investment and trade law create a 'chilling effect' on States which legislate to protect human rights. Indeed, the increasing number of claims by companies against States threatens their financial capacity to implement human rights. At the same time, arbitration tribunals operate as a private judicial system, outside the States' domestic court system, with arbitrators whose independence is questionable: they often have close ties with the corporate sector (some having even been members of corporate boards) and evidently have a vested interest in investors bringing arbitration cases.[29]
g) There is an increasing undue influence of the most powerful TNCs in public policy standard-setting processes and governance, which has been alleged to undermine human rights protection. The situation is so strong that civil society actors are speaking about 'corporate capture' of policy spaces. This happens both at national and international level.[30]

---

against Women, 'General Recommendation No. 34 on the rights of rural women', UN Doc CEDAW/C/GC/34, 2016; UN Committee on the Rights of the Child, 'General Comment No. 16 on State obligations regarding the impact of the business sector on children's rights', UN Doc CRC (2013) UN Doc CRC/C/GC/16.

27 E.g. *Kiobel v. Royal Dutch Petroleum. Co.*, a case before the US Supreme Court, is an example of the retrogression in the interpretation of the Alien Tort Statute. See also G Skinner, R McCorquodale and O De Schutter, *The Third Pillar: Access to Judicial Remedies for Human Rights Violations by Transnational Business*, ICAR, CORE, ECCJ, 2013, pp 19–20, <http://icar.ngo/wp-content/uploads/2013/02/The-Third-Pillar-Access-to-Judicial-Remedies-for-Human-Rights-Violation-by-Transnational-Business.pdf> accessed 01.12.2016.

28 The Global Campaign to Reclaim Peoples' Sovereignty, Dismantle Corporate Power and Stop Impunity, 'Building a UN Treaty on Human Rights and TNCs: A Way Forward to Stop Corporate Impunity' (2016) 22–26, <www.stopcorporateimpunity.org/wp-content/uploads/2016/10/SIX-points_ENG.pdf> accessed 24.11.2016; UNHRC, 'Report of the Independent Expert on the Promotion of a Democratic and Equitable International Order', UN Doc A/HRC/33/40, 2016.

29 UNHRC, 'Report of the Independent Expert on the Promotion of a Democratic and Equitable International Order, Alfred-Maurice De Zayas', UN Doc A/HRC/30/44, 2015; P Eberhardt and C Olivet, 'Profiting from Injustice: How Law Firms, Arbitrators and Financiers are Fueling an Investment Arbitration Boom', Corporate Europe Observatory and Transnational Institute, 2012. <www.tni.org/files/download/profitingfrominjustice.pdf> accessed 01.12.2016.

30 See e.g. Global Policy Forum, *Fit for Whose Purpose: Private Funding and Corporate Influence in the United Nations*, Global Policy Forum, 2015 <www.globalpolicy.org/images/pdfs/images/pdfs/Fit_for_whose_purpose_online.pdf> accessed 27.01.2017; Right to Food and Nutrition

h) There has been an increase in criminalization and psychological and physical harassment of human rights defenders and trade unionists by TNCs and other business enterprises.[31]
i) There still exists a big gap between the affected individuals' and communities' perception of the reality and that of the delegations present in the UN human rights system – although the two first sessions of the Intergovernmental Working Group on transnational corporations and other business enterprises with respect to human rights have contributed to closing this gap.

3. THE RESPONSE FROM THE TREATY ALLIANCE

Although NGOs, CSOs and social movements have been campaigning for a long time against impunity for crimes committed by TNCs as well as for binding standards regulating their activities, the adoption of the UN Guiding Principles on Business and Human Rights by the UN Human Rights Council in 2011 spurred yet further mobilisation. In a statement submitted to the Human Rights Council on 30 May 2011, 28 CSOs drew the Council's attention to the insufficiencies of the Guiding Principles, in particular:[32]

a) their failure to go beyond mechanisms such as the OECD Guidelines on Multinational Enterprises and UN Global Compact by depending on the voluntary action of businesses instead of on binding national and international regulations;
b) the lack of consistency with existing international human rights law interpretations from UN Treaty Bodies, with regard to, for instance, States' extraterritorial obligations to take measures to avoid abuses committed by their corporations overseas;
c) failure in focusing particular attention on the existing challenges in regulating TNCs individually as well as through international cooperation, which was the original mandate of the Special Representative.

Watch, *Who Decides about Global Food and Nutrition? Strategies to Regain Control*, Right to Food and Nutrition Watch, 2012 <http://www.righttofoodandnutrition.org/sites/www.righttofoodandnutrition.org/files/R_t_F_a_N_Watch_2012_eng.pdf> accessed 10.03.2017; ESCR-net, 'Corporate Capture Project', <https://www.escr-net.org/corporateaccountability/corporatecapture> accessed 14.03.2017.

31 See FIAN International, 'Civil society condemns murder of Berta Cáceres' <www.fian.org/fr/actualites/article/civil_society_condemns_murder_of_berta_caceres/> accessed 08.10.2016; UNGA, 'Report of the Special Rapporteur on the situation of human rights defenders', UN Doc A/68/262, 2013.

32 FIAN International, 'Civil Society Organizations respond to Ruggie's Guiding Principles regarding human rights and transnational corporations and other business enterprises', FIAN, 2011 <www.fian.org/fileadmin/media/publications/2011.05_Statement_to_Delegations_on_the_Human_Rights_Council_2011.pdf> accessed 31.01.2017.

The next important call from civil society came from Medellin, Colombia in August 2013, where CSOs created an alternative forum to the Regional Forum on Business and Human Rights for Latin America and the Caribbean organised by the UN Working Group on the issue of human rights and transnational corporations and other business enterprises (the body which promotes the dissemination and implementation of the Guiding Principles). On this occasion, over 100 organisations signed a declaration calling on the Human Rights Council to make progress 'towards the adoption of a binding international instrument on States, Business and Human Rights'.[33] The Medellin Declaration also strongly addressed the issue of corporate capture of policy spaces in the midst of the appointment of members of the Working Group with a strong link to TNCs having committed human rights abuses. The signatory organisations urged States, the UN and other intergovernmental organisations to prohibit the participation of corporations in policy making.

These calls found support in the UN Human Rights Council from the African Group, the Arab Group, Pakistan, Sri Lanka, Kyrgyzstan, Cuba, Nicaragua, Bolivia, Venezuela, Peru and Ecuador during the Council's 24th Session in September 2013. In an oral statement, this group of States declared: 'The increasing cases of human rights violations and abuses by some Transnational Corporations reminds us of the necessity of moving forward towards a legally binding framework to regulate the work of transnational corporations.'[34] The States supporting the statement finally renewed their 'commitment to work towards the elaboration of a legally binding instrument on the basis of a careful and serious assessment of options available in the framework of the Human Rights Council'.

The first annual Peoples' Forum on Human Rights and Business some months later in November 2013 represented an important milestone towards the creation of the Treaty Alliance. In Bangkok, the participants of the forum convened by ESCR-net and Forum-Asia drafted a joint statement, which built on the momentum created by the States at the Human Rights Council, calling for a legally binding instrument in September 2013. What was later to become the Treaty Alliance's first joint statement called on the Human Rights Council to take steps towards the elaboration of a treaty and to that end create an open-ended working group tasked with such a mandate.[35] In the Bangkok

33 FIAN International, 'Declaration of Alternative Forum on Business and Human Rights in Colombia', FIAN, 2013 <www.fian.org/fileadmin/media/publications/Declaration_Busines_and_HR_Regional_Forum_Medellin_EN.pdf> accessed 05.12.2016.

34 The African Group, the Arab Group, Pakistan, Sri Lanka, Kyrgyzstan, Cuba, Nicaragua, Bolivia, Venezuela, Peru and Ecuador, 'Statement on behalf of a Group of Countries at the 24th Session of the Human Rights Council', 2013 <https://business-humanrights.org/sites/default/files/media/documents/statement-unhrc-legally-binding.pdf> accessed 10.10.2016.

35 Treaty Alliance, '2013 Bangkok Joint Statement: Call for an international legally binding instrument on human rights, transnational corporations and other business enterprises', Treaty Alliance, 2013 <www.treatymovement.com/statement-2013> accessed 28.09.2016.

statement, civil society gathered around some key points with regard to the provisions which this future treaty should include:[36]

a) confirmation that States have an obligation to regulate TNCs and other business enterprises under their jurisdiction, including when they operate abroad;
b) States must provide for the legal liability of TNCs and other business enterprises which commit human rights abuses;
c) host States and home States of TNCs and other business enterprises having committed human rights abuses must provide for access to effective remedies, in accordance with States' territorial and extraterritorial human rights obligations;
d) the creation of monitoring and accountability mechanisms at the international level;
e) a reminder that States should guarantee the protection of human rights defenders, affected people and communities and whistleblowers that seek to prevent, expose or ensure accountability in cases of corporate abuse.

So far, the Bangkok statement has been signed by 620 organisations and over 400 individuals in 95 countries.[37] It marked the beginning of the mobilisation of a wide alliance of international networks, organisations and social movements worldwide for an international treaty to deal with corporate human rights abuses.

The Treaty Alliance was formally set up at the start of 2014 when the most involved NGOs, networks and campaign groups to have signed the Bangkok statement agreed on the need to better coordinate their actions, especially in view of the eventual proposal by some States for the creation of an Intergovernmental Working Group of the Human Rights Council mandated to elaborate a binding instrument.

It was under these premises that an open group of some of the most active organisations began to meet regularly, through virtual means, to analyse the situation and strategise over their advocacy work towards the creation of this Intergovernmental Working Group. To this end, Treaty Alliance members undertook content discussions, consultations, capacity building, awareness-raising campaigns and advocacy work in Geneva and at the national level, involving meetings with government representatives, staff working for ministries and ambassadors, among others. The Alliance has always worked in a flexible manner, with activities being implemented by its members individually or jointly in their own names. At least once a year, the members of the Alliance are invited by the facilitation group to participate in face-to-face meetings in order to discuss content-related issues as well as to strategize collectively.

36 ibid.
37 ibid.

After the creation of the Treaty Alliance, the side-event organised by Ecuador and South Africa during the March 2014 session of the Human Rights Council represented another important moment. During this event, international law experts, State representatives and CSOs discussed the need for, as well as the added value of, the demanded binding instrument, departing from the state of the art of international law. The event furthermore served to gain additional support among the Human Rights Council member States and other interested actors.

During the June 2014 session of the Human Rights Council, Ecuador and South Africa, with the support of other States,[38] presented a resolution establishing an Open-ended Intergovernmental Working Group mandated to elaborate a legally binding instrument, which civil society had been vigorously demanding. This draft resolution was frowned upon by some States who perceived the process towards a legally binding instrument as competing with the UN Guiding Principles on Business and Human Rights, which led to a strong polarisation within the Human Rights Council.

On the one side, a large group of States, mainly industrialised States, insisted on the pertinence of maintaining a non-binding approach to the issue and working towards the implementation of the Guiding Principles on Business and Human Rights. Another bloc of States, mainly composed of developing States, and supported by a large sector of civil society, emphasised the need to work towards the adoption of binding regulations. While the first group expressed its concern over the risks of breaching the alleged existing consensus built around the Guiding Principles on Business and Human Rights, the proponents of the resolution insisted on the complementary character of both processes and the importance of nurturing an intergovernmental democratic debate instead of leaving the discussion in the hands of independent experts. For the approximately 60 civil society representatives present during the session, initiating a treaty process was the natural step in the evolution of the human rights architecture.

The efforts from both groups to bring together these two initiatives in a single resolution failed. Instead, each group presented its resolution for approval by the Human Rights Council. Resolution 26/22 supporting the Guiding Principles on Business and Human Rights was adopted by consensus.[39] However, Resolution 26/9 establishing an Open-ended Intergovernmental Working Group (OEIGWG) was approved by the Council through a majority vote, mainly supported by the African Group of States, some Asian States and the Bolivarian Alliance for the Americas (ALBA) States.[40] An intergovernmental

[38] UNHRC Res 26/9, above n 1, co-sponsored by Bolivia, Cuba, Ecuador, South Africa, Venezuela.

[39] UNHRC Res 26/22, UN Doc A/HRC/RES/26/22, 2014.

[40] *In favour*: Algeria, Benin, Burkina Faso, China, Congo, Côte d'Ivoire, Cuba, Ethiopia, India, Indonesia, Kazakhstan, Kenya, Morocco, Namibia, Pakistan, Philippines, Russian Federation,

process towards a legally binding instrument on transnational corporations and other business enterprises with respect to human rights was finally born.

4. RESOLUTION 26/9

Resolution 26/9, entitled 'Elaboration of an international legally binding instrument on transnational corporations and other business enterprises with respect to human rights',[41] establishes the OEIGWG, whose mandate is to 'elaborate an international legally binding instrument to regulate in international human rights law, the activities of transnational corporations and other business enterprises'.[42]

The resolution additionally specifies that the first two sessions of the OEIGWG 'shall be dedicated to conducting constructive deliberations on the content, scope, nature and form of the future international instrument'[43] and tasks the Chairperson-Rapporteur (currently the Ambassador of Ecuador) with preparing 'elements for the draft legally binding instrument for substantive negotiations at the commencement of the third session'[44] of the OEIGWG.

One aspect of the resolution which received heavy criticism from some States and NGOs was the footnote in the title, which specifies that '"Other business enterprises" denotes all business enterprises that have a transnational character in their operational activities, and does not apply to local businesses registered in terms of relevant domestic law'.[45] The concern relates mainly to the double standards which this scope could create, as locally registered enterprises would not be covered under the treaty and impunity would therefore persist for abuses committed by these enterprises. Certain CSOs have furthermore criticised the footnote by pointing to the fact that affected people rarely care whether it is a transnational corporation or a domestic enterprise which has impaired their human rights.[46] It was additionally argued that many international investors

South Africa, Venezuela (Bolivarian Republic of), Vietnam. *Against*: Austria, Czech Republic, Estonia, France, Germany, Ireland, Italy, Japan, Montenegro, Republic of Korea, Romania, the former Yugoslav Republic of Macedonia, United Kingdom of Great Britain and Northern Ireland, United States of America. *Abstaining*: Argentina, Botswana, Brazil, Chile, Costa Rica, Gabon, Kuwait, Maldives, Mexico, Peru, Saudi Arabia, Sierra Leone, United Arab Emirates.

41 Above n 38.

42 ibid, para. 1.

43 ibid, para. 2.

44 ibid, para. 3.

45 ibid.

46 See e.g. Franciscans International, 'Submission of Franciscans International to the first session of the Open-ended Intergovernmental Working Group on Transnational Corporations and Other Business Enterprises with Respect to Human Rights', Franciscans International, 2015 <www.ohchr.org/Documents/HRBodies/HRCouncil/WGTransCorp/Session1/Franciscans International.pdf> accessed 05.01.2017.

operate through national companies under opaque links in order to escape any corporate liability. This complex articulation between economic actors therefore requires international regulation of national companies so as to ensure that they are held accountable when linked to transnational corporations.

5. THE PRE-SESSIONAL PERIOD

The tension between the proponents of the OEIGWG process and those preferring to stick with the UN Guiding Principles on Business and Human Rights remained. Of special concern to civil society was the position of the European Union, which permanently opposed the treaty initiative and which set four conditions (diplomatically called parameters) for its participation in the first session of the OEIGWG.

First, the EU requested in various meetings that the chair of the working group be an independent and impartial person. This condition was politically delicate since it implicitly suggested that the Ambassador of Ecuador was not respectful of diversity and could become partial. Some civil society actors interpreted this as a possible interest of the EU to once again see an independent expert leading the process. Despite this, the EU was not able to influence the normal practice and the Ambassador of Ecuador was elected as Chairperson-Rapporteur of the OEIGWG.

Second, the EU requested that the States supporting the treaty process should begin implementing the Guiding Principles on Business and Human Rights. This was seen by some sectors of civil society as an unfair condition, taking into account the voluntary nature of the principles.

Third, the EU requested that the footnote to the title of Resolution 26/9 be changed so as to ensure that the treaty refers to all businesses without any distinction. With regard to this point, the views from civil society were varied. Some reaffirmed the need for the future instrument to avoid any distinction between different types of businesses (as the arguments presented above illustrate), while others firmly believed that a focus on transnational corporations was necessary. This was justified by suggesting that TNCs drive most of the global economy and control many domestic businesses. Second, due to their flexibility, complex structures, power and the fact that they are almost always in a different jurisdiction from the individuals and communities they affect, TNCs' parent or controlling companies have been able to escape liability, leaving affected people without any remedy.[47]

[47] FIAN, Franciscans International, CCFD-Terre Solidaire, The Colombian Commission for Jurists, La Plataforma Internacional Contra la Impunidad, Society for International Development, 'Written Submission by FIAN International, Franciscans International, CCFD-Terre Solidaire, the Colombian Commission of Jurists, La Plataforma Internacional

Despite these different opinions, the facilitation group of the Treaty Alliance was united in affirming that there was room for interpreting the footnote, which the working group should dedicate itself to debating, instead of instrumentalising the footnote in bad faith so as to hinder the process.

Finally, the EU demanded that business enterprises be part of the process. The majority of the facilitation group of the Treaty Alliance disagreed on this point, considering that in the current context of corporate capture of governance spaces at different levels,[48] providing a space for companies within the debate could weaken the result of the intergovernmental process. Many Treaty Alliance members pointed to the process on the Framework Convention on Tobacco Control as an example of the importance of excluding companies from the process.[49]

6. FIRST SESSION OF THE OPEN-ENDED INTERGOVERNMENTAL WORKING GROUP

Despite the efforts of the EU to disrupt the process, the first session took place just over a year after the adoption of Resolution 26/9, from 6 to 10 July 2015.

The polarisation among States during the adoption of both TNCs- and human rights-related resolutions during the Council's 26th session continued to be reflected in the first session of the OEIGWG. Many European and North American delegations, strongly opposed to the creation of the working group, did not attend the session or abstained from participating in the discussions. Additionally, the adoption of the programme of work for the first session witnessed intense discussions. The programme presented by the Chairperson-Rapporteur, Ecuadorian Ambassador María Fernanda Espinosa Garcés,

---

Contra la Impunidad and Society for International Development for the second session of the open-ended intergovernmental working group (OEIGWG) on transnational corporations and other business enterprises with respect to human rights', 2016 <www.ohchr.org/EN/HRBodies/HRC/WGTransCorp/Session2/Pages/WrittenContributions.aspx> accessed 05.01.2017.

48 On corporate capture see e.g. B Adams and J Martens, *Fit for whose purpose: Private funding and corporate influence at the United Nations*, Global Policy Forum, 2015 <www.globalpolicy.org/images/pdfs/images/pdfs/Fit_for_whose_purpose_online.pdf> accessed 27.01.2017; Right to Food and Nutrition Watch, *Peoples' Nutrition Is Not a Business* (2015) 7 *Right to Food and Nutrition Watch* <www.righttofoodandnutrition.org/sites/www.righttofoodandnutrition.org/files/R_t_F_a_N_Watch_2015_eng_single-page_Web.pdf> accessed 27.01.2017.

49 Corporate Accountability International, 'Corporate Accountability International submission to the second session of the United Nations' Open-ended Intergovernmental Working Group on Transnational Corporations and Other Business Enterprises with Respect to Human Rights', Corporate Accountability International, 2016 <www.stopcorporateabuse.org/sites/default/files/resources/corporate_accountability_international_oeiwg_written_submission.pdf> accessed 05.01.2017.

included sessions on (i) the principles for an international legally binding instrument; (ii) the scope of coverage; (iii) the human rights to be covered; (iv) the obligations of States; (v) the responsibility of TNCs and other business enterprises; (vi) the legal liability of TNCs and other business enterprises; and (vii) the national and international mechanisms for access to remedy. However, the EU delegation made two proposals for amending the programme of work, which were to include an additional panel entitled 'Implementation of the United Nations Guiding Principles on Business and Human Rights – a renewed commitment by all States' and to add 'all' before 'business enterprises' wherever it appeared in the programme of work. After intense discussions and informal consultations, the Chairperson-Rapporteur revised the programme in order to include a panel on the UN Guiding Principles on Business and Human Rights, but rejected the second amendment proposal due to significant opposition from other participating delegations.

Over the course of a week the discussions showed the diversity of views which exists among States and also within civil society, and which is part of and defines any democratic debate. Having played a vital role in the adoption of Resolution 26/9, civil society actively intervened during all of the panel discussions of the first session. The Treaty Alliance was strongly mobilised before and during the session and released a joint statement before the session with signatures from over 400 organisations. The statement reiterated many of the points from the first Treaty Alliance statement with regard to the content, scope, nature and form of the prospective treaty, demonstrating the Treaty Alliance's unity around certain core issues (States' extraterritorial obligation (ETOs) to protect, access to judicial remedies in TNCs' home States, protection of human rights defenders, corporate legal liability and liability of company managers and directors).[50] The Treaty Alliance statement also reiterated, with regard to the process of the OEIGWG, the need for States to participate in good faith and to safeguard the working group's integrity from any undue influence from private sector actors 'whose primary interest in the process falls outside the objective of promotion and protection of human rights'.[51]

Despite certain delegations' attempts to label the treaty process as opposition to the UN Guiding Principles on Business and Human Rights process, both the Treaty Alliance and the majority of State delegations came to agree at the end of the session that there is no contradiction between the Guiding Principles and a legally binding instrument on TNCs and other business enterprises. They are rather complementary and even mutually reinforcing processes.[52]

---

50 Treaty Alliance, 'Enhance the International Legal Framework to Protect Human Rights from Corporate Abuse', Treaty Alliance, 2016 <www.treatymovement.com/statement/> accessed 29.11.2016.

51 ibid.

52 South Centre, 'Business and Human Rights: Commencing Discussions on a Legally Binding Instrument' (2015) 87–88 *South Bulletin*, p. 7.

Another point of consensus among participants was that the future instrument should cover all human rights and not be confined to gross human rights violations. This consensus was based on the fact that human rights are universal, indivisible, interdependent and interrelated, as laid down in the 1993 Vienna Declaration and Programme of Action, it therefore making little sense to exclude certain human rights from the future treaty.[53] Civil society furthermore proved in their oral and written statements that abuses and crimes by TNCs and other business enterprises that they had documented affect a broad scope of civil, political, and economic, social and cultural rights. The imprecise definition of 'gross violations', which in general only refers to civil and political rights and excludes in most cases violations or abuses of economic, social and cultural rights, would not achieve the aim of the treaty of guaranteeing effective prevention and remedy mechanisms for the individuals and communities affected by the activities of business enterprises.[54]

There were nonetheless also some 'sticky points' or points where delegations had divergent points of view during the first session. The two most notable related to the scope of coverage and to the holders of human rights obligations under the future instrument. The issue of whether the treaty should cover all business enterprises or specifically TNCs and business enterprises of transnational character had already been the subject of heated debate during the adoption of Resolution 26/9 and was again a divisive issue during the first session. Proponents of the 'all business enterprises' option argued that the prospective instrument should not create separate standards for TNCs, but a level playing field for all businesses, while opponents believed that a focus on TNCs was required in order to fill current existing gaps in protection in the context of globalisation.

On the second issue regarding the holders of human rights' obligations under the future instrument, a group of participants envisaged that the treaty would impose human rights obligations on TNCs, while others preferred States to be the duty-bearers of human rights, as is traditionally the case under human rights law. The latter argument stems from the risks of corporate capture by defining transnational corporations as duty-bearers of human rights under the future legally binding instrument. According to this position, human rights law mandates States to realise the human rights of their populations whereas TNCs and other business enterprises are mandated by their shareholders and investors and not by the public. In addition, these actors, by their very nature, do not

---

53 'Vienna Declaration and Programme of Action' World Conference on Human Rights, UN Doc A/CONF.157/23, 1993.

54 Franciscans International, 'Submission of Franciscans International to the first session of the Open-ended Intergovernmental Working Group on Transnational Corporations and Other Business Enterprises with Respect to Human Rights', 2015 <http://www.ohchr.org/Documents/HRBodies/HRCouncil/WGTransCorp/Session1/FranciscansInternational.pdf> accessed 20.03.2017.

work for the public good but for private profit. Human rights are a fundamental element for democracy and the rule of law and therefore only States should continue to hold human rights obligations and be held accountable for human rights violations. This position also reduces the risk that companies claim to hold human rights as a corollary to their human rights obligations, which has been the case at the European level and in a recent advisory opinion requested by Panama of the Inter-American Human Rights Court (leading to Advisory Opinion OC 22/16 of 22 February 2016). Preserving States as the duty-bearers under human rights law does not mean that transnational corporations and other business enterprises should be free from any form of regulation. These actors should be held accountable for the harm they cause to the enjoyment of human rights under administrative, civil or criminal law and hold 'direct obligations' under such laws.

7. SECOND SESSION OF THE OEIGWG, 24–28 OCTOBER 2016

The second session of the OEIGWG began in a more promising climate. As opposed to the first session a year before, the European Union announced prior to the session its commitment to constructively participate as an agreement was found with the Chairperson-Rapporteur on the content of the programme of work, which was later adopted by the working group without incident and in fact to the relieved applause of the assembly. While the EU delegation stayed in the room during the whole week and did not show any intention of hindering the session's proceedings, they nonetheless remained silent during most of the discussions, failing to fully engage in the debates on the issues it had expressed as being problematic. The other promising factor was the important mobilisation of the Treaty Alliance, which counted on the participation of approximately 100 of its members during the entire week and contributed to making the Human Rights Council a space for affected individuals and communities to voice their concerns. Through their numerous substantive oral and written statements and activities, both in and outside of the UN, the Treaty Alliance members demonstrated how civil society is an important driving force behind this process.[55] The Treaty Alliance members also proved to be crucial in guaranteeing the participation of the European Union by actively engaging with and lobbying European delegations.

Other NGOs representing the business sector came to the OEIGWG well prepared and determined to actively engage during the session. The International

55 See UNHRC, 'Report on the second session of the open-ended intergovernmental Working Group on transnational corporations and other business enterprises with respect to human rights', UN Doc A/HRC/34/47.

Organization of Employers as well as the International Chamber of Commerce, both holding UN Economic and Social Council consultative status, delivered oral statements during each of the panel discussions, presenting the corporate sector's views as well as their 'no-goes' with regard to the treaty process.[56] In their opinion, a legally binding instrument is not necessary as they consider that there are already sufficient existing standards available with regard to the regulation of TNCs and that what is lacking is their enforcement. Limiting the instrument's scope to TNCs, imposing direct human rights obligations on businesses and expanding extraterritoriality were some of the red lines that the business community expressed.

Concrete proposals on the content, scope, nature and form of the prospective treaty emerged out of this session. For instance, proposals were made with regard to extraterritorial obligations of States concerning the regulation of the activities of TNCs. On reducing barriers to access to justice, experts, delegations and civil society often expressed the need for the treaty to scrap the principle of *forum non conveniens* and to provide for class action, the piercing of the corporate veil, the reversal of the burden of proof and choice of forum (home or host State of the corporation) for affected people. On the form of the treaty, concrete suggestions were made as to whether adopting a framework treaty with annexes and protocols to be expanded by the Conference of the Parties or going for a detailed treaty with substantive and procedural matters already spelled out.

Although many of the 'sticky points' resulting from the first session remained unresolved after this second session, it was possible to see the gaps between certain positions being bridged. For instance, regarding the scope of the treaty, many CSOs and State delegations proposed to interpret the expression 'transnational corporations and other business enterprises' as well as the footnote in a flexible manner, so as to encompass all business enterprises linked to global supply chains, which naturally includes many domestic companies.[57] It was furthermore stated that the future instrument could reaffirm States' existing obligations to regulate all business enterprises domestically, as a way of finding consensus with the proponents of a scope covering all business enterprises.[58]

---

56 ibid.

57 See e.g., Joint Written Contribution of FIAN, Franciscans International, CCFD-Terre Solidaire, the Colombian Commission of Jurists, la Plataforma Internacional Contra la Impunidad and Society for International Development <www.ohchr.org/EN/HRBodies/HRC/WGTransCorp/Session2/Pages/WrittenContributions.aspx>.

58 A Zarro, 'Oral Statement delivered by FIAN, Franciscans International, CCFD-Terre Solidaire, La Plataforma Internacional Contra la Impunidad and the Society for International Development – Panel IV: Open debate on different approaches and criteria for the future definition of the scope of the international legally binding instrument', Second session of the intergovernmental working group on transnational corporations and other business enterprises with respect to human rights, Geneva 2016 <www.ohchr.org/Documents/HRBodies/HRCouncil/WGTransCorp/Session2/PanelIV/FIAN_FI_CCFD_PICI_SID.pdf> accessed 23.11.2016.

The Chairperson-Rapporteur, civil society and different States welcomed the constructive exchanges, general positive climate and manner in which much of the polarisation on this topic was overcome during the session. Unlike in the first session, discussions during the second session were mostly centred on what a future treaty would look like instead of on whether such a treaty was legitimate or not. With this session, the treaty process has gained a new momentum and entered a new phase: the negotiation phase. As Resolution 26/9 stipulates, the third session will be dedicated to substantive negotiations, according to the draft elements presented by the Chairperson-Rapporteur.

8. CONCLUSIONS: THE ADDED VALUES OF THE PROCESS AND THE WAY AHEAD

Regardless of the outcome of the intergovernmental process at the Human Rights Council towards the establishment of a treaty on TNCs and other business enterprises with respect to human rights, the process in itself is already having a positive mark in many different ways.

First, it has provided a space worldwide to give more visibility to the views of those affected by the harm caused by the activities of TNCs and other businesses abusing human rights.

Second, thanks to this process, existing spaces at the UN have been occupied by the voices of those suffering the impacts of corporate human rights abuses, of their supporters and of those involved in the legal, political and economic analysis of this phenomenon.

Third, it has enabled debates at the Human Rights Council on business and human rights to be reframed from a solely voluntarist approach to an obligatory approach, thus shifting the focus from CSR to legal corporate accountability.

Fourth, the treaty process has provided an impulse to the development of national action plans under the UN Guiding Principles on Business and Human Rights, highlighting the role of national laws in the regulation of TNCs and other business enterprises, and the need for binding regulations and extraterritorial obligations of States.

Fifth, this international process has stimulated similar debates on the regulation of transnational corporations and other business enterprises with respect to human rights at the regional level.

Sixth, it has energised the convergence of diverse CSOs and social movements which would not normally have worked together, and as a consequence it has strengthened the human rights movement.

Seventh, the process has contributed to providing visibility to existing international standards and legal dissertations on the extraterritorial obligations of States with regard to the regulation of transnational companies, trade and investment agreements, climate change and tax justice, among other topics.

Finally, the process has opened up an opportunity to continue developing the still incomplete legal architecture of human rights. It has generated more space for comparative legal analyses in diverse areas of international and national law (human rights law, environmental law, criminal law, international private law, tort law, competition law, tax law, trade law) as well as for the analysis of the interaction between these areas of law and the regulation of transnational corporations in the frame of an intergovernmental democratic debate.

Resolution 26/9 establishing the OEIGWG stipulates that the Chairperson-Rapporteur shall present elements of a draft legally binding instrument for substantive negotiations at the upcoming third session of the working group to take place in October 2017. At the date of publication of this chapter, it remains unclear whether this will be in the shape of a document presenting the elements for the binding instrument or if a first draft of the instrument will be made available in order to commence the negotiations. The intensified convergence of the Treaty Alliance members on the content, nature, scope and form of the future instrument means that it will continue and strengthen its advocacy and analysis work during 2017 in the hope of achieving an adequate international legal instrument to put an end to corporate impunity. With a view to the third session of the OEIGWG, the Treaty Alliance has been developing common positions which include, inter alia, States' extraterritorial obligations to respect, protect and fulfil human rights in the context of the activities of TNCs and other business enterprises, States' obligations to hold TNCs and other business enterprises accountable under their domestic laws, and States' obligations to remove barriers for affected individuals and communities to access justice and provide them with effective remedies.

The path ahead will certainly be a long one, filled with challenges of various kinds that will threaten the process. To begin with, the increase in right-wing governments worldwide as well as the political instability in certain regions or States that were originally sponsors of this process, such as Brazil and the Philippines, will be a key challenge. The ever-changing political context exemplified by Brexit, the general rise of extreme right-wing parties and policies in Europe, the presidency of Donald Trump in the United States and the upcoming presidential elections in Ecuador are some of the political situations which the process will have to contend with.

The increasing political power of the business sector and in particular its influence in standard-setting processes at all levels will undeniably represent one of the greatest challenges to this process. For the first time in its history, the UN General Assembly has admitted a business organisation, namely the International Chamber of Commerce (ICC), as an Observer of the body. As illustrated by the UN Global Compact, the UN Guiding Principles on Business and Human Rights and the Sustainable Development Goals, these actors have been influential in softening the international human rights architecture and therefore in the weakening of human rights protection in the context of business activities. Beyond a threat to this treaty process, the 'corporate capture' of policy spaces contributes more generally to the watering down of human rights to morals or desirable goals instead of legally justiciable entitlements.

The World Health Organization (WHO) is an example of how 'corporate capture' is already a reality of international governance spaces, and represents a precedent which should alert us. The WHO has increasingly been relying on earmarked government funding and philanthropic foundations, which have as a consequence influenced the organisation's agenda and framing of policies in a way which serves their interests. For example, the Bill & Melinda Gates Foundation, as the second largest donor to the WHO in 2014, has undoubtedly contributed to the organisation's drift away from a public health, social determinant approach into the adoption of vertical technological interventions, which supposedly provide technical, rapid and visible solutions to global health problems.[59] Another trend has been the increasing pressure on the WHO to leave aside its norm- and standard-setting role and to take on more of an emergency response profile, which is not in line with the WHO's mission and structure.[60]

In the midst of all of this, individuals and communities around the world supporting the treaty process and denouncing corporate human rights abuses continue to face a hostile environment in many parts of the world, where they are criminalised, threatened and even assassinated. Protecting human rights defenders and guaranteeing their safe participation in this process will be a vital and priority struggle for civil society moving forward.

The impressive and intensified engagement of civil society during the sessions of the OEIGWG is, however, a tremendous source of hope. The Treaty Alliance has become a space for the convergence of organisations and movements working in different areas. Trade unions, peasant movements, indigenous peoples' rights organisations, human rights organisations, environmental organisations, academics, movements and organisations from the health sector, and tax justice organisations inter alia, will continue to join forces and increase in numbers and strength. Civil society has been the driving force behind the creation of this process and the engagement of States in the process (most notably in engaging the EU to participate in the second session) and will only get stronger until an international legally binding instrument is finally adopted and enforced.

---

59 Above n 30.

60 ibid.

PART III
REGIONAL APPROACHES

BUSINESS AND HUMAN RIGHTS IN THE AMERICAS: DEFINING A LATIN AMERICAN ROUTE TO CORPORATE RESPONSIBILITY

Humberto Cantú Rivera

1. INTRODUCTION

Since the endorsement of the Guiding Principles on Business and Human Rights[1] (hereinafter the 'Guiding Principles' or the 'UNGPs') by the UN Human Rights Council in 2011, several voices have called for the development of

[1] Special Representative of the Secretary-General on the issue of human rights and transnational corporations and other business enterprises, *Guiding Principles on Business and Human Rights: Implementing the United Nations 'Protect, Respect and Remedy' Framework*, A/HRC/17/31 (21.03.2011).

binding standards to regulate corporate conduct in the field of human rights.[2] Although businesses generally tend to have a positive impact on social and economic development, the negative consequences of their activities need to be addressed in order to protect human rights, especially of the most vulnerable groups in society. An important global movement in favour of corporate responsibility in the field of human rights, based on the UNGPs and other international instruments and led mostly by some developed economies, has nevertheless had a relatively low impact in the areas where such rules are required the most: in developing countries. It is precisely in some of these countries – and notably in Ecuador, where the activities of national and foreign oil companies have had a severe impact on the environment and local communities[3] – that such abuses have led to a call to develop stronger human rights obligations for corporations.

Different areas of Africa, Asia and Latin America are among the regions where such standards have yet to make an important – or even significant – impact. Particularly in the case of Latin America, the UNGPs are just starting to become referred to by governments and companies, despite the support received in the process leading to their adoption in 2011.[4] This situation has been generally reflected in the process related to the establishment of the Open-ended Intergovernmental Working Group on transnational corporations and other business enterprises with respect to human rights, and later on during its two initial sessions. It is therefore necessary to scale up the efforts in the region to ensure that corporations respect human rights and that States are aware of their duties under international human rights law; such efforts, however, need to be implemented both nationally and regionally if progress is to be achieved.

This chapter, divided into three substantive sections, will first address the position of Latin American States regarding the treaty process, including during the initial two sessions of the Intergovernmental Working Group. Secondly, the initial steps being taken in the region will be analysed, including the recent

---

2 Office of the High Commissioner for Human Rights, *Council establishes Working Group on human rights and transnational corporations and other business enterprises* (16.06.2011), available at <http://www.ohchr.org/en/NewsEvents/Pages/DisplayNews.aspx?NewsID=11165> (accessed 28.01.2016); S Deva, 'Treating Human Rights Lightly: A Critique of the Consensus Rhetoric and the Language Employed by the Guiding Principles' in S Deva and D Bilchitz (eds), *Human Rights Obligations of Business: Beyond the Corporate Responsibility to Respect?*, Cambridge University Press, Cambridge 2013, pp 90–91.

3 For a full review and profile of the Ecuadorian saga, which led to the start of the treaty process, see Business & Human Rights Resource Centre, *Texaco/Chevron lawsuits (re Ecuador)*, available at <http://business-humanrights.org/en/texacochevron-lawsuits-re-ecuador> (accessed 27.05.2016).

4 E Godoy, 'Lip-Service but Little Action on UN Business and Human Rights Principles in Latin America', *Inter-Press Service* (21.03.2015), available at <http://www.ipsnews.net/2015/03/lip-service-but-little-action-on-u-n-business-and-human-rights-principles-in-latin-america/> (accessed 29.01.2016).

institutional and country developments in this field, as well as the involvement of the UN Working Group on Business and Human Rights in promoting and facilitating the use of the UN Guiding Principles in the Americas. Finally, a brief analysis will be made on the role that the Inter-American Human Rights System needs to play in the field of business and human rights, in order to contribute indirectly to the global standard-setting effort in this field.

2. THE TREATY RESOLUTION AND THE POSITION OF LATIN AMERICAN STATES DURING THE FIRST AND SECOND SESSIONS OF THE TREATY PROCESS

During the 26th session of the Human Rights Council in June 2014 the South African delegation filed a motion to start a process to develop a binding international instrument on the responsibilities of transnational corporations and other business enterprises with regard to human rights. This motion, supported by the Ecuadorian delegation (which was not a Council member at the time), was the result of a call by Ecuador[5] to develop a binding instrument on business and human rights in September 2013, largely as a result of its (still) ongoing dispute with Chevron over environmental damage and resulting human rights violations in the Lago Agrio region.[6]

The draft resolution, recalling the UN Guiding Principles on Business and Human Rights endorsed by the Human Rights Council in 2011 and recognising the differentiated but complementary roles corresponding to the State, corporations and civil society in relation to human rights, advocated for the establishment of an Open-ended Intergovernmental Working Group to develop under international human rights law a binding international instrument to regulate transnational corporations and other business enterprises.[7]

As was largely expected, the South African proposal was met with support from numerous Global South countries and with opposition from most of

---

5 Republic of Ecuador, *Statement on behalf of a Group of Countries at the 24rd Session of the Human Rights Council* (01.09.2013), available at <http://business-humanrights.org/sites/default/files/media/documents/statement-unhrc-legally-binding.pdf> (accessed 29.01.2016).

6 On this case, see PM Barret, 'Amazon Crusader. Chevron Pest. Fraud?', *Bloomberg Businessweek* (09.03.2011), available at <http://www.bloomberg.com/bw/magazine/content/11_12/b4220056636512.htm> (accessed 29.01.2016); see also Business & Human Rights Resource Centre, *Ecuador*, available at <http://business-humanrights.org/en/regions-countries/americas/ecuador> (accessed 29.01.2016) for updated information on the Chevron oil pollution case in Ecuador.

7 Human Rights Council, *Elaboration of an international legally binding instrument on transnational corporations and other business enterprises with respect to human rights*, A/HRC/RES/26/9 (26.06.2014) §1.

the Western group. Those in favour included most countries of the African group,[8] several Asian nations,[9] and Cuba and Venezuela from the Group of Latin America and the Caribbean (GRULAC) States. The sharply divided vote, however, was far from the expected North–South division:[10] with 13 abstentions (mostly from market-oriented economies from Latin American, Asian and some African States),[11] it was a clear indication that the globalisation process and the preference for a market economy had reached several developing countries, which would rather not commit to a cause that may endanger much-needed foreign direct investment for the economic and social well-being of the country.[12]

In the case of Latin American States, it is remarkable how divided the position of most countries was in the voting pattern, considering their previous preferences in past UN efforts to further corporate accountability.[13] The fact that most GRULAC countries decided to abstain from voting,[14] particularly those with pro-free market economic policies, reveals the enormous discrepancy – and the lack of a singular regional approach – within the Latin American region as to the need to establish specific regulations directed to business.

While it was expected that Organisation for Economic Co-operation and Development (OECD) member States or candidates (Mexico, Chile, Colombia

---

8 Algeria, Benin, Burkina Faso, Congo, Côte d'Ivoire, Ethiopia, Kenya, Morocco, Namibia and South Africa.

9 China, India, Indonesia, Kazakhstan, Pakistan, Philippines, Russian Federation and Vietnam.

10 O De Schutter, 'Towards a New Treaty on Business and Human Rights' (2015) 1 *Business and Human Rights Journal* 41, 43, where he argues that the gap between States 'is less wide than the voting patterns seem to suggest'.

11 The abstaining States were Argentina, Botswana, Brazil, Chile, Costa Rica, Gabon, Kuwait, Maldives, Mexico, Peru, Saudi Arabia, Sierra Leone and the United Arab Emirates.

12 On this topic, see L Colen, M Maertens and J Swinnen, 'Foreign Direct Investment as an Engine for Economic Growth and Human Development: A Review of the Arguments and Empirical Evidence' in O De Schutter, J Swinnen and J Wouters (eds), *Foreign Direct Investment and Human Development: The Law and Economics of International Investment Agreements*, Routledge, London 2013.

13 Consider, for example, the position of most developing countries during the new international economic order era (where Mexico, for example, was a strong supporter of the development of a new international economic balance), or specifically in relation to the development of a code of conduct on transnational corporations (where again, Mexican and Chilean diplomats played a pivotal role during the negotiations, both at the Working Group created to that end or during the ensuing negotiations at the UN Commission on Transnational Corporations). On this experience, see T Sagafi-Nejad and JH Dunning, *The UN and Transnational Corporations: From Code of Conduct to Global Compact*, Indiana University Press, Bloomington 2008. It is also important to consider how all GRULAC States voted in favour of endorsing the UN Guiding Principles in 2011 (however, see n 2).

14 R Freedman and J Mchangama, 'Expanding or Diluting Human Rights?: The Proliferation of United Nations Special Procedures Mandates' (2016) 38 *Human Rights Quarterly* 164, 176: 'Countries may abstain from the vote, which in itself can be quite telling. Abstentions are a method of registering non-acceptance of a particular provision or of the need for a mandate even if a country agrees with the right itself.'

and Costa Rica, as well as other partner States such as Brazil) would not be particularly favourable to such a proposal, the lack of a clear position is a glimpse of the delicate balance on which attracting foreign direct investments rests, as well as of the pressure that emerging economies are subjected to by their more developed peers. It may also reflect how most countries are beginning to consider how to move forward from the relative 'success' of the Guiding Principles, and perhaps also the belief that more time is needed to evaluate their actual impact in curbing negative effects on human rights as a result of business activities. Whichever may be the case, it is clear that Ecuador has been pushing for binding international human rights standards for corporations for a long time, and thus, seeing the relatively slow pace at which States and corporations were starting to use the UN Guiding Principles, decided to call for a 'harder' approach to corporate human rights responsibility.

The first session of the Open-ended Intergovernmental Working Group on transnational corporations and other business enterprises with regard to human rights (hereinafter referred to as the 'treaty process' or the 'Intergovernmental Working Group') took place in early July 2015.[15] With the presence of most Latin American States, as well as many African and Asian delegations (and a limited number of Western delegations, including France and the European Union), the session was interrupted abruptly shortly after it started.

The EU and some of its member States called for the inclusion of a panel – in a particularly full agenda – on the relevance and degree of implementation of the UNGPs, and for the modification of Resolution 26/9 to include the word 'all' before 'other business enterprises' in its controversial footnote;[16] as a result of these requests, diplomatic negotiations ensued in order to overcome the impasse that delayed the start of the session for half a day. The Western group threatened that lack of inclusion or accommodation of such requests would be 'non-starters' for them, which would be a particularly discouraging start to the session for the rest of the participating delegations, given their interest in having a broad representation.

15 For a more accurate analysis of the different aspects that were discussed and addressed during the first session of the Intergovernmental Working Group, see H Cantú Rivera, '¿Hacia un tratado internacional sobre la responsabilidad de las empresas en el ámbito de los derechos humanos? Reflexiones sobre la primera sesión del Grupo de trabajo intergubernamental de composición abierta' (2016) XVI *Anuario Mexicano de Derecho Internacional* 425. See also C Lopez and B Shea, 'Negotiating a Treaty on Business and Human Rights: A Review of the First Intergovernmental Session' (2015) 1 *Business and Human Rights Journal* 111.

16 Human Rights Council, *Elaboration of an international legally binding instrument on transnational corporations and other business enterprises with respect to human rights*, A/HRC/RES/26/9 (26.06.2014). The resolution includes the following footnote: '"Other business enterprises" denotes all business enterprises that have a transnational character in their operational activities, and does not apply to local businesses registered in terms of relevant domestic law.' The purpose of the modification was to make the proposed instrument binding on all business enterprises, regardless of their national or transnational character.

A proposal by the Mexican delegation to focus globally on corporations regardless of the transnational or national character of their operations, as well as to accommodate the panel on the UNGPs, given the precise reference of Resolution 26/9 to the Guiding Principles, helped to unblock the negotiations. Another proposal by Uruguay, supported by Chile and Mexico, to postpone the debate on whether the footnote should be modified, in order to start the session, finally allowed the participating delegations to overcome the procedural impasse.

Under the lead of Ecuador (whose ambassador was elected Chair of the Intergovernmental Working Group as a result of prior negotiations), the modified agenda for the session unfolded in an orderly fashion and without further interruptions.[17] It must be noted that the ideological gap that was evident in the voting patterns on Resolution 26/9 was reproduced throughout the first session: with the exception of Ecuador, Cuba, Venezuela and Bolivia (who actively proposed the establishment of a binding treaty for transnational corporations), the rest of the Latin American delegations barely participated, and when they did it was notably to pose questions to the panellists on specific points of interest or to make general statements, rather than to relay their positions vis-à-vis certain issues or questions.

While some of those questions did contribute to the general debate during the session (particularly in relation to the normative hierarchy under international law, or regarding universal civil jurisdiction and the use of *forum necessitatis*),[18] a more active role would have been useful to provide a clearer insight on the possible route or position that the region as a whole would be adopting. However, the clear support for the UNGPs and the reluctance to engage more actively in the treaty discussions already speaks to the difficulties that most States (not only in Latin America, but elsewhere) will have to face: either to continue encouraging corporations to adopt measures to respect human rights with the corresponding national differences and the oversight of States, or to pursue the development and eventual adoption of an international, legally binding instrument, with the risk of facing rejection and divestment in host States by corporations who may feel threatened by their position regarding the treaty. While theoretically such a binding instrument could be directly applicable to corporations under international human rights law,[19] the most likely form that such a treaty would

---

17 However, during the second day, most Western States' delegations decided to abandon the session, or to leave minimal personnel to cover the discussions, without intervening substantively for the remainder of the panels.

18 On the concept and (sporadic) use of *forum necessitatis*, see S Redfield, 'Searching for Justice: The Use of Forum Necessitatis' (2014) 45 *Georgetown Journal of International Law* 893.

19 This was one of the main arguments posited by Professor Chip Pitts during the first session of the treaty process; see generally J Letnar Černič and T Van Ho (eds), *Human Rights and Business: Direct Corporate Accountability for Human Rights*, Wolf Legal Publishers, Nijmegen 2015.

adopt – if States effectively look to ensure the largest ratification possible – would be a traditional, State-centric approach to regulate corporate activities and behaviour within their corresponding jurisdiction.[20]

The second session of the treaty process took place in late October 2016, and contrary to the first session, EU Member States did engage in the discussions, although limitedly and especially in relation to the necessary implementation of the UNGPs in order to effectively protect human rights. Some other States, such as Brazil, had a more active approach to the discussions, insisting on several legal issues and concepts and showing a genuine interest in pursuing the development of an international legally binding framework on business and human rights. The rest of the Latin American States attending the session (with the exception of Cuba, Venezuela, Bolivia and Ecuador, who repeated their role of the first session) engaged in moderate participation, suggesting elements from other legal forums that could be important for the negotiation stage, such as the domestic implementation method suggested by the project on crimes against humanity of the International Law Commission.[21] While going into detail as to the width and depth of discussions during the second session is beyond the scope of this chapter,[22] two main key points emerged: the apparent general belief that any prospective treaty will necessarily have to be built upon the foundations laid down by the Guiding Principles, and that it will have to focus on covering the existing governance and policy gaps at the domestic and international level in order to ensure more effective access to remedy for victims; and inter-State cooperation in the investigation, prosecution and execution of judgments in civil and criminal cases involving human rights violations by corporate actors.

In relation to the first point, it is relatively clear that there is sufficient political support beyond the Guiding Principles to have them as a starting point for the treaty negotiations – even from those States that are in favour of developing binding international standards and that have been critical of the UNGPs. That fact is not to be understated, given the complex relationship between law and politics that exists in any treaty-drafting process, and the necessary degree of consensus among States with different legal, political, social and economic realities to move the project forward.[23] The second point is also important: an effective

20 De Schutter, above n 10, pp 44–66.

21 International Law Commission, *Report of the International Law Commission*, A/71/10 (2016), §84, art. 5.7. This point was raised by the Mexican delegation.

22 For further references on the second session of the Intergovernmental Working Group, see C López, 'Struggling to Take Off?: The Second Session of Intergovernmental Negotiations on a Treaty on Business and Human Rights' (2017) 2 *Business and Human Rights Journal* 365; H Cantú Rivera, 'Negotiating a Treaty on Business and Human Rights: The Early Stages' (2017) 40 *UNSW Law Journal* (forthcoming).

23 W Tijerina Sepúlveda, 'Post-Cold War Implications on Comparative Law: The Misguided Enthusiasm for Legal Transplants and its Effects on Latin America' (2014) 2 *International Relations and Diplomacy* 518, 524ff.

treaty is not likely to focus on developing entirely new standards, but rather on filling the legal lacunae that exist at the international level, in order to standardise national approaches towards specific aspects of the business and human rights field, in particular those that sit on grey areas that allow for human rights abuses to go unpunished.

It is certainly unrealistic to expect all States to have a defined position regarding the adoption of a treaty on business and human rights without at least the completion of a draft instrument.[24] That is exactly the reason why the first two sessions were devoted to the analysis of the basis for the proposed international instrument.[25] However, precisely in order to define the content that should be included in said instrument – particularly now that the Intergovernmental Working Group is entering the negotiating stage – wide participation of States is necessary to ensure that all the experiences – both positive and negative – in hosting businesses with transnational operations in their territories are clearly (and collectively) reflected upon, as well as ensuring commitment from home States in developing adequate and accessible remedies. As this treaty project moves forward, the different Latin American governments should undertake profound national consultations with the participation of all stakeholders – including victims, civil society organisations and government officials – in order to define a preliminary position in relation to the issues and topics that will be addressed.[26]

3. FIRST STEPS TOWARDS THE IMPLEMENTATION OF THE UN GUIDING PRINCIPLES IN THE AMERICAS

The Latin American region has taken cautious steps in the implementation of the UNGPs. While numerous developments that intersect the different aspects addressed by the UNGPs have been on the regional agenda for the better part of the last three decades (such as due diligence or the rights of indigenous peoples), few (albeit relevant) steps have been taken to bring the three pillars of the UN instrument into the regional sphere and onto its political and legal agendas. A series of institutional and country developments have started to pave the way for a larger role of the Guiding Principles in the continent, while several actions in partnership with the UN Working Group on Business and Human Rights have contributed to provide more visibility to the UNGPs in the region.

---

24 In effect, that has been the position of most Latin American and other States: not to pronounce themselves in any sense until a draft instrument has been completed.

25 Human Rights Council, *Elaboration of an international legally binding instrument on transnational corporations and other business enterprises with respect to human rights*, A/HRC/RES/26/9 (26.06.2014) §2.

26 Lopez and Shea, above n 15, p 116.

3.1. INSTITUTIONAL DEVELOPMENT IN THE ORGANISATION OF AMERICAN STATES

The General Assembly of the Organization of American States (OAS) adopted a resolution[27] in June 2014 whereby it requested the Committee on Juridical and Political Affairs to hold a special meeting in order to exchange best practices and experiences in relation to the promotion and protection of human rights in the business sphere in early 2015.[28] The Committee held the special session in January 2015 with the participation of numerous Latin American States, OAS officials, civil society organisations, the Latin American member of the UN Working Group on Business and Human Rights[29] and business representatives. While the session was held for the exchange of best practices, on several occasions the contributions of States centred on how they promoted corporate social responsibility within their jurisdictions,[30] which conceptually is very different from the legally oriented discourse on the obligation of business to respect human rights.[31] Ecuador, on the other hand, continued promoting the need to establish a binding international instrument to regulate corporate behaviour and impact on human rights.[32]

The first session on this topic at the OAS was followed in late June 2015 by a second meeting between the (newly appointed) Latin American member of the UN Working Group on Business and Human Rights and several OAS missions, to discuss the state of implementation of the UNGPs and challenges faced by the different States.[33] In addition, a cooperation agreement between

---

27 General Assembly, *Promotion and Protection of Human Rights in Business*, AG/RES. 2840 (XLIV-O/14 (04.06.2014) §5.

28 This decision was the result of two previous developments: first, a report adopted by the Inter-American Juridical Committee on 'Guidelines Concerning Corporate Social Responsibility in the Area of Human Rights and the Environment in the Americas' (CJI/doc.449/14 rev.1), presented a few months earlier, in March 2014; and secondly, as a continuation of the First Latin America and Caribbean Regional Forum on Business and Human Rights, which will be commented upon later.

29 At the time Alexandra Guáqueta, a Colombian national, replaced in April 2015 by Dante Pesce from Chile.

30 Committee on Juridical and Political Affairs, *Summary of the meeting of January 29, 2015*, CP/CAJP/SA-560/15 (18.02.2015). Notable exceptions were the contributions of Chile and Colombia, two of the leading Latin American States working on business and human rights.

31 For an analysis of this difference, see A Ramasastry, 'Corporate Social Responsibility Versus Business and Human Rights: Bridging the Gap Between Responsibility and Accountability' (2015) 14 *Journal of Human Rights* 237.

32 The footnote added to the resolution requesting the meeting sets forth: 'Ecuador wishes to underscore the efforts undertaken in the United Nations and in other bodies to develop a binding international instrument on Human Rights and Transnational Enterprises …'; General Assembly, *Promotion and Protection of Human Rights in Business*, AG/RES. 2840 (XLIV-O/14) (04.06.2014). The Ecuadorian delegation insisted on this position during the special meeting.

33 For a more thorough discussion on the specific contents addressed at the meeting, see P Muñoz Quick, 'UN Working Group on Business and Human Rights meets with OAS

the Danish Institute for Human Rights and the Inter-American Commission on Human Rights to develop capacity in the region was signed,[34] and the topic has been included in the work stream of the (recently created) Special Rapporteur on Economic, Social and Cultural Rights of the Inter-American Commission.[35] Finally, a couple of resolutions addressing this question were adopted during the 46th session of the General Assembly of the OAS in Santo Domingo in 2016, one focusing on fostering the implementation of the Guiding Principles,[36] the other one on actively participating and engaging with the global treaty initiative, as well as with any other that may develop regionally.[37]

While these developments are important, it would be particularly convenient for the OAS and its different bodies (including the Inter-American Commission on Human Rights) to design a regional action plan on this issue, in order to have a clear scheme that would allow it to scale up the efforts and abandon the piecemeal approach that so far has characterised its work.[38] Such an approach could probably address important questions, such as the adoption of regional policies to improve the work and capacities of national human rights institutions in this field, the development of regional multi-stakeholder forums on corporate responsibility in the field of human rights, and even strategic initiatives in the work of the Inter-American Human Rights System.[39]

3.2. NATIONAL DEVELOPMENTS IN RELATION TO THE BUSINESS AND HUMAN RIGHTS AGENDA

In addition to the institutional initiatives that have been taking place in the regional organisation, some country developments are also starting to appear

Missions', *B&HR in the Americas* (05.07.2015), available at <https://bhramericasblog.wordpress.com/2015/07/05/un-working-group-on-business-and-human-rights-meets-with-oas-missions/> (accessed 29.01.2016).

34 The Danish Institute for Human Rights, *Collaboration on human rights and business starts with the Americas* (29.05.2015), available at <http://www.humanrights.dk/news/collaboration-human-rights-business-starts-americas> (accessed 29.01.2016).

35 It is important to note that the Unit on Economic, Social and Cultural Rights of the Inter-American Commission (pending the final establishment of the position of Special Rapporteur) is currently considering issuing its 2017 thematic report on the topic of business and human rights.

36 General Assembly, *Promotion and Protection of Human Rights*, AG/RES. 2887 (XLVI-O/16) (14.06.2016), §§I.ii (*Promotion and Protection of Human Rights in Business*).

37 *Ibid.*, §§I.iii (*Conscious and Effective Regulation of Business in the Area of Human Rights*).

38 It must be noted that the 2017–2021 Strategic Plan of the Commission does include several strategies to continue advancing the implementation of the UNGPs in the region. For a comparison with the EU process, see H Cantú Rivera, 'Regional Approaches in the Business & Human Rights Field' (2013) 35 *L'Observateur des Nations-Unies* 53.

39 For a more detailed analysis of possible work streams, see H Cantú Rivera, 'The UN Guiding Principles in the Americas: Moving Forward?', *Measuring Business & Human Rights* (24.12.2015), available at <http://blogs.lse.ac.uk/businesshumanrights/2015/12/24/un-forum-series-the-un-guiding-principles-in-the-americas/> (accessed 29.01.2016).

in the Americas. While referring to particular cases or legislative developments in specific countries is beyond the scope of this chapter,[40] it is nevertheless important to address the overall situation in the region to identify the speed at which domestic policies are being adopted to deal with business and human rights issues.

At the time of writing, five States in the region (Chile, Argentina, Brazil, Mexico and Guatemala) are at different phases in the development of National Action Plans[41] (NAP) to implement the UNGPs. So far, only one Latin American State has produced a NAP: Colombia, where its Action Plan on Human Rights and Business[42] was adopted in December 2015. While going into detail on Colombia's National Action Plan would be a particularly interesting exercise due to its focus not only on the general business and human rights discussion, but also on its role in the construction of peace, the following remarks will have to be relatively succinct, due to space constraints and the need to address other relevant issues and situations developing in the Americas.

Colombia's Action Plan on Human Rights and Business follows the structure of the UN Guiding Principles, and is thus divided into three sections (related to State action and its duty to protect, the corporate responsibility to respect human rights, and the need for adequate access to remedy). It is the result of a significant number of multi-stakeholder consultations undertaken in 2012 and 2013, which produced the *Guidelines for a Public Policy on Human Rights and Business*[43] in 2014. These guidelines were the baseline for the adopted NAP, which follows several principles that mirror some of John Ruggie's own recommendations in the Guiding Principles,[44] while also denoting a specific

40 Further references can be found in the Government Action Platform of the Business & Human Rights Resource Centre's website, available at <http://business-humanrights.org/en/government-action-platform> (accessed 29.01.2016).

41 The UN Working Group understands National Action Plans as 'evolving policy strategies developed by States to prevent and protect against human rights abuses by business enterprises in conformity with the Guiding Principles on Business and Human Rights. In national action plans, States take stock of what they are already doing to implement the Guiding Principles and identify gaps which require further policy action to implement the Guiding Principles'. Working Group on the issue of human rights and transnational corporations and other business enterprises, *Human rights and transnational corporations and other business enterprises. Note by the Secretary-General*, A/69/263 (05.08.2014) §6. *Cf.* H Cantú Rivera, 'Planes de acción nacional sobre empresas y derechos humanos: sobre la instrumentalización del derecho internacional en el ámbito interno' (2017) XVII *Anuario Mexicano de Derecho Internacional* 113.

42 Gobierno de Colombia, *Plan Nacional de Acción sobre Derechos Humanos y Empresas*, 2015.

43 Gobierno de Colombia, *Lineamientos para una Política Pública de Derechos Humanos y Empresas* (2014).

44 For example, the NAP focuses on the need to adopt a human rights-based approach, on the need for coherence with international standards, and on the importance of coordination and articulation with other public policies.

focus in creating a national framework that can be useful to the overall human rights and development strategy and needs of the country.[45]

The Action Plan contains 11 action guidelines, which are being developed (or will be developed) throughout the different governmental structures and administrative regions, with the active participation of corporations and civil society. The action guidelines will be steered by a Working Group on Human Rights and Business – integrated by officials from the different national ministries and public institutions – who will act as the steering and oversight body in charge of coordinating the national strategy. In addition to the role played by the Working Group, an expert commission – integrated with civil society organisations, unions, universities, the Colombian National Human Rights Institution and other entities – will undertake an advisory role in the implementation of the NAP.[46] The role of these two bodies, as well as their complementarity, will be instrumental for the proper implementation of the different actions foreseen in the Action Plan, as well as in ensuring a coordinated and efficient work stream.

In relation to the State duty to protect human rights, Colombia's NAP establishes several functions and principles to be performed by its institutions, such as the need for institutional coherence[47] (coordinated by the two aforementioned bodies), the role of the State as an economic actor[48] (particularly in relation to public procurement,[49] the inclusion of human rights clauses or criteria in commercial negotiations with other States,[50] or in the addition of human rights criteria in environmental impact assessments),[51] or the need to guarantee effective participation and monitoring by civil society.[52] Additionally, the Action Plan recognises the importance of providing guidance to companies on respecting human rights[53] in order to ensure their full understanding and involvement in the national strategy, as well as on defining human rights due diligence, providing guidance and developing mechanisms and tools to foster easier implementation by companies.[54] One noteworthy omission, however, is the lack of a formal reference to the need to instate corporate human rights due

45 Several autochthonous aspects of Colombia's NAP are its differential approach (to ensure that vulnerable groups are covered by the plan) and its territorial emphasis on former and current conflict zones, on addressing the role of business in a post-conflict context, and on the need for leadership in its implementation.

46 Gobierno de Colombia, *Plan Nacional de Acción sobre Derechos Humanos y Empresas* (2015) 10–12.

47 *Ibid* 10–12.

48 *Ibid* 12–13.

49 *Ibid* §2.1.

50 *Ibid* §2.3.

51 *Ibid* §2.6.

52 *Ibid* 13–14.

53 *Ibid* 14–15.

54 *Ibid* 16–17.

diligence as a legal requirement. The fact that this standard is not considered as a binding requirement under domestic law, but rather as a risk-measuring tool, can importantly undermine its effectiveness, and thus be used as a public relations exercise or instrument with no effect for the adequate protection of human rights.[55]

On the corporate responsibility to respect human rights, Colombia's NAP establishes the need to develop a corporate human rights culture that adds to its peace-building process,[56] with a particular emphasis on fostering the use of due diligence mechanisms.[57] In addition, it highlights the need to develop a culture that recognises respect for human rights as a competitive advantage and the use of yet-to-be defined incentives to support this development.[58] Finally, it addresses the importance of ensuring that corporate social responsibility actions revolve around the respect of human rights[59] in order to promote sustainability, risk-prevention and the advancement in the fulfilment of human rights.

As to the third pillar of the UNGPs, the NAP outlines the need to clearly identify existing obstacles that hinder effective access to judicial remedy[60] (including the need to map those challenges),[61] as well as the need to strengthen and foster the use of non-judicial mechanisms for access to remedy based on dialogue, mediation and/or arbitration.[62] Finally, in order to evaluate and follow up on the results of the Action Plan, the NAP establishes a timeline of three years during which it will be valid, before a global and final evaluation must be undertaken of its achievements and what challenges remain in its implementation.[63]

It is expected that Chile and Mexico will be the next States in Latin America to publish their own NAPs. Brazil, Guatemala and Argentina are still in the earlier stages of development of these projects. Regardless of the time it takes for them to fulfil their commitments, it is particularly important that their foreign policy on human rights is matched domestically by actions and policies that confirm those commitments, in order to avoid what would be an incoherent policy gap.

---

55 On the State duty to protect and the need to enact domestic legal requirements or modify legislation to give effect to the UN Guiding Principles, see JG Ruggie, *Just Business: Multinational Corporations and Human Rights*, W.W. Norton, New York 2013, pp 107–10. On corporate human rights due diligence and the need for binding legal requirements, see J Nolan, 'The Corporate Responsibility to Respect Human Rights: Soft Law or Not Law?' in S Deva and D Bilchitz (eds), *Human Rights Obligations of Business: Beyond the Corporate Responsibility to Respect?*, Cambridge University Press, Cambridge 2013, p 156.

56 Gobierno de Colombia, *Plan Nacional de Acción sobre Derechos Humanos y Empresas* (2015) 18.

57 *Ibid* 19–20.

58 *Ibid* 20–21.

59 *Ibid* 21–22.

60 *Ibid* 23.

61 *Ibid* §§10.2, 10.4.

62 *Ibid* 24.

63 *Ibid* 25.

Particularly for those States that have not pledged to develop a NAP (such as several of those most active in the treaty process), the adoption of domestic measures is necessary to ensure that potential victims of human rights abuses related to corporate activity have access to an effective remedy,[64] as well as to set forth the governmental expectation (or even the legal requirement) that corporations must respect human rights throughout their operations, and influence their supply chains to do so as well. In fact, as long as the appropriate legislative or regulatory adjustments are made, and public policies to address the impact of corporations on human rights are adopted, States do not need to undertake the development of a NAP.[65] To consider that there is only one way to address the issue of business and human rights is not necessarily correct; States have different forms of governance and levels of development, and thus the imposition of a model structure would not necessarily satisfy the particular needs of every single country. As John Ruggie himself recognised during his tenure as Special Representative on human rights and transnational corporations, one size does not necessarily fit all the different needs.

While it may appear easier to coordinate a national strategy through one single policy scheme, it is not necessarily the only way in which such issues can be addressed and thus different approaches could also be successful. Of particular importance is the need to ensure that legislative and regulatory reforms to address corporate responsibility in the field of human rights are adopted; without the permanent effect of a domestic legal requirement, public policies (and priorities) may change over time and thus leave potential or actual victims of corporate human rights abuses without protection.[66]

3.3. THE UN WORKING GROUP ON BUSINESS AND HUMAN RIGHTS IN THE AMERICAS: STRENGTHENING THE DISCUSSION, FURTHERING STATE ACTION

The UN Working Group on Business and Human Rights has had an increasingly involved relationship with the regional structures and States in the Americas. From the country visits to the United States of America in April 2013, to Brazil in December 2015, to Mexico in September 2016, and to Peru in 2017; to the first-ever Regional Forum on Business and Human Rights in Medellín, Colombia in September 2015; to the first meeting with OAS missions in June 2015,

64 S Deva, 'Guiding Principles on Business and Human Rights: Implications for Companies' (2012) 9(2) *European Company Law* 101, 104–05, where the author argues that States should take steps to overcome legal, practical or procedural barriers that could deny access to remedy.

65 Cantú Rivera, above n 41, 117.

66 S Deva, *Regulating Corporate Human Rights Violations: Humanizing Business*, Routledge, London 2012, p 209.

the regional consultation in Chile to discuss the issue of NAPs[67] in partnership with the Economic Commission for Latin American and the Caribbean in March 2016, and the regional seminar on the role of State-owned enterprises in relation to human rights[68] in Argentina in August 2016, the presence and activity of the Working Group in the region has successively increased. The same can be said of its work in relation to victims, where the use of communications has become an interesting tool for the UN Working Group to engage senior-level government officials (and four companies) in investigating and providing remedy to victims of corporate human rights violations.[69]

This increase has helped to foster dialogue on the convenience of using an authoritative framework such as the UNGPs in the region, as well as on adopting public policies to ensure positive contributions of businesses to the protection and fulfilment of human rights. It has also been instrumental in identifying and highlighting some of the main issues that are present in the region in relation to the impact of business in human rights. Considering the regional needs in terms of socioeconomic development, it is necessary to ensure that the common scenario throughout Latin America allows for 'win-win' situations where corporations can work profitably while also contributing to human rights and sustainable development.[70]

---

67 'Actores estatales y privados buscan estrategias para implementar estándares de empresas y derechos humanos en América Latina y el Caribe' (02.03.2016), available at <http://acnudh.org/actores-estatales-y-privados-buscan-estrategias-para-implementar-estandares-de-empresas-y-derechos-humanos-en-america-latina-y-el-caribe/> (accessed 21.11.2016).

68 'Primer Seminario Regional sobre Derechos Humanos y empresas de propiedad del Estado', (23.08.2016), available at <http://www.onu.org.ar/primer-seminario-regional-sobre-derechos-humanos-y-empresas-de-propiedad-del-estado/> (accessed 21 November 2016).

69 This does not necessarily mean that victims have had effective access to remedies; rather, it points to the fact that the Working Group has been in touch with Latin American governments to bring to their attention the communications sent by alleged victims. As the last communications report of Special Procedures shows (and the reports after the 23rd session of the Human Rights Council, when the Working Group started receiving allegation letters or urgent appeals from victims), 17 out of a total of 68 communications have been sent by the Working Group to different Latin American countries (Brazil has received four; Guatemala, four; Colombia, two; Honduras, two; Nicaragua, two; Mexico, Peru and Suriname, one each), and five have been sent to several companies (IAMGOLD Co., regarding its operations in Suriname; and BHP Billiton, Samarco Mining and Vale for the environmental disaster in Brazil). Eight of the communications sent to States have received responses, and all communications submitted to companies have been responded to. Human Rights Council, *Communications report of Special Procedures*, A/HRC/33/32 (09.09.2016); on the use and effectiveness of communications procedures, see C Rivera Diaz, 'Victims, Communications and the Special Procedures of the Human Rights Council' in H Cantú Rivera (ed), *The Special Procedures of the Human Rights Council*, Intersentia, Cambridge 2015, pp 127–44.

70 Such was the position of the UN Working Group prior to the first regional forum: 'The region needs jobs as well as social and economic inclusiveness. The UN Guiding Principles provide a solid platform to align business activities with human rights and sustainable development. Latin American culture has never questioned human rights. The region has a unique

One important obstacle, however, is the lack of awareness in relation to the implications of the UNGPs (and of human rights in general) for companies,[71] or the confusion of this debate with voluntary corporate social responsibility initiatives.[72] Another obstacle is the ineffectiveness of sanctions in civil law regimes, due to the fact that they are not deterrent (given the strict legality principle that usually limits economic sanctions to insignificant amounts)[73] or fail to address or effect change in harmful practices or policies.[74] These and other issues and obstacles were identified by the Working Group in its first Regional Forum in 2013, which nevertheless served to increase sensibility on this topic in the regional and national agendas, as well as to raise awareness on the need to address these types of issues from a human rights perspective.

The visit of the Working Group to Brazil in December 2015 served to measure more precisely and in a fact-finding manner the issues that exist generally in the country, but which replicate themselves throughout the region. In its end-of-visit statement,[75] the Working Group identified an alarming lack of awareness on the Guiding Principles, as well as a non-existent translation of the provisions in them into management activities of those companies that were aware of them. Of particular significance is the understanding by corporations of human rights risks as risks to the company, rather than as risks to the rights of vulnerable rights holders. While this is a more or less common trait worldwide, it does highlight the ineffectiveness of the initiatives undertaken so far to ensure that corporations appropriately understand their responsibility to respect human

---

opportunity to become a champion on business and human rights, bolster its competitiveness in the global market, and respond to social needs ...'. Working Group on the issue of human rights and transnational corporations and other business enterprises, *The impact of businesses on human rights in Latin American and the Caribbean – First regional debate* (26.08.2013), available at <http://www.ohchr.org/EN/NewsEvents/Pages/DisplayNews.aspx?NewsID=13658&LangID=E> (accessed 29.01.2016).

71 Working Group on the issue of human rights and transnational corporations and other business enterprises, *Report on the First Latin America and Caribbean Regional Forum on Business and Human Rights*, A/HRC/26/25/Add.2 (24.04.2014) §20. The report highlights, for example, that companies have difficulties in cases dealing with consumer protection, land use, or the respect of the rights of indigenous peoples, while some other core issues, such as labour standards or children's rights, are more easily dealt with.

72 *Ibid* §6.

73 Although it must be mentioned that some recent examples have proved otherwise (i.e. the cases of Chevron in Ecuador, and BHP Billiton and Vale in Brazil), where important economic sanctions have been imposed on perpetrators of environmental damage and human rights violations.

74 Working Group on the issue of human rights and transnational corporations and other business enterprises, *Report on the First Latin America and Caribbean Regional Forum on Business and Human Rights*, A/HRC/26/25/Add.2 (24.04.2014) §27.

75 Working Group on the issue of human rights and transnational corporations and other business enterprises, *Statement at the end of visit to Brazil by the United Nations Working Group on Business and Human Rights* (16.12.2015), available at <http://www.ohchr.org/EN/NewsEvents/Pages/DisplayNews.aspx?NewsID=16891&LangID=E> (accessed 29.01.2016).

rights.[76] Several of these patterns were also found by the Working Group during its visit to Mexico in August and September 2016.[77]

Both visits also raised concerns about the lack of instruction or guidance from governments to companies in relation to the UNGPs, and to the low level of oversight on projects once they had been approved and the licences awarded. In relation to Brazil, the Working Group highlighted the need to ensure that regulation by the State is not undermined by its investment commitments or development projects, and that there is a growing need to avoid corporate capture of regulatory and policy-making processes.[78] This same reality was recognised in the case of Mexico.[79]

These issues, shortcomings and obstacles are to a greater or lesser degree common throughout Latin America. In particular, the power imbalance when negotiating bilateral investment agreements with developed economies, and the powerlessness to stand against powerful corporate actors to regulate or legislate for the public good (under the threat of arbitration), have greatly reduced the State's ability to protect human rights, and thus, to fulfil its international obligations.[80] Nevertheless, not all of these issues can be attributed to such obstacles; when making balancing decisions, States must realise that it is realistically possible to ensure that both sustainable development and human rights protection are compatible with development projects and foreign direct investment. Adopting a position that allows them to negotiate projects that can positively contribute to social and economic development, while also setting forth clauses that ensure human rights protection and the regulatory capacity of the State, is necessary in order to ensure that both corporations and States

---

76 Working Group on the issue of human rights and transnational corporations and other business enterprises, *Report of the Working Group on the issue of human rights and transnational corporations and other business enterprises on its mission to Brazil*, A/HRC/32/45/Add.1 (12.05.2016).

77 Working Group on the issue of human rights and transnational corporations and other business enterprises, *Statement at the end of visit to Mexico by the United Nations Working Group on Business and Human Rights* (07.09.2016), available at <http://www.ohchr.org/EN/NewsEvents/Pages/DisplayNews.aspx?NewsID=20466&LangID=E> (accessed 21.11.2016).

78 *Ibid.*

79 Working Group on the issue of human rights and transnational corporations and other business enterprises, *Report of the Working Group on the issue of human rights and transnational corporations and other business enterprises on its mission to Mexico*, A/HRC/35/32/Add.2 (27.04.2017).

80 On the issue of investment protection and corporate capture of policy space, see JE Alvarez, *The Public International Law Regime Governing International Investment*, Brill, Leiden 2011, pp 413–14; for a more nuanced approach focused on the possible interactions between the UNGPs and the investment arbitration regime, see E Prieto Ríos and A Amaya, 'Los Principios Rectores sobre empresas y derechos humanos y la práctica legal en el arbitraje de inversión respecto del derecho internacional de los derechos humanos' in H Cantú Rivera (ed), *Derechos humanos y empresas: reflexiones desde América Latina*, IIDH, San José 2017, pp 405–21.

fulfil their own responsibilities while also obtaining benefits. The role of the UN Working Group will be of particular relevance to continue embedding the discussion on business and human rights in government policies and legislation, as well as to ensure that this topic continues advancing steadily throughout the region, both at institutional and country levels.

In general, these first steps in the region to introduce the UN Guiding Principles on Business and Human Rights into legal frameworks, public policies and the daily activities of States and businesses have had a positive effect. However, it is important that more States commit to ensuring that their domestic legal frameworks and policies have the appropriate focus and sufficient force to ensure that corporations respect human rights, be it through a National Action Plan or through other policies or regulations. One way in which such developments could be accelerated would be through cooperation in the work of the regional human rights institutions, which to some extent are well respected by the States in the Americas. In this sense, the Inter-American Human Rights System has an important role to fulfil in order to close the gap existing among States in relation to the protection of human rights from business-related negative impacts.[81]

4. A CHANGING ROLE FOR THE INTER-AMERICAN HUMAN RIGHTS SYSTEM: HUMAN RIGHTS DUE DILIGENCE

Writing about how the Inter-American Human Rights System may play a vital role in advancing the business and human rights discussion in the Americas could easily command (and deserves) a thorough exploration. However, this section will address a pivotal aspect that goes along the lines of work that have been so often explored by the two regional institutions in charge of the protection of human rights in the Americas, at the risk of neglecting many other important issues that are relevant to the reality of the region.[82] In this sense, the section will briefly address the question of human rights due diligence, with a particular emphasis on how the Inter-American System could contribute to ensuring that

[81] On this point, see K Salazar, 'Business and Human Rights: A New Challenge for the OAS?' (2015) 20 *Aportes DPLF* 9.

[82] For an extraordinary analysis on how the Inter-American system of human rights may contribute to developing the business and human rights agenda in the region, see N Carrillo Santarelli, 'La promoción y el desarrollo de la protección de los derechos humanos frente a abusos empresariales en el sistema interamericano' in H Cantú Rivera (ed), *Derechos humanos y empresas: reflexiones desde América Latina*, IIDH, San José 2017.

both States and corporations comply with their corresponding responsibilities stemming from the UN Guiding Principles on Business and Human Rights.[83]

The widely known dictum of *Velásquez Rodríguez* indicates that States will be internationally responsible not only for actions that are in violation of their international human rights commitments, but also for the actions of non-State actors[84] that may result in said violations, due to their lack of due diligence (omissions) in preventing them.[85] The due diligence doctrine has been explored in further detail in other judgments, including in several cases related to the rights of indigenous peoples dealing with private or communal property,[86] where it has evolved into a series of requirements that the State must satisfy in order to fulfil its international obligations. Such is the case, for example, for the obligation to perform environmental impact assessments as an element of the right to free, prior and informed consultation[87] with indigenous peoples before any activity or project that may impact upon their livelihoods is undertaken, and to provide timely information in a bidirectional and open dialogue with them. As can be observed (and has been widely discussed), this entails obligations of means, which imply for the State the need to discharge its positive obligations to avoid a breach of international law.

As is also known, the Inter-American Human Rights System usually relies not only on its own international standards (either conventional or case law), but also on external sources of international law, including European human rights jurisprudence, UN resolutions and reports, and other conventions or treaties that may directly contribute to ensuring more inclusive human rights protection. In the case of the rights of indigenous peoples, for example, it has frequently referred to International Labour Organization Convention 169 on the rights of indigenous peoples, as well as to the UN Declaration on the Rights of Indigenous Peoples, or to the reports issued by the Special Rapporteur on this theme. This constant interaction between international human rights systems allows for a progressive and dynamic interpretation that seeks to foster the

---

83 It has already taken its first steps: *Case of the Kaliña and Lokono Peoples v. Suriname* (IACtHR, 25.11.2015) §§222–226; *Case of the Hacienda Brasil Verde Workers v. Brazil* (IACtHR, 20.10.2016) §317.

84 O de Frouville, 'Private Individuals' in J Crawford, A Pellet and S Olleson (eds), *The Law of International Responsibility*, Oxford University Press, Oxford 2010, p 257.

85 *Velásquez Rodríguez v. Honduras* (IACtHR, 29.07.1988) §172. On this point, see also F Latty, 'Actions and Omissions' in J Crawford, A Pellet and S Olleson (eds), *The Law of International Responsibility*, Oxford University Press, Oxford 2010, p 355.

86 Some of the most recent examples involving indigenous peoples' rights are *Case of the Saramaka People v. Suriname* (IACtHR, 28.11.2007) §§129, 146, 154; *Case of the Kichwa Indigenous People of Sarayaku v. Ecuador* (IACtHR, 27.06.2012) §§177ff.

87 See U Khatri, 'Indigenous Peoples' Right to Free, Prior, and Informed Consent in the Context of State-Sponsored Development: The New Standard Set by Sarayaku v. Ecuador and its Potential to Delegitimize the Belo Monte Dam' (2013) 29(1) *American University International Law Review* 165.

pro homine principle,[88] and thus to provide the greatest protection possible to the rights of vulnerable groups.

These two elements (the concept of human rights due diligence and the use of international standards) are of particular relevance for the Inter-American Human Rights System in relation to corporate responsibility in the field of human rights. First of all, the fact that Inter-American case law has recognised the existence of a State obligation to act diligently in order to prevent human rights abuses by non-State actors includes a duty to protect from abuses caused by third parties such as corporations. This duty entails, of course, obligations to prevent, investigate, sanction and provide redress for human rights violations committed by corporations; however, it also implies that the State must adopt the appropriate policies, legislation and regulations necessary to ensure that such abuses are adequately covered by its legal framework.[89]

In this sense, taking into consideration the margin of action that the State has to adopt domestic measures that aim to prevent human rights violations (including by non-State actors), it is conceivable that States would be inclined to regulate within their domestic sphere the activities of corporations in relation to their impact on human rights, in order to fulfil their obligations of means[90] under international human rights law.[91] If such a route were to be adopted, States could impose upon corporations direct duties to undertake their own human rights due diligence as a matter of domestic law, in order to make sure that their operations do not infringe upon the rights of stakeholders that may be affected by their activities. This corporate human rights due diligence could include the duties to perform human rights impact assessments prior to and

88 The *pro homine* principle, also known as *pro persona* principle, is an interpretative method commonly used by the Inter-American Human Rights System, based on the search for the most protective principle under international human rights law. See A Rodiles, 'The Law and Politics of the *Pro Persona* Principle in Latin America' in HP Aust and G Nolte (eds), *The Interpretation of International Law by Domestic Courts: Uniformity, Diversity, Convergence*, Oxford University Press, Oxford 2016, p 162: 'In doctrine, it has been defined as "the hermeneutic criterion that informs the whole universal *corpus* of human rights". Departing from this, it is said that pro persona enables the judge to depart as much as possible, "in a positive sense", from the core of the human right at hand, in order to construe its widest expression.'

89 Special Representative of the Secretary-General on the issue of human rights and transnational corporations and other business enterprises, *Guiding Principles on Business and Human Rights: Implementing the United Nations 'Protect, Respect and Remedy' Framework*, A/HRC/17/31 (21.03.2011) §1.

90 CP Economides, 'Content of the Obligation: Obligations of Means and Obligations of Result' in J Crawford, A Pellet and S Olleson (eds), *The Law of International Responsibility*, Oxford University Press, Oxford 2010, p 371.

91 Indeed, the Court seems to suggest such a position when it says '... because the State did not ensure that an independent social and environmental impact assessment was made prior to the start-up of bauxite mining, *and did not supervise the assessment that was made subsequently*, it failed to comply with this safeguard ...' (emphasis added); see *Case of the Kaliña and Lokono Peoples v. Suriname* (IACtHR, 25.11.2015) §226.

during project cycles, and to communicate those results both to the authorities and to potentially affected stakeholders.

Through the establishment of said regulatory measures, States could fulfil their international obligations while at the same time directly contributing not only to ensuring that corporate activities are respectful of human rights, but also to solidifying a standard[92] that has been internationally recognised in the UN Guiding Principles on Business and Human Rights and in other international instruments, such as the OECD Guidelines for Multinational Corporations.[93] Furthermore, the results of corporate human rights impact assessments could be analysed jointly with the environmental impact assessments mandated by Inter-American case law in order to ensure that environmental and human rights aspects are equally taken into account when deciding upon the feasibility of a given project.

The Inter-American System, through its decisions and judgments, could contribute to establishing a clear State duty to regulate corporate activities in a manner that is compatible with human rights, and particularly with the standards of the UNGPs. Together with a thorough examination of the different characteristics of the two impact assessments mentioned before, which could give way to a solidified impact assessment standard that requests that the State and third parties under its jurisdiction fulfil certain requirements in order to discharge their obligations of means, these measures could contribute to directly integrating the UNGPs into the Inter-American *jus commune*,[94] while also contributing to the development of some of their principles under international human rights law. A political statement or declaration in the regional sphere on this topic could also help to define a common position in relation to the expectations of States vis-à-vis corporate conduct in the Americas.[95]

---

92 H Cantú Rivera, 'Business & Human Rights: From a "Responsibility to Respect" to Legal Obligations and Enforcement' in J Letnar Černič and T Van Ho (eds), *Human Rights and Business: Direct Corporate Accountability for Human Rights*, Wolf Legal Publishers, Nijmegen 2015, pp 310ff; see also J Letnar Černič, 'Corporate Accountability for Human Rights: From a Top-Down to a Bottom-Up Approach' in J Martin and KE Bravo (eds), *The Business and Human Rights Landscape: Moving Forward, Looking Back*, Cambridge University Press, Cambridge 2016, pp 216–18.

93 Additionally, the organs of the Inter-American System could also base their judgments and decisions on other reports issued by the former Special Representative on the issue of human rights and transnational corporations and other business enterprises, or on those by the Working Group on business and human rights, who have examined the issues of indigenous peoples' rights in the context of corporate activity, or the ideal requirements for the development of NAPs, among others.

94 A Von Bogdandy, H Fix-Fierro and M Morales Antoniazzi (eds), *Ius Constitutionale Commune en América Latina: Rasgos, Potencialidades y Desafíos*, UNAM/Max Planck/IIDC, Mexico 2014. It has arguably already started to do so, following the judgments against Suriname in the case of the Kaliña & Lokono Peoples, and against Brazil in the case of the Hacienda Brasil Verde.

95 Cantú Rivera, above n 39.

The inclusion of such measures in the work of the Inter-American Commission on Human Rights and the Court could potentially also contribute to the development of State practice in the field of human rights and business, which could be useful for the treaty process currently underway. As a reflection of the current status of international human rights law in this topic, as well as adjudicative and regulatory measures by regional courts and States, respectively, these standards could probably contribute to ascertaining more clearly what may be acceptable rules to be imposed upon States in order to protect victims from corporate human rights abuses. The role of the Inter-American Commission and the Court in this field is particularly relevant, and their determinations in current or future cases involving corporate activity and State human rights due diligence could potentially help to move the discussion forward on the responsibilities – or obligations – of corporations under international human rights law.

5. CONCLUDING THOUGHTS

Having reviewed the positions of Latin American States during the process leading to and during the initial two sessions of the Intergovernmental Working Group on the elaboration of a binding international instrument on human rights and transnational corporations, as well as the different developments taking place regionally and nationally throughout the Americas, it is clear that efforts need to be scaled up if corporate responsibility in the field of human rights is to become a reality in the region. States need to play a much more proactive role in defining their priorities in this discussion,[96] as well as in adapting their domestic legal frameworks and public policies to rein in negative impacts of corporations on human rights. These actions are only some of the required first steps to be taken by States, which could nevertheless complement the treaty process by defining basic standards that are acceptable for inclusion in the draft instrument (or 'elements paper') that is to be presented in 2017.

The Inter-American System of Human Rights, on the other hand, can indirectly fill some of the gaps that may appear in this field through a constant use of the existing international standards on corporate responsibility in their decisions and judgments. Their role, perhaps yet unsuspected, will be essential in defining what the status quo is under international human rights law, and in ascertaining ways in which States can appropriately protect populations from human rights violations related to business activity.

---

96 Lopez and Shea, above n 15.

THE APPLICABILITY OF HUMAN RIGHTS TREATIES TO BUSINESS ENTERPRISES: A CASE STUDY OF INDIA

Manoj Kumar SINHA

1. INTRODUCTION

By the end of the 1970s India had acquired a reputation as one of the most protected and heavily regulated economies in the world. Although, some positive steps were taken in the mid-1970s and then later in the 1980s, the full fledged transformation only took place in 1991.[1] The government's main objective in liberalising the economy in 1991 was to reduce the public debt and stabilising the economy. These paths of reducing the fiscal deficit resulted in pruning down the expenditure in social sectors and in the longer run have affected the development and growth of the social sector by curtailing its new infrastructure and other resources. This reform led to remarkable change in the Indian economy, which deviated from the traditional values held since independence in 1947, such as self-reliance and socialist policies of economic development. India is widely afflicted with disturbing economic disparity among urban, semi-urban and rural populations. This disparity has further been widened after globalisation largely because of transnational corporations (TNCs). The emerging business culture of profit and competition has had a serious impact on various social welfare issues such as health, education and social security for the vulnerable sections of society.

2. BUSINESS AND HUMAN RIGHTS

International human rights law places the primary responsibility for implementing and ensuring protection of human rights on the States. When non-State actors commit acts that are harmful to human rights, States are obliged under international law to take action to prevent and stop the violations and to provide victims with appropriate remedies and relief. States therefore have a duty to ensure that private corporations respect human rights. They must create the legal and institutional framework to enforce this obligation. The treaty bodies are the main international accountability and monitoring mechanism for the implementation of the treaties. Businesses are increasingly focused on the impact they have on individuals, communities and the environment. It is clear that one of the central measures of a company's social responsibility is its respect for human rights. And while most companies recognise the moral imperative to operate consistently with human rights principles, recognition is growing that respect for human rights also can be a tool for improving business performance. The increasing attention businesses have shown to States' regulation and adjudication of corporate acts is an important and welcome development.

International human rights standards have traditionally been the responsibility of governments, aimed at regulating relations between the State and individuals and groups. But with the increased role of corporate actors, nationally and internationally, the issue of business's impact on the enjoyment

---

1 A Kotwal, B Ramaswami and W Wadhwa, 'Economic Liberalisation and Indian Economic Growth: What's the Evidence', discussion papers published by Indian Statistical Institute, New Delhi, 2011.

of human rights has been placed on the agenda of the United Nations. Over the past decade, the United Nations human rights machinery has been considering the scope of business's human rights responsibilities and exploring ways for corporate actors to be accountable for the impact of their activities on human rights. As a result of this process, there is now greater clarity about the respective roles and responsibilities of governments and business with regard to protection and respect for human rights. Most prominently, the emerging understanding and consensus have come as a result of the UN 'Protect, Respect and Remedy' Framework on human rights and business, which was elaborated by the Special Representative of the UN Secretary-General on the issue of human rights and TNCs and other business enterprises. On 16 June 2011 the UN Human Rights Council endorsed the Guiding Principles on Business and Human Rights for implementing the UN 'Protect, Respect and Remedy' Framework, providing – for the first time – a global standard for preventing and addressing the risk of adverse impacts on human rights linked to business activity.[2]

3. ENFORCEMENT OF HUMAN RIGHTS

Since all human beings are born free and equal in dignity and rights, everyone, simply by virtue of being human, is entitled to all the rights and freedoms enshrined in the Universal Declaration of Human Rights (UDHR).[3] This entitlement applies without discrimination, whether by race, skin colour, sex, language, religion, political or other views, national or social origin, property, birth or any other criteria. The State and its institutions bear primary responsibility for ensuring that human rights are respected, protected and fulfilled. International law establishes that States have a duty to protect against non-State human rights abuses within their jurisdiction, and that this duty extends to protection against abuses by business entities. The duty to protect exists under the core United Nations human rights treaties as elaborated by the treaty bodies, and is also generally agreed to exist under customary international law. Moreover, the treaty bodies unanimously affirm that this duty requires steps by States to regulate and adjudicate abuses by all social actors including businesses. Failure to abide by these obligations may amount to a violation of the State's treaty obligations. These duties cannot be delegated to any other organ of society. The reference to the State and its institutions as primary bearers of responsibility does not, however, mean that other actors have no obligations. The Preamble of

2 SL Seck, 'Corporate Law Tools and Guiding Principles for Business and Human Rights' in MK Sinha (ed), *Business and Human Rights*, Sage Law, New Delhi 2013, pp. 93–130.

3 N Robinson, *The Universal Declaration of Human Rights: Its Origin, Significance, Application and Interpretation*, Institute of Jewish Affairs, New York 1958.

the UDHR states that every individual and every organ of society 'shall strive by teaching and education to promote respect for these rights and freedoms and by progressive measures, national and international, to secure their universal and effective recognition and observance'. Increasingly, human rights groups draw on this statement as a basis for numerous far-reaching demands on companies.

Indeed, it is vital that the treaty bodies continue to provide guidance to States on how they can fulfil their role in effectively regulating and adjudicating the acts of business enterprises in relation to human rights. Such guidance as well as deliberations among treaty bodies about this particular issue would not only assist States, but also provide more clarity to rights-holders and business enterprises as to States' obligations in this respect. To this end, the treaty bodies could also consider issuing specific General Comments or Recommendations on this issue. National laws are the most important instruments in protecting human rights, as they are legally binding and apply to all actors in a given country, including all businesses, regardless of size or home country. Therefore, governments' performance in promoting and protecting human rights should be assessed not only on the basis of what laws they have enacted but more importantly on the basis of how effectively these laws are enforced. This gap between legal standards and their implementation in practice is the most pressing human rights issue today. Priority should therefore be given to improving the capacity of national governments to effectively protect and promote human rights, both in national law and by respecting their international obligations.

4. HUMAN RIGHTS AND THE INDIAN CONSTITUTION

The Indian Constitution[4] envisages a noble democracy which ensures freedom under the law and the dignity of the individual. Part III of the Indian Constitution enumerates the fundamental rights[5] and Part IV sets out the Directive Principle of State Policy.[6] The Indian Constitution provides certain rights for individuals in Part III of the Constitution which are known as the 'Fundamental Rights'.

[4] D Das Basu, *Commentary on the Constitution of India*, S.C. Sarkar, Calcutta 1994; MP Jain, *Indian Constitutional Law*, Tripathi Private Ltd. Bombay 1986; H. Seervai, *Constitutional Law of India: A Critical Commentary*, 4th edn., N.M. Tripathi, Bombay 1991.

[5] Articles 12 to 35 of the Indian Constitution deal with Fundamental Rights. The Indian Constitution groups the Fundamental Rights under several sub-heads: (a) Right to Equality (Arts. 14–18); (b) Right to Freedom (Arts. 19–22); (c) Right against Exploitation (Arts. 23–24); (d) Right to Freedom of Religion (Arts. 25–26); (e) Cultural and Educational Rights (Arts. 29–30); (f) Right to Constitutional remedies (Art. 32).

[6] Articles 38–51-A contain the Directive Principles of State Policy. The idea to have such principles in the Constitution has been borrowed from the Irish Constitution. The Directive Principles are not enforceable by a court of law.

The word 'fundamental' means that these rights are inherent in all human beings and basic and essential for the individual. These rights represent the basic values of a civilised society and the Constitution makers declared that they should be given pride of place in the Constitution. These rights are aimed at protecting the dignity of the individual and create conditions in which every human being can develop his personality to the fullest extent. No law, ordinance, custom, usage or administrative order can abridge or take away one's fundamental rights. The Indian Constitution has laid down the implementation procedure in Parts III and IV. While the former guarantees certain rights to the individual, the latter gives direction to the State to provide economic and social rights to its people in specified matters. They together constitute the conscience of the Constitution.

4.1. IMPLEMENTATION MECHANISM AT NATIONAL LEVEL

The fundamental rights enumerated in Part III of the Constitution would remain ineffective if there were no strict implementation mechanism. The framers of the Indian Constitution were fully aware that the supreme importance of judicial remedies to enforce fundamental rights was evident from the fact that not only did they expressly lay down that any law which contravened any of the fundamental rights should be 'void', but they also incorporated in the Constitution itself certain extraordinary remedies for enforcing these rights against any deviant State action, legislative or executive. Further, the right to make use of these constitutional remedies is itself made a fundamental right guaranteed by the Constitution, so that nothing short of an amendment of the Constitution can take away the power of the superior courts, that is, the Supreme Court and the State High Courts, to apply these constitutional remedies for the protection of individual rights guaranteed by the Constitution. The Courts have made it clear that they cannot refuse to entertain an application for an appropriate constitutional remedy where a fundamental right has been infringed. Indeed, it is doubtful if the powers of the High Courts and the Supreme Court can be abridged even by a constitutional amendment.[7] The justiciability of fundamental rights is itself guaranteed under Article 32 of the Constitution. Article 32 has been described as 'the Cornerstone of the democratic edifice'.[8]

The responsibility for the enforcement of the fundamental rights lies on the Supreme Court by virtue of Article 32. It is often alleged that this would

---

7 PN Bhagwati, 'Human Rights in the Criminal Justice System' (1985) 27 *Journal of the Indian Law Institute* 1–22.

8 *Prem Chand v. Excise Commissioner*, AIR 1963 SC 996; 'the fundamental rights guaranteed by Part III which have been made justiciable, form the most outstanding and distinguishing feature of the Indian Constitution' (para. 2), p. 998.

involve the Court making decisions on policy,[9] which in reality is a matter to be left to the legislature, and that this would contravene the constitutional framework for the separation of powers. The general principle is that any person whose fundamental right is violated can seek remedy under Article 32 of the Constitution. The violation of a fundamental right of the petitioner is the condition precedent for moving the Court under Article 32.[10] To be actionable, it is not necessary for actual infringement of the fundamental right; a petition can be moved even if there is an imminent danger of infraction of a fundamental right.[11] The Courts has widened its jurisdiction for enforcement of fundamental human rights under public interest litigation (PIL).[12]

4.2. ROLE OF THE NATIONAL HUMAN RIGHTS COMMISSION OF INDIA IN PROMOTION OF HUMAN RIGHTS

The establishment of an autonomous commission for the promotion and protection of human rights by the government of India reflects its genuine intention for effective implementation of human rights provisions under national and international instruments. In 1993 the National Human Rights Commission[13] (NHRC) was constituted by the adoption of the Protection of Human Rights Act 1993 by the Indian Parliament. The Protection of Human Rights Act was

---

9 AIR 1984 SC 802 at p. 812; see also WE Dellinger, 'Of Rights and Remedies: The Constitution as a Sword' (1971) 85 *Harvard Law Review* 1532.

10 *Romeshwar Prasad v. Commrs., LRsJ*, AIR 1959 SC 498. 'It is well settled that no petition under Article 32 is maintainable, unless it is shown that the petitioner has some fundamental rights. The fundamental right claimed in these case is that the property which the State of Madhya Pradesh Bharat (now Madhya Pradesh) is not permitting the petitioners to remove from the forests is property which they have right to hold and dispose off. This could only be so if the property in the trees or the charcoal or katha which have been manufactured passed to the petitioners. No such property, however, passed to the petitioners. In the circumstances they have no right to hold and dispose of their property, in the absence of any law authorising the state to deprive them of it'.

11 *Hans Muller v. Supdt. Presidency Jail*, AIR 1955 SC 367.

12 SK Aggarwal, *Public Interest Litigation in India*, Indian Law Institute Publications, New Delhi 1986; NR Madhav Menon, 'Public Interest Litigation: A Major Breakthrough in the Delivery of Social Justice' (1982) 5 *Journal of Bar Council of India* 150–58; CD Cunningham, 'Public Interest Litigation in Indian Supreme Court: A Study in the Light of American Experience' (1988) 30 *Journal of the Indian Law Institute* 19–44; J Cassels, 'Judicial Activism and Public Interest Litigation in India: Attempting the Impossible?' (1989) 37 *American Journal of Comparative Law, 495–519;* A Hingorani, 'Public Interest Litigation' (2014) 50 *Annual Survey of Indian Law* 995–1038.

13 The Commission was constituted by an Act of Parliament. The Protection of Human Rights Act was adopted in 1993 and was amended in 2006. The Act is divided into eight Chapters consisting of 43 articles. Special powers are conferred on the NHRC under Article 10(c), which provides that '[t]he Commission shall regulate its own procedure'. There are 19 articles under Procedural Regulations.

amended in 2006 to enlarge its scope and remove the ambiguities. Section 2(d) of the Protection of Human Rights Act, defines human rights and provides that '"human rights" means the rights relating to life, liberty equality, and dignity of the individual guaranteed by the Constitution or embodied in the International Covenants and enforceable by courts in India'. Wide powers and functions have been given to the Commission under section 12 of the Protection of Human Rights Act. Paragraph (a) of section 12 provides that the Commission can enquire *suo moto*[14] action against any public servant against whom a complaint has been registered for violation of human rights. A considerable increase in public awareness of the work of the Commission has been observed. This was reflected in the vast increase in the number of complaints of human rights violations received by the Commission.[15] Many of the cases received by the Commission were of great poignancy but could not be entertained by the Commission, falling as they did under the categories listed in Regulation No. 8[16] of the Commission. The Indian judiciary and the National Human Rights Commission of India have been working continuously for the promotion and protection of human rights of individuals and on many occasions the Supreme Court of India has directed the government of India to adopt legislation necessary for protection of human rights.

5. RIGHT TO WORK

As the world's largest democracy, India adheres strictly to the socio-economic welfare of the people.[17] Part IV of the Indian Constitution deals with the Directive Principles of Policy, which enjoin the State to make effective provisions for securing the right to work[18] and the right to public assistance in cases of

---

14 The Commission took *suo moto* action on the basis of a press report on 12.01.1994 concerning the alleged tattooing of the words 'jeb katri' on the forehead of an alleged pickpocket by Amritsar police personnel, *Annual Report*, National Human Rights Commission, New Delhi 1993–94, p. 22.

15 Currently, 36,956 complaints have attracted the consideration of the Commission. The Commission had disposed of 4,013 cases, with directions by the Commission to the appropriate authorities for action at their end, by 19.07.2013 <http://www.nhrc.nic.in> accessed 23.12.2016.

16 Under this regulation, the Commission had decided not to entertain cases relating to (a) events which happened more than one year before the making of the complaint, (b) matters which are *sub judice*, (c) matters that are vague, anonymous or pseudonymous, (d) matters that are frivolous in nature, or (e) matters which are outside the purview of the Commission.

17 In India there are 29 States and 7 Union Territories <http://goidirectory.nic.in/stateut.htm> accessed 17.11.2016.

18 VH Devi, Sayed Maswood and B Yuvakumar Reddy, 'Right to Work as Fundamental Right: Illusion or Reality?' (2002) 44 *Journal of the Indian Law Institute* 269–72; CB Ramulu and PN Rao, 'Poverty Alleviation Programmes and Right to Work to Rural Poor' (1997) *Indian Journal of Public Administration*, pp. 680–694.

unemployment. Article 41 of the Constitution provides that 'the State shall within the limits of its economic capacity and development, make effective provision for securing the right to work, to education and to public assistance in cases of unemployment, old age, sickness and disablement, and in other cases of undeserved want'.[19] It is interesting to note that the word 'right' is used only in Article 41 of Part IV. The constitutional provision under Article 41 may be read with Article 43, which provides for a minimum wage and a decent standard of living for all workers. Article 38 of the Constitution states that the State shall strive to promote the welfare of the people and Article 39(a) provides that the State shall, in particular, direct its policy towards securing that 'citizens, men and women, have the right to have an adequate means of livelihood'. In addition to these rights reflected under the Directive Principles of State Policy, Article 19(1)(g), which is part of the Fundamental Rights mentioned under Part III of the Constitution, guarantees fundamental freedom to all citizens to practise any profession or to carry out any occupation, trade or business.

5.1. EMPLOYMENT POLICY RECORD

India has the distinction of developing one of the most comprehensive labour laws in the world. Since labour is a concurrent subject in India, both the Central and State governments have made laws covering almost all aspects of work. The laws cover practically all aspect of workers' lives, including industrial relations, service conditions, wages and benefits, and social security. The Constitution of India under Article 19(1)(c) guarantees freedom of association to all citizens, including government servants. However, reasonable restrictions may be imposed on the exercise of this freedom by the State in the interest of the sovereignty and integrity of India or public order or morality.[20] The judgments of the courts in India are relevant on this aspect.[21] The Indian industrial working class largely belongs to the poorest section of Indian society. The history of the labour movement can be traced in India from 1890, when the Bombay Milhand Association was formed. The Association acted merely as a clearing house for the grievances of the Bombay Mill workers and thus could be regarded as a trade union in the real sense. The labour policy of the government of India derives its philosophy and contents from the Directive Principles of State Policy as laid down

---

19 PM Bakshi, *The Constitution of India: With Selective Comments*, Universal Publishing House, Delhi 2000, p. 72.

20 Article 19(4) of the Constitution.

21 *Kulkarni v. State of Bombay*, AIR 1954 SC 73; *O.K.Ghosh, v. Joseph*; AIR 1963 SC 812; *All India Bank Employees Association v. National Industrial Tribunal*; AIR 1962 SC 171; *Delhi Police Sang v. Union of India*, AIR 1987 SC 379.

in the Constitution of India.[22] This policy has been evolving in response to the specific needs of the situation and to suit the requirements of planned economic development and social justice.[23] An independent ministry of the government of India is entrusted with the task of protecting and safeguarding the interests of workers in general, and poor and deprived sections of society in particular. It also works for the promotion of welfare and providing social security to the labour force, both in the organised and unorganised sectors, in tandem with the process of liberalisation. At present there are 44 labour-related statutes that have been enacted by the government, dealing with minimum wages, accidental and social security benefits, occupational safety and health, and conditions of employment, formation of trade unions and industrial relations. Since labour is in the Concurrent List, the State government is also empowered to legislate.

5.2. THE MAHATMA GANDHI NATIONAL RURAL EMPLOYMENT GUARANTEE ACT 2005

The Mahatma Gandhi National Rural Employment Guarantee (MGNREGA) Act 2005 was enacted on 7 September 2005 and is a historic piece of legislation for the simple reason that it has put the onus of providing employment on the government.[24] The Act provides for assured employment for not less than 100 days.[25] A person is entitled to unemployment allowance'[26] subject to a

22 G Saibaba, 'Core Labour Standards, Human Rights and Structural Adjustments: The Indian Experience and Perspectives' in G Saibaba and KS Rao (eds.), *Structural Adjustment and Implications of Human Rights*, Serials Publications, New Delhi 2003, pp. 71–96.

23 Economic and Social Council, *Initial Report submitted by States Parties to the Covenant concerning Rights covered by Articles 6 to 9*, E/1984/6Add.13, 07.01.1986, para. 17.

24 The Mahatma Gandhi National Rural Employment Guarantee (MGNREG) Act 2005, No. 42 of 2005, entered into force 02.02.2006 <http://rural.nic.in/rajaswa.pdf> accessed 24.07.2016.

25 *Ibid.* According to section 4(1) of the MGNREG Act: 'For the purposes of giving effect to the provisions of section 3, every State government shall, within six months from the date of commencement of this Act, by notification, make a Scheme, for providing not less than one hundred days of guaranteed employment in a financial year to every household in the rural areas covered under the Scheme and whose adult members, by application, volunteer to do unskilled manual work subject to the conditions laid down by or under this Act and in the Scheme: provided that until any such Scheme is notified by the State Government, the Annual Action Plan or Perspective Plan for the Sampoorna Grameen Rozgar Yojana (SGRY) or the National Food for Work Programme (NFFWP) whichever is in force in the concerned area immediately before such notification shall be deemed to be the action plan for the Scheme for the purposes of this Act'.

26 *Ibid* According to section 7(1) of the MGNREG Act: 'If an applicant for employment under the Scheme is not provided such unemployment employment within fifteen days of receipt of his application seeking employment or from allowance the date on which the employment has been sought in the case of an advance application, whichever is later, he shall be entitled to a daily unemployment allowance in accordance with this section.'

minimum of Rs. 60 (around 1 euro) a day.[27] The Act seeks to empower the rural poor through a rights-based law, thus trying to put in place an institutional arrangement for ensuing grass-roots democracy through transparency and involvement of local institutions. The productive absorption of under-employed and surplus labour force in the rural sector has been a major focus of planning for rural development for many years.

The MGNREGA constitutes a pioneering endeavour to secure waged employment for households in rural areas as a guaranteed entitlement. It takes into account the experience of 30 years gained under the Employment Guarantee Scheme in Maharashtra.[28] The MGNREGA effectively benefited 67 per cent of the population below the poverty line (BPL). This helped in increasing their purchasing power and thereby gave a significant impetus to overall economic development. The scheme also helped to check migration from rural to urban areas and solve the problem of urban slums. No doubt it is a visionary attempt to remove poverty, but how to ensure its sustainability should be the central issue.[29]

5.3. JURISPRUDENCE ON THE RIGHT TO WORK

The Supreme Court of India has delivered some significant judgments on the right to work, and the Court viewed the right to work in a much broader perspective and linked the right to work with the right to life. Article 21 of the Indian Constitution guarantees the right to life and liberty.[30] The courts in India have consistently maintained that the right to life does not mean mere animal existence. In a case of forced eviction of pavement dwellers, the apex court extended the scope of the right to life to include the right to livelihood.[31] The Supreme Court of India clarified its position with regard to livelihood in

27 *Ibid.* According to section 6(1) of the MGNREG Act: 'Notwithstanding anything contained in the Minimum Wages Act, 1948, the Central Government may, by notification, specify the wage rate for the purposes of this Act: Provided that different rates of wages may be specified for different areas: Provided further that the wage rate specified from time to time under any such notification shall not be at a rate less than sixty rupees per day.'

28 S Narayan, 'Unemployment and Migration' <http://www.indiatogether.org> accessed 15.10.2016. The Maharashtra Employment Guarantee Scheme was launched in 1972 and aims to provide unskilled manual employment on demand for wage labourers. The programme innovatively draws its corpus of funds, which is funded up to 90 per cent, by imposing a tax on white-collar professionals and traders in the cities, especially Bombay, and imposing an additional motor vehicle and sales tax. These funds are used to create labour-intensive public works, for example digging wells, building roads, etc. Employment is guaranteed in the vicinity of the village or the transport cost to the place of work is reimbursed.

29 *Ibid* MP Jain, *Indian Constitutional Law*, Bombay 1986.

30 Article 21 of the Constitution states that 'no person shall be deprived of his life or personal liberty except according to procedure established by law'.

31 *Olga Tellis v. Bombay Municipal Corporation*, AIR 1986 SC 180.

Delhi Development Horticulture Employee's Union v. Delhi Administration,[32] stating that 'there is no doubt that broadly interpreted and as a necessary logical corollary, right to life would include the right to livelihood and therefore, right to work'.[33] The Court also opined in this case that though the right to livelihood has not so far become part of fundamental rights, this is because the country has not attained the capacity to guarantee it and not because it considers it any the less fundamental to life.[34] In *Postal & Telegraph Department v. Union of India*[35] the issue was of regularising the services of a large number of non-permanent workers in the posts and telegraphs department of the government. In this case the Court did not hesitate to invoke the Directive Principles of State Policy to direct such regularisation.[36] The Court held that the State cannot deny at least the minimum pay in the pay scales of regularly employed workmen even though the government may not be compelled to extend all the benefits enjoyed by regularly recruited employees.[37] The government cannot take advantage of its dominant position and compel any worker to work even as a casual labourer on starvation wages. The government should be a model employer. The Court observed that on the facts and in the circumstances of this case the classification of employees into regularly recruited employees and casual employees for the purpose of paying less than the minimum wage payable to employees in the corresponding regular cadres, particularly in the lowest rungs of the department where the pay scales are the lowest, was not tenable.[38] It further made clear that all these rights cannot be extended simultaneously. But they do indicate the socialist goal. The degree of achievement in this direction depends upon economic resources, the willingness of the people to produce, and, above all, the existence of industrial peace throughout the country. For those rights the question of security of work is of utmost importance.[39]

For protection against the arbitrary termination of employment, the Industrial Disputes Act 1947 has a provision under Article 25-F, which provides that no workman employed in any industry who has been in continuous service for not less than one year under an employer shall be retrenched by the employer until the workman has been given one month's notice and reasons for retrenchment,[40]

---

32 *Delhi Development Horticulture Employee's Union v. Delhi Administration*, AIR 1992 SC 789.

33 *Ibid.*

34 *Ibid.*

35 *Postal & Telegraph Department v. Union of India* (1988) 1 SCC 122.

36 *Ibid.*

37 *Ibid.*

38 *Ibid.*

39 Daily Rated Casual Labour Employed under *P & T Department v. Union of India* (1988) 1 SCC 122 at paras. 7 and 9. Similar orders were made in *Dharwad P. W. D. Employees Association* v. *State of Karnataka* (1990) 2 SCC 396; *Jacob M. Puthuparambil* v. *Kerala Water Authority* (1991) 1 SCC 28; *Air India Statutory Corporation* v. *United Labour Union* (1997) 9 SCC 425.

40 Section 25(F)(a) of the Industrial Disputes Act 1947.

compensation shall be paid to the employee,[41] and notice shall be served in the prescribed manner.[42]

The problem of unemployment is in urgent need of redress in India. India has about 250 million people who are so unimaginably poor that they cannot cross the poverty line, which is set way below what can be considered necessary for human existence.[43] The phenomenon of low productivity due to overcrowding and cyclical unemployment has important implications for future generations in terms of education as it affects their labour market options to improve their skills and vertical mobility. Therefore it is imperative to protect the right to work in the second most populous nation on earth. Today the nation is facing the daunting challenge of unemployment. With restructuring, even formal sector jobs have been shed. While employment options abound for the core circle of skilled professionals, the periphery of the unskilled and semi-skilled is worsening. Most workers in the unorganised sector are poor and many are in debt to labour contractors, to whom they are forced to pledge their labour. Although bonded labour was prohibited India by the Bonded Labour System (Abolition) Act 1976, cases of bonded labour have been noticed regularly. Thus, it is important that those who are responsible for implementation of the laws ensure that they are indeed implemented.

5.4. REMUNERATION

Article 43 of the Constitution provides that the State shall endeavour to secure by suitable legislation or economic organisation to all workers a living wage and conditions of work and ensure a decent standard of life and full employment of leisure and cultural opportunities. Another provision has been added under Article 43 of the Constitution by the 42nd Constitutional Amendment 1976.[44] In addition to the constitutional safeguards, the government adopted the Minimum Wages Act in 1948.[45] The Minimum Wages Act is an Act to provide for fixing minimum rates of wages in certain employments.[46] The Act is applicable

41 Section 25(F)(b) of the Industrial Disputes Act 1947.

42 Section 25(F)(c) of the Industrial Disputes Act 1947.

43 Devi, above n 18.

44 Ins, by the Constitution (Forty-Second Amendment) Act 1976, section 9 (w.e.f. 03.01.1977). Article 43A: 'The State shall take steps, by suitable legislation or in any other way, to secure the participation of workers in the management of undertakings, establishments or other organizations engaged in any industry.'

45 The process of considering minimum wages was begun during British rule by the constitution in 1929 of a Royal Commission on Labour to consider this subject. On 11.04.1946 a Minimum Wages Bill was introduced but the passage of the Bill was considerably delayed because of the constitutional changes in India. However, the Minimum Wages Bill was finally adopted in 1948.

46 A Singh, *Introduction to Labour & Industrial Law*, Wadhwa Publications, Nagpur 2002, pp. 257–61.

to all the States of India. It applies to a number of employments, which are listed in a Schedule appended to the Act[47] and may be extended by the appropriate government, Central or State, as the case may be, to any employment in respect of which it is of the opinion that minimum rates of wages should be fixed under the Act.[48] Every person who provides labour or services to another person is entitled to minimum wages.[49] It is the statutory responsibility of the appropriate government to review the minimum wages at intervals not exceeding five years and revise them if necessary.[50] It can hardly be disputed that securing living wages for labourers, which ensures not only physical subsistence, but also the maintenance of health and decency, is conducive to the general interest of the public.[51] Careful study of the various provisions of the Act and the machinery set up by it shows that they do not contravene Article 19(1) of the Constitution nor do they infringe the equal protection clause mentioned under Article 14 of the Constitution. Article 39(d) of the Indian Constitution envisages that equal pay should be given to men and women for equal work. The total population of women in the country is about 495.74 million as per the 2011 census and thus represents 48.3 per cent of the country's total population of 1,210.19 million.[52] In India the female labour force comprises a section of the working population that is exposed to exploitation. The majority of women work in the unorganised sector for low wages and at low levels of skill. A number of legislative measures have been taken for the protection of women. The government of India ratified International Labour Organization (ILO) Convention No. 100 in 1958 concerning equal remuneration for men and women for work of equal value.[53] In the age of globalisation it is equally important that TNCs implement the above-mentioned legislation, but unfortunately, in practice, non-compliance with these laws by TNCs is common. None of the major ILO Conventions dealing with occupational safety and health has been ratified.[54]

The 'right to strike' refers to the cluster of rights, immunities and protections that allow a group of workers to cease work without terminating their employment relationship with their employer and without exposing themselves to civil

47 The object of the Act is to provide for the fixing of minimum rates of wages in employment in which labour is vulnerable to exploitation, being not well organised and having no effective bargaining power. Such employments are listed in Part I and Part II of the Schedule to the Act.

48 *Ibid.*, pp. 257–58.

49 *Ibid. Patel Ishwerbhai Prahaladbhai v. Taluka Development Officer* (1983) 1 *Lab LJ* 237 (SC).

50 Report, above n 5, para. 29.

51 *Ibid.*, p. 260.

52 Annual Report 2014–15, the Department of Women and Child Development, Ministry of Human Resource & Development, Government of India <http://www.wcd.nic.in> accessed 12.06.2015.

53 *Ibid.*

54 *Ibid.*

liability for their actions.[55] Most countries distinguish between legal and illegal strikes. The right to strike thus refers to taking protected industrial action within the legal framework of a particular country.[56] The right to form associations or unions is recognised as a fundamental right under the Indian Constitution.[57] The right to strike is not a fundamental right but a legal right, and with this right statutory restriction is attached in the Industrial Disputes Act 1947. While these provisions effectively grant workers and unions the right to legally strike, the recognition of this right in India has been inconsistent. The right to strike is an important weapon in the armoury of workers, recognised by almost all democratic countries as a mode of redress. The blanket ban on the right to strike also transgresses the limits of the Conventions of the ILO. Therefore, by virtue of being a member of the ILO, India is under an obligation to satisfy at least the fundamental rights promoted by the Conventions, irrespective of its having ratified them or not.

The right to strike is not a fundamental and absolute right in India; it is a conditional right, only available after certain pre-conditions are fulfilled. The right to strike must be a weapon of last resort because its misuse will lead to problems in production and affect the financial profits of industry. This would ultimately affect the country's economy. Today, most countries, especially India, are dependent upon foreign investment and in these circumstances it is necessary that countries seeking foreign investment keep some safeguards in their respective industrial laws so that there will be no misuse of the right to strike.

6. RIGHT TO SOCIAL SECURITY

The concept of social security is as old as the history of man. The oldest institution of social security is the family, which includes the extended family. The Industrial Revolution in Europe saw the growth of urban and industrial centres, which affected rural joint families, thereby disrupting the institution of social security in the joint family system.[58] The purpose of any social security measure is to give individuals and families the security that their standard of living and quality of life will not be eroded by social or economic eventuality.[59]

55 'Right to Strike Indispensable for Workers' Rights', HRF/121/05, 24.06.2005 <http://www.hrdc.net> accessed 25.11.2016.

56 *Ibid.*

57 Article 19(1)(c) of the Constitution.

58 UNDP Report, Livelihood Opportunities for Persons with Disabilities (UNDP, India, 2012); PM Rao, 'Social Security for Persons with Disabilities in India' <http://www.disabilityindia.org> accessed 01.12.2016.

59 *Ibid.*

The contingencies of social security are to provide medical care and income security against the consequences of defined contingencies.[60] Thus, the main strength of the social security system is that it acts as a facilitator, helping people to plan their own futures through insurance and assistance.[61] The success of social security schemes, however, requires the active support and involvement of employees and employers.

India has always had a joint family system that takes care of the social security needs of all the members provided the family has access to material assets like land. In keeping with its cultural traditions, family members and relatives have always discharged a sense of shared responsibility towards one another. To the extent that the family has resources to draw upon, this is often the best relief for the special needs and care required by the aged and those in poor health. In India the State bears the primary responsibility for developing appropriate systems for providing protection and assistance to its workforce.

6.1. WORKFORCE IN INDIA

The dimensions and complexities of the problem in India can be better understood by taking into consideration the extent of the labour force in the organised and unorganised sectors.[62] The organised sector includes primarily those establishments which are covered by the Factories Act 1948,[63] the Shops and Commercial Establishments Acts of State governments, the Industrial Employment Standing Orders Act 1946 etc. This sector already has a structure through which social security benefits are extended to workers covered under these pieces of legislation.

The unorganised sector, on the other hand, is characterised by a lack of labour law coverage, the seasonal and temporary nature of occupations, high labour mobility, dispersed functioning of operations, casualisation of labour, lack of organisational support, low bargaining power, etc., all of which make it vulnerable to socio-economic hardship.[64] The nature of work in the unorganised sector varies between regions and also between the rural areas and the urban

60 *Ibid.*

61 General Overview: 'Why Do We Need Social Security?' <http://www archive.is/labour.nic.in.> accessed 28.11.2016.

62 According to the NSSO's survey of 1999–2000, the workforce increased to about 397 million, out of which only 28 million were in the organised sector.

63 The Employees' State Insurance Act 1948 (ESI Act), which covers factories and establishments with 10 or more employees and provides for comprehensive medical care to the employees and their families as well as cash benefits during sickness and maternity, and monthly payments in case of death or disablement.

64 SC Srivastava, 'Machinery for Fixation of Minimum Wages of Sweated Labour in India: Problems and Prospects' (1981) 23 *Journal of the Indian Law Institute* 495–521.

areas, which may include the remote rural areas as well as sometimes the most inhospitable urban concentrations. In the rural areas the unorganised sector is comprised of landless agricultural labourers, small and marginal farmers, share croppers, persons engaged in animal husbandry, fishing, horticulture, bee-keeping, toddy tapping, forest workers, rural artisans, etc. In the urban areas it is comprised mainly of manual labourers in construction, carpentry, trade, transport, communication etc. and also includes street vendors, hawkers, head load workers, cobblers, tin smiths and garment makers.[65]

6.2. DIRECTIVE PRINCIPLES OF STATE POLICY AND SOCIAL SECURITY

Matters relating to social security are listed in the Directive Principles of State Policy and the subjects in the Concurrent List. The following social security issues are mentioned in the Concurrent List.[66] Article 41 of the Constitution provides for the right to work, to education and to public assistance in certain cases. The State shall, within the limits of its economic capacity and development, make effective provision for securing the right to work, to education and to public assistance in cases of unemployment, old age, sickness and disablement, and in other cases of undeserved want.[67] Under Article 42 the State shall make provision for securing just and humane conditions of work and for maternity relief and Article 43 of the Constitution speaks of the State's responsibility to provide social security to the citizens of the country. The International Covenant on Economic, Social and Cultural Rights (ICESCR) under Article 9 recognises the right of everyone to social security including social insurance. India has also ratified some Conventions of the ILO.[68]

---

65 SC Srivastava, 'Constitutional Protection to Weaker and Disadvantaged Section in Labour' (2000) 42 *Journal of the Indian Law Institute* 232–62.

66 List III in the Seventh Schedule of the Constitution of India – Item No. 23: Social Security and insurance, employment and unemployment. Item No. 24: Welfare of Labour including conditions of work, provident funds, employers' liability, workmen's compensation, invalidity and old age pension and maternity benefits.

67 Available at <http://www.labour.nic.in/ss/welcome.html> accessed 28.11.2016.

68 *Ibid.* The Workmen's Compensation, (Occupational Diseases) – No. 18 and revised Convention No. 42 of 1934; Equality of Treatment (Accident Compensation) – No. 19 of 1925; and Equality of Treatment (Social Security) – Nos. 1 & 8 of 1962. The other relevant acts are: the Workmen's Compensation Act 1923 (WC Act), which requires payment of compensation to the workman or his family in case of employment-related injuries resulting in death or disability; the Maternity Benefit Act 1961 (MB Act), which provides for 12 weeks' wages during maternity as well as paid leave in certain other related contingencies; the Payment of Gratuity Act 1972 (PG Act), which provides 15 days' wages for each year of service to employees who have worked for five years or more in establishments having a minimum of 10 workers. ILO Convention 102, however, has not been ratified by India.

6.3. PROTECTION AND ASSISTANCE SHOULD BE ACCORDED TO THE FAMILY

In India the family[69] is perceived as a unit of two or more persons united by the ties of marriage, blood, adoption or consensual unions, generally constituting a single household, and interacting and communicating with each other. It is considered the basic unit of society, to meet the needs of individuals and those of other societal institutions. It determines the development of individuals, in that it is a major source of nurturance, emotional bonding and socialisation. Families in a large and culturally diverse country such as India are fairly well developed, strong and based on a range of kin-extensions. The normative family composition types in India are the extended joint family and elementary nuclear family. In many rural areas, the traditional joint family system is still very strong, where a child grows up in the company of his/her own siblings, cousins and grandparents. The term 'joint family' is used more commonly than 'extended family' in India. The elementary or nuclear family comprises couples and their unmarried children and is generally financially independent of other families. This structure appears to be becoming the norm in most urban areas.

Religious and personal laws traditionally govern family relations in India. The major religious communities have their separate personal laws. Their respective religious laws in matters of marriage, divorce, succession, adoption, guardianship and maintenance govern them. The personal laws of minority communities have been left untouched on the basis of the policy of non-interference in the personal laws of any community unless the demand for change comes from within those communities. The family in India is often understood as an ideal homogeneous unit with strong coping mechanisms. However, it is important to recognise that there may be inherent problems within the family. Moreover, families have a plurality of forms that vary with class, ethnicity and individual choices, requiring specific interventions.

---

[69] A family is defined by the Civil Procedure Code, 1908, in Order XXXII-A6 as follows:

(a) (i) a man and his wife living together,
(ii) any child or children, being issue of theirs; or of such man or such wife;
(iii) any child or children being maintained by such man and wife;

(b) a man not having a wife or not living together with his wife, any child or children, being issue of his, and any child or children, being maintained by him;

(c) a woman not having a husband or not living together with her husband, any child or children being issue of hers, and any child or children being maintained by her;

(d) a man or woman and his or her brother, sister, ancestor or lineal descendant living with him or her; and

(e) any combination of one or more of the groups specified in (a), (b), (c) or (d) of this rule.

6.4. PROTECTION OF CHILDREN AND YOUNG PERSONS

The concept of family responsibility for children in the earlier systems in the region, while humane in its approach, was combined with a corresponding concept of sweeping family authority. Early legal systems did not recognise the concept of the personal autonomy of the child. In many cases, the family was and is also the source of inequality, exploitation and violence in addition to its idealistic picture of the source of nurturance, emotional bonding and support.

Both the Constitution and specific statutes prohibit forced or compulsory labour, and bonded labour, as a form of compulsory labour, is also prohibited by statute; however, such practices are widespread. In India various national laws have been adopted, some dating back to the 1930s, offering protection from exploitation to India's working children. The Bonded Labour System (Abolition) Act 1976 is the most significant and far-reaching of these laws. It outlaws all debt bondage, including that of children, and it requires government intervention and rehabilitation of the bonded worker.[70] The Bonded Labour System (Abolition) Act, the Child Labour (Prohibition and Regulation) Act 1986, and the other pieces of protective legislation that apply in varying circumstances to the situation of the bonded child labourer, are weakened by an extremely low rate of enforcement.[71] In addition, under the Indian Penal Code (IPC) rape, extortion, causing grievous hurt, assault, kidnapping, abduction, wrongful confinement, buying or disposing of people as slaves, and unlawful compulsory labour are criminal offences, punishable by up to 10 years' imprisonment and fines.

6.5. PROTECTION UNDER THE INDIAN CONSTITUTION

Article 21 of the Constitution of India guarantees the right to life and liberty. The Indian Supreme Court has interpreted the right to liberty to include, among other things, the right of free movement, the right to eat, sleep and work when one pleases, the right to be free from inhuman and degrading treatment, the right to integrity and dignity of the person, the right to the benefits of protective labour legislation, and the right to a speedy trial.[72] The practice of bonded labour violates all of these constitutionally mandated rights. Article 23 of the Constitution prohibits the practice of debt bondage and other forms of slavery, both modern and ancient, and it states that 'traffic in human beings and *begar*

70 Human Rights Watch Children's Rights Project, *The Small Hands of Slavery. Bonded Child Labor In India*, Human Rights Watch/Asia, 1996, available at <http://www.hrw.org> accessed 02.12.2016.

71 M Jain, *Bonded Labour: Justice Through Judiciary*, Manak Publications, New Delhi 1997.

72 MK Sinha, *Implementation of Basic Human Rights*, Lexis Nexis, New Delhi 2013; The Government of India has not ratified ILO Convention 182 on the worst forms of child labour.

and other similar forms of forced labour are prohibited and any contravention of this provision shall be an offence punishable in accordance with the law'. *Begar* is an ancient caste-based obligation, a form of forced labour under which a person is compelled to work without receiving any remuneration.[73] Other similar forms of forced labour were interpreted extensively by the Supreme Court in 1982, when it ruled in the *Asiad Workers'* Case[74] that both unpaid and paid labour were prohibited by Article 23, so long as the element of force or compulsion was present in the worker's ongoing services to the employer.[75] All labour rewarded with less than the minimum wage, then, constitutes forced labour and violates the Constitution of India.

Article 24 prohibits the employment of children in factories, mines and other hazardous occupations. Work by children under 14 years of age is barred completely in 'hazardous industries', which include, among other things, passenger, goods and mail transport by railway. Together, Articles 23 and 24 are placed under the heading Right against Exploitation, part of the Fundamental Rights under Part III of the Indian Constitution. Article 39(e) and (f)[76] requires the State to direct its policy towards securing health and strength of workers.

The enforcement of child labour laws is the responsibility of the state governments. Enforcement is inadequate, especially in the informal sector, in which most children who work are employed. Labour inspectors at the State and local level have overwhelming caseloads and in many cases do not receive adequate support or protection to challenge employers, who often have direct access to government officials. On the occasions when inspectors refer violations for prosecution, long court backlogs and inadequate funding for legal counsel frequently result in acquittals. The continuing prevalence of child labour is attributed to social acceptance of the practice.

Indian civilisation recognised education as one of the pious obligations of human society. To establish and administer educational institutions is considered a religious and charitable object. The Preamble of the Indian Constitution promises to secure justice in social, economic and political fields for the citizens. The objective of the Preamble cannot be achieved and will remain on paper unless the people of the country are educated. It is only education that equips

---

73 Human Rights Watch Project, above n 70.

74 *People's Union for Democratic Rights v. Union of India* (Asiad Workers' Case), AIR 1982 SC 1473.

75 *Ibid.*

76 Article 39(e): the health and strength of workers, men and women and the tender age of children are not abused and that citizens are not forced by economic necessity to enter avocations unsuited to their age or strength. Article 39(f): children are given opportunities and facilities to develop in a healthy manner and in conditions of freedom and dignity and that childhood and youth are protected against exploitation and against moral and material abandonment. This section was inserted by the 42nd Amendment of the Indian Constitution 1976 and came into effect from 01.03.1977.

the citizen to participate in achieving the objectives enshrined in the Preamble. The framers of the Indian Constitution were aware of the fact that more than 70 per cent of the people of India were illiterate and that human dignity and respect for human rights will have no meaning for them unless they are educated. The two articles, namely Article 41[77] and Article 45[78] of the Constitution reflect the intention of the framers to give importance to education. It is important to note that Article 45 is the only article among all the articles in Part IV of the Indian Constitution which speaks of a time limit within which this right should be made justiciable. Thus, it is clear that when the Constitution of India was adopted in 1950, the framers of the Constitution were aware that for the realisation of a person's capabilities and for full protection of her rights, education was an important tool. Article 46 further requires that the 'State shall promote with special care the educational and economic interests of the weaker sections of the people, and in particular, of the Scheduled Castes and the Scheduled Tribes, and shall protect them from social injustice and all forms of exploitation'. Though education is in the Concurrent List of the Constitution, the State governments play a very major role in the development of education, particularly in the primary and the secondary education sectors.

A significant development took place in 2002 with the 86th Amendment of the Indian Constitution, by which primary education was made free. The government has amended the Constitution to make primary education a fundamental right of all children up to 14 years of age. The Constitution (86th Amendment) Act 2002,[79] notified on 13 December 2002, inserted a new Article 21-A on Right to Education under Part III of the Indian Constitution, which deals with Fundamental Rights of the Constitution. Article 21-A states that 'the State shall provide free and compulsory education to all children of the age of six to fourteen years in such manner as the State may, by law, determine'.[80] Further, this amendment has inserted new clauses in Articles 45[81] and 51A[82]

---

77 Article 41 states that 'the State shall, within the limits of its economic capacity and development, make effective provision for securing the right to work, to education and to public assistance in cases of unemployment, old age, sickness and disablement, and in other cases of undeserved want'.

78 Article 45 provides that 'the State shall endeavour to provide, within a period of ten years from the commencement of this Constitution, for free and compulsory education for all children until they complete the age of fourteen years'.

79 Available at <http://indiacode.nic.in/coiweb/welcome.html> accessed 22.12.2014.

80 Annual Report 2013–14, 'Overview' <http://www.education.nic.in/> accessed 20.12.2014.

81 According to the 86th Amendment, Article 45 of the Constitution, the following article shall be substituted, namely: Provision for early childhood care and education to children below the age of six years. 'The State shall endeavour to provide early childhood care and education for all children until they complete the age of six years.'

82 Part IV A of the Constitution refers to the Fundamental Duties from Article 51A (a) to (j). This Part was added to the Indian Constitution by the 42nd Amendment of the Constitution. By the 86th Amendment a new clause was added to Article 51A of the Constitution, after

of the Indian Constitution. Pursuant to the above, the Right to Education Act was adopted in 2009 and it came into force from 1 April 2010.[83] States have demanded that additional expenses that accrue in giving compulsory education to children of the 6–14 age group be borne by the Centre. The Right to education Act stipulates that free education must be made available to at least 25 per cent of children of weaker sections in partially aided and unaided schools.

7. UN TREATY ON BUSINESS AND HUMAN RIGHTS: INDIAN EXPERIENCE

Businesses are increasingly focused on the impact they have on individuals, communities and the environment. It is clear that one of the central measures of a company's social responsibility is its respect for human rights.[84] And while most companies recognise the moral imperative to operate consistently with human rights principles, recognition is growing that respect for human rights also can be a tool for improving business performance.[85] Ensuring that business operations are consistent with these legal principles helps companies to avoid legal challenges to their global activities. In recent years in the United States and in other countries, courts have considered lawsuits alleging that multinational corporations (MNCs), sometimes through their business partners, have contributed to human rights violations in their global operations.[86] Initiatives were taken by all stakeholders to ensure effective implementation of the UN Guiding Principles for Business and Human Rights (UNGPs), however the government has not taken adequate steps to ensure adherence to the guidelines by MNCs in their operations and supply chain. Unfortunately, the contributions of NGOs and civil society organisations in the field of business and human rights are minimal in India and that affects the implementation of the UNGPs. There is an urgent need for active involvement of NGOs and civil society organisations to play an active role in dissemination and implementation of the UNGPs framework.

---

clause (j), the following clause shall be added, namely:- '(k) who is a parent or guardian to provide opportunities for education to his child or, as the case may be, ward between the age of six and fourteen years.'

83 Right to Education Act 2009 <http://www.education.nic.in/> accessed 20.12.2014.

84 D Nayyar, 'Alleviating Poverty: Role of Good Governance and Constitutional Reform' (2000) *Economic and Political Weekly* 3739–42.

85 G Alfredsson, *Human Rights and Good Governance. Building Bridges*, Martinus Nijhoff Publishers, The Hague 2002.

86 International Human Rights Law Group, *U.S. Legislation Relating Human Rights to U.S. Foreign Policy*, W.S. Hein, New York 1991.

In the wake of economic reforms in 1991 the government realised that many provisions of the Companies Act had become obsolete and were not conducive to the growth of the Indian corporate sector in the changing environment. This led to the adoption of the Companies Act 2013 on 29 August 2013, which replaced the Companies Act 1958. The new Companies Act provides the corporate sector with an opportunity for self-regulation, while mandating greater transparency and enhanced disclosure for improved compliance. The Companies Act came into effect on 1 April 2014 and makes it mandatory for certain companies to spend 2 per cent of profit on corporate social responsibility (CSR) activities. According to section 135, the companies which have had a net profit of Rs.5 crore or more, a net worth of Rs. 500 crore or a turnover of Rs.1000 crore or more in any financial year have to spend 2 per cent of profit on CSR activities. The Act applies to a holding company, its subsidiary and even a foreign company with a branch or project office in India.[87] Every company that meets the net profit, net worth, or turnover criteria of the Act has to constitute a CSR committee on its Board. The CSR committee has to formulate and recommend a CSR policy for the company to the company Board. The CSR policy must indicate the activities to be undertaken by the company as per Schedule VII of the Companies Act.

A large number of companies in India were contributing to CSR long before the concept of CSR crystallised at the international level. Notable among these company are Birla and Tata, both of which have established educational institutions and temples in many parts of the country. Interestingly, several trade and industry associations in India have already incorporated CSR principles and UN Global Compact principles in their codes of conduct. However, practice in the corporate sector is uneven and much remains to be done to persuade trade and industry that human rights is good for business, not in conflict with it. The adoption of the National Voluntary Guidelines on Social, Environmental and Economic Responsibilities of Business (NVGs) in 2011–12 was an extraordinary effort of the government and civil society towards fixing responsibility on business. The NVGs were adopted by the Ministry of Corporate Affairs and are currently under revision. This was the first initiative that led to the crystallisation of the concept of CSR in the core business. However, the emerging development was short-lived because the amended Companies Act 2013 provided under section 135 of the Act that a company has to pay 2 per cent of profit towards CSR, those who fall in the criteria laid down under this section. The criteria of profit, turnover and worth have brought approximately 16,000 companies within its ambit where companies have to spend 2 per cent of their net profit for CSR. The Indian government has taken adequate steps in formulating strict guidelines in fixing social responsibility for companies. India must play an important role

---

87 Section 2(42) of the Companies Act.

at the international level to support the adoption of a legally binding regime at the international level.

8. CONCLUSION

It is clear from the above discussion that primary responsibility has been fixed on the State for the welfare of the people by providing employment, social security, education, health and in other important areas. The government took appropriate steps by adopting policies and made an attempt to implement these constitutional goals set under Chapter IV of the Constitution. There is a manifold increase in India's commitment to fulfil the aspirations of the people because it has ratified a number of international human rights instruments which place obligations on the government to ensure that business enterprises operating within its territory or jurisdiction do not violate human rights. Thus, there is an urgent need for adoption of a UN Business and Human Rights (BHR) Framework. A national BHR framework would be useful even if a legally binding international instrument to impose human rights obligations on companies were adopted in the future. The Indian government has adopted a number of significant CSR initiatives in recent years – e.g., the NVGs 2011, and CSR provisions in the Companies Act 2013 and the Model Bilateral Investment Treaty (BIT) 2015. Today, CSR goes far beyond the old philanthropy of the past, when money was donated to good causes at the end of the financial year, and is instead an all-year-round responsibility that companies accept for the environment around them, for the best working practices, for their engagement in their local communities and for their recognition that brand names depend not only on quality, price and uniqueness, but on how, cumulatively, they interact with their workforce, community and environment.

Companies are increasingly being assigned moral responsibility. While the dimension and complexity of these expectations often makes it difficult to satisfy all stakeholders, the human rights-related expectations should be dealt with in a constructive and positive way. No company competing with integrity can justify collateral human rights damage in its endeavours to achieve its profit targets. Enlightened companies will therefore take a *rights-aware approach*, which is their willingness to accept universally accepted human rights and take appropriate action to strive to respect human rights.

RECKLESS BUSINESS: CORPORATE ACCOUNTABILITY FOR ATROCITIES

Dan Kuwali

1. INTRODUCTION

As a result of globalisation, corporations that operate across national borders have gained unprecedented power and influence across the world. As noted in the case of *Nigeria: Social and Economic Rights Action Centre (SERAC) and Another* v. *Nigeria*,[1] companies operating across borders are often involved in

[1] *Nigeria: Social and Economic Rights Action Centre (SERAC) and Another* v. *Nigeria*, African Human Rights Law Report (AHRLR) 60 (ACHPR 2001). See also Communication 155/96,

severe abuses, such as forced labour or forcibly relocating communities from their lands. Addo has aptly noted that '[a]mid rapid economic growth and new investments in land and natural resources, there is an increasing awareness of why human rights must be brought into business strategies and operations'.[2] Amnesty International has exposed countless instances where corporations exploit weak and poorly enforced domestic regulation with devastating effects on people and communities. Abuses are particularly stark in the extractive industry, with companies competing against each other to mine precious resources. Traditional livelihoods are destroyed as land is contaminated and water supplies polluted.

In its publication, *Injustice Incorporated*, Amnesty International has revealed four cases of the effects of corporate action on human rights, namely: Trafigura (2006) concerning the dumping of toxic waste in Abidjan, Côte d'Ivoire (in violation of Dutch and European Union law); Bhopal (1984) involving a gas leak and continuing environmental contamination; Omai (1995) relating to the failure of the waste containment system at the Omai gold mine in Guyana; and Ok Tedi (1984) exposing the failure of the waste containment system at the Ok Tedi gold and copper mine in Papua New Guinea and continuing environmental contamination.[3] Using their financial muscle, companies have used legal fictions and political power to evade meaningful accountability and deny victims their right to remedy.[4] In this regard, Professor John Ruggie has aptly summarised that:

> The question that confronted the international community is how, in a world of profit maximizing firms and states jealously guarding their sovereign prerogatives, can multinational corporate conduct be regulated to prevent or mitigate such human costs? The core challenge is that globally operating firms are not regulated globally. Instead, each of their component entities is subject to the individual jurisdiction in which it operates. Yet even where national laws exist prohibiting abusive conduct, which cannot always be taken for granted, states in many cases fail to implement them – because

The Social and Economic Rights Action Center and the Center for Economic, and Social Rights/Nigeria. Decided at the 30th ordinary session, October 2001, 15th Annual Activity Report.

2 The Chair of the United Nations Working Group on Business and Human Rights, Michael K Addo, speaking at the African Regional Forum, held from 16 to 18 September 2014 in Addis Ababa. See Office of the High Commissioner for Human Rights (OHCHR), 'UN and AU commit to advance business and human rights agenda in Africa', <http://www.ohchr.org/EN/NewsEvents/Pages/DisplayNews.aspx?NewsID=15053> (accessed 15.03.2017).

3 Amnesty International, *Injustice Incorporated: Corporate Abuses and Human Right to Remedy*, 07.03.2014, <www.amnesty.org/en/library/info/POL30/001/2014/en> accessed 15.03.2017.

4 Ibid.

> they lack the capacity, fear the competitive consequences of doing so, or because their leaders subordinate the public good for private gain.[5]

Focusing on Africa, apart from the pandemonium in the oil and mining industries, there has been an increasing role for religious institutions at national and international levels, which have invested in unscrupulous business enterprises. Likewise, multi-party democracy has brought about the proliferation of political parties together with stiff competition for financial resources among political parties. With the increased influence of these institutions on the general public, their irresponsible business dealings have called for public scrutiny.[6] The media has been awash with financial scandals involving religious organisations and political parties, thereby awakening public opinion to the problem of illicit financing and corruption in these institutions, which are built on trust. Although such negative publicity has not diminished the importance of religious institutions and political parties, it has become evident that clear rules for involvement of these organisations in business are required to prevent the financial activities of these organisations from interfering with the rights of their followers and the communities they operate in. Therefore, the proposed treaty of business and human rights should seize the opportunity to seal this oversight vacuum.

The 2000 Global Compact,[7] the 2003 Norms on the Responsibilities of Transnational Corporations and Other Business Enterprises with Regard to Human Rights ('the Norms')[8] and the 2011 Guiding Principles on Business and Human Rights ('Guiding Principles')[9] and the concomitant National Action Plans have not been able to effectively prevent human rights violations by

---

5 JG Ruggie, 'Just Business: Multinational Corporations and Human Rights', 2013 Raymond and Beverly Sackler Distinguished Lecture, Round Table Report, *Implementing the UN Guiding Principles on Business and Human Rights*, 28.02.2013, Thomas J Dodd Research Center, University of Connecticut, p 2.

6 More generally, religious and political activities involve expenses which are necessary and unavoidable costs in running the affairs of such institutions. In order to carry out their core activities, religious institutions and political parties need appropriate funding. The Council of Europe, *Financing Political Parties and Election Campaigns – Guidelines*, Making Democratic Institutions Work Integrated Project, p 11.

7 United Nations (UN), *The Ten Principles*, UN Global Compact, <http://www.unglobalcompact.org?AboutTheGC/index.html> (accessed 20.02.2017).

8 In 2003 the United Nations Sub-Commission on the Promotion and Protection of Human Rights unanimously adopted the Norms on the Responsibilities of the Responsibilities of Transnational Corporations and Other Business Enterprises with Regard to Human Rights ('Norms'). See A McBeth, J Nolan and S Rice, *International Law of Human Rights*, Oxford University Press, Oxford 2012, pp 615, 620.

9 Special Representative of the Secretary-General, *Report on the Issue of Human Rights and Transnational Corporations and Other Business Enterprises, Guiding Principles on Business and Human Rights: Implementing the United nations 'Protect, Respect and Remedy Framework*, UN Doc A/HRC/17/31 (21.03.2011) (by J Ruggie) ('the Guiding Principles').

corporations. Religious institutions and political parties have been left out in the United Nations (UN) regime of regulating multinational non-state actors. Yet some religious organisations and political parties have also been used as conduits to facilitate financial crimes and such other unethical actions due to compromised oversight mechanisms in these institutions. In some cases, the proceeds of crime have contributed to the perpetrations of unimaginable violations of human rights of innocent citizens, particularly in cases where the laundered money has been invested in illegal businesses.

The UN regulatory regime for business and human rights, therefore, should not only be limited to business enterprises but should also focus on the role and influence the finances of organisations have on the enjoyment of human rights by their members and the general public. Using this theory, influential corporations cannot slip through the cracks of financial accountability. Against this background, therefore, this chapter seeks to address the question whether, and if so how, the proposed international legally binding instrument on transnational corporations and other business enterprises with respect to human rights can strengthen oversight mechanisms for business and human rights in order to contribute to the prevention of human rights violations, protection of human rights and the provision of reparations to victims of human rights violations occasioned by corporations.

2. MAPPING OUT THE BUSINESS AND HUMAN RIGHTS AGENDA IN AFRICA

The heralding of the business and human rights agenda in Africa can be traced as far back as March 1996 in the watershed *SERAC and Another* v. *Nigeria* cited earlier,[10] When two non-governmental organisations (NGOs) lodged a complaint before the African Commission for Human and Peoples' Rights ('the African Commission' or 'the Commission'). The NGOs, the Nigeria-based SERAC and New York-headquartered Centre for Economic and Social Rights (CESR) lodged a complaint alleging violations of human rights of the Ogoni people in Nigeria by the then military government. The complaint alleged that the Nigerian government had been directly involved in irresponsible oil development practices in the Ogoni region. The State oil company, Nigerian National Petroleum Company (NNPC), formed a joint venture with Shell Petroleum Development Corporation (SPDC), whose activities in the Ogoni region had allegedly caused environmental degradation and health problems among the Ogoni people, resulting from the contamination of the environment.

[10] *SERAC and Another* v. *Nigeria*, above n 1.

The complaint noted that these activities violated several right under the African Charter on Human and Peoples' Rights ('the African Charter'), particularly Article 2 (non-discriminatory enjoyment of rights), Article 4 (right to life), Article 14 (right to property), Article 16 (right to health), Article 18 (family rights), Article 21 (right of peoples to freely dispose of their wealth and natural resources) and Article 24 (right of peoples to a satisfactory environment). The Commission considered the communication under Article 55 of the African Charter and concluded that the Nigerian government had failed to exercise due diligence with respect to the activities of the oil companies and their effects upon the population of Ogoni Land. The Commission reasoned that, among other things, the practice of the Nigerian government '[fell] short of the minimum conduct expected of governments, and therefore, is in violation of … the African Charter'.[11]

Today, Constitutions of countries in Africa such as Malawi and South Africa expressly impose human rights obligations on juristic or legal persons such as corporations in sections 15 and 8 of their respective Constitutions. In line with this prevailing constitutional paradigm, Judge Dennis Davies of the Cape High Court has reasoned thus:

> There is no reason why, at the end of the 20th century, we should not see multinational companies as being able to exert even greater power over individuals than is in fact the case with the state – for example, Bill Gates is richer than South Africa. In other words, if multinationals have the capacity to exert extraordinary influence over the lives of individuals, why then do we still persist with a laissez-faire division between public power and private power?[12]

It is not surprising, therefore, that South Africa was among the first countries to propose the adoption of a legally binding instrument on transnational corporations and other business enterprises with respect to human rights.[13] One of the reasons may be that Africa has seen some of the worst human rights effects of corporate activity, especially in the extractive industries such as mining and oil exploration.[14] Apart from the adverse effects of business enterprises on

---

11 Ibid, §§53–66. See also F Coomans, 'The Ogoni Case before the African Commission on Human and Peoples' Rights' (2003) 52 *International and Comparative Law Quarterly* 749–60.

12 D Davies, 'Charting the Statutory Implementation of the Values of the Bill of Rights in the Business World: Past and Future', in *Business and Human Rights in South Africa*, Human Sciences Research Council, Pretoria, South Africa, 1999, pp 39–46, at p 40.

13 The United Nations Human Rights Council, *Resolution on Elaboration of an International Legally Binding Instrument on Transnational Corporations and Other Business Enterprises With Respect to Human Rights* (Bolivia (Plurinational State of), Cuba, Ecuador, South Africa, Venezuela (Bolivarian Republic of)): draft resolution, A/HRC/26/L.22/Rev.1, 25.01.2014, para. 1. <http://daccess-ddsny.un.org/doc/UNDOC/LTD/G14/064/48/PDF/G1406448.pdf?OpenElement> (accessed 13.06.2017).

14 See *SERAC and Another* v. *Nigeria*, above n 1. See also Amnesty International, above n 3.

human rights, there has recently been a disturbing trend in many countries in Africa whereby some individuals have joined politics and religion as a business and as a means for their personal survival. In politics, this trend has been exemplified by 'politics of the belly' and the 'it is our time to eat attitude'.[15] Since traditional methods of raising money are no longer profitable, political parties are tempted to venture into other business enterprises which are economically more attractive.[16]

The growing importance of other sources of party financing such as corporate financing and private donations, poses a challenge for the legitimacy of party financing. Such practices may be susceptible to corruption and have given rise to allegations of human rights violations,[17] the reason being that certain economic activities may very well profit from favourable political decisions.[18] There has been growing concern about the improper influence of money on political decisions and about corrupt practices linked to political parties. In addition to corruption-related issues, organised crime is an issue connected with the financing of political activities in some countries. Finances of political parties have traditionally not been subject to public scrutiny because of the traditional perception that they are private associations, not subject to interference by States in their activities. Complete transparency of the financing of political parties should be ensured with a view not only to avoiding any potentially undesirable influence of money on party politics, but also to preserve the trust and confidence of the members in their parties and to avoid their involvement in human rights violations.[19]

The other challenge facing Africa is the proliferation of religious institutions, which generally have fewer oversight mechanisms than other major institutions built on the trust and confidence of their members. Although some religious organisations have voluntarily implemented different accountability mechanisms, others remain stand-alone organisations centred on magnetic personalities who control the purse strings and exercise undue influence over their members through their charismatic leadership.[20] These religious leaders have been labelled 'pastorneurs' or 'propheteers' also 'profiteers' for their love of money and often flamboyant and extravagant lifestyles. Unlike other non-profit

15 The Council of Europe, above n 6, pp 9–11.

16 Ibid, p 19.

17 For example, political parties have developed commercial activities in areas such as marketing, shopping centres, and house construction through companies owned or shared by the party. See ibid.

18 Ibid, p 19.

19 Ibid, pp 9–13.

20 The point is that money should not be allowed to buy access to decision-making power nor dent the image of the organisation. Ibid, pp 9–11.

organisations, these 'pastorneurs' can exert ostensible religious authority over their followers.[21]

Some 'pastorneurs' have used charitable gifts to enrich themselves, pushing the legal boundaries of what is considered reasonable compensation for their 'calling'.[22] The dubious donations made in religious institutions have been used to acquire mines and other lucrative businesses that have contributed to the perpetration of unimaginable violations of human rights of helpless citizens.[23] The conduct of these institutions has contributed to erosion of public trust and, in some cases, violations of human rights, especially in cases where money from these institutions has been invested in multinational corporations that have a propensity for breaking the law.

The agenda for business and human rights in Africa has mainly been driven by the African Coalition for Corporate Accountability (ACCA), which is a civil society group of at least 89 organisations from over 28 African countries. The ACCA supports communities and individuals in Africa whose human rights are adversely impacted by activities of corporations. The involvement of civil society in Africa can be seen to have derived from the frustration created among affected communities and their advocates by the existing voluntary standards, which have proved unable to provide effective protection of victims and to ensure liability of errant companies, especially in the cases of human rights abuses caused by transnational corporations beyond the borders of their home countries.

Most prominent African perspectives on business and human rights were highlighted at the first African Forum on Business and Human Rights, which ended with a strong call for action to make business a force for improving human rights in Africa.[24] The resolve of Africans to end corporate impunity was

---

21 Some religious leaders have proclaimed themselves to be 'prophets' and even invoked verses in religious scriptures to convince congregants that God has called them to be in their positions of authority and that their followers have a God-given duty to submit to them at all costs. See letter from C Grassley, United States Senator, to Randy and Paula White, Without Walls International Church (05.11.2007), <http://grassley.senate.gov/releases/2007/110620071.pdf> (accessed 20.03.2017). See also L Goodstein, 'Senator Questioning Ministries on Spending', *New York Times*, 07.11.2007, p 21. See also Press Release, Senator Chuck Grassley, Grassley Seeks Information from Six Media-based Ministries (06.11.2007), <http://grassley.senate.gov/news/Article.cfm?customel_dataPageID_1502=12011> (accessed 20.03.2017).

22 To the extent that costly electoral campaigns largely determine the outcome of elections, it is clearly undesirable that parties depend on or represent the interests of closely allied financial contributors. J Montague, 'The Law and Financial Transparency in Churches: Reconsidering the Form 990 Exception' (2013) 35 *Cardozo Law Review* 203, 207.

23 Ibid, p 239.

24 The African Regional Forum, held from 16 to 18 September 2014 in Addis Ababa, brought together 200 representatives of governments, business, civil society, and national human rights institutions to debate the defining challenges of Africa. The Regional Forum was convened by the United Nations Working Group on Business and Human Rights, with the support of the African Union Commission, the United Nations Economic Commission for Africa and the Office of the United Nations High Commissioner for Human Rights.

poignantly pointed out by the African Union (AU) Commissioner for Political Affairs, Aisha Abdullahi: '[a]ll too often have human rights concerns fallen by the wayside in the race to attract foreign investment. We have to fundamentally break with this logic and ensure that business and respect for human rights go hand-in-hand.'[25] According to Abdalla Hamdok, the Deputy Executive Secretary of the United Nations Economic Commission for Africa, '[n]ot only is this the only way to ensure the interest and welfare of the people of Africa, it is also good business and critical for the sustainability of investments'.[26]

Participants at the 2014 African Forum, which included senior government officials and experts, underlined that the AU and the UN should join forces to support responsible business practices in line with fundamental human rights standards. To this end, the participants committed to work jointly to advance the business and human rights agenda. Specific steps to advance the agenda include the development of practical tools adapted to the realities in African countries to implement the UN Guiding Principles.[27] Participants from across Africa called for responsible business practices that respect human rights, provide adequate safeguards to protect against business-related rights abuses, and ensure victims can seek redress.[28] According to experts in Africa, National Action Plans are an important tool to advance the business and human rights agenda. Such plans should be developed though inclusive consultative processes, bringing on board all stakeholders, to identify problems and find solutions.[29] It is for this reason that all stakeholders are required to promote the effective use of the panoply of human rights instruments available under the African Charter as part of any strategy to implement and enforce corporate accountability and liability in Africa and beyond.[30]

3. WHY A TREATY? CLOSING THE CORPORATE ACCOUNTABILITY GAP

The International Court of Justice in the *Democratic Republic of the Congo* v. *Uganda* case held that States have a responsibility to protect human rights of

25 OHCHR, above n 2.

26 Ibid.

27 A Abdullahi, AU Commissioner for Political Affairs, ibid.

28 See, for example, OHCHR, above n 2.

29 OHCHR, above n 2.

30 African Coalition for Corporate Accountability (ACCA), 'Statement by the African Coalition for Corporate Accountability on the occasion of the first-ever African Regional Forum on Business and Human Rights', 09.10.2014. The African Coalition for Corporate Accountability is a coalition of 89 organisations from 28 African countries supporting communities in Africa and individuals whose human rights are adversely impacted by activities of corporations.

individuals within their territories and where they have effective control.[31] However, as noted in *SERAC and Another* v. *Nigeria*,[32] many States have not been able to effectively discharge their duty to protect human rights, especially in relation to operations of multinational corporations. There are several reasons for States' failure to protect their populations from human rights violations arising from corporate activity, for example because many States do not have the capacity to engage or censure influential corporations; their dependence on the corporation as an investor; or because the enforcement machinery of some States is compromised due to their susceptibility to corruption.

The 1948 Universal Declaration of Human Rights (UDHR) requires that 'every individual and every organ of society [should] strive by teaching and education to promote respect for these rights and freedoms and … to secure their universal and effective recognition and observance, both among the peoples of Member States themselves and among the peoples of territories under their jurisdiction'.[33] In this way, the UDHR places human rights responsibilities on individuals, as well as on every organ of society, which would undoubtedly include corporations.[34] Although it is now widely accepted that corporations have a responsibility to respect human rights, the profit motive of corporations has overridden their obligation to respect the rights of communities, thereby occasioning violations in some cases.

In spite of the existence in many countries of legislation that allows corporations to be criminally liable or sued under civil actions, some governments have been unwilling or unable to even investigate wrongdoing by influential corporations. When communities have attempted to access justice, their efforts have been thwarted by ineffective or compromised legal systems, a lack of access to relevant information concerning the activities of the corporations, and corruption where governments shield errant corporations. Akin to the proverbial David and Goliath scenario, most of the victims are indigent such that they cannot afford protracted and complex legal battles against super-rich corporations to secure redress. This uneven playing field provides an opportunity for corporations to exploit poor communities with impunity. These difficulties are even greater when multinational corporations have perpetrated those abuses. The global nature of multinational companies, and their political and financial

31 *Armed Activities on the Territory of the Democratic Republic of the Congo (Democratic Republic of the Congo* v. *Uganda)* (Request from the Indication of Provisional Measures), <www.icj-cij.org/decisions/summaries/iCO_summary_20000704.html.> (accessed 12.03. 2017).

32 *SERAC and Another* v. *Nigeria*, above n 1.

33 United Nations, 'Universal Declaration of Human Rights', General Assembly Resolution 217A (III), UN Doc. A/RES/217(III), preamble, adopted10.12.1948.

34 See D Weissbrodt, 'Human Rights Standards Concerning Transnational Corporations and Other Business Entities' (2014) 23 *Minnesota Journal of International Law*, 135, 136.

power, raise very specific challenges for the right to effective remedy. Current law and policy does not adequately address these particular obstacles.[35]

The fact that there have been persistent attempts to negotiate a legally binding international instrument on business and human rights entails that the other existing regulatory initiatives do not offer effective prevention, protection and reparation mechanisms for the victims of corporate human rights abuses.[36] It for this reason that there is a need to enhance the international legal framework to protect human rights in the context of business operations.[37] However, the debate as to whether or not there should be a legally binding international treaty on corporate human rights responsibilities has exposed deep cleavages in opinions. For example, most of the countries in the Global South generally support the idea of having a legally binding treaty whereas several countries in the Global North are against the idea.[38] At the same time, while civil society groups support the need for a binding treaty, corporations themselves are generally not in favour of the idea. Surprisingly, one of the most persuasive dissenting voices is that of South Africa's Entrepreneur, Mahlaphe Sello:

> Systematic, voluntary and committed engagement in all the issues discussed above inculcates in society an understanding, appreciation and strong respect for human rights. Failure to voluntarily act raises the need for legislative intervention which, although well intentioned, is not always in the best interests of society. Over-legislation invariably pits one set of rights against the other, stifles the exercise of rights and itself can become a threat to the development of human rights. It is imperative that this be avoided where possible. And business has not only the ability to ensure that this does not happen, but also a vested interest.[39]

On the one hand, opponents contend that the UN Human Rights Council has already endorsed the UN's Guiding Principles on Business and Human Rights. In this vein, corporate lobbyists have ceaselessly campaigned to ensure that the Guiding Principles remain entirely voluntary. On the other hand, proponents argue that although the Guiding Principles are the global authoritative standard for preventing and addressing negative human rights impacts linked to business activity, the reality is that governments and businesses alike have failed to make the Guiding Principles meaningful. This loophole points to the need for

35 Amnesty International, above n 3.

36 That is to say, existing initiatives such as including the Guiding Principles on Business and Human Rights.

37 Treaty Alliance, 'Enhance the International Legal Framework to Protect Human Rights from Corporate Abuse', <http://www.treatymovement.com/statement> (accessed 18.03.2017).

38 The UN Human Rights Council, above n 13.

39 M Sello, 'The Role of the Business Community in the Evolution of a Human Rights Culture in South Africa', in *Business and Human Rights in South Africa*, above n 12, p 47, at p 53.

accountability to be mandated by an international legal regime as opposed to self-regulatory mechanisms.

Therefore, balancing the pros and cons of having a legally binding treaty on business and human rights, a reasonable view is that international binding law on corporations and human rights is the only effective way to tackle corporate abuse of rights, given the impunity of powerful corporations and the voluntary nature of the Guiding Principles. Thus, adoption of a treaty would provide an additional route and more clear opportunity in which local communities and individual victims of corporate human rights violations may seek redress against errant corporations and governments. It should be noted that the development of such a treaty does not mean abandoning the UN Guiding Principles but rather building on them and making its key provisions mandatory.

Far from eroding the relevance of the Guiding Principles, a legally binding international treaty will strengthen and provide enforcement mechanisms for existing instruments to prevent impunity for human rights violations occasioned by corporations.[40] In this way, the adoption of an international treaty on business and human rights would effectively end the debate as to whether or not corporations have binding human rights obligations, thereby buttressing the position that the Guiding Principles are not merely voluntary, but binding. As a matter of fact, strict oversight mechanisms are good for the business of corporations themselves as they can help them earn the trust and confidence of the communities they are involved in. It therefore makes good business sense to strengthen oversight mechanisms of corporations to avoid unethical and atrocious conduct associated with human rights violations.

As it is now generally agreed that corporations have human rights obligations, it is conceivable to argue that there is a social expectation on the part of corporations' stakeholders that they will behave ethically and respect human rights in the way they conduct the affairs of their organisations.[41] This social expectation is what Ruggie has called the organisation's 'social license to operate'.[42] Failure to meet this responsibility can subject organisations to courts of public opinion – comprising also all those involved in, affected by, or able to influence such organisations and the general public as a whole.[43] As the ancient Greek Philosopher Plato noted, 'a person who is habitually just will enjoy important reputational benefits'.[44] To achieve this, progressive business enterprises should

40 Treaty Alliance, above n 37.

41 See, for example, section 8(2) of the Constitution of the Republic of South Africa, which binds natural as well as juristic persons, if and to the extent that it is applicable, taking into account the nature of the right and the nature of the duty imposed by the right. See also section 15(1) of the Constitution of the Republic of Malawi.

42 See Special Representative of the Secretary-General, above n 9.

43 Ibid. See also WEISSBRODT, above n 34, p 139.

44 See also SF JOHNSON, 'Making Ethical Decisions', <http://www.sfjohnson.com/acad/ethics/making_ethical_decisions.pdf> (accessed 27.08.2015).

embrace corporate responsibility to help them establish a good reputation in the environment in which they operate. It is easy to argue that institutions that treat each stakeholder in a humane and professional manner and display a strong work ethic when discharging transactions or responsibilities invariably develop positive goodwill with stakeholders as well as the general public.

However, in considering the adoption of a treaty, Professor Ruggie has cautioned that '[h]uman rights treaties can take a long time to negotiate and enter into force. Generally, the broader their scope and the more controversial the subject, the longer the duration.'[45] As the prospective treaty will be negotiated and adopted by some of the very same States that may have been compromised by power corporations, States should safeguard their integrity from undue influence by actors from, or related to, the private sector, whose primary interest in the process falls outside the objective of promotion and protection of human rights.[46] In the spirit of complying with their duty to protect the human rights of their populations, States should actively participate in good faith and constructively in the development of this treaty. More importantly, the process of elaboration of the prospective treaty should address the needs and realities of the people and communities whose human rights have been infringed, or are being threatened, by corporate conduct.[47]

4. FROM CORPORATE IMPUNITY TO CORPORATE ACCOUNTABILITY: TOWARDS RESPONSIBLE BUSINESS CONDUCT

The 2000 Global Compact,[48] the Norms[49] and the 2011 Guiding Principles have left out religious organisations and political parties from their respective oversight radars. Therefore, the UN regulatory regime for business and human rights should not only focus on multinational business enterprises, but also address the role and influence the finances of an organisation have on the enjoyment of human rights by its members and the general public. On this basis, given their growing influence, religious organisations and political parties should be subjected to accountability when they venture into businesses. The gap left by the UN voluntary regulatory regime should be closed through formulation of the proposed treaty on business and human rights.

It cannot be denied that a treaty is needed to improve access to justice and effective remedy for victims and to stop corporate human rights abuses. A legally

45 Ruggie, above n 5, p 3.
46 Treaty Alliance, above n 37.
47 Ibid.
48 United Nations, above n 7.
49 See McBeth, Nolan and Rice, above n 8, p 620.

binding treaty will complement other instruments and initiatives in the field of business and human rights.[50] Recognising that business and human rights challenges cannot be met by States, corporations and civil society acting on their own, the treaty should take a similar format to the Guiding Principles, which Ruggie calls 'polycentric governance' that weaves together three different rationales into a single normative platform.[51] Thus, first, for States, it should spell out the legal obligations they have under the international human rights regime to protect human rights abuses by third parties, in the form of corporations; secondly, for corporations, the treaty should outline the duty to prevent involvement in human rights abuses, which requires acting with due diligence to avoid infringing the rights of others, and to address harm where it does occur; and thirdly, for affected individuals and communities, the treaty should provide mechanisms for accessing justice and realisation of their right to remedy, both judicial and non-judicial.[52]

In negotiating and drafting the treaty, it is important to have recourse to Amnesty International's seminal publication, *Injustice Incorporated*, which makes proposals for change in three core areas: legal hurdles to extraterritorial action; lack of information; and corporate–State relationships. Amnesty International calls for legal and policy change to make it easier to hold parent companies responsible for human rights abuses arising in their global operations. For example, it suggests that there should be improvements in the disclosure of information about corporations and their human rights impacts, particularly when handling toxic substances. It also addresses some of the more problematic aspects of corporate–State relationships, including calling for disclosure of all government meetings with companies.[53]

It should be remembered that States are required to actively promote the welfare and development of their people by progressively adopting and implementing policies and legislation aimed at achieving public trust and good governance. For example, this can be achieved by introducing measures which protect human rights, guarantee accountability, and which, by virtue of their effectiveness and transparency, will strengthen confidence in public institutions.[54] Going by this reasoning, a treaty will enable States to fulfil their duty to protect populations against all human rights abuses, including those caused by corporate abuse and negligence.

---

50 Treaty Alliance, above n 37.

51 RUGGIE, above n 5, p 4.

52 Ibid, p. 4.

53 Amnesty International, above n 3.

54 For example, section 13(o) of the Constitution of the Republic of Malawi, which provides for principles of national policy. See Malawi Government, The Constitution of the Republic of Malawi, 2004, <http://www.chr.up.ac.za/undp/domestic/docs/c_Malawi.pdf> (accessed 02.08.2015).

For example, the treaty could clearly set out the parameters of the state's duty to protect in the context of business operations, including with regard to parent and controlling companies of multinational groups active in more than one country. In this way, the treaty would also help to standardise how States relate to business. Such a treaty should also require each state to pass laws to make corporate human rights due diligence mandatory, and introduce sanctions and legal liability for companies that fail to act responsibly. More importantly, the treaty should require corporations to be transparent and accountable. It is only when corporations are held accountable that they will be diligent and responsible in their conduct. Corporations should be required to share information and technical and financial resources, including cooperation in terms of ensuring corporate accountability and people's access to remedy. Against this backdrop, below are suggestions of some of the elements that should be considered in the proposed treaty on business and human rights.

4.1. THE TREATY SHOULD IMPOSE A DUTY TO CONDUCT DUE DILIGENCE AND SANCTIONS FOR NON-COMPLIANCE

The proposed treaty should require States to adopt legislation and other measures to impose a duty to prevent human rights violations by requiring all corporations and other business enterprises to take steps and adopt policies and procedures aimed at identifying, preventing, stopping and redressing human rights abuses wherever they operate or cooperate. These measures should also cover business operations and relationships taking place in countries other than the countries where the business may be domiciled or headquartered.[55] The proposed treaty should require corporations to exercise due diligence as it contributes to informed decision making and is key to making a correct and informed decision.[56] To embody due diligence, the treaty should also provide for an avenue for victims to sue for corporate negligence. Therefore, companies should be subjected to appropriate sanctions for their failure to adopt such policies and procedures.[57]

---

55 Treaty Alliance, above n 37.

56 Due diligence is the idea that reasonable investigation is necessary before certain kinds of relief are requested. See RE Hoskisson, MA Hitt and RD Ireland, *Competing for Advantage*, South-Western/Thomson Learning, Ohio 2004, p 251. See also CE Chapman, *Conducting Due Diligence*, Practicing Law Institute, New York 2006.

57 Treaty Alliance, above n 37.

4.2. THE TREATY SHOULD ENHANCE TRANSPARENCY AND ACCOUNTABILITY

The proposed treaty should enhance transparency and accountability for corporations by requiring States to ensure that companies are held accountable for abuses they commit. Accountability is answerability of responsibility for actions and the expectation of account-giving.[58] The treaty should oblige States to demand corporations to be transparent in the way they operate so that it is easy for affected communities to see what actions are performed, including feasibility studies of projects.[59] Transparency is the linchpin of compliance such that when corporate activities are visible to all, the possibility of abuse is reduced.[60] It is suggested that corporations should be required to file relevant information relating to their compliance with human rights and that such information should be available for public inspection.[61] As discussed earlier, it is easy to see that corporations themselves would benefit from increased transparency and accountability.[62] The treaty should, thus, require States to enact legislation that encompasses the obligation for corporations to report, explain and be answerable for resulting consequences of their actions. Over and above this, the treaty should also require States to be more transparent in their relationships with corporations.

4.3. THE TREATY SHOULD SPELL OUT CONDUCT GIVING RISE TO CRIMINAL AND CIVIL LIABILITY

The treaty should clarify the kind of corporate conduct that will give rise to legal liability, that is to say, civil, criminal and administrative actions. Through the proposed international instrument, States should have the obligation to translate these standards into national legislation and enforce them. For example, offences committed against the environment and adversely impacting human rights should be included.[63]

---

58 CA Dykstra, 'The Quest for Responsibility' (1939) 33(1) *American Political Science Review* 1–25. See also R Williams, *Leadership Accountability in a Globalizing World*, Palgrave Macmillan, London 2006.

59 AK Schnackenberg and EC Tomlinson, 'Organizational Transparency: a New Perspective on Managing Trust in Organization-Stakeholder Relationships' (2014) 37 *Academy of Management Journal* 1302–34.

60 *Hearing on Tax-Exempt Charitable Organizations Before the Subcomm. on Oversight of the H. Comm. on Ways & Means*, 110th Cong. 11 (2007) [hereinafter *Hearing on Tax-Exempt Charitable Organizations* (2007)] (statement of Steven T Miller, Commissioner, Tax Exempt and Government Entities Division, IRS).

61 Tax Reform Act of 1969, H.R. 13270, 91st Cong. §101(d) (as passed by House, 07.08.1969).

62 Montague, above n 22, p 246.

63 Treaty Alliance, above n 37.

4.4. THE TREATY SHOULD PROVIDE A MECHANISM FOR ACCESS TO LEGAL REDRESS FOR VICTIMS

The treaty should require States to provide access to legal redress so that the people whose rights have been abused by corporations must be able to access justice and effective remedy. The treaty should allow people with a claim access to reparations not only in their own home States, but in all other States that have jurisdiction over the business enterprise concerned. The jurisdiction of national courts of these States should extend to deal with these cases separately and jointly, and effectively guarantee access to justice to the victims.[64]

4.5. THE TREATY SHOULD PENETRATE THE VEIL OF INCORPORATION

It should be remembered that violations are incited, facilitated and committed by individuals and not really abstract entities called corporations. For this reason, the treaty should elaborate on the modalities in which corporations and other business enterprises participate in the commission of human rights abuses, including corporate complicity and parent company responsibility for the offences committed by their subsidiaries. Corporate legal responsibility for human rights violations should include the legal responsibility of company directors as well as managers.[65] In this way, directors of the corporation will have an incentive to pay closer attention to the organisation's activities and to be more vigilant about their oversight role when they know that others can look over their backs.[66] Even when nothing illegal has occurred, directors of the company will be likely to be more conscientious about ensuring that organisations seem clean and efficient.

4.6. THE TREATY SHOULD PROVIDE A VICTIM ASSISTANCE PROGRAMME AND COOPERATION AMONG STATES

The treaty should contain provisions requiring States that are in a position to do so to provide assistance to victims of human rights abuse by corporations. States should also be required to respect, protect and facilitate the work of human rights defenders and whistle-blowers. The right to access to information of public importance and relevant to cases of business-related abuse should

---

64 Ibid.

65 Ibid.

66 Swords, *The Form 990 as an Accountability Tool for 501(c)(3) Nonprofits*, p 582.

be guaranteed.[67] To ably assist the victims, the treaty should require more cooperation between and among States. To this end, the treaty should have provisions that promote international legal and judicial cooperation among countries to facilitate the investigation and prosecution of cases of a transnational nature.[68] Cooperation should also be required in terms of sharing of information and technical and financial resources as well as cooperation in terms of ensuring corporate accountability and people's access to remedy.

4.7. THE TREATY SHOULD PROVIDE FOR AN INTERNATIONAL MONITORING AND ACCOUNTABILITY MECHANISM

The treaty should establish an oversight body composed of independent members who should be provided with sufficient means (including investigative powers, financial resources and technical equipment) for effectively exercising their monitoring function.[69] To this end, Amnesty International has suggested that a dedicated unit or centre within the UN may improve the international capacity for independent research and analysis and for monitoring the practices of transnational corporations and other business enterprises.[70] However, to achieve this, the needs and feasibility of a complementary international jurisdiction should be explored.[71]

4.8. THE TREATY SHOULD PROVIDE FOR EXTRATERRITORIAL APPLICATION OF CORPORATE RESPONSIBILITY

The treaty should require States to enact legislation demanding corporations to protect human rights beyond borders. The treaty should, thus, require the home States of multinational companies to act to prevent abuses by corporate actors, including abuses that occur outside their territory.[72] Therefore, the prospective treaty should oblige home States of the multinational corporation involved to enact legislation to ensure that corporate perpetrators of human rights abuses domiciled or headquartered within their territory are held criminally and/or

67 Treaty Alliance, above n 37.
68 Ibid.
69 Council of Europe, above n 6, p 13.
70 Treaty Alliance, above n 37.
71 Ibid.
72 For example, home states should place parent or controlling companies of multinational corporations domiciled or headquartered in their countries under an express legal duty of care towards individuals and communities whose human rights are affected by their global operations. See Amnesty International, above n 3, p 143. See also G Quijano, 'Justice for Corporate Atrocities' (2016) 57 *Online Symposium* 31.

civilly accountable, regardless of where the abuses took place.[73] It has been noted that 'the prospect of effective sanctions and an adverse legal finding in the home state can provide companies at the headquarter level with the incentive to put measures in place to ensure that no human rights abuses occur in the context of their global operations'.[74] The reasoning is that if companies operate across borders, the law must also operate across borders to protect people's rights.[75]

5. CONCLUSION

It is acknowledged that the UN Guiding Principles provide globally agreed standards on how to make business and human rights work together. Given their voluntary nature and the impunity of influential corporations for human rights violations, it is an uphill battle to translate these standards into concrete action plans and implementation tools tailored to the realities of African countries.[76] The 2000 Global Compact, the Norms and the 2011 Guiding Principles have not been able to prevent some of the most powerful non-state actors in the world from committing human rights violations or from being held accountable for violations. It should be noted that with power should come responsibility. Therefore, the regulation of ethical conduct should focus adequately on these extremely potent non-state actors.[77]

The players in the battle for justice between corporations and victims reflect the proverbial David and Goliath scenario. On the one side is a multitude of helpless victims searching for truth, justice and compensation; and on the other side are influential corporations who have been effectively protected by governments from accountability. Victims of human rights abuses frequently face significant challenges when seeking remedy.[78] Although domestic legislation in several countries allows for criminal prosecution of corporations and civil suits, it has proved difficult to ensure corporate responsibility for human rights violations. The challenges range from ineffective or compromised legal systems, impediments to accessing relevant information faced by victims, and the protection offered to corporations by governments due to their influence or sheer corruption. The likelihood of impunity posed by these challenges buttresses the fact that corporate accountability for human rights violations

---

73 See Amnesty International, above n 3, p 143.

74 Ibid.

75 Treaty Alliance, above n 37.

76 OHCHR, above n 2.

77 D Weissbrodt and M Kruger, 'Norms on the Responsibilities of Transnational Corporations and Other Business Enterprises with Regard to Human Rights (2003) 97 *American Journal of International Law* 901, p 901.

78 Amnesty International, above n 3.

should be mandated by an international legal regime as opposed to voluntary regimes. Therefore, far from the fear expressed by Ruggie, among others, that the proposed treaty may undermine the consensus garnered by the Guiding Principles, the adoption of an internationally binding treaty may actually increase the incentives for States and corporations to conform to the Guiding Principles by formulating credible National Action Plans and adopting policies to respect human rights at all times.[79]

By focusing on some of the current challenges faced by business activities on human rights on the African continent, the main argument made in this chapter is that a legally binding international treaty to ensure corporate responsibility for human rights violations is not only necessary but also imperative to close the impunity gap exposed by powerful multinational corporations. Such a treaty will complement the existing mechanisms by providing an enforcement mechanism. A treaty will enable States to fulfil their duty to protect people against all human rights abuses, including those caused by corporate abuse and negligence. A treaty could clearly set out what the state duty to protect means in the context of business operations, including with regard to parent and controlling companies of multinational groups active in more than one country. A treaty should require each state to enact legislation that makes corporate human rights due diligence mandatory, and provide sanctions and legal liability for companies that fail to act responsibly.

It is important that the process of elaboration of the prospective treaty should address the needs and realities of the affected populations and communities whose human rights have been violated, or are being threatened, by corporate conduct. Therefore, to avoid being compromised, States should actively and constructively negotiate this prospective human rights treaty. In doing so, States should safeguard their integrity from undue influence by corporate lobbyists whose primary interest in the process is profit and not the objective of promotion and protection of human rights.[80] All in all, the proposed international legally binding instrument on transnational corporations and other business enterprises with respect to human rights will complete the panoply of instruments aimed at arresting corporate activities that have occasioned human rights violations, by using the law to empower the victims and to redress the imbalances that have resulted from failure to ensure corporate accountability.

---

79 C Macchi, 'A Treaty on Business and Human Rights: Problems and Prospects' in this volume.

80 Treaty Alliance, above n 37.

EUROPEAN PERSPECTIVES ON THE BUSINESS AND HUMAN RIGHTS TREATY INITIATIVE

Jernej Letnar Černič

1. INTRODUCTION

The European Union and the Council of Europe have, since their foundation, been committed to the rule of law, human rights and accountability. However, the approach of European states, within the European Union and the Council of Europe, to the Business and Human Rights Treaty Initiative has so far been cautious and conservative.[1] For instance, the European Commission has advocated for 'a smart mix of voluntary policy measures and, where necessary, complementary regulation, for example to promote transparency, create market incentives for responsible business conduct, and ensure corporate accountability'.[2] Nonetheless, it appears that both the European Union and the

---

1 See J Letnar Černič, 'Towards a Holistic Approach to Business and Human Rights in the European Union' (2016) 10(1) *Human Rights and International Legal Discourse* 160–80. This chapter is a considerably extended and updated version of J Letnar Černič, 'Desarrollos internacionales recientes en el ámbito de los derechos humanos y las empresas' in H Cantú Rivera (ed) *Derechos Humanos y Empresas : Reflexiones desde América Latina* (San José, C.R.: Instituto Interamericano de Derechos Humanos, 2017), pp. 137–156.

2 A renewed EU Strategy 2011–2014 for Corporate Social Responsibility. Communication from the Commission to the European Parliament, the Council, the European Economic and Social Committee and the Committee of the Regions. Brussels, 25.10.2011. EU Doc. COM(2011)681, p 7.

Council of Europe clearly favour voluntary approaches to human rights and business, before binding regulation.

This chapter will therefore present and analyse European approaches to business and human rights, and particularly the proposed UN Treaty on Business and Human Rights. It is divided into five sections. Section 2 first describes and analyses the European approach to the UN Guiding Principles on Business and Human Rights and to the Business and Human Rights Treaty Initiative. Section 3 examines initiatives of the Council of Europe in the business and human rights field, whereas Section 4 studies and analyses different approaches within the European Union, with both sections trying to draw out lessons concerning the understanding of current developments in Europe. Equipped with this knowledge, Section 5 considers and argues how to move forward with the possibility of adopting a holistic approach to business and human rights within and beyond the European Union and the Council of Europe. All in all, the conclusion raises the need for a victims-orientated approach to business and human rights in the European Union and argues that there exist strong legal and moral grounds for European support of the Business and Human Rights Treaty Initiative.

2. THE UN GUIDING PRINCIPLES AND THE EUROPEAN STATES

The UN Human Rights Council adopted the UN Guiding Principles on Business and Human Rights in June 2011 by 'consensus'.[3] They rest on three pillars: the protect, respect and remedy framework. First, states primarily have responsibility to protect individuals from corporate conduct that may result in corporate human rights violations.[4] Second, the Guiding Principles on Business and Human Rights impose responsibilities to on corporations to respect human rights.[5] Such obligations on businesses not to harm human rights are not straightforward and should be expected, however the real power of the UN Guiding Principles lies in Principles 13–15, which indirectly also include corporate obligations to

3 S Deva, 'Treating Human Rights Lightly: A Critique of the Consensus Rhetoric and the Language Employed by the Guiding Principles' in S Deva and D Bilchitz (eds), *Human Rights Obligations of Business: Beyond the Corporate Responsibility to Respect?* (Cambridge: Cambridge University Press, 2013), pp 78–104.

4 Special Representative of the Secretary-General on the Issue of Human Rights and Transnational Corporations and Other Business Enterprises, 'Guiding Principles on Business and Human Rights: Implementing the United Nations "Protect, Respect and Remedy" Framework' [hereinafter *The Guiding Principles*], UN Doc A/HRC/17/31 (21.03.2011), Principles 1–2.

5 ibid. Principle 11.

protect and fulfil human rights in their business activities. Its principal author, Ruggie, argues that those obligations derive from societal expectations not from legal norms.[6] Therefore possibly their most striking shortcoming is that they recognise that businesses do not have legal obligations to respect, but only 'responsibility to respect', which 'is not an obligation under international human rights law imposed directly upon companies'.[7] Finally, the third pillar includes access of individuals to remedy for human rights violations.

The apparent division created by the UN Guiding Principles was later echoed by the adoption of the recent resolutions on business and human rights.[8] The Guiding Principles have received a mixed response. One of the most vocal criticisms was concentrated on corporate influence in the drafting process of the Principles.[9] Nonetheless, they were taken up by several international organisations as benchmark standards in business and human rights.[10] Some European states, such as Denmark, Finland, Germany, Italy, Lithuania, the Netherlands, Norway, Spain, Sweden, Switzerland and the United Kingdom, have subsequently adopted National Action Plans to implement the UN Guiding Principles.[11] However, most European states have remained very passive[12] in developing their national plans and strengthening their national systems towards greater corporate human rights accountability, far behind the consensus reached at the time the UN Guiding Principles were adopted.[13] It appears unlikely that the majority of European states will adopt national plans to implement the UN Guiding Principles anytime soon. In contrast, the UN Guiding Principles have

---

6 JG Ruggie, 'Regulating Multinationals: The UN Guiding Principles, Civil Society, and International Legalization' (2015) Regulatory Policy Program Working Paper RPP-2015-04. Cambridge, MA: Mossavar-Rahmani Center for Business and Government, Harvard Kennedy School, Harvard University, 3.

7 C Woods, '"It Isn't a State Problem": The Minas Conga Mine Controversy and the Need for Binding International Obligations on Corporate Actors' (2015) 46 *Georgetown Journal of International Law* 629–683, 649.

8 International Organisation of Employers, 'Consensus on Business and Human Rights Is Broken With the Adoption of the Ecuador Initiative' (26.12.2014). See also A Rhodes, 'The False Promise of an International Business and Human Rights Treaty', *The World Post* (10.07.2014), C Rees, 'Treaties & The UN Guiding Principles on Business & Human Rights: The Way Forward', *CSR Wire*, 07.07.2014.

9 See Misereor, Global Policy Forum, Brot für die Welt, *Corporate Influence on the Business and Human Rights Agenda of the United Nations*, Working paper (June 2014).

10 See, for example, Section 3 below on the developments with the Council of Europe.

11 Business and Human Rights Resource Centre, National Action Plans, <https://www.business-humanrights.org/en/un-guiding-principles/implementation-tools-examples/implementation-by-governments/by-type-of-initiative/national-action-plans> accessed 22.05.2017.

12 Business and Human Rights Resource Centre, Government comparative survey, <http://business-humanrights.org/en/government-survey-compare?keywords=&filtertype=economicregion&economicregions[]=5&actions[]=11512> accessed 22.05.2017.

13 See also recent developments in Switzerland: Swiss Coalition for Corporate Justice, 'Swiss Parliament Motion for mandatory human rights due diligence narrowly turned down Conservative backlash blocks increased corporate accountability', 13.03.2015.

been welcomed by the business community. Transnational corporations such Microsoft,[14] Adidas Group,[15] Rio Tinto,[16] Cisco Systems,[17] Barclays,[18] Credit Suisse,[19] UniCredit,[20] Unilever,[21] Repsol[22] and others operating in Europe now refer to the UN Guiding Principles in their human rights and/or corporate social responsibility policies. What is more, there have been several references to the UN Guiding Principles in reports by non-governmental and international organisations.

All in all, the added value of the UN Guiding Principles lies particularly in their relevance for the corporate sector as they leave corporations with a 'free hand' as to how to incorporate human rights into their business activities and do not provide any sanctions for alleged corporate human rights abuses. Not surprisingly, European states have been their strongest supporter and they find themselves therefore nowadays in the camps of opponents of the proposed UN Treaty on Business and Human Rights. Despite some initial success, their practical value remains to be proven, particularly when assessing their contribution to the protection of rights of vulnerable groups and victims. Particularly, their added value for victims' access to justice is particularly problematic. Nonetheless, they should not and cannot be discarded as irrelevant as John Ruggie can be attributed with having placed a movement for corporate accountability at the heart of the agenda of the international community and this is no small feat. Time will show how their role and relevance will develop in the light of new initiatives in the field of business and human rights. However, for European states to focus all their efforts only on the Guiding Principles would be counter-productive.

---

14 Microsoft, Corporate Citizenship, <http://www.microsoft.com/about/corporatecitizenship/en-us/working-responsibly/principled-business-practices/human-rights/> accessed 22.05.2017.

15 Adidas Group, Human Rights and Responsible Business Practices, <http://www.adidas-group.com/media/filer_public/2013/11/14/human_rights_responsible_business_practices_qa_july_2011_en.pdf> accessed 22.05.2017.

16 Rio Tinto, Why Human Rights Matter, January 2013, <http://www.riotinto.com/documents/ReportsPublications/Rio_Tinto_human_rights_guide_-_English_version.pdf> accessed 22.05.2017.

17 Cisco Systems, Human Rights policy, <http://csr.cisco.com/cdnorigin/media/documents/Human-Rights_129973805781330000.pdf> accessed 22.05.2017.

18 Barclays, Human Rights, <http://www.barclays.com/citizenship/the-way-we-do-business/human-rights.html> accessed 22.05.2017.

19 Credit Suisse, Corporate Social Responsibility, <https://www.credit-suisse.com/bh/en/about-us/corporate-responsibility/banking/international-agreements/global-compact.html> accessed 22.05.2017.

20 Statement by the Thun Group of Banks, <http://business-humanrights.org/sites/default/files/media/documents/thun_group_statement_final_2_oct_2013.pdf> accessed 22.05.2017.

21 Unilever, Advancing Human Rights across our operations, <http://www.unilever.com/sustainable-living-2014/enhancing-livelihoods/fairness-in-the-workplace/advancing-human-rights-across-our-operations/> accessed 22.05.2017.

22 Repsol, Respecting Human Rights, Public Commitment, <http://memorias.repsol.com/memoria2013/en/responsabilidadCorporativa/nuestrosCompromisos/respetarDerechosHumanos/compromisoPublico.html> accessed 22.05.2017.

3. WORKINGS WITHIN THE COUNCIL OF EUROPE

The Council of Europe has been involved in the work on business and human rights for many years. On 6 October 2013 the Parliamentary Assembly of the Council of Europe adopted Resolution 1757, which recognises the shortcoming of the European system of human rights relating to business activities. It notes that:

> The Assembly is also concerned about the existing imbalance in the scope of human rights protection between individuals and businesses. While a company may bring a case before the European Court of Human Rights claiming a violation by a state authority of its rights protected under the European Convention on Human Rights, an individual alleging a violation of his or her rights by a private law company cannot effectively raise his or her claims before this jurisdiction.[23]

The resolution interestingly called member for 'the implementation of the United Nations "Norms on the responsibilities of transnational corporations and other business enterprises with regard to human rights" by business entities registered within their jurisdiction'[24] and proposed 'devising a toolkit on mainstreaming best practices in the field of human rights protection into every aspect of a business and on how to conduct human rights impact assessments, in co-operation with business organisations and human rights groups'.[25] Such wording is quite interesting as in autumn 2010 the Norms were already dead and Ruggie had already in 2008 formulated his framework of the 'Respect, Protect and Fulfil' framework. Thereafter, the Committee of Ministers of the Council of Europe asked the Steering Committee for Human Rights (CDDH) to elaborate a study on the feasibility and the added value of new standard-setting work of the Council of Europe in human rights and business.[26] The state representatives of the Committee of Ministers deliberately moved away from the existing language of the Council of Europe, preferring to use 'corporate social responsibility' instead of human rights and business, as it had used previously.[27] It seems that

---

23 Resolution 1757 (2010), Human rights and business, *Assembly debate* on 06.10.2010 (32nd Sitting) (see Doc. 12361, report of the Committee on Legal Affairs and Human Rights, Rapporteur: Mr Haibach; and Doc. 12384, opinion of the Committee on Economic Affairs and Development, Rapporteur: Mr Elzinga). Text adopted by the Assembly on 06.10.2010 (32nd Sitting), 4.

24 ibid. 7.2.

25 ibid. 7.4.1.

26 Steering Committee for Human Rights (CDDH), Feasibility Study on Corporate Social Responsibility on the field of human rights, Strasbourg, 30.11.2012 CDDH(201 2) R76, Addendum VII, < https://www.coe.int/t/dghl/standardsetting/cddh/CDDH-DOCUMENTS/CDDH(2012)17_EN.pdf accessed 22.05.2017.

27 Corporate social responsibility in the field of human rights, <http://www.coe.int/t/dghl/standardsetting/hrpolicy/Other_Committees/HR_and_Business/Default_en.asp> accessed 22.05.2017.

such a change signals the move from a more binding to more voluntary approach. Such a move has not been fully implemented, as the dedicated Council of Europe webpage refers to 'Corporate social responsibility in the field of human rights', whereas its website address still has 'human rights and business' in its name.[28]

The Steering Committee thereafter prepared a draft preliminary study examining the state of the art on human rights and business within the Council of Europe. The Steering Committee first produced a draft preliminary report in June 2012, which explored some issue in the area of human rights and business but did not include any guidance on how to proceed.[29] This was later followed by the feasibility report in November 2012.[30] Alas, the report did not provide any new insights in the field of human rights and business, particularly in the sub-areas of children's rights, social rights and the internet and can rather be characterised as an awareness-raising document.

Thereafter, the Council of Europe asked the Steering Committee 'to elaborate a declaration of the Committee of Ministers supporting the UN Guiding Principles and to submit it to the Committee of Ministers by 30 June 2014' and by the end of 2015 'to elaborate – in co-operation with the private sector and civil society – a non-binding instrument'.[31] The Committee of Ministers thereafter adopted a declaration stating that 'the effective implementation, both by States and business enterprises, of the UN Guiding Principles is essential to ensure respect for human rights in the business context, and [the Committee of Ministers] expresses its willingness to contribute to their effective implementation at the European level, by identifying and analysing specific gaps and proposing appropriate solutions'.[32] However, the approach of the Council of Europe nevertheless has taken forward the initiative of the UN Guiding Principles by asking the Member States of the Council of Europe to 'take appropriate steps to protect against human rights abuses by business enterprises', 'formulate and implement policies and measures to promote that all business enterprises respect human rights throughout their

---

28 ibid.

29 Steering Committee, Draft Preliminary Study on Corporate Social Responsibility in the field of human rights: Existing Standards and Outstanding Issues, Strasbourg, 04.06.2012, CDDH(2012)012, Strasbourg, 04.06.2012 85th meeting of the CDDH-BU, <http://www.coe.int/t/dghl/standardsetting/hrpolicy/Other_Committees/HR_and_Business/Documents/CDDH_2012_012_Study_EN.pdf> accessed 22.05.2017.

30 Steering Committee for Human Rights (CDDH), Feasibility Study on Corporate Social Responsibility on the field of human rights, Strasbourg, 30.11.2012 CDDH(201 2) R76, Addendum VII, < https://www.coe.int/t/dghl/standardsetting/cddh/CDDH-DOCUMENTS/CDDH(2012)17_EN.pdf> accessed 22.05.2017.

31 Steering Committee for Human Rights (CDDH), 1160th meeting – 30.01.2013, Item 4.1a,b, <https://wcd.coe.int/ViewDoc.jsp?Ref=CM/Del/Dec%282013%291160/4.1&Language=lanEnglish&Ver=original&Site=CM&BackColorInternet=DBDCF2&BackColorIntranet=FDC864&BackColorLogged=FDC864> accessed 22.05.2017.

32 Declaration of the Committee of Ministers on the UN Guiding Principles on business and human rights adopted by the Committee of Ministers on 16.04.2014 at the 1197th meeting of the Ministers' Deputies), 9.

operations, within and beyond their national jurisdictions', 'take appropriate steps to ensure that when such abuses occur within their territory and/or jurisdiction those affected have access to effective remedy', and 'develop national action plans on the implementation of the UN Guiding Principles'.[33]

More specifically, the Council of Europe recognises that its Member States have extraterritorial obligations to control corporations that are based on their territory when they do business abroad.[34] In contrast, the UN Guiding Principles only provide that states have territorial obligations to comply with human rights obligations. Nonetheless, the Council of Europe's approach has translated the approach of the UN Guiding Principles on Business and Human Rights to its documents. Such approach is also due to the support of the European states for the 2014 Norway UN resolution favouring the work of the UN Working Group on Business and Human Rights, which promotes and disseminates the UN Guiding Principles. What is more, the Council of Europe's Committee of Ministers' Resolution expressly mentioned that its decisions have to follow the workings of other international organisations.[35] Section 9 of the Recommendation to the States, which the Committee of Ministers of the Council of Europe adopted on 2 March 2016, provides that 'Member States should support the work of the United Nations, including in particular the UN Working Group on Business and Human Rights, to promote the effective and comprehensive dissemination and implementation of the UN Guiding Principles on Business and Human Rights'.[36] Further, the Recommendation noted that 'in their implementation of the UN Guiding Principles on Business and Human Rights, member States should take into account the full spectrum of international human rights standards and ensure consistency and coherence at all levels of government'.[37]

However, in order for Council of Europe's work to complement the existing initiatives on human rights and business, it would have to identify additional added value of its approach. It could be argued that the Council of Europe

---

33 ibid. Section 10.

34 See recent developments of the liability of parent corporations for subsidiaries in France – Elodie Aba, 'Opportunity for France to hold companies legally responsible for human rights abuses by subsidiaries abroad, Business and Human Rights Resource Centre', <http://business-humanrights.org/en/opportunity-for-france-to-hold-companies-legally-responsible-for-human-rights-abuses-by-subsidiaries-abroad> accessed 22.05.2017. See Loi n° 2017-399 du 27 mars 2017 relative au devoir de vigilance des sociétés mères et des entreprises donneuses d'ordre publiée, Official Journal, 28.03.2017, <http://www.assemblee-nationale.fr/14/dossiers/devoir_vigilance_entreprises_donneuses_ordre.asp>, accessed 22.05.2017.

35 ibid.

36 Council of Europe, Recommendation of the Committee of Ministers to member States on human rights and business, CM/Rec(2016)3, 02.03.2016, Section 9. See also Council of Europe, Steering Committee for Human Rights (CDDH) – Explanatory Memorandum to Recommendation CM/Rec(2016)3 of the Committee of Ministers to member States on human rights and business.

37 ibid. Section 3.

could offer a European approach to human rights and business/corporate social responsibility, particularly focusing on the Europe-based corporations. However, even in this respect it is questionable what the Council of Europe's approach should be as the European Union is quite industrious in this area. An approach of focusing on particular rights or sectors would be one way to go (as already identified by the feasibility study),[38] however it would be also advisable for the Council of Europe to focus on practical tools and measures which could assist corporations in meeting their human rights obligations. Another approach would be to streamline the case law of the European Court of Human Rights[39] and the European Committee on Social Rights in order to reaffirm state responsibility to protect in their decisions[40] by also applying the European Convention on Human Rights and Fundamental Freedoms and the European Social Charter extraterritorially where European corporations do business. This would not require extending jurisdiction of the European Court, as some authors suggest,[41] but only that the European Court applies its approach to extraterritoriality also with respect to the conduct of European corporations. In other words, it is more useful to raise awareness of judges concerning potential consequences of the conduct of European corporations outside their borders and state obligations to protect individuals outside their borders from harmful conduct of corporations based on their territory. All in all, the Council of Europe has been active in voluntary regulation in the business and human rights field. However, there is no evidence that Member States of the Council of Europe nor the institution itself have been in favour of the initiative on the Business and Human Rights Treaty.

4. THE EUROPEAN UNION AND BUSINESS AND HUMAN RIGHTS

4.1. INSTITUTIONAL INITIATIVES WITHIN EU INSTITUTIONS

The Treaty on European Union provides in Article 2 that

> the Union is founded on the values of respect for human dignity, freedom, democracy, equality, the rule of law and respect for human rights, including the rights of persons

---

38 Council of Europe, Feasibility study, paras. 15–25.

39 See European Court of Human Rights, *López Ostra v. Spain*, no. 16798/90, 09.12.1994; *Taşkin and Others v. Turkey*, no. 46117/99, 10.12.2004; *Fadeyeva v. the Russian Federation*, no. 55273/00, 09.06.2005; *Tatar v. Romania*, no. 67021/01, 27.01.2009 where the European Court of Human Rights found violations of state obligation to protect individuals in the enjoyment of human rights.

40 See, for example, the European Committee of Social Rights. *Marangopoulos Foundation for Human Rights v. Greece*, no. 30/2005, decision of 06.12.2006.

41 S Khoury and D Whyte, *New Mechanisms of Accountability for Corporate Violations of Human Rights*, University of Liverpool, February 2015, p 3.

> belonging to minorities. These values are common to the Member States in a society in which pluralism, non-discrimination, tolerance, justice, solidarity and equality between women and men prevail.[42]

It further states in Article 3(5) that

> in its relations with the wider world, the Union shall uphold and promote its values and interests and contribute to the protection of its citizens. It shall contribute to peace, security, the sustainable development of the Earth, solidarity and mutual respect among peoples, free and fair trade, eradication of poverty and the protection of human rights, in particular the rights of the child, as well as to the strict observance and the development of international law, including respect for the principles of the United Nations Charter.

Those provisions also provide a platform for the functioning of the European Commission in the field of business and human rights.[43] More specifically, the European Commission has recently noted that

> trade policy can be a powerful tool to further the advancement of human rights in third countries in conjunction with other EU policies, in particular foreign policy and development cooperation. Human rights breaches that may be found in global supply chains such as the worst forms of child labour, forced prison labour, forced labour as a result of trafficking in human beings and land grabbing deserve particular attention.[44]

However, the binding sources of law on business and human rights have so far, with a few exceptions,[45] been outstanding. In this context, the Council of the European Union and the European Commission noted in their 2013 EU Strategic Framework and Action Plan on Human Rights and Democracy that 'the EU will encourage and contribute to implementation of the UN Guiding Principles on Business and Human Rights'.[46] Moreover, section 25 of its Action Plan on Human Rights and Democracy provides that one of its goals is to '(a) ensure implementation to [*sic*] the Commission Communication on Corporate Social Responsibility, in particular by developing and disseminating human rights guidance for three business sectors (ICT; oil and gas; employment

---

42 See Černič, above n 1.

43 ibid.

44 European Commission (2015), *Trade for All: Towards a More Responsible Trade and Investment Policy*, Luxembourg, Publications Office, pp 25–26.

45 See, for example, EU Directive 2014/95/EU on disclosure of non-financial and diversity information by certain large undertakings and groups (OJ L330, 15.11.2014).

46 EU Strategic Framework and Action Plan on Human Rights and Democracy, 25.06.2012, <http://www.consilium.europa.eu/uedocs/cms_data/docs/pressdata/EN/foraff/131181.pdf> accessed 22.05.2017, p 3.

and recruitment agencies), and for small and medium-sized enterprises'.[47] At the 2013 UN Business and Human Rights Forum, the EU delegation argued that

> the EU remains fully committed to the Guiding Principles, as emphasised in the European Commission's current strategy on Corporate Social Responsibility. The EU believes that governments have an important role to play as they are first and foremost responsible for the protection of human rights by law and in practice. Businesses, on the other hand, should carefully consider their impacts on society and a) plan and carry out operations in compliance with legal frameworks and b) integrate environmental, social, ethical, human rights and consumer concerns into their business strategies and operations.[48]

Such commitments have so far been mostly rhetorical as not many changes have been seen in business and human rights practice. Lack of efficient victims' access to justice has been an ongoing obstacle to advancement in the business and human rights field in the European Union. However, one cannot but agree that the European Union's 'success will be measured against the capacity to prevent human rights violations and to ensure effective access to remedy when such violations occur'.[49] However, effective access to remedies for abuses that occurred outside the European Union has so far been lost in the rhetorical pledges of its high officials. On the other hand, other European institutions have been more industrious in advancing victims' access to justice. For instance, the European Parliament in 1999, in its 'Resolution on EU standards for European enterprises operating in the developing countries: towards a European Code of Conduct',[50] requested

> … the Commission and the Council to make proposals, as a matter of urgency, to develop the right legal basis for establishing a European multilateral framework governing companies' operations worldwide and to organise for this purpose consultations with companies' representatives, the social partners and those groups in society which would be covered by the code.[51]

The European Parliament's Report on EU standards for European enterprises operating in developing countries requests in paragraph 24 that

> the European Council … confirm the interpretation in the 1968 Brussels Convention that, for cases of basic duty of care, legal action may be taken against a company in the

---

47 ibid. p 19.

48 EU statement at the 2013 UN Business and Human Rights Forum, Geneva, 03.12.2013, <http://eeas.europa.eu/delegations/un_geneva/documents/eu_statments/human_right/2013-1203_forum_buz_hr-panel-i.pdf>, accessed 22.05.2017, p 2.

49 ibid.

50 European Parliament, Resolution A4-0508/98.

51 European Parliament (1999), 'Resolution on EU standards for European enterprises operating in developing countries: towards a European code of conduct', A4-508/98, Official Journal of the European Communities, C 104, Part II, 1, 04 04.1999, pp 180–84. See in detail Černič, above n 1.

> EU country where its registered office is, in respect of any third country throughout the world, and calls on the Commission to study the possibility of enacting legislation, which open European courts to lawsuits involving damage done by MNEs, thus creating a precedent for developing customary international law in the field of corporate abuse.[52]

Further, on 13 March 2006 the European Parliament approved a report entitled 'Corporate Social Responsibility: A New Partnership',[53] which encourages the Commission to improve access to justice for victims, including third-country nationals, seeking accountability of European corporations for human rights abuses in the national courts of the Member States.[54] The report also asked the Commission 'to organise and promote awareness campaigns and monitor the implementation of the application of direct foreign liability according to the Brussels Convention'.[55] More recently, the European Parliament adopted a resolution condemning land grabbing in Tanzania.[56] It emphasised the 'importance of full transparency and accountability of the operations of EU companies and financial institutions in large-scale agri-business investments and land acquisitions in Tanzania, and calls for a strong and efficient EU mechanism to monitor these operations'.[57] Finally, the European Parliament on 25 October 2016 adopted a resolution on 'Corporate liability for serious human rights abuses in third countries', which inter alia asks Member States:

> to take any appropriate steps, in cooperation with international partners, to ensure, through judicial, administrative, legislative or other appropriate means, that when such human rights violations occur, those affected have access to an effective remedy, when a corporation based in the given states holds, directs or controls companies that are responsible for human rights violations in other countries; calls on said states to take appropriate steps to eliminate legal, practical and other relevant barriers that could lead to a denial of access to remedy and to establish appropriate procedural means to enable those affected in third countries to have access to justice in both the civil and criminal courts; in this regard, calls on states to pierce the veil of the legal personality, which may obfuscate the effective ownership over certain corporations.[58]

---

52 European Parliament, 17.12.1998, A4-0508/98, Report on EU standards for European Enterprises operating in developing countries: towards a European code of conduct, Committee on Development and Cooperation, Rapporteur: Richard Howitt, European Parliament.

53 (2006/2133(INI)), Committee on Employment and Social Affairs, European Parliament, 20.12.2006, Rapporteur: Richard Howitt.

54 ibid. para. 34 of the Report.

55 ibid. para. 40 of the Report.

56 European Parliament, Resolution of 12.03.2015 on Tanzania, 2015/2604(RSP), para. 13, <http://www.europarl.europa.eu/sides/getDoc.do?pubRef=-//EP//TEXT+TA+P8-TA-2015-0073+0+DOC+XML+V0//EN&language=EN>, accessed 22.05.2017.

57 ibid. para. 13.

58 European Parliament resolution on corporate liability for serious human rights abuses in third countries (2015/2315(INI)), 25.10.2016, para. 25, <http://www.europarl.europa.eu/sides/getDoc.do?type=TA&reference=P8-TA-2016-0405&language=EN&ring=A8-2016-0243> accessed 22.05.2017.

All in all, the European Parliament has in past decades adopted several reports and resolutions, however its voice has not been fully taken into account in business and human rights developments in other European institutions and Member States.

4.2. THE EUROPEAN UNION'S APPROACH TO THE TREATY INITIATIVE ON BUSINESS AND HUMAN RIGHTS

The European Union has favoured the implementation of the UN Guiding Principles, which was illustrated by the support of its Member States for Norway's resolution supporting the implementation of the UN Guiding Principles in June 2014.[59] This also follows from the rejection by some EU Member States of the resolution calling work to be started on the UN Business and Human Rights Treaty.[60] The EU Member States have from the beginning been cautious about this binding initiative. Such caution also derives from the 2016 Council of the European Union conclusions, which recall the 'global consensus reached on the UN Guiding Principles five years ago and stress[] that any possible further steps regarding the international legal framework for business and human rights at UN level must be inclusive, firmly rooted in the UN Guiding Principles and address all types of companies'.[61]

Aside from some general observations, the European proponents, particularly in European civil society, of a binding treaty on business and human rights have been silent on what exactly the treaty should entail. The proposal on the binding treaty on business and human rights has a number of advantages and disadvantages. Proponents of the treaty often name several arguments for the adoption of the treaty. Bilchitz, for instance, lists four: 'Bindingness, Norm Development, Competing Obligations, Access for Remedies'.[62] Arguably, access

59 UN Human Rights Council, Human rights and transnational corporations and other business enterprises, proposed by Norway, 26.06.2014, A/HRC/26/L.1 (adopted by the UN Human Rights Council on 27.06.2014), <http://daccess-dds-ny.un.org/doc/UNDOC/LTD/G14/062/40/PDF/G1406240.pdf?OpenElement> accessed 22.05.2017. The resolution sought 'the effective implementation of the Guiding Principles' (para. 2).

60 UN Human Rights Council, Resolution on Elaboration of an International Legally Binding Instrument on Transnational Corporations and Other Business Enterprises with respect to Human Rights (Bolivia (Plurinational State of), Cuba, Ecuador, South Africa, Venezuela (Bolivarian Republic of)): draft resolution, A/HRC/26/L.22/Rev.1, 25.06.2014, para. 1, <http://daccess-dds-ny.un.org/doc/UNDOC/LTD/G14/064/48/PDF/G1406448.pdf?OpenElement> accessed 22.05.2017.

61 Council Conclusions on Business and Human Rights, Brussels, 20.06.2016 (OR. en), 10254/16, <https://ec.europa.eu/anti-trafficking/sites/antitrafficking/files/council_conclusions_on_business_and_human_rights_foreign_affairs_council.pdf> accessed 22.05.2017.

62 D Bilchitz, 'The Moral and Legal Necessity for a Business and Human Rights Treaty', Business and Human Rights Resource Centre (February 2015), <https://business-humanrights.org/

to justice is the principal area any potential treaty on business and human rights or any other initiative within or beyond the European Union and/or the Council of Europe shall and should concentrate on. However, even though such arguments in favour of the treaty are valid and strong, they include some major and minor weaknesses. The main objection to the development of an international treaty on human rights and business is that it is not very clear what added value it would bring to the protection of individual's rights against business activity. There are many international treaties that have not created added value for the everyday lives of individuals as they depend on the consent of states. It is also doubtful that the creation of the treaty would enhance or simplify the access of individuals to courts as such a change would again depend on the goodwill of state parties. Even an established treaty such as the International Covenant for Economic, Social and Cultural Rights[63] has only recently had its complaint procedures established with the coming into force of the Optional Protocol,[64] which at the time of writing has only 20 ratifications.[65] However, positive examples also exist. For instance, in the little over four years since it was adopted, the Arms Trade Treaty has already acquired 92 ratifications.[66]

Even if a treaty on business and human rights were to achieve a high number of ratifications and become binding on a large number of states, it would still impose obligations to protect individuals' human rights against human rights-impacting activities of corporations, primarily on *states*. However, it is already generally accepted (not least as a result of the Guiding Principles, which promote themselves as a mere restatement of international law) that states have obligations to protect human rights. Therefore, again this objection of added value comes to light. The complaints procedure could, at best, be established in the form of quasi-judicial or quasi-legal procedure such as now exists before the UN Human Rights Committee and other UN human rights bodies. However, even in such cases it is questionable whether such decisions are meaningful as they are mostly adopted in the form of recommendations and are not binding upon states. It is overly utopian to believe that states will ever agree upon the establishment of the World Court of Human Rights, which would also hear cases against corporations. What is more, it would be futile to expect that the

sites/default/files/documents/The%20Moral%20and%20Legal%20Necessity%20for%20a%20Business%20and%20Human%20Rights%20Treaty%20February%202015%20FINAL%20FINAL.pd> accessed 04.08.2017.

63 International Covenant on Economic, Social and Cultural Rights, GA Res. 2200A (XXI), 21 UNGAOR Supp. (No. 16) at 49, UN Doc. A/6316 (1966), 993 UNTS 3, 03.01.1976.

64 Optional Protocol to the International Covenant on Economic, Social and Cultural Rights, GA Res. 63/117 (2008).

65 ibid. Status of ratification on 22.03.2015, <https://treaties.un.org/pages/viewdetails.aspx?src=ind&mtdsg_no=iv-3-a&chapter=4&lang=en> accessed 22.03.2017.

66 Arms Trade Treaty, adopted on 02.04.2013, entered into force on 24.12.2014.

UN could ever effectively monitor the activities of thousands of corporations if it has problems monitoring the activities of fewer than 200 states.

It is therefore quite understandable in the light of above objections that the European Union is putting so much emphasis on implementation of the UN Guiding Principles. Moreover, even though the EU Member States initially opposed the idea of starting work on the potential UN Business and Human Rights Treaty, recent developments suggest that some states are beginning to change their positions and are considering participation in the working group on the elaboration of the Treaty.[67] Initially, only nine out of the 28 EU Member States participated in the first meeting of the UN open-ended intergovernmental working group on transnational corporations and other business enterprises with respect to human rights (hereinafter : UN intergovernmental working group).[68] This eventually changed in the second meeting of the UN intergovernmental working group, where the EU Member States actively participated. Sixteen of the 28 Member States of the European Union actively participated in the proceedings, which illustrated the increased importance of the work of the UN intergovernmental working group.[69] The European Union also submitted a concise written statement, which argues that

> While respecting resolution 26/9, the EU continues to believe that it is important to ensure that the scope of the discussion and the Programme of Work are not limited to transnational corporations. The European Union also reiterates that the Programme of Work of the second session of the Intergovernmental Working Group should include a dedicated agenda Item to reaffirm the commitment by all States to implementing the UN Guiding Principles on Business and Human Rights. Also, for a comprehensive discussion on business and human rights, it remains important that all relevant stakeholders, including NGOs, trade unions and the business community, are given a chance to contribute their views and expertise. The EU position is also supported by a range of countries across different regions.[70]

Further, the European Union also intervened orally during the second session of the UN intergovernmental working group and argued that 'the European

---

67 European Parliament, Subcommittee on Human Rights, DROI, delegation to UN Human Rights Council, Geneva, 19.03.2015 <https://polcms.secure.europarl.europa.eu/cmsdata/upload/a6f26747-16d1-4d66-ac9e-8ee28e0f5387/HRC%2028%20delegation%20Geneva%20 19_03_2015.pdf> accessed 22.05.2017.

68 M Kourabas, 'Is a Binding Treaty the Way Forward for Business and Human Rights?', 14.07.2015, <http://www.triplepundit.com/2015/07/binding-treaty-way-forward-business-human-rights> accessed 22.05.2017.

69 United Nations, 2nd Session of the Intergovernmental group, <https://documents-dds-ny.un.org/doc/UNDOC/GEN/G17/000/94/PDF/G1700094.pdf?OpenElement> accessed 22.05.2017.

70 European Union contribution in view of the second session of the Inter-governmental Working Group on Transnational Corporations and Other Enterprises with respect to human rights, 29.08.2016, para. 4.

Union values the global consensus reached on the UN Guiding Principles on Business and Human Rights five years ago and stresses that any possible further steps regarding the international legal framework for business and human rights at the UN level must be inclusive, firmly rooted in the UN Guiding Principles and address all types of companies'.[71] Such wording is hardly a surprise as the European Union has to date employed a cautious approach to the Treaty Initiative that favours continuous work on the UN Guiding Principles. This has gone so far that even John Ruggie, the author of the UN Guiding Principles, has recently expressed his discontent with the European Union's strategy towards business and human rights.[72] All in all, the EU Member States should clearly employ more precise, targeted and binding strategies in the field of business and human rights, thereby strengthening responsibility and accountability of European-based corporations when and where they are involved in corporate human rights abuses committed at home and outside European borders and also by adopting a more industrious and engaged approach in the next sessions of the UN intergovernmental working group.

5. HOW TO MOVE FORWARD?

A million dollar question revolves around the question how to effectively move forward. How can corporations be made more responsible and victims' access to justice more simple and effective? How could the European Union contribute to advancing the business and human rights field? Responsible corporations that observe human rights are arguably those which employ preventive measures and do not shy away from proposals for more effective enforcement of accountability. Allen observes that '... corporations as independent social actors ... do not simply owe contract or other legal duties to those affected by its operations, but owe loyalty in some measure to all such persons as well'.[73] Porter and Kramer argue that 'strong regulatory standards protect both consumers and competitive companies from exploitation'[74] and rightly observe that 'by providing jobs, investing capital, purchasing goods, and doing business every day, corporations

71 Open-ended intergovernmental working group on transnational corporations and other business enterprises with respect to human rights, 2nd session (2410.2016–28.10.2016), EU intervention for Day 4 under Panel V Subtheme 2 ('The relation between the UN Guiding Principles and the elaboration of an international legally binding instrument on TNCs and other business enterprises').

72 J Ruggie, Letter to European Commission President Jean-Claude Juncker, 24.02.2017.

73 WT Allen, 'Our Schizophrenic Conception of the Business Corporation' (1992) 14 *Cardozo Law Review* 271.

74 ME Porter and MR Kramer, 'Strategy and Society: The Link Between Competitive Advantage and Corporate Social Responsibility' (2006) 84(12) *Harvard Business Review* 83.

have a profound and positive influence on society'.[75] It appears that a corporation should pursue a substantive dimension of corporate responsibility as opposed to employing corporate responsibility as a camouflage for public eyes. Finally, Porter and Kramer note that corporations must start thinking in terms of 'corporate social integration' rather than in terms of 'corporate social responsibility'.[76] In this way, corporations would integrate human rights into their business policies without moving away from their primary objectives of generating revenues and profit.

Despite very slow progress in the global business environment, the majority of corporations now recognise that they have a role to play in guaranteeing human rights in a given society. Such a development has not occurred overnight and would not have taken place if it had not been for various industrious efforts in international civil society to regulate corporations. Those efforts later resulted in the adoption of several international, mostly quasi-legal, documents. The initiative for a business and human rights treaty has been developed in response to growing pressure from international civil society that something be done to enhance corporate accountability and the positions of victims. A valid initiative should offer a way to move forward, however some have been more dedicated than others when it comes to enhancing victims' rights and enforcing corporate accountability for human rights. For instance, the proposed UN Treaty on Business and Human Rights, if ever adopted, would represent a small step in the right direction, although it is doubtful whether it would certainly mean the end of such initiatives. Nonetheless, Woods observes that 'binding human rights obligations on corporations are necessary to ensure protection of individual human rights in relation to MNCs'.[77] In fact, a treaty would, at best, only recognise that corporations have binding human rights obligations; it would not be able to immediately enhance access to justice for victims of alleged human rights abuses. The European Union, the Council of Europe and their Member States could recognise that any treaty would therefore represent only the first step in the quest to improve the rights of victims in the field of business and human rights, and would have to be followed by further steps towards bringing justice closer to victims. A UN Treaty on Business and Human Rights would make sense if it created incentives for states to adopt binding statutes that would require corporations to take preventive measures, ensure liability of parent companies for the actions and omissions of their subsidiaries, and increase civil and criminal liability for corporations.

The Declaration on Business and Human Rights is often mentioned as the potential by-product of the movement for a Business and Human Rights Treaty,

---

75 ibid. 91.

76 ibid. 92.

77 Woods, above n 7, 683.

to which European states could also contribute without compromising their support for the UN Guiding Principles. It seems likely that the discussion on the Treaty on Business and Human Rights will finally result in compromise, which could be reached in the form of a Declaration on Business and Human Rights of the United Nations General Assembly. Surya Deva has observed that 'we should start with drafting a Declaration on the Human Rights Obligations of Business (Declaration) along the lines of the Universal Declaration of Human Rights'.[78] Such a proposal has been aired several times before. In light of this, the real question is what would be the added value of such a declaration, particularly bearing in mind the nature and scope of the UN Guiding Principles. Declarations are usually non-binding 'soft law' documents, which do not initially create international legal obligations for states. After the passage of time, some of their content could be transformed into customary international law if there is consent. What should such a declaration entail? First, it would have to reiterate that corporations have obligations to respect, protect and fulfil human rights, and that the existence of such obligations is complementary to those of states. Secondly, it would have to argue for impartial, independent, fair and transparent judicial and quasi-judicial mechanisms for victims to be able to invoke the responsibility and accountability of corporations. Thirdly, it would need to propose new ways, ex ante and ex post facto, to ensure that corporations effectively include human rights in their operations. However, it would remain to be seen what effect the Declaration would have for the rights of victims. For instance, the United Nations Declaration on the Rights of Indigenous Peoples has not gained recognition as a useful mechanism for enforcement of indigenous rights.[79] The fate of the latter declaration does not mean that the Declaration on Business and Human Rights would not be successful.

Responsible European corporations would take all the necessary and appropriate measures to prevent human rights abuses, as they would submit themselves to independent due process to examine whether they or their executives and employees have committed any abuses. Such procedures should be established through the combination of voluntary and binding approaches. In this way they may able to attract and keep consumers and employees if they comply with human rights. One may point to concerns that recent initiatives in business and human rights have undermined each other as they follow different objectives and employ different means in their attempts to meet such objectives.

---

78 S Deva, 'Corporate human rights abuses and international law: brief comments', 28.01.2015, <http://jamesgstewart.com/corporate-human-rights-abuses-and-international-law-brief-comments> accessed 22.05.2017.

79 United Nations Declaration on the Rights of Indigenous Peoples art. 25, UN Doc. A/RES/61/295 (13.09.2007), 46 ILM 1013 (2007).

Even though such initiatives may be scattered around different areas on the spectrum of human rights, they all appear to improve the current state of affairs by making companies more responsible for human rights by taking preventive measures and improving victims' access to justice if abuses do occur.

Common to all initiatives within and beyond the European Union and the Council of Europe is that they at least theoretically improve victims' access to justice in cases of alleged corporate human rights abuses. Not all of them have the same objectives; the UN Guiding Principles are more geared towards business sectors, whereas the impetus for a binding treaty comes more from civil society sectors and victims' organisations. Moreover, all the different initiatives take divergent paths to achieve their goals and may even turn out to be contradictory in assessing situations and offering remedies. However, this pluralistic debate and collection of diverse initiatives enriches the field of human rights and business by developing the notions of corporate accountability and the rights of victims in multiple forums. Each of them can contribute to the applicability of other initiatives. As in any other field, there is no single solution to the challenges presented in business and human rights. If there is an initiative that offers a single solution to all the problems in this field, it should be taken and examined with a suspicious mind. A pluralistic approach operates on values of openness, inclusiveness and transparency and, in particular, offers a forum where victims can voice their concerns. Nonetheless, all of the identified initiatives are working towards a greater responsibility for the business operations of local and transnational corporations within more accountable national and international normative settings. They stimulate a pluralistic debate about the potential way forward in business and human rights, which has been absent from the agenda in past years.[80] A pluralistic approach also goes hand in hand with the holistic approach, which concentrates not only on the obligations and responsibility of corporations, but also on the responsibility of other actors who take part in business activities or should have control over the businesses which conduct their operations. States and individuals should also have responsibilities to protect individuals' human rights against corporate conduct. States also have positive obligations to prevent abuses of individual's rights during the business operations of the corporations based on their territory and outside it. Individuals can be held responsible for taking decisions within the companies violating human rights.

---

80 J Letnar Černič and T Van Ho, 'Introduction', in J Letnar Černič and T Van Ho (eds), *Human Rights and Business* (Oisterwijk: Wolf, 2015), p 24. See also J Kyriakakis, 'The Debate about having a debate about a business and human rights treaty' (17.02.2015), <http://castancentre.com/2015/02/17/debateaboutbusinessandhumanrights> accessed 22.05.2017.

Figure 1. A potential way forward for business and human rights in Europe

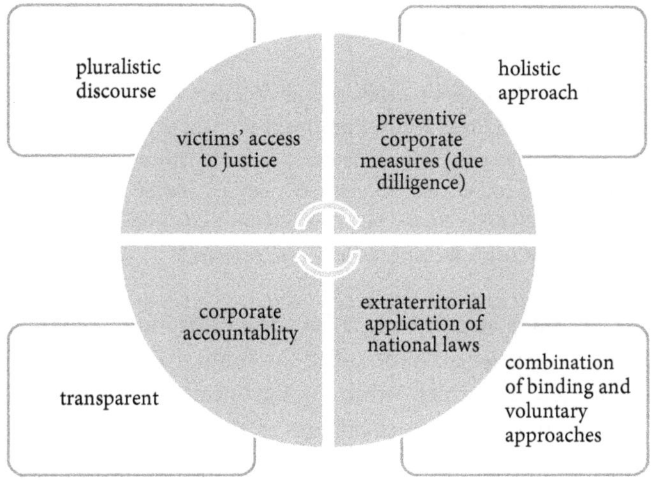

Source: Produced by the author

Rather than advocating for a particular initiative or approach, it is more appropriate for the European Union to identify the areas and issues which any effective proposal on how to move forward in business and human rights should include. Figure 1 illustrates the areas/issues that would have to be included in any initiative carrying the possibility of success. A successful initiative would employ both pluralistic and holistic approaches to the field of business and human rights that would consider the perspectives of both businesses and victims. Such an initiative would have to be based on a combination of binding and voluntary approaches. The following four issues are particularly important in strengthening the field of business and human rights: preventive (corporate) measures (due diligence), victims' access to justice, corporate accountability/liability and the extraterritorial application of national administrative, criminal and civil laws. States are under a primary obligation to protect human rights, not only within their territory, but also outside it where they exercise control over their corporations ('their' referring to corporations registered on their territory). National legal systems have to do a better job of securing human rights against the activities of corporations as they need to provide victims with more effective avenues of access to justice.[81] The European Union Agency for Fundamental Rights recently observed that 'the EU should mandate a platform for EU Member States to have a dedicated exchange on how best to address extra-territoriality

81 See, for example, European Union Agency for Fundamental Rights, 'Improving access to remedy in the area of business and human rights at the EU level', FRA Opinion – 1/2017, Vienna, 10.04.2017.

in legislation and through other measures, including subsidiary jurisdiction, to improve access to remedy for victims of business-related human rights abuse across the EU'.[82] It further argued that

> the EU should provide further incentives to all Member States to adopt, implement and review National Action Plans which implement the UN Guiding Principles, including access to remedy. The inclusion of more specific measures could strengthen these national action plans to facilitate access to remedy … The EU should ensure a regular peer review of EU Member States' National Action Plans and the progress made as to actions, not the least when it comes to access to remedy.[83]

However, corporations also have to meet their obligations and enable victims to enforce their potential accountability for human rights abuses. All in all, for existing and new initiatives within the European Union and the Council of Europe to effectively respond to challenges in the field of business and human rights, they would have to include and effectively address each of the issues identified above.

6. CONCLUSION

It appears that the European Union, the Council of Europe and the majority of their Member States have considered that not all initiatives in business and human rights are worth considering and all the focus should be steered towards the national implementation of the non-binding UN Guiding Principles. Moreover, the insistence on the UN Guiding Principles is not consensual as only a few EU and Council of Europe Member States have adopted National Action Plans. Most European states have therefore initially been suspicious of the initiative for a UN Treaty on Business and Human Rights, although it appears that this cautious approach has been melting away in recent months, particularly given the lack of national implementation of the UN Guiding Principles. Surely, from the point of view of victims it would be erroneous and dangerous to concentrate only on voluntary approaches, as the European Union, the Council of Europe and the majority of their Member States have done in the past.

Therefore, European states are obliged to uphold their commitments so that corporations should be aware that they do not operate in a vacuum, completely exempt from all civilisation's values and the principles of human rights and fundamental freedoms. In order to strengthen business and human rights worldwide, states and corporations must improve their performance, become

---

82 ibid. FRA opinion 6, p 10.

83 ibid. FRA opinion 18, p 16.

more transparent, and enable effective enforcement of corporate accountability for alleged human rights abuses. The current negotiations under the initiative for a UN Treaty on Business and Human Rights can in the next years contribute to more efficient and effective access to justice in national judicial systems. Corporations based or operating in European states not only have moral and ethical obligations, but are already at this point in time subject to domestic constitutional and statutory human rights obligations to respect and protect human rights of individuals, minorities and indigenous peoples against corporate abuses. It is essential to extend such binding protections of victims' individual rights to extra-territorial operations of European corporations. All in all, though the present situation may appear disheartening, consensus should be growing in Europe for meaningful and continued improvements of the legal underpinnings of national legal systems so that individuals have the right to full judicial protection against corporate human rights abuses.

PART IV

LESSONS FROM OTHER REGIMES OF INTERNATIONAL LAW

A CONVENTION OR A RECOMMENDATION? THE EXPERIENCE OF INTERNATIONAL LABOUR LEGISLATION

Ago Shin-Ichi

1. INTRODUCTION

The question whether to opt for a legally binding instrument or not, i.e. a treaty or a resolution, has always been a difficult one for decision-makers in public international law. Our current task of evaluating the decision taken by the United Nations Economic and Social Council (ECOSOC) to formulate a Treaty on Business and Human Rights is, therefore, not a new one. We can recall the development of international human rights norms at the UN, for instance. The General Assembly, in its early years, decided to adopt an International Bill of Human Rights by opting for a non-binding Universal Declaration of

Human Rights first. The binding Covenants followed later. International labour legislation, represented by the adoption of international labour standards, has a long history in facing this question. We may learn a lesson from the experience of the International Labour Organization (ILO) when considering the issue of the UN instrument on business and human rights. It is not only significant for its long history, but the ILO instruments are of particular importance to the discussion on business and human rights because they set labour standards, which largely contain human rights principles and which are jointly formulated by, and partly addressed to, non-state entities, namely employers' organisations or corporate entities. In other words, the prospective legally binding instrument is not operating in a vacuum, but has been preceded by a large number of ILO Conventions and Recommendations, regulating business and human rights.[1]

The following sections first outline essential features of international labour standards in their adoption process (Section 2), in the importance of constitutional obligations under Article 19 (Section 3) and in the 'division of labour' between a Convention and a Recommendation (Section 4). A parallel is drawn between such a two-tier system and the proposed UN instrument, with some preliminary findings (Section 5). The analysis then turns to the ILO's Tripartite Declaration on Multinational Enterprises and explores its strengths and weakness, comparing it with the Organisation for Economic Co-operation and Development (OECD) Guidelines on Multinational Enterprises (Section 6). A general conclusion is that the existence of a follow-up mechanism is most important in making the original instrument work. The endeavour to make the Protect, Respect and Remedy framework work should carefully study the lessons learnt from the ILO's experience, both in its regular standard-setting process, as well as the Tripartite Declaration (Section 7).

2. LEGAL NATURE OF INTERNATIONAL LABOUR INSTRUMENTS

International labour legislation dates back to the beginning of the twentieth century, not counting its sporadic predecessors at the end of the nineteenth century,[2] when the Peace Treaty of Versailles set up the International Labour

1 It is fair to say that an important part of the prospective UN instrument (labour rights as human rights: trade union freedom, prohibition of forced labour, discrimination in employment, child labour) has already been covered by the ILO instruments. The ILO instruments have even greater value in terms of the scope of application, as they are formulated in collaboration with employers' and workers' organisations, and can, therefore, partly solve the deficiency of a normal treaty, in which non-State parties are not directly involved.

2 Berlin Conference on 15.03.1890, described in N Valticos, *Droit international du travail*, Dalloz, Paris 1983, pp 19–22.

Organization with its unique tripartite structure. This uniqueness has seen no rival during nearly a hundred years of operations, and – even today – there is no inter-governmental institution that has incorporated non-State entities (as full components) in a comparable way. The ILO's experience is particularly important for those who seek to involve non-State actors in the application of international legal instruments today.

It is therefore understandable that active discussions were held during the Versailles Peace Conference as to the best way of incorporating employers' and workers' organisations into the legislative and supervisory processes of the international labour standard (ILS). A compromise of a 2-1-1 ratio for the Conference and the Governing Body configuration, namely two seats going to the government and one each to the employer and the worker, respectively, was struck after a long debate.[3] A similar debate also surrounded the discussion about what sort of instrument the ILO should adopt, namely a legally binding Convention or a non-binding Recommendation.[4]

The ILO was established primarily to set ILS. It was, unlike today's ILO, which is half a technical co-operation agency, a largely norm-creating institution from the outset. The work of the ILO in its initial stages, therefore, concentrated in setting ILS, namely International Labour Conventions and International Labour Recommendations (hereinafter referred to as ILO Conventions and ILO Recommendations, or simply Conventions and Recommendations). It was, therefore, of crucial importance to decide on the legal nature of the instruments to be adopted. At the Preparatory Committee for drafting the ILO Constitution, or Part XIII of the Peace Treaty of Versailles, some countries (Italy supported by France) wanted to see the prospective instruments given supra-national power. In other words, they proposed the International Labour Conference to adopt Conventions, which would automatically bind Member States, without awaiting their ratification. That would have amounted to supra-national legislation, far too radical to be accepted by the majority of the delegates at the Preparatory Committee.[5] The British proposal, on the other hand, was somewhat less radical, giving States a one-year time limit to derogate from the treaty obligations. It was a kind of 'opting out' scheme, later found in a few specialised agencies of the UN.[6] However, this proposal was rejected by the US delegation, which worried that its federal system would not allow the federal government to enter into international legal commitments that could apply directly to federal States. The US delegation proposed, instead, that the ILO only adopt Recommendations, which would eventually be submitted to national parliaments for appropriate

---

3 Valticos, above n 2, p 45.
4 ibid pp 46–51.
5 ibid p 47.
6 ICAO: Arts. 37 and 38 of the Convention on International Civil Aviation, 1944. WHO: Art. 22 of the Constitution of the World Health Organization.

action, including legislation, but which would be deprived of any international legal obligation after the said legislative body decided not to act. This proposal was now too much of a retreat and could not be accepted by the majority of the delegation. At this juncture, the discussion at the Preparatory Committee entered into an impasse and apparently came to a halt for a number of days.[7] With a view to ending the impasse, a sub-committee was created to come up with a solution. It proposed a formula that was eventually accepted by the whole committee. Its gist was as follows: the ILO would adopt not only Conventions, but also Recommendations, both of which would be submitted to the competent authority for appropriate action within one year. In the case of a Convention, a Member State would communicate the ratification instrument to the ILO when its competent national authority consented to the implementation of the Convention. In the case of a Recommendation, the Member States would only report to the ILO on measures they had taken.

This formula slightly deviates from traditional international treaty making, but its basic idea essentially keeps the sovereign right of States intact in that a Member State retains discretion as to its commitment to a particular treaty. Namely, adoption of a Convention by a two-thirds majority at the International Labour Conference does not automatically bind Member States of the Organization. However, the drafters of the ILO Constitution were innovative in various aspects. They not only went a step forward towards international legislation by making it obligatory for all the Member States to bring the newly adopted instruments before their national parliaments for possible ratification and/or actual implementation, but also designed a two-tier system in which a Convention could be adopted, which would be supplemented by a Recommendation. Article 19 of the current ILO Constitution, which does not differ from the original text of 1919, is one of the most important provisions of the Constitution and it is a long one. We will analyse it by looking more closely into its specific provisions.

3. A 'SOFT DRIVE' TOWARDS RATIFICATION OF AN ILO CONVENTION

Paragraph 5(a) and (b) of Article 19 of the Constitution provides:

> In the case of a Convention:
>
> (a) the Convention will be communicated to all Members for ratification;
> (b) each of the Members undertakes that it will, within the period of one year at most from the closing of the session of the Conference, or if it is impossible

7 Valticos, above n 2, p 49.

> owing to exceptional circumstances to do so within the period of one year, then at the earliest practicable moment and in no case later than 18 months from the closing of the session of the Conference, bring the Convention before the authority or authorities within whose competence the matter lies, for the enactment of legislation or other action;

Although paragraph 5(a) provides that a newly adopted Convention shall be communicated 'for ratification', it does not mean that Member States are obliged to ratify it. The wording of paragraph 5(b) – 'bring the Convention before the authority or authorities within whose competence the matter lies, for the enactment of legislation or other action' – read together with paragraph 5(a), has given rise to some confusion. This was especially so after a large number of newly independent States entered the ILO, because some governments had interpreted it to mean that the Constitution obliged Member States to 'ratify' the Convention. With a view to eradicating the misunderstanding, the Governing Body of the ILO adopted a *Memorandum concerning the obligation to submit Conventions and Recommendations to the competent authorities*, which clearly stated that 'governments remain entirely free to propose any action which they may judge appropriate in respect of Conventions or Recommendations. The aim of submission is to encourage a rapid and responsible decision by each State on instruments adopted by the Conference.'[8]

While the traditional principle of international treaty law has been kept intact, there was an important step forward to make ILO standards a little more binding.

Paragraph 5(e) continues:

> If the Member does not obtain the consent of the authority or authorities within whose competence the matter lies, no further obligation shall rest upon the Member except that it shall report to the Director-General of the International Labour Office, at appropriate intervals as requested by the Governing Body, the position of its law and practice in regard to the matters dealt with in the Convention, showing the extent to which effect has been given, or is proposed to be given, to any of the provisions of the Convention by legislation, administrative action, collective agreement or otherwise and stating the difficulties which prevent or delay the ratification of such Convention.

This seemingly negative form of expression – 'no further obligation shall rest upon ...' – implies, however, an important obligation to 'report to the Director-General ...'. While it is perhaps a modest expression, it creates a very special situation in international law. That is to say, a nation is sovereign in deciding whether to enter into a treaty obligation or not, but the ILO obliges a sovereign nation to report on something which it is not legally bound to implement.

8 Most recently revised by the Governing Body in 2005. GB292/LILS/1(Rev.) and GB.292/10(Rev.). Appendix I.

In other words, implementation is not obligatory (a treaty may be ratified or not), but reporting on what they have done or not done has become obligatory. This is a new technique in international legislation, which the world had not known before.

The same situation is found in the case of a Recommendation. Paragraph 6(d) of the ILO Constitution states:

> Apart from bringing the Recommendation before the said competent authority or authorities, no further obligation shall rest upon the Members, except that they shall report to the Director-General of the International Labour Office, at appropriate intervals as requested by the Governing Body, the position of the law and practice in their country in regard to the matters dealt with in the Recommendation, showing the extent to which effect has been given, or is proposed to be given, to the provisions of the Recommendation and such modifications of these provisions as it has been found or may be found necessary to make in adopting or applying them.

A government is constitutionally obliged to report to the ILO on what it is not legally bound, a peculiar situation that is not frequently found in other international legal instruments. The reporting obligation under normal human rights treaties, such as the International Covenant on Civil and Political Rights (ICCPR), is not particularly special because the Covenant obliges Member States to report on what they had committed to implement by ratifying the Covenant. In this sense, the reporting obligation under Article 22 of the ILO Constitution is the same, in that ILO members are obliged to report on the ratified Conventions. However, Article 19 reporting is different and a special case.

This innovative idea may have lost its importance if a sophisticated system of supervision had not backed it up. The Constitution itself is silent about this, however Article 19 has implied that the Organization would monitor the reporting process. As a matter of fact, the International Labour Conference immediately started formally acknowledging receipt of reports sent in by ratifying countries, as soon as very first reports under Article 22 began arriving in 1921.[9] Furthermore, this established the important practice of examining them. The examination of reports transformed itself to a monitoring mechanism, which was further developed by the creation of an independent committee consisting of eminent legal experts. A double-layer monitoring system exercised by the Committee of Experts[10]

9 Six Conventions were adopted in 1919 and a number of countries ratified them as early as in 1920. According to the standard final provisions of a Convention, ratification will take effect one year after the registration of the ratification and governments are requested to report one year after the ratification has taken effect in their countries.

10 The Committee of Experts on the Application of Conventions and Recommendations, hereinafter referred to as the Committee of Experts.

and a tripartite Conference Committee[11] has continued since then up to the present and has given a tremendous impetus to this unique idea of obliging governments to report on instruments by which they are not legally bound. A large number of works have been written on the success and the significance of the ILO's supervision in the past[12] and this is not the place to repeat the exercise here. It is, however, noteworthy to reiterate the important effect of the ILO's supervision on the realisation of the constitutional obligation to report on non-ratified Conventions and Recommendations.

4. CONVENTIONS AND RECOMMENDATIONS AS A SET

Our quest for an appropriate choice of instrument, i.e. whether to opt for a treaty or a non-binding instrument, was provisionally solved by the drafters of the ILO Constitution in Versailles in the following way:

Paragraph 1 of Article 19 provides:

> When the Conference has decided on the adoption of proposals with regard to an item on the agenda, it will rest with the Conference to determine whether these proposals should take the form: (a) of an international Convention, or (b) of a Recommendation to meet circumstances where the subject, or aspect of it, dealt with is not considered suitable or appropriate at that time for a Convention.

As we have seen, in the first discussion at the drafting committee of the ILO Constitution in 1919, the initial proposal was to adopt a binding treaty, which was opposed by the US delegation, who wished to have the ILO adopt only Recommendations. The compromise was the formula, in which a Convention or a Recommendation was to be adopted. The above-cited provision of the Constitution is clear that it is a choice of a binding Convention 'or' a non-binding Recommendation. What happened, in practice, was the establishment of a custom to adopt a Convention 'and/or' a Recommendation.

The original idea was that a non-binding instrument was to be chosen, if it were 'not considered suitable or appropriate at that time for a Convention'. The rationale behind this provision was that there might be situations in which a binding instrument was deemed unworkable due to the immaturity of the substance to be formulated in a legally binding treaty. There was also a concern about the differences in economic, social and other development in different

---

11 The Committee on the Application of Standards, hereinafter referred to as the Conference Committee.

12 EA Landy, *The Effectiveness of International Supervision: Thirty Years of I.L.O. Experience*, Stevens & Sons, London 1966, for instance.

Member States. This latter consideration was eventually addressed by inserting paragraph 3, which read:

> In framing any Convention or Recommendation of general application the Conference shall have due regard to those countries in which climatic conditions, the imperfect development of industrial organization, or other special circumstances make the industrial conditions substantially different and shall suggest the modifications, if any, which it considers may be required to meet the case of such countries.

What then are the circumstances warranting that a proposed instrument be 'down-graded' to a non-binding Recommendation? According to Valticos, there are three reasons.

First, a Recommendation is preferred when a subject is not ripe enough for the adoption of a Convention. Valticos and von Potobsky cite cases in which the adoption of a Recommendation 'has paved the way for the adoption of a Convention on the same subject, several years later'.[13] This is the same situation, as already mentioned above, with respect to the process leading to the adoption of the International Covenants on Human Rights. Similarly, one can mention the adoption of the Outer Space Treaty in 1966, which was preceded by the adoption by the General Assembly of a Declaration on the same subject three years before. If we were to take the adoption of the UN Guiding Principles (UNGP) as a sort of prelude to a legally binding instrument, the currently proposed Treaty on Business and Human Rights could perhaps be regarded as the ultimate outcome of the UNGP. However, it does not look like it. It is probably because the preparation is not ripe enough to transform the UNGP into a treaty. In the case of the Outer Space Treaty, for example, there was already a general consensus in the UN at the time of the adoption of the Declaration that the principles enshrined therein become law.[14] Furthermore, we should also take into consideration the background, which was that the UNGP were adopted solely because it was deemed inappropriate to adopt a binding instrument. The Commission on Human Rights rejected the proposal of its working group to adopt a resolution ('Norms') containing normative principles related to

---

13 N Valticos and G von Potobsky, *International Labour Law*, Kluwer, Deventer 1995, p 62. 'Recommendations on Labour Inspection, 1923 (No. 20) and on Social Security, 1944 (Nos. 67 and 69) and on the Termination of Employment, 1963 (No. 119). A number of Conventions on labour inspection, social security and termination of employment were adopted at a later stage, such as Convention No. 81 on Labour Inspection in 1947, Convention No. 102 on Social Security (Minimum Standards) in 1952 and Convention No. 158 on Termination of Employment in 1982.

14 In this case, however, the adoption of the Treaty took place within three years and one author arguably called this event an 'instant custom'. B Cheng, 'United Nations Resolutions on Outer Space: "Instant Customary Law"?' (1965) 5 *Indian Journal of International Law* 23.

human rights and business activities.[15] The Commission on Human Rights did not endorse an instrument, which was even less legally binding than a treaty, and it gave a mandate to a Special Representative of the Secretary-General (John Ruggie) to work out a substitute for the 'Norms'. As such, it is apparent that the eventual product of the Special Representative, the UNGP, were not meant to be further elaborated to become an internationally legally binding instrument. Having said this, it is worth pointing out that among the three pillars of the UNGP, the first 'Protect' and the third 'Remedy' pillars are basically addressing Member States and the normative potentials can be found therein.

Secondly, a Recommendation can supplement the contents of a corresponding Convention. This is a function which, according to Valticos and von Potobsky, has become increasingly important and

> Now it is common practice followed in the case [of] approximately eighty Conventions, to adopt, on the same subject, a Convention laying down the basic rules and a Recommendation containing more detailed provisions for their application which might furnish guidelines for governments without the Recommendation having the binding force of a Convention.[16]

Twenty years have lapsed since Valticos and von Potobsky wrote this book and now we can count more than 90 Conventions adopted with corresponding Recommendations. It can fairly be said that it has become almost a rule to adopt a Convention together with a supplementary Recommendation. The ILO's supervisory machinery has again made use of this custom to strengthen the contents of both Conventions and Recommendations. That is to say, it has occasionally been observed that the Committee of Experts has referred to provisions in a Recommendation to interpret certain provisions in a corresponding Convention. When a Convention has set standards in vague terms, such as requiring ratifying States 'to adopt and develop comprehensive and co-ordinated policies and programmes',[17] the Committee of Experts has referred to relevant provisions in a corresponding Recommendation[18] to indicate to a ratifying State what 'comprehensive and co-ordinated policies' were. In this way, a non-binding Recommendation has been made binding by 'jurisprudence'. This is an interesting development, which may also be applied in the case of the UN Treaty on Business and Human Rights. Suppose the UN Treaty were adopted and the wording were vague or simply declaratory of a principle, the UNGP might be utilised to concretise the vague content of the Convention.

---

15 Norms on the Responsibilities of Transnational Corporations and Other Business Enterprises with Regard to Human Rights, UN Doc. E/CN.4/Sub.2/2003/12/Rev.2 (2003).

16 Valticos and von Potobsky, above n 13, p 62.

17 Art. 1, Human Resources Development Convention (No. 142) of 1975.

18 Human Resources Development Recommendation (No. 150) of 1975.

For this to happen, however, we would need a supervisory mechanism attached to the prospective Treaty and the UNGP.

Thirdly, a Recommendation deals with matters in respect of which the standards laid down have to be of so technical and detailed a character that they may call for frequent adjustment to the situation in different countries, or the nature of which is such that there are wide variations in circumstances and practices from one country to another. Valticos and von Potobsky cite subject matters, such as industrial relations, training and workers' housing, to fall under this category.[19] It is debatable whether the question of industrial relations is of a highly technical nature, but there exists a great variety of situations, in which legal standards are difficult to set. There are a small number of Recommendations, which were adopted independently from any corresponding Convention, and they mostly fall into this category of instrument. The prospective UN Treaty on Business and Human Rights cannot be described as a legal instrument of a highly technical nature, such as workers' housing or training, but in so far as it aims at setting human rights standards, it should be legally relevant and uniformly applicable, regardless of specific situations of Member States.

5. LESSONS LEARNT FROM THE ILO'S CHOICE OF LEGAL INSTRUMENTS

We should be careful to draw a parallel between the ILO's standard-setting and general international law-making, because the background of international labour legislation is different from the norm-creating function at the UN. In the case of the ILO, there is already a consensus available among the stakeholders, at the outset, to set labour standards. By entering into the Organization, a country commits itself to make efforts to achieve social justice. The Preamble of the Constitution, read together with the Philadelphia Declaration of 1944, which forms an integral part of the Constitution, is clear about it. In the case of the UN, on the other hand, while a similar situation is described in the Preamble of the Charter, as well as in Articles 1 and 55, the economic and social aspect of the UN mandate is provided for in a progressive and declaratory manner. Consequently, the norm-creating function in this field by the UN had been entrusted to a time consuming customary law formation by adding up a series of resolutions. Given this difference in background, a parallel cannot be drawn too simplistically.

On the other hand, when it comes to international law creation, the means are limited and less institutionalised when compared to the domestic situation, and there appear to be certain similarities between international labour legislation

[19] Valticos and von Potobsky, above n 13, p 63. Cf. Workers' Housing Recommendation, 1961 (No. 115).

and the UN legislative function in economic and social matters. In other words, there is reason to believe that international law-making by the UN can learn something from the ILO's experience.

The foregoing analysis in the light of the ILO's experience in setting standards in two ways, Conventions and Recommendations, and that in a set, drives us to a tentative conclusion that the UN Treaty on Business and Human Rights should be regarded as an arm of the UNGP. In other words, in order to make the Treaty legally relevant, a positive link must be created between the proposed Treaty and the UNGP. It is important to have a monitoring system to combine the two instruments. As we saw in the ILO's case, the functional relationship between a Convention and a Recommendation has been materialised by the efficient mechanism of the supervision.

Unlike the ILO Constitution, which provides for a reporting obligation of a country with respect to a Recommendation (under Article 19), UNGP is not equipped with such an obligation so far. Under these circumstances, there is a challenge to connect the UNGP to the Treaty. However, this might be an idea to be explored when the Treaty will be shaped. It may not be a straight-forward provision for establishing a new obligation to the UNGP, but it can be done in a way to make the proposed Treaty to refer to UNGP all the time, when it addresses issues covered by the UNGP, for instance. Practical proposals for making the drafting of the Treaty more meaningful will be further elaborated in the concluding section of this paper.

6. LESSON FROM THE ILO'S TRIPARTITE DECLARATION ON MULTINATIONAL ENTERPRISES

In the foregoing part of the chapter, we explored the possibility, albeit with some difficulties, of transplanting the ILO's standard-setting experience into the current UN's endeavour to draft a treaty. It did not, however, address another challenge the proposed UN Treaty faces, namely the applicability of the instrument to corporate entities, i.e. non-State actors. The ILO Conventions and Recommendations have not been able to overcome these difficulties. It is therefore interesting to see how the ILO has tried to overcome them, especially with regard to multinational enterprises.[20]

[20] A remarkable development occurred during the writing of this chapter: The ILO Governing Body substantially revised the Declaration in February 2017. It has become more substantial in its content compared to the original one, but the weakness in its implementation seems to persist. Therefore the basic argument developed in this section does not need to be altered.

6.1. A PECULIAR LEGAL INSTRUMENT

The biggest challenge of the proposed UN Treaty on Business and Human Rights lies obviously in the fact that an international treaty cannot directly make enterprises accountable because they are private persons, even if some of them may be as economically and politically influential as some nation States, and they are not subjects of international law. As indicated at the beginning of this chapter, the ILO is better off in this aspect because it is a tripartite body and representatives of enterprises are officially involved, at least in the legislative and supervisory processes. From the point of view of individuals whose human rights are infringed, ILO Conventions may even be directly applied. Some of the ILO Conventions, those on freedom of association and forced labour in particular, provide a strong basis for victims of human rights infringement to support their claims in domestic courts.[21] In other words, an individual person, who is not a subject of international law, can directly derive a remedy for human rights violation from the Convention. However, the same cannot be said for the relationship of ILO Conventions and Recommendations with private enterprises.

It is under these circumstances that the Tripartite Declaration on Multinational Enterprises (hereinafter referred to as the Tripartite Declaration) was adopted in 1977. As stated in paragraph 4, the 'principles set out in this Declaration are commended to the governments, the employers' and workers' organisations of home and host countries and to the multinational enterprises themselves'. Paragraph 5 further states:

> These principles are intended to guide the governments, the employers' and workers' organizations and the multinational enterprises in taking such measures and actions and adopting such social policies, including those based on the principles laid down in the Constitution and the relevant Conventions and Recommendations of the ILO, as would further social progress.

Paragraph 4 is clear in addressing employers' and workers' organisations, as well as enterprises themselves. This was made possible by the use of a declaration adopted by the Governing Body. If it were a regular ILO Convention or a Recommendation, enterprises would not be made accountable because an international treaty cannot normally bind an individual directly. This is why the ILO came up with the novel idea of adopting a declaration by the Governing Body.

The international legal nature of a Governing Body declaration is, however, unclear. It is not based on the Constitution of the ILO. The unclear nature of the

21 In some countries, such as Japan, where ratified international treaties are given the status of national law, ILO Conventions can be directly applied in a court of law. There have been many cases in Japan where the court referred to ILO Conventions Nos. 29 and 87. Cf Cases listed in S Ago, 'ILO's supervision and Japan' (1995) 38 *Japanese Annual of International Law* 17.

instrument was, perhaps, considered better suited to address non-State entities. When the ILO Tripartite World Employment Conference in June 1976 discussed questions related to multinational enterprises, the Workers' Group, as well as the Group of 77, recommended that a Convention on the social aspects of the activities of multinational enterprises be adopted. The Employers' Group did not share this view but agreed on the usefulness of a Tripartite Declaration of Principles, which would be of a voluntary character. The Governing Body thus adopted the Tripartite Declaration in November 1977.

There were various reasons for the ILO to adopt a code of conduct as a Governing Body declaration, instead of an ordinary ILO Convention or a Recommendation. First, the target entities are neither States nor ILO constituents, but private enterprises. Multinational enterprises, being by nature multinational and conducting their activities across borders, cannot, in many cases, be regulated by nation States. Even if a country is bound by a treaty and assumes certain international duties to control multinational enterprises, the latter frequently bypass national jurisdictions and the realisation of the treaty objectives is curtailed. Multinational enterprises cannot be effectively regulated by traditional ILO Conventions or Recommendations. Secondly, the Employers' Group of the ILO, which largely represents the interests of multinational enterprises, was strongly against adopting a legally binding instrument. This is shown in the fact that the administrative back-up of the instrument is not exercised by the ILS Department, which is the secretariat for the supervision of ILS, but rather the ILO had to create a *sui generis* division called MULTI outside the ILS Department, within the secretarial structure of the Enterprises Department, along with the Small and Medium Enterprises Unit (SME), Cooperatives Branch (EMP/COOP) and Social Finance Programme (EMP/SFP). In other words, supervision of the Declaration was not contemplated.

From this development, one can see the legal importance (or rather lack of importance) attached to the instrument. There was a consensus that the Declaration would not be adopted in the form of the regular ILS, i.e. neither a Convention nor a Recommendation. The ILO members agreed not to provide legal substance to the Declaration, hence the adoption of the instrument as a Governing Body instrument. Furthermore, the consequence of the adoption of a legal instrument with little relevance blurred the question of who precisely is an addressee of the instrument and facilitated private individuals (enterprises) to be directly addressed.

6.2. 'ENFORCEMENT' OF THE TRIPARTITE DECLARATION

As indicated above, the Tripartite Declaration is, therefore, a legally non-binding instrument. However, like the OECD Guidelines, it is more than just a policy statement of an inter-governmental institution. It also has a follow-up machinery attached to the substantive provisions. The follow-up is conducted in the form of periodic reports requested by the Governing Body and by 'interpretation by the ILO', a procedure approved by the Governing Body in 1980 and revised in 1986.[22]

6.2.1. *The Periodical Survey*

A reporting exercise began when the Governing Body at its 205th Session (February–March 1978) invited governments to report periodically on the effect given to the Declaration after full consultation with the national employers' and workers' organisations.[23] The action taken by the Governing Body was confirmed and reinforced in a resolution adopted at the 65th Session of the International Labour Conference in June 1979.[24] Consequently, the first such reports, for the years 1978 and 1979, were examined in September 1980 by an ad hoc committee of the Governing Body. The committee recommended, in particular, a second round of government reports covering the years 1980, 1981 and 1982, the creation of a standing Governing Body Committee on Multinational Enterprises entrusted with the follow-up, a procedure for the examination of disputes concerning the application of the Tripartite Declaration (also referred to as the interpretation procedure) and a series of studies which the Office would undertake in areas specifically relevant to it. The Governing Body endorsed the above proposals at its 214th Session (November 1980).[25] The second government reports on the Declaration were examined by the Committee on Multinational Enterprises and its report was approved by the Governing Body during its 224th Session (November 1983).[26] In 1984 the Governing Body[27] decided that the third round of government reports should cover 1983, 1984 and 1985 and that the next full-scale report (fourth survey) on the Declaration should be undertaken for 1986, 1987 and 1988. The fifth and sixth reports (1980–82; 1983–85; 1986–88; 1989–91; and 1992–94) and seventh and eighth Surveys for the years 1996–99 and 2000–04 followed.[28] This reporting exercise continued

---

22 Procedure for the examination of disputes concerning the application of the Tripartite Declaration of Principles concerning Multinational Enterprises and Social Policy by means of interpretation of its Provisions. *Official Bulletin*, Geneva, ILO [1986] Vol. LXIX, Series A, No. 3 pp 196–97 (to replace Part IV of the Procedures adopted by the Governing Body at its 214th Session [November 1980]). See *Official Bulletin* [1981] Vol. LXIV, Series A, No. 1 pp 89–90.

23 GB.205/10/2, para 9 and GB.205/PV(Rev.) p VI/4.

24 'Resolution concerning follow-up to the World Employment Conference', International Labour Conference, 65th Session, Record of Proceedings (Geneva, International Labour Office [1979]), section on multinational enterprises XCV–XCVI.

25 GB.214/6/3, para 85; GB.214/PV(Rev.) p IV/11.

26 GB.224/17/30.

27 GB.228/19/24, paras 12, 14.

28 Para 7 of the GB.301/MNE/4 301st Session 2008.

until 2006, when the Governing Body decided to postpone it, in view of concern about the low rate of response to the Eighth Survey, as well as the lack of detail contained in the responses.[29]

A conference called 'MultiForum 07' was convened by the Governing Body in 2007, in which top executives and worker representatives from more than 100 innovative global companies, as well as government officials from around the world, were invited to mark the 30th Anniversary of the Tripartite Declaration.

After postponing the discussion of the form of periodical survey for a number of years, the ILO Governing Body, at its 320th session in March 2014, adopted a new follow-up mechanism on the Tripartite Declaration, comprised of promotional activities and an information-gathering mechanism, thus practically abandoning the periodical review exercise conducted over the past 30 years. As part of the information-gathering process, the Office will collect prior to each ILO Regional Meeting country-level experiences on harnessing opportunities and addressing challenges related to foreign direct investment (FDI) and activities of multinational enterprises as well as on the promotion of the principles of the Tripartite Declaration. This information gathering will be done through a short questionnaire addressed to governments and employers' and workers' organisations of the region. The input received through the questionnaire will inform a report that then forms the basis for a discussion by the tripartite constituents during the regional meetings. After four regional meetings, a global report will be presented to the ILO Governing Body that will allow for the identification of lessons learnt and good practices as well as for an assessment of the ILO Member States' needs and the effectiveness of promotional activities related to the Tripartite Declaration.

6.2.2. Interpretation Procedure

The 'Procedure for the Examination of Disputes Concerning the Application of the Tripartite Declaration of Principles Concerning Multinational Enterprises and Social Policy by Means of Interpretation of its Provisions', adopted by the Governing Body in March 1986, provides for the submission of requests for interpretation in cases of disputes on the meaning and application of its provisions. The importance of this procedure lies in its ability to contribute to the harmonious development of labour relations, either by its use or by its availability, the latter of which may encourage disputants to confront their difficulties and to gain a perspective capable of mutual accommodation. It is not designed to solve conflicts or determine findings or provide Recommendations. It is not a form of supervision, such as the examination by the Committee of Experts on the Application of Conventions and Recommendations, which concludes findings and even suggests (recommends) amendment to, or abolition

29 GB.294/10(Rev.).

of, legislative texts, to make the Member States abide by their obligations under the ILO instruments. On the other hand, the Interpretation Procedure of the Tripartite Declaration was designed to function, at least, as a sort of supervision without explicitly calling it so. If there had been a consensus to regard it as a quasi-supervisory procedure, the system would have worked. However, unlike in the case of the OECD Guidelines, the ILO's procedure has not been fully utilised. To date there have only been five cases in which the Governing Body of the ILO issued 'official' interpretations of the relevant provisions of the Tripartite Declaration. Nonetheless, a 'successful' conclusion was reported in one case, where paragraph 26 of the Declaration was 'interpreted' as to the duties of a multinational enterprise to give reasonable prior notice of changes, which would have major employment effects. The ILO (Governing Body), referring to the Termination of Employment Convention 1982 (No. 158) as a guide, maintained that paragraph 26 requires reasonable prior notice of intended changes in operations to be given to workers' representatives and their organisations where such organisations are identifiable under national law and practice, and if such representatives and organisations exist it is insufficient to inform the workers affected on an individual basis.[30]

The fact that no more cases on multinational enterprises are reported on the ILO's website these days suggests that the procedure has not been particularly successful. Many ILO Conventions are now referred to in the OECD Guidelines and the latter appears to have overtaken the ILO's function in pursuing the aims of the non-binding instrument. Although there is no clear mention about the non-application of the Interpretation Procedure of 1986, the ILO appears now to have shifted the emphasis to promotional activities rather than sticking to the 'interpretation' method for the implementation of the Tripartite Declaration. On 20 March 2014 the Governing Body adopted a decision on the 'Implementation strategy for the follow-up mechanism of and promotional activities on the Tripartite Declaration of Principles concerning Multinational Enterprises and Social Policy',[31] which is mainly comprised of promotional activities and an information-gathering system.

6.3. LESSONS LEARNT FROM THE POOR RECORD OF THE TRIPARTITE DECLARATION

The idea was unique, in 1977, to adopt an instrument as a declaration of the Governing Body to address the issue of multinational enterprises in a

30 ILO, 'Interpretation Procedure at Work: BIFU Case (1984–1985)', Multi: Multinational Enterprise and Social Policy, <http://www.ilo.org/public/english/employment/multi/tripartite/cases.htm>, accessed 13.02.2009. However, this URL was recently removed from the ILO's website.

31 Document GB.320/POL/10.

non-conventional manner. However, despite its existence over 30 years, the instrument has apparently not achieved its basic objective. The periodical review process may have achieved better results and the 'interpretation' procedure might have created a working system of supervision, if it had been more frequently utilised. The restrictive manner of its application, such as limiting the initiator of the interpretation only to the traditional tripartite constituents of the ILO[32] and making such requests receivable, only when all other means have been exhausted, has meant that the Tripartite Declaration is not user friendly.[33]

The greatest difference between the relatively successful record of the application of the OECD Guidelines and that of the ILO Tripartite Declaration appears to lie in the composition of the bodies to look into the cases. In the case of the ILO, it is the Office (Secretariat), which will 'prepare a draft reply in consultation with the Officers of the Committee on Multinational Enterprises'.[34] In the case of the OECD, it will be a National Contact Point (NCP), which looks into the question and suggests a solution. The fact that a secretariat is the body to propose eventual changes to the activities of multinational enterprises makes the weight of the product lighter. The NCP, on the other hand, is a body authorised by the OECD Guidelines to follow up the original instrument and it can be assimilated as a 'treaty body', such as the Human Rights Committee established by the ICCPR. The OECD Guidelines are, obviously, not an international treaty[35] but the OECD has endeavoured to make it closer to a treaty[36] by using a treaty-like procedure, such as 'adherence' to the Guidelines, which is similar to 'ratification' of a Convention and creates a supervisory mechanism with an international administrative function.

The difference between the ILO's instrument and the OECD's is found in their follow-up mechanisms. There was a fundamental difference in the

---

32 Para 5 of the Procedure, above n 29.

33 Para 2 of the Procedure, above n 29. 'The procedure should in no way duplicate or conflict with existing national or ILO procedures. Thus, it cannot be invoked: (a) in respect of national law and practice; (b) in respect of international labour Conventions and Recommendations; (c) in respect of matters falling under the freedom of association procedure. The above means that questions regarding national law and practice should be considered through appropriate national machinery; that questions regarding international labour Conventions and Recommendations should be examined through the various procedures provided for in Arts 19, 22, 24 and 26 of the Constitution of the ILO, or through government requests to the Office for informal interpretation; and that questions concerning freedom of association should be considered through the special ILO procedures applicable to that area.'

34 Para 7 of the Procedure, above n 29.

35 The OECD has adopted treaties, such as the Anti-Bribery Convention or the Model Tax Convention, but in the case of multinational enterprises, it did not choose to adopt the Guidelines as a treaty.

36 'The *Guidelines* provide voluntary principles and standards for responsible business conduct consistent with applicable laws and internationally recognized standards. However, the countries adhering to the *Guidelines* make a binding commitment to implement them in accordance with the Decision of the OECD Council on the OECD Guidelines for Multinational Enterprises' (OECD Guidelines, Preamble, para 1).

degree of consensus at the time of the adoption of the instrument. The ILO Governing Body was clear in its decision not to adopt it as a Convention or a Recommendation and therefore outside the ambit of the regular supervisory mechanism of ILS. The Tripartite Declaration was to be deprived of all and any elements of ILS, thus making the periodical reporting and 'interpretation' completely outside the scope of the ILO's regular and special supervision. It is therefore understandable that the reporting exercise has not been rigorously pursued, nor the 'interpretation' machinery frequently relied on.

7. TREATY OR GUIDELINES: CONCLUDING REMARKS

7.1. VIABILITY OF A TREATY

A treaty is obviously clear in its content and fully legally binding when ratified. That is why the United Nations Charter promotes codification of customary law (Article 13, paragraph 1(a). The drawback is that it only binds countries ratifying a treaty. A multilateral treaty that is not widely ratified is less effective than a customary rule. Lessons learnt from the ILO show us that genuine consensus must precede formulation of a treaty. The degree of consensus is defined not only by the numerical majority at the adoption of the instrument, but also the nature of consensus, whether there is a sincere commitment by the parties concerned, especially those who are the target of the treaty.[37] We have already seen significant doubt cast by industrialised countries in the formulation of the Norms on the Responsibilities of Transnational Corporations and Other Business Enterprises with Regard to Human Rights and we now see clear objections expressed by the home countries of the multinational enterprises in the adoption of a treaty. In the case of the ILO, as soon as the Member States face problems in drafting a Convention, it quickly changes its effort to draft a Recommendation instead.

There was a case in the ILO where a consensus had not existed at the initial stage of the adoption of a Convention. In 1964, when the Conference discussed the adoption of ILS on employment policy, the original proposal made by the Governing Body was adoption of a Recommendation. However, during the drafting stage of the instrument, the Workers' Group strongly pushed for a Convention and it eventually succeeded in persuading the Conference to adopt it as Convention No. 122. The Convention initially lacked concreteness in its provisions and it appeared to be promotional. It was only thanks to the established system of supervision that the Convention remained a valid legal instrument

37 ILO Conventions on migrant workers (Nos. 97 and 143) have been ratified by many worker-sending countries, but by few receiving countries. Most of the requirements under these Conventions are targeted at the receiving countries.

and it acquired an important place among other priority Conventions. The prospective UN Treaty might become legally relevant if there existed a well-functioning system of supervision. As it is very unlikely that such a system can be established soon, it would appear more appropriate pursue a non-binding instrument, i.e. substantiation of the UNGP.

7.2. SUBSTANTIATION OF THE UNGP

The UNGP has been adopted as a resolution of the Human Rights Council, i.e. a subsidiary body of the General Assembly. It can therefore be assimilated to a resolution of other subsidiary bodies of the General Assembly, such as the Final Acts of the United Nations Conference on Trade and Development (UNCTAD). 'The Set of Multilaterally Agreed Equitable Principles and Rules for the Control of Restrictive Business Practices', worked out by UNCTAD and eventually adopted by the General Assembly,[38] is another example. More generally, the UNGP is a non-binding instrument adopted by a universal inter-governmental institution, sometimes referred to as 'soft law', which needs special attention in the legal debate.

Resolutions of the General Assembly, ECOSOC and their subsidiary organs, such as the Human Rights Council and UNCTAD, are neither treaty nor customary law so that they cannot legally bind Member States. However, a significant number of studies have already been undertaken on this subject matter and the general conclusion is that although these instruments are not legally binding, they may become legally relevant if various necessary conditions are met. These conditions include the degree of consensus, degree of concreteness and existence of a follow-up mechanism.[39] Seen from this perspective, one can say that the UNGP can meet some of the standards required for an instrument to be qualified as a legally relevant instrument, but there are a few obstacles to be overcome. One of the most significant conditions is the availability of a mechanism of follow-up. The follow-up can take various forms and one of them is to set up a subsidiary body to work out a legally binding instrument. We would here recall the experience of ECOSOC, which mandated the Commission on Human Rights to draw up the International Bill of Human Rights and which eventually came up with the non-binding Universal Declaration, on the one hand, and the binding International Covenants, on the other. This process led the initially non-binding Universal Declaration to become more legally relevant.

---

38 GA Resolution 35/63 of 05.12.1980.

39 OY Asamoah, *The Legal Significance of the Declarations of the General Assembly of the United Nations*, Martinus Nijhoff, The Hague 1966 pp 1–274. S Ago 'Follow-up of UN Resolutions' (1995) 61 *Journal of Law and Politics* (Kyushu U, Japan) 34–82.

Some of the principles enshrined in the Declaration are sometimes claimed to have attained the status of customary international law.

To the extent that the proposed UN Treaty on Business and Human Rights can be conceived as a follow-up process, it has a favourable effect on the legal relevance of the UNGP. On the other hand, as the ILO's experience has shown, when there is no genuine consensus to make a binding instrument, the process will not be easy. It is, therefore, preferable to stick to non-binding resolution, i.e. the UNGP, and try to make it more legally relevant by various means, in particular by 'following up' the instrument.

One of the means of follow-up is reporting, especially if that is supported by a monitoring mechanism. In a way, the Global Forum, which has been organised in November/December of every year since 2012 at the European Headquarters of the UN in Geneva, is a sort of monitoring, in the sense that the stakeholders get together and governments and enterprises report on what measures they have taken to apply the UNGP, while delegates from civil society critically review their statements. In order to make this mechanism work properly, a resolution will have to be adopted by the Human Rights Council or the General Assembly to request governments and enterprises to report specifically to the Forum. The Forum has so far achieved a certain degree of awareness of the UNGP and business and human rights issues overall, but it appears to be too large a gathering to monitor the original instrument. The ILO provides another experience here. When a huge number of reports sent by the governments in accordance with Articles 19 and 22 of the ILO Constitution began reaching the ILO, the general conference of the ILO (the International Labour Conference) could no longer cope with the volume of the reports and entrusted their examination to the Committee of Experts on the Application of Conventions and Recommendations, an independent body of specialists, to examine the consistency of national laws and practices with the provisions of the ILO Conventions. A similar mechanism could possibly be created in the case of the UNGP too.

It is in the method of following up the UNGP that the objectives enshrined therein can be substantiated and the original instrument made legally more relevant. If the monitoring system begins to work, the effect of the UNGP may be more strongly felt than the proposed UN Treaty being adopted but not ratified by the majority of countries that are the target of the treaty.

LESSONS FOR THE TREATY PROCESS FROM THE INTERNATIONAL LAW COMMISSION AND INTERNATIONAL ENVIRONMENTAL LAW

Sara L Seck*

1. INTRODUCTION

In March 2014 Amnesty International published *Injustice Incorporated: Corporate Abuses and the Human Rights to Remedy.*[1] *Injustice Incorporated* details four case studies described by Amnesty as 'emblematic' for the way in which they demonstrate how 'corporate political and financial power intertwined with specific legal obstacles … allow companies to evade accountability and deny, or severely

* With thanks to Kirsten Stefanik, PhD Candidate, Western Law, and Jessica Buckerfield, JD candidate, Western Law, for excellent research assistance.

1 Amnesty International, *Injustice Incorporated: Corporate Abuses and the Human Right to Remedy*, 07.03.2014 <http://www.amnesty.org/en/documents/POL30/001/2014/en/> accessed 26.05.2017.

curtail, remedy'.[2] *Injustice Incorporated* concludes with recommendations for legal reform, yet does not call for a 'binding international treaty' as a necessary mechanism for implementation of the reforms. Instead, recommendations are focused upon measures that could be implemented through state practice, whether of legislatures or courts. Yet Amnesty, together with many other civil society groups and states of the Global South, have thrown their support behind the negotiation of a 'binding' treaty in the business and human rights context.[3]

Drawing upon the case studies presented in *Injustice Incorporated*, this chapter will examine the treaty debate through the lens of international environmental law, with attention to the work of the International Law Commission (ILC). Amnesty highlights that the chosen case studies have in common a wide-ranging and, at most, only partially successful search for remedy and justice over many years and in many fora. Also notable, but not explicitly identified by Amnesty, is that each case study may be characterised as an example of transnational environmental harm[4] with corporate power of a rich country externalising environmental costs to a poor one – whether, as in the first three cases, by transfer of potentially hazardous industrial technologies through foreign direct investment, or, in the fourth case, the physical transfer of hazardous waste. Thus, all involve environmental harm with associated violations of human rights. This is important as Ecuador, a key player in the push towards a binding treaty, is known for the notorious and never-ending Chevron-Ecuador oil pollution dispute – another environmental case.[5] Moreover, *Kiobel*, the case that led to the decision emanating from the United States Supreme Court limiting the application of the Alien Tort Statute by US courts to cases that do not violate the 'presumption against extraterritoriality', may be seen as arising out of an effort to seek justice for the deaths of environmental activists voicing concerns over oil pollution on Ogoni lands in Nigeria.[6] Indeed, it is increasingly common to hear

---

2 Ibid 11.

3 S Shetty, 'Corporations have rights. Now we need a global treaty on their responsibilities', Amnesty International, 21.01.2015 <https://www.amnesty.org/en/articles/blogs/2015/01/corporations-have-rights-now-we-need-a-global-treaty-on-their-responsibilities/> accessed 26.05.17. See further information on the binding treaty process, <http://business-humanrights.org/en/binding-treaty> accessed 26.05.2017; Intergovernmental Working Group, <http://www.ohchr.org/EN/HRBodies/HRC/WGTransCorp/Pages/IGWGOnTNC.aspx> accessed 26.05.2017.

4 SL Seck, 'Transnational Business and Environmental Harm: A TWAIL Analysis of Home State Obligations' (2011) 3(1) *Trade, Law & Development* 164, 174–76.

5 See Resolution co-sponsored by South Africa and Ecuador on the need for a BHR treaty <http://business-humanrights.org/en/binding-treaty> accessed 26.05.17. See also Texaco/Chevron lawsuits (re Ecuador), as described on the Business and Human Rights Resource Centre website <http://business-humanrights.org/en/texacochevron-lawsuits-re-ecuador> accessed 26.05.17.

6 SL Seck, 'Kiobel and the E-word: Reflections on Transnational Environmental Responsibility in an Interconnected World', *Law at the End of the Day*, 05.07.2013 <http://lcbackerblog.blogspot.ca/2013/07/sara-seck-on-kiobel-and-e-word.html> accessed 26.05.2017.

expressions of concern over the persecution of 'environmental rights defenders', whether or not they self-identify as indigenous peoples.[7] Yet discussions of the treaty debate in the business and human rights context are generally divorced from existing lessons within international environmental law.

The chapter will first examine each of the Amnesty case studies in order to document the state practice identified and the gaps that need to be filled. The chapter will then consider the work of the ILC in its progressive codification of the law on prevention and loss allocation with respect to transboundary harm arising from hazardous activities, culminating in draft Articles[8] and draft Principles,[9] respectively, in 2001 and 2006. The modest claim of this chapter is that as the key United Nations body responsible for the progressive development and codification of international law, the work of the ILC should surely be of relevance to the treaty debate. Bringing together the Amnesty case studies with the work of the ILC, the chapter will consider whether in fact there are lessons for the treaty debate to be learned from this body of work.

2. THE AMNESTY CASE STUDIES

The Amnesty report *Injustice Incorporated* details four case studies: (1) the 1984 Bhopal gas disaster in India; (2) the 1995 Omai mine tailings dam rupture in Guyana; (3) the three-decades-long dumping of mine waste at the Ok Tedi mine in Papua New Guinea beginning in the 1980s; and (4) the 2006 dumping of toxic waste in Abidjan in Côte d'Ivoire by Trafigura. Each will be briefly examined in turn.

2.1. THE 1984 BHOPAL GAS DISASTER IN INDIA

The Bhopal gas plant tragedy has elicited extensive commentary, and rightly so given the horrific events and failure of satisfactory legal remedy and accountability.[10] On 2 December 1984 toxic gas leaked from a methyl

---

7 See, for example, United Nations Secretary-General, *Situation of Human Rights Defenders*, UNGA 68th Sess., UN Doc A/68/262 (05.08.2013) paras 15–18; M. Sekaggya, Report of the Special Rapporteur on the Situation of Human Rights Defenders, UN Doc A/HRC/19/55 (21.12.2011), paras 60–87, 124–26.

8 International Law Commission, *Draft Articles on Prevention of Transboundary Harm from Hazardous Activities*, Report of the International Law Commission: Fifty-third Session, UN Doc A/56/10 (2001) 366–436.

9 International Law Commission, *Draft Principles on the Allocation of Loss in the Case of Transboundary Harm Arising from Hazardous Activities*, Report of the International Law Commission: Fifty-eighth Session UN Doc A/61/10 (2006) 101–82.

10 In addition to Amnesty International, above n 1, see the extensive writings of Upendra Baxi on Bhopal. See, for example, <http://upendrabaxi.in/> accessed 26.05.2017.

isocyanate (MIC) storage tank at the Union Carbide India Limited (UCIL) pesticide manufacturing plant in Bhopal, India. Majority owned by United States-based Union Carbide Corporation (UCC), the UCIL plant had been built in 1968 close to 'densely populated slum areas' which expanded over the years to accommodate rural migrants.[11] According to Amnesty, the leak was responsible for the death of between 7,000 and 10,000 people within three days of the accident, and more than 570,000 people were exposed to 'damaging levels' of the gas, 'leading to a range of chronic and debilitating illnesses' with consequences still felt today.[12] While evidence suggests management at UCC had been aware of safety problems at the Bhopal plant for years, cost-cutting measures and a lack of local laws relating to hazardous industries combined to create a situation in which no comprehensive emergency plans existed to warn the local communities about what to do in the event of a leak, even though such plans were in effect at a comparable Union Carbide plant in the United States.[13] Moreover, the withholding of timely and accurate information with regard to the toxicological properties of the chemicals involved and appropriate treatments exacerbated health problems in the aftermath and over the long term.[14]

The Amnesty report details numerous legal actions, both criminal and civil, brought in the courts of India and the United States over many years, which resulted in a 1989 civil settlement agreement of US$470 million bestowing civil and criminal immunity on UCC and UCIL, despite an initial claim by India for US$3.3 billion.[15] This settlement was reached in India after US courts dismissed actions brought by victims and consolidated into one claim brought by India, on the basis of the doctrine of *forum non conveniens*.[16] In 2010 criminal negligence

11 Amnesty International, above n 1, 33.

12 Ibid 35. For a detailed discussion of the health effects see R Dhara, 'Health Effects of the Bhopal Gas Leak: a Review' (Spring 1994) *New Solutions* 40.

13 Ibid.

14 Ibid 37.

15 The Supreme Court of India upheld the civil settlement and civil immunity granted in the settlement, but quashed the decision to grant criminal immunity in *Union Carbide Corporation v Union of India*, Supreme Court of India (1991) 4 SCC 584; AIR 1992 SC 248.

16 Amnesty International, above n 1, 43–46. *The Union of India v Union Carbide Corporation*, US Southern District Court of New York, 08.04.1985, reproduced in APPEN Report, *The Bhopal Tragedy: One Year After* (Sahabat Alam Malaysia 1985) 223–28, dismissed by Judge Keenan in *In Re Union Carbide Corporation Gas Plant Disaster* 634 F Supp 842 (SDNY 1986). Subsequent attempts to bring additional civil cases in the United States have been made and have also been unsuccessful. In *Bi v Union Carbide Chems. and Plastics Co.*, 984 F 2d 582 (2d Cir) cert. denied 510 US 862, 114 S Ct 179, 126 L Ed 2d 138 (1993) class action lawsuits were dismissed on the grounds of *forum non conveniens* by Judge Keenan, who held that his analysis and conclusions from the 1986 decision were still appropriate. In November 1999 a group of victims filed a suit under the Alien Tort Claims Act against UCC and its former CEO, Warren Anderson. This claim was dismissed by Judge Keenan on the grounds that the plaintiffs lacked standing and because proceedings were barred by the 1989 settlement, see *Bano v Union Carbide Corporation*, 273 F3d 120 (2d Cir. 2001). In November 2004

convictions were finally handed down against UCIL and seven accused, but not against UCC or Warren Anderson, the chairman of UCC at the time of the disaster, who had previously been declared an absconder and subject to an extradition request.[17] Notably, the civil settlement agreement provided that if it was insufficient to address the costs of personal injuries and compensation, the government of India would be responsible for any shortfall.[18] However, as noted by Amnesty, 'the settlement agreement did not take into account damages for environmental pollution generated by the plant's operations. As a result, the award was not calculated to cover or compensate for damage to the environment, life, health or property resulting from plant contamination.'[19]

In addition to the inadequacy of the economic settlement and its fraught implementation process, the Amnesty report highlights the ongoing health effects of the gas leak and the ongoing environmental pollution at Bhopal, including groundwater contamination.[20] As yet unresolved civil claims for environmental damage and clean-up have been brought in US courts and public interest litigation commenced in Indian courts.[21] Meanwhile, UCC divested from UCIL, and was subsequently purchased by Dow Chemical. Dow denies any responsibility for the Bhopal disaster.[22]

2.2. THE 1995 OMAI MINE TAILING DAM RUPTURE IN GUYANA

The Omai mine tailings dam rupture is much less well known than the Bhopal gas plant disaster, although the Canadian case law emerging out of the failed attempt to litigate against Canadian-based Cambior Inc. was the subject of

claims were filed against UCC and its former CEO, Warren Anderson for damage arising from alleged water pollution caused by the Bhopal plant and were, again, dismissed by Judge Keenan, *Sahu v Union Carbide Corporation* 2006 WL 3377577 (SDNY 20.11.2006) No 04 Civ 8825 (JFK), reinstated by the Court of Appeal on technical grounds, *Sahu v Union Carbide Corporation*, 2012 WL 2422757 (SDNY 26.06.2012) (No 04 Civ 8825 (JFK)), and ultimately dismissed again by Judge Keenan, *Sahu v Union Carbide Corporation* No 04 Civ 8825 (JFK) (SDNY 2012).

17 Amnesty International, above n 1, 41–42. *State of Madhya Pradesh v Warren Anderson (Absconder) and Others, in the Court of Chief Judicial Magistrate Bhopal, Madhya Pradesh*, Cr. Case No 8460/1996 – Date of Institution 01.12.1987, Judgment of 07.06.2010.

18 Amnesty International, above n 1, 49.

19 Ibid.

20 Ibid 50–54.

21 Ibid 47, 53–59. In July 2004, Bhopal Gas Peedith Mahila Udyog Sangathan filed proceedings in the Madhya Pradesh High Court against a number of defendants, including the government of India, the Madhya Pradesh state government, UCC, Eveready (formerly UCIL) and Dow. The plaintiffs seek damages of US$3.3 billion for environmental pollution, environmental remediation and medical assistance for victims. This case is ongoing.

22 Amnesty International, above n 1, 4–57.

detailed analysis in a paper published by the author in 1999.[23] Omai Gold Mines Limited (OGML) was a joint venture of Cambior Inc., US-based Golden Star Resources, and the government of Guyana, established to operate OGML in accordance with a Mineral Agreement and accompanying Environmental Impact Statement (EIS).[24] OGML began operations in 1993, and in August 1995 the banks of its tailings dam ruptured and collapsed, spewing effluent laced with cyanide and heavy metals into the Omai and then Essequibo rivers.[25] Indigenous Guyanese villagers who relied upon the Essequibo River for 'transport, food harvesting and subsistence fishing, drinking water, animal husbandry, irrigation, bathing and recreation' noticed changes in the river, including scores of dead fish, and stopped using the water or consuming the fish even before being notified of the problem.[26] It took five days for the spill to be contained, and three days for official government notification of the environmental disaster.[27] Yet, shortly thereafter the government declared the water quality met Canadian standards and lifted the water ban.[28] As documented in the Amnesty report, an earlier spill had occurred at a time when OGML was seeking to discharge higher concentrations of cyanide in wastewater than was permitted under the EIS, and subsequent discharges were allowed in 1996.[29]

The extent to which the spill in fact impacted people's health has been controversial, due in part to conclusions of a Guyanese government Commission of Inquiry to the effect that 'there had been no serious risks to the health of riverian communities'.[30] Yet community concerns about water quality persisted due to a lack of government environmental monitoring coupled with a lack of assessment of health effects.[31] While the mine was allowed to resume operations under new environmental protection legislation, the Amnesty report highlights the lack of governmental financial and technical capacity to effectively regulate compliance.[32]

Immediately after the spill, Cambior offered very small amounts of compensation to some affected people as full and final settlement of OGML's liability.[33] These settlements were criticised as inadequate and unjust as many

---

23 SL Seck, 'Environmental Harm in Developing Countries Caused by Subsidiaries of Canadian Mining Corporations: The Interface of Public and Private International Law' (1999) 37 *Canadian Yearbook of International Law* 139, 154–68, 188–89.
24 Amnesty International, above n 1, 65.
25 Ibid 66.
26 Ibid 66–67.
27 Ibid 67.
28 Ibid.
29 Ibid 67–68.
30 Ibid 69.
31 Ibid.
32 Ibid 72–73.
33 Ibid 73.

of those who signed were illiterate and had not received legal advice.[34] A class action lawsuit was commenced in Canadian courts in 1997 on behalf of an estimated 23,000 victims but this was dismissed on the basis of the doctrine of *forum non conveniens*.[35] Legal actions brought in Guyana were unsuccessful for various reasons,[36] and in 2001 Cambior acquired Golden Star Resources' share in the mine. In 2006 Canadian company Iamgold bought Cambior's share and ran the mine until it closed in 2008.[37]

2.3. THE DUMPING OF MINE WASTE AT THE OK TEDI MINE IN PAPUA NEW GUINEA

The third case in the Amnesty report also involves mining, but this time instead of a tailings dam spill, the problem was the dumping of mine waste directly into

34 Ibid. See further, A McIntosh, 'Cambior pays off poor Guyanese at $150 a pop', *The Montreal Gazette*, 09.09.1995; R Ramraj, 'The Omai Disaster in Guyana' (2001) 43(2) *Geographical Bulletin* 88.

35 Ibid 74–76. *Recherches Internationales Québec v Cambior Inc and Home Insurance and Golder associés ltée, corespondents* [1998] QJ No 2554, Québec Super Ct (Class Action), 14.08.1998. See analysis of this decision in Seck, above n 23.

36 Amnesty International, above n 1, 76–78. In August 1998 an action on behalf of 23,000 riverian Guyanese was brought against Cambior, OGML and others. The plaintiffs sought compensation of around US$150 million and injunctions to (1) prevent the defendants from discharging further cyanide and other heavy metals into the rivers; (2) to direct the defendants to remediate the damage caused by the 1995 spill; and (3) to provide the residents with reliable supplies of potable water. *Judith David and Elizabeth David v Cambior Inc, Golder and Associates, Home Insurance, and Omai Gold Mines Limited*, the High Court of the Supreme Court of the Judicature (Civil Jurisdiction) Demerara, No 867-W, Statement of Claim, 16.08.1999. This action was dismissed against plaintiffs outside Guyana on 28.03.2000, leaving OGML as the sole defendant. The action against OGML was dismissed on 12.02.2002 by the Guyana High Court with no written reasons provided. See, for example, International Human Rights Clinic, 'All that Glitters: Gold Mining in Guyana: The failure of government oversight and the human rights of Amerindian communities' (March 2007) Human Rights Program, Harvard Law School, 39. A second case was brought against Cambior, OGML, Golden Star Resources and others in the Guyanese courts in May 2003. The plaintiffs sought: (1) US$2 billion in damages; (2) injunctions ordering the defendants to provide potable water and meet the costs of medical monitoring of the Essequibo population; (3) the discontinuation of effluent dumping into the rivers; (4) various measures to ensure that improved management and contingency plans were put in place at the mine; and (5) US$1 billion in punitive damages. The case was dismissed in October 2006 with no written reasons provided. Justice Carl Singh provided a verbal judgment articulating the finding of the representative nature of the suit 'inappropriate' and 'bad in law' and ruling that the residents did not share common interest. *Judith David, Richard Bowens, and Lilmattie v Cambior Inc, Golder associés ltée and Associates, Home Insurance, and Omai Gold Mines Limited, Knight Piesold, Golden Star Resources, The Attorney General on Behalf of Government of Guyana/Ministry of Public Works, JP Morgan Canada, the Royal Bank of Canada, Société Générale Canada, Credit Lyonnais, Banque ABN AMRO NV SUCC Du Canada, National Bank of Canada and Citibank of Canada*, the High Court of the Supreme Court of the Judicature (Civil Jurisdiction) Demerara, Civil Jurisdiction.

37 Amnesty International, above n 1, 66, 78.

a river over the course of 30 years. Australia's Broken Hill Proprietary Company Limited (BHP) was the majority owner and operator of Ok Tedi Mining Limited (OTML), and the mine was one of Papua New Guinea (PNG)'s most important contributors to the economy.[38] However, while the original mining agreement provided that waste was to be stored in a tailings dam, OTML was allowed to operate without one after a landslide destroyed the dam's foundations in 1984 while it was under construction.[39] The ongoing riverine waste disposal cumulatively has had a devastating impact on the environment and the 250 indigenous communities who rely upon the water in the Ok Tedi and Fly rivers and adjacent forests for subsistence.[40] Yet, the PNG government never ordered OTML to mitigate the environmental impact or to rehabilitate the river system.[41]

In 1994 claims were brought against BHP in Australian courts on behalf of 30,000 indigenous villagers, while other claims were filed in PNG courts.[42] This Australian litigation was also the subject of detailed analysis in the 1999 article published by the author.[43] Notably, the remedy sought included not only civil damages for the destruction of subsistence livelihoods, but also court orders to stop further dumping and to construct a tailings dam.[44] Claims based on nuisance and trespass were dismissed on the basis of the Mozambique principle, according to which courts do not have jurisdiction to hear cases relating to foreign property rights, while other claims were dismissed on the basis of other doctrines.[45] Ultimately, some claims did proceed, although only those for which a damages remedy could be ordered.[46] Notably, while *forum non conveniens* was argued, the Australian version of the doctrine provides the court with more discretion and so did not lead to dismissal from Australian courts as had been the case in both Bhopal (United States) and Cambior (Canada).[47]

---

38 Ibid 81–82.

39 Ibid 82.

40 Ibid 81–82.

41 Ibid 83.

42 Ibid 84. The cases brought in the Australian courts were: *No. 5782 of 1994 Rex Dagi and Others v The Broken Hill Proprietary Company Limited* (CAN 004 028 077) *and Ok Tedi Mining Limited; No. 5980 of 1994 Barry John Shackles; Daru Fish Supplies Pty. Ltd. v The Broken Hill Proprietary Company Limited* (CAN 004 028 077) *and Ok Tedi Mining Limited; No 6861 of 1994 Baat Ambetu and Others v The Broken Hill Proprietary Company Limited* (CAN 004 028 077) *and Ok Tedi Mining Limited; No. 6862 of 1994 Alex Maun and Others v The Broken Hill Proprietary Company Limited* (CAN 004 028 077) *and Ok Tedi Mining Limited.*

43 Seck, above n 23, 171–74, 193–96.

44 Amnesty International, above n 1, 84.

45 Ibid 45. The Mozambique principle originates from *British South Africa Co v Companhia de Moçambique* [1893] AC 602. The *Dagi* case was dismissed on the basis of this principle. Portions of the *Shackles*, *Ambetu* and *Maun* cases were dismissed on the basis of the 'act of state' principle, which dictates that the courts of one state will not judge the sovereign acts of another state within its own territory.

46 Amnesty International, above n 1, 45.

47 Seck, above n 23, 157–74.

The Amnesty report details the attempts by BHP and the PNG government to legislatively block victims from pursuing their claims by criminalising the filing of lawsuits in foreign courts, and the contempt of court actions brought in response in Australian courts against OTML and BHP.[48] BHP and all plaintiffs ultimately reached a settlement in 1996, according to which BHP was to pay compensation to affected villagers, provide an equity share in the mine in trust for local communities, consider rehabilitation measures, and implement a tailings containment.[49] However, subsequent studies of the environmental impact of the mine led BHP to conclude that these would be greater than predicted and mitigation measures would be unsuccessful.[50] As the PNG government wanted to keep the mine open, BHP began to divest from the mine, and secured an agreement with the PNG government granting it immunity from further liabilities even as OTML decided against implementation of a tailings containment system.[51] Under the agreement, BHP transferred all its shares to a Singaporean company (the PNG Sustainable Development Program Limited) in 2002.[52] Meanwhile, Community Mine Continuation Agreements offering compensation packages were signed between OTML and local communities in order to keep the mine operating,[53] yet, as environmental impacts were worse than imagined, compensation was enhanced in 2007.[54]

In 2013 the PNG Parliament passed a Bill giving itself complete ownership of OTML and removing all legal liability limits against BHP (now BHP Billiton).[55]

---

48 Amnesty International, above n 1, 85–87.

49 Ibid 87. The agreement was codified as the Mining (Ok Tedi Restated Eighth Supplemental Agreement) Act 1995 in PNG. Under the agreement BHP agreed to pay around US$86 million to affected villagers along the river and an additional US$31 million to those most severely affected in the lower OK Tedi river area. Under the agreement the plaintiffs retained the right to recommence legal action in the Supreme Court of Victoria with regard to any dispute related to the settlement. The PNG government further passed the Compensation (Prohibition of Foreign Legal Proceedings) Act 1995, imposing fines or imprisonment for anyone who brings proceedings in a foreign court in relation to compensation claims arising from any mining and petroleum projects in PNG.

50 Amnesty International, above n 1, 88.

51 Ibid. In April 2000, two new actions were brought in the Supreme Court of Victoria against BHP and OTML, seeking to enforce commitments made in the *Eighth Supplemental Agreement*, which had allegedly not been honoured, specifically the failure to construct a tailings containment system to mitigate environmental damage. *Rex Dagi v The Broken Hill Proprietary Company Limited and Ok Tedi Mining Limited* No 5002 of 2000; *Gabia Gagarimabu v The Broken Hill Proprietary Company Limited and Ok Tedi Mining Limited* No 5003 of 2000. However, before these cases were heard the PNG government and BHP came to a new agreement, the *Ok Tedi Mine Continuation (Ninth Supplemental) Agreement (The Mining Act 2001)*.

52 Amnesty International, above n 1, 89.

53 Ibid.

54 Ibid 91.

55 Ibid 93.

In early 2014 a PNG court issued an interim order restraining OTML from further dumping of mine waste, an order that the PNG government planned to appeal.[56]

2.4. THE 2006 DUMPING OF TOXIC WASTE IN ABIDJAN, CÔTE D'IVOIRE BY TRAFIGURA

This case has a slightly different character from the three other examples in the Amnesty report, as the transnational character here is not the transfer of potentially hazardous industrial technology, but rather the direct transfer of the hazardous waste itself. In August 2006 hazardous waste was dumped in nearly 20 different locations around the city of Abidjan, 'close to houses, workplaces, schools, fields, and the city prison'.[57] The waste was dumped by Compagnie Tommy, a small newly licensed Ivorian company without the 'means or expertise to handle hazardous waste' that had been contracted to dispose of the waste by Trafigura, 'the world's third largest independent trader of crude and oil products'.[58] According to Amnesty, the contract called for Compagnie Tommy to 'discharge' the waste in an 'open dumpsite for domestic waste, located in a poor residential district of Abidjan' with 'no facilities for storing or processing hazardous waste'.[59] Nor did the contract call for any such treatment.

Trafigura had purchased coker naphtha from a Mexican state-owned petroleum company and used a process of caustic washing to refine it, which took place on board the *Probo Koala* in the Mediterranean, a ship chartered by Trafigura.[60] Trafigura's intention was to sell the refined product as a 'cheap blendstock for gasoline' and to dispose of the waste subsequently stored in the ship. Having chosen this method of refinement over a different process that would have produced a less harmful waste, Trafigura contemplated disposing of the waste safely through a Dutch specialist company. However, this would have been very expensive.[61]

According to Amnesty, people living or working near the waste sites in Abidjan experienced symptoms ranging from nosebleeds and vomiting to skin lesions and respiratory problems, which were found by the World Health Organization to be consistent with exposure to this type of waste.[62] At least 100,000 people sought treatment at health facilities while others sought traditional healers or received no treatment at all (the elderly). While

---

56 Ibid 94. *Bagari and Others v Minister for Finance of Papua New Guinea and Others*, WS 14 of 2014, Order of the National Court of Justice of Papua New Guinea (24.01.2014).

57 Amnesty International, above n 1, 97.

58 Ibid.

59 Ibid.

60 Ibid 97–98.

61 Ibid 98.

62 Ibid 99.

the government provided free medical treatment for thousands, Trafigura never made public full information about the exact composition of the waste, and disputes the possibility that it could have long-term consequences.[63] The government took initial steps to remove the waste and clean it up, yet sources, including Amnesty, have documented that the decontamination process was not complete despite settlement money paid by Trafigura that was designated for this purpose.[64]

A National Commission of Enquiry concluded that there had been systemic failings of Ivorian institutions, including enforcement of licence requirements, but also that there were clearly failings of corporate actors and individuals who must have known of the inability of Compagnie Tommy to safely dispose of the waste.[65] Criminal prosecutions were brought against various individuals in Côte d'Ivoire courts. However, a settlement agreement entered into between the government and Trafigura provided immunity to all members of Trafigura, including, in practice, individual Trafigura executives and employees who had been charged criminally and released on bail.[66] Two individuals were ultimately convicted, neither from Trafigura or the government of Côte d'Ivoire.[67]

The settlement agreement was entered into in 2007, before a full determination had been made of the number of victims and the nature of the harm, and without prior consultation with victims. The amount was US$200 million, and it was intended for compensation and clean-up costs, with Côte d'Ivoire agreeing to compensate the victims and to take responsibility for any future claims.[68] Yet the method of distributing the compensation has been critiqued for failing to include victims who chose traditional healers, victims whose medical forms were not properly completed by medical staff at the time of the emergency, and victims who did not have official identify cards.[69]

---

63 Ibid.

64 Ibid 100.

65 Ibid 101. Republic of Côte d'Ivoire, *National Commission of Enquiry on the toxic waste in the district of Abidjan*, 15.11.2006.

66 Amnesty International, above n 1, 102. In September 2006 state prosecutors in Côte d'Ivoire brought criminal charges against a number of individuals alleged to have been involved in the dumping of the toxic waste. The accused included local port and customs officials, employees of local companies implicated in the dumping, and the CEO and two employees of the Trafigura Group. *Yao Essaie Motto & Others v Trafigura Limited and Trafigura Beheer BV*, High Court of Justice, Queen's Bench Division, Claim No HQ06X03370. The government of Côte d'Ivoire and Trafigura reached a settlement, the *Protocol of agreement (Protocole d'accord) between the State of Côte d'Ivoire and the Trafigura Parties*, 13.02.2007, which effectively ended all actions in the Côte d'Ivoire against members of Trafigura.

67 Amnesty International, above n 1, 102–03. Salomon Ugborugbo (head of Compagnie Tommy) and Essoin Kouao (shipping agent from WAIBS (West African International Business Services), the port agent used by Trafigura who had recommended Compagnie Tommy) were ultimately convicted in relation to the incident. *Arrêt No 14 du 22/10/2008*, Cour d'Assises, Cour d'Appel Abidjan.

68 Amnesty International, above n 1, 103.

69 Ibid 104.

Legal actions were also brought in foreign courts. A civil action in 2006 in UK courts resulted in a 2009 US$49 million settlement agreement between Trafigura and 30,000 claimants.[70] Terms of the settlement included that Trafigura would not admit liability, the law firm would not bring any further claims against Trafigura relating to the waste, and confidentiality was imposed upon independent experts who examined medical evidence as well as the claimants and their lawyers. However, a joint public comment was released that stated in part that the plaintiffs' law firm acknowledged 'the slops could at worst have caused a range of short term low level flu like symptoms and anxiety'.[71] Distribution of the settlement funding to victims was met with fraud and irregularities, with thousands left unpaid. Ultimately, victims who had not been included in this action were left without access to necessary information and expertise.

A criminal prosecution was brought by the Dutch Public Prosecutor against Trafigura Beheer BV (TBBV), the group holding company incorporated in the Netherlands,[72] as well as one against the London-based employees of Trafigura Limited (a wholly owned subsidiary of TBBV incorporated in the UK) and the Captain of the *Probo Koala*.[73] Separate charges were brought in the Netherlands against Trafigura's chairman.[74] After some successful convictions under EU and Dutch law, including a €1 million fine imposed on TBBV, many of which were appealed, an out-of-court settlement was reached ending all legal proceedings, which obliged TBBV to pay the fine and imposed fines on individuals as well.[75] However, the company took the position that despite this no executives of Trafigura had accepted a conviction or made any admission of liability or guilt.[76] Meanwhile, Trafigura Limited was never investigated or prosecuted in the UK.[77]

---

70 Ibid 105.

71 Ibid. The joint statement was approved by the High Court, *Motto & Ors v Trafigura Ltd & Anor* [2011] EWHC 90201 (Costs) (15.02.2011), paras 70, 109.

72 Amnesty International, above n 1, 97.

73 Ibid 107.

74 Ibid 108.

75 Ibid. The Dutch Court of First Instance found TBBV, Naeem Ahmed (a London-based employee of Trafigura Ltd), and Captain Chertov guilty. See Amnesty International English translation of verdict on Trafigura Beheer BV, LJN (National Case Law Number): BN2149, District Court of Amsterdam, 13/846003-06 (PROMIS), 23.07.2010. The Court of Appeal annulled the verdict against Naeem Ahmed in July 2011. This was appealed by the Public Prosecutor. The Court of Appeal upheld the €1 million fine against TBBV, though the ruling was appealed by both TBBV and the Public Prosecutor. All legal proceedings were ended in November 2012 when the Dutch Public Prosecutor and TBBV, Claude Dauphin and Naeem Ahmed reached a settlement. As a result, the Court of Appeal ruling obliging TBBV to pay the €1 million fine became final. In addition, the settlement provided for TBBV to pay a further €300,000, Claude Dauphin (Trafigura's CEO) a €67,000 fine, and Naeem Ahmed a €25,000 fine. Amnesty International, above n 1, 108–09.

76 Amnesty International, above n 1, 108–09.

77 Ibid 110.

2.5. CONCLUSIONS

In sum, the case studies presented in Amnesty's *Injustice Incorporated* illustrate that environmental contamination issues may feature prominently in relation to transnational corporate human rights violations, and, while host and home state practice has emerged attempting to address remedy for victims, this practice is sporadic and inadequate. The rights violated in these examples include rights of local people to health, food, water, livelihood and a clean environment.[78] However, home and host states have failed at working cooperatively to meet their obligations to provide access to effective remedy for victims. These failures have been compounded by allegations of corruption at multiple levels, which inhibit both the awarding of compensation in the first place and its delivery once awarded.[79]

The case studies also suggest that it is not simply a question of rectifying doctrines such as the much-criticised common law doctrine of *forum non conveniens*. As the Ok Tedi litigation in particular illustrates, even where home state courts accept jurisdiction over a case and a settlement is reached, clean-up, justice and accountability may still be out of reach. Ultimately, *Injustice Incorporated* identifies three major obstacles to remedy:[80] (a) 'extraterritorial' legal issues, such as separate legal personality, limited liability, and jurisdictional hurdles; (b) corporate control over information leading to a lack of access to information by victims; and (c) the nature of 'corporate–state relationships' that impact the 'willingness and ability of States to uphold human rights, including the right to remedy'.

3. CONTRIBUTIONS OF THE INTERNATIONAL LAW COMMISSION

3.1. STATE RESPONSIBILITY, LIABILITY, AND 'DO NO HARM'

The work of the ILC will be the subject of attention in this section.[81] In 1947 the UN General Assembly established the ILC with the mandate to 'initiate studies and make recommendations for the purpose of … encouraging the progressive development of international law and its codification'.[82] The ILC has since that

78 Ibid 82, 98. See further on the topic of environmental rights, J Knox, *Report of the Independent Expert on the Issue of Human Rights Obligations Relating to the Enjoyment of a Safe, Clean, Healthy and Sustainable Environment, John H. Knox: Mapping Report*, UNHRC, 30.12.2013, UN Doc A/HRC/25/53.

79 See, for example, Amnesty International, above n 1, 50, 76, 107, 110.

80 Ibid 199.

81 See generally International Law Commission <http://legal.un.org/ilc/> accessed 26.05.2017.

82 Ibid. The ILC was created in accordance with Art 13(1)(1) of the Charter of the United Nations.

time issued many reports and studies that have been considered influential by the International Court of Justice, whether or not they codify or progressively develop customary international law, and has also prepared draft treaties for '[m]any of the most important international conventions'.[83] Importantly, the ILC has considered analogous issues to those of concern in the business and human rights treaty debate. The work of the ILC deserves serious attention and reflection.

As is well known, in the 1950s the ILC began work on the codification of the international law of state responsibility[84] – which resulted in 2001 in draft *Articles on the Responsibility of States for Internationally Wrongful Acts* [hereinafter DARS].[85] The DARS have been well received by international courts and tribunals, including the International Court of Justice.[86] In the business and human rights context, scholars frequently cite DARS Article 8 for the proposition that the conduct of non-state actors, including businesses, cannot be directly attributed to the state unless the business was acting under the 'instructions of, or under the direction and control of' that state (the effective control test).[87] Contested interpretations of this and related Articles that raise the possibility of attribution of transnational corporate conduct to the state have received

83 See generally MN Shaw, *International Law*, 7th edn, Cambridge University Press, 2014, pp 84–86; A Boyle and C Chinkin, *The Making of International Law*, Oxford University Press, 2007, especially pp 171–204. Boyle and Chinkin note that the ILC has tended not to draw a 'sharp distinction between codification and progressive development', enabling international tribunals to rely on ILC work 'without overtly enquiring whether particular articles represent existing law, revision of existing law or a new development of the law'. Boyle and Chinkin, ibid, p 200.

84 'State Responsibility' in *Summaries of the Work of the International Law Commission* <http://legal.un.org/ilc/summaries/9_6.shtml> accessed 26.05.2017.

85 International Law Commission, *Draft Articles on Responsibility of States for Internationally Wrongful Acts*, Report of the International Law Commission: Fifty-third Session, UN Doc A/56/10 (2001) pp 43–365.

86 Boyle and Chinkin, above n 83, pp 183–85. For example, an early version of the DARS was relied upon by the International Court of Justice (ICJ) in *Case concerning the Gabčíkovo-Nagymaros Project (Hungary v Slovakia)*, Judgment, 25.09.1997, ICJ Reports 1997, 7, paras 47, 79, 83. The ICJ further commented in *Application of the Convention on the Prevention and Punishment of the Crime of Genocide* (*Bosnia v Serbia*) ICJ Reports 2007, 7, para 420, that Art 16 of DARS dealing with coercion of a state or another international organisation is reflective of customary international law.

87 See generally SL Seck, 'Conceptualizing the Home State Duty to Protect Human Rights' in K Buhman, M Morsing and L Roseberry (eds), *Corporate Social and Human Rights Responsibilities: Global Legal and Management Perspectives*, Palgrave Macmillan, 2011, pp 25, 39–40. For a small sample of sources see NMCP Jägers, *Corporate Human Rights Obligations: In Search of Accountability*, Intersentia, 2002, pp 169–72; O de Schutter, 'The Accountability of Multinationals for Human Rights Violations in European Law' in P Alston (ed), *Non-State Actors and Human Rights*, Oxford University Press, 2005, pp 235–37; R McCorquodale and P Simons, 'State Responsibility for Extraterritorial Violations by Corporations of International Human Rights Law' (2007) 70(4) *Modern Law Review* 598.

much attention in the business and human rights literature, including Article 5 (agency), Article 7 (governmental authority), Article 9 (conflict zones) and Article 11 (adoption of conduct).[88] As I have argued elsewhere, other Articles of DARS are clearly relevant to conceptualising the state duty to protect, including Article 4 which draws attention to the conduct – both actions and omissions – of state organs, including organs of the home state.[89] Indeed, it follows from Article 4 of DARS that as judicial organs are state organs too, home states have a duty of due diligence to prevent and remedy human rights violations by transnational corporations, including a duty of both courts and legislatures to provide victims of human rights violations with access to justice through home state courts.[90] Moreover, this argument is strengthened, not weakened, by Principle 25 of the UN Guiding Principles.[91]

What has received far less attention in the business and human rights scholarly and advocacy communities is the parallel work undertaken by the ILC initially conceptualised as International Liability for Injurious Consequences arising out of Acts not Prohibited by International Law. Begun in the 1970s, this plan of work was specifically designed to consider secondary rules for acts such as industrial activities that were not in themselves wrongful under international law, but which could cause international harms such as transboundary pollution impacting the territory of another state.[92] This approach was strongly criticised by many, including notably Professor Ian Brownlie, who described this approach as 'fundamentally misconceived' in its confusion of primary and secondary rules, and its failure to appreciate that 'much of state responsibility … is concerned with categories of lawful activities which have caused harm'.[93]

88 Seck, above n 87, pp 39–42 and sources cited therein. See also Art 16 (aiding or assisting) for the possibility of direct state complicity. Ibid p 46 citing McCorquodale and Simons, above n 87, 611–15.

89 Seck, above n 87, pp 43–44.

90 Ibid pp 43, 45–46.

91 Principle 25 states: 'As part of their duty to protect … States must take appropriate steps to ensure, through judicial, administrative, legislative or other appropriate means, that when such abuses occur within their territory and/or jurisdiction those affected have access to effective remedy.' UN Guiding Principles, Principle 25, p 22. While the scope of meaning of 'jurisdiction' is clearly contested (and undermined by those who unnecessarily argue in favour of 'extraterritorial' obligations), the reference in the Commentary to Principle 25 to National Contact Points of the OECD Guidelines for Multinational Enterprises clearly supports an interpretation that this Principle applies to home states. See further SL Seck, 'Canadian Mining Internationally and the UN Guiding Principles for Business and Human Rights' (2011) 49 *Canadian Yearbook of International Law* 51, 111–12.

92 Boyle and Chinkin, above n 83, 197–98.

93 I Brownlie, *System of the Law of Nations: State Responsibility (Part I)*, Clarendon Press, 1983, p 50. See also Boyle and Chinkin, above n 83, who describe the original conceptualisation as 'fundamentally confused' and 'extraordinary' in part for 'appear[ing] to believe that

In 1997 the ILC's work on international liability was subdivided into two separate streams, one on the Prevention of Transboundary Damage from Hazardous Activities, which resulted in 2001 in draft Articles (Prevention Articles);[94] while the other resulted in 2006 in draft Principles on the Allocation of Loss in the case of Transboundary Harm Arising out of Hazardous Activities (Loss Allocation Principles).[95] These two bodies of work are now considered a contribution to the codification of primary rules of international environmental law designed to address transboundary environmental risk management.[96] However, relegating the relevance of this body of work to the environmental arena would be a grave mistake, although an easy one to make in light of the problem of fragmentation in international law.[97]

As I have discussed elsewhere,[98] the kind of environmental harms identified in the second and third Amnesty case studies, if not the first, may be classified as 'intra-territorial' problems, which, if examined through the lens of Principle 2 of the 1992 Rio Declaration,[99] fall within the exclusive territorial jurisdiction of the host state. This is because the starting point of Principle 2 is the sovereign right of states to exploit their natural resources in accordance with their own environmental and developmental policies (reflecting the principle of permanent sovereignty over natural resources).[100] That these environmental policies need not be so rigorous as those of the 'first world' is also embedded in the Rio Declaration (all Principles of which were re-endorsed in the 2012 Rio +20 process culminating in *The Future We Want*).[101] Specifically, Principle 11 provides that while all states must enact effective environmental regulation, the application of standards and management practices from rich countries within

no primary obligations of environmental protection existed' and 'unable to grasp that international law might … impose obligations of regulation, diligent control, and prevention of harmful emissions even in respect of lawful activities without either prohibiting the activities or excluding the possibility of state responsibility for breach of these activities.' Ibid.

94 International Law Commission, above n 8.

95 International Law Commission, above n 9.

96 On the conceptualisation as primary rules, see ibid 'Principle 1: Commentary' para 6.

97 See, for example, International Law Commission Study Group, 'Fragmentation of International Law: Difficulties arising from the Diversification and Expansion of International Law', *Report of the Study Group of the International Law Commission*, finalised by Martti Koskenniemi, A/CN.4/L.682 and Corr.1, 13.04.2006.

98 Seck, above n 4, 170; see also SL Seck, 'Human Rights and Extractive Industries: Environmental Law and Standards', *Human Rights Law and Extractive Industries*, Paper No 12, pp 12-1–12-42 (Rocky Mt Min L Fdn 2016).

99 Rio Declaration on Environment and Development, Rio de Janeiro, 14.06.1992, UN Doc. A/CONF.151/26 (vol. 1); 31 ILM 874 (1992).

100 Ibid Principle 2.

101 United Nations General Assembly, *The Future We Want*, Rio de Janeiro, 11.09.2011, UNGA 66th Sess., UN Doc. A/RES/66/288.

developing countries may 'be inappropriate and of unwarranted economic and social cost'.[102]

However, examining these cases through an international human rights lens, as does the Amnesty report, highlights that this interpretation of Principle 11 is fundamentally flawed. Local communities in host states anticipate that environmental standards applied by transnational corporations will be equally rigorous wherever in the world businesses operate. Environmental human rights include both procedural rights protections and substantive rights protections, as well as additional protections for vulnerable groups.[103] While substantive environmental rights that may be classified as second-generation social, economic and cultural rights, or third-generation peoples' rights,[104] may arguably be interpreted as requiring progressive realisation by states, this does not mean that businesses with a responsibility to respect human rights and thus to do no harm are off the hook. Indeed, it is precisely when states are failing in their duty to protect human rights by failing to pass and enforce appropriate regulatory standards that the business responsibility to respect rights requires businesses to go beyond strict compliance with domestic host state law and embrace their independent responsibility to respect rights. Importantly, the responsibility of the state and businesses will be separately engaged for breaches of their independent duties.

A different question is whether the 'do no harm' principle, embedded within the second half of Rio Principle 2, applies to home states as well as host states. This principle is widely understood to reflect customary international law, although its precise meaning and scope are contested. The Principle arose initially out of international disputes such as the 1930s Canada–United States international arbitration over air pollution arising from the Trail Smelter in British Columbia, Canada, and harming farmers in the United States.[105] According to Principle 2, while engaging in activities within their jurisdiction or control, states may not cause harm to the territory of other states (transboundary harm) or areas beyond the jurisdiction of any state (global commons harm). This 'do no harm' principle is generally understood as requiring the exercise of due diligence,[106] and provides a basis for the ILC's Prevention Articles and Loss Allocation Principles. An unanswered question is whether the ILC's work, and the 'do no harm' principle more generally, are relevant for what I and others classify

102 Rio Declaration, above n 99, Principle 11.

103 Knox, above n 78.

104 S Bavikatte and T Bennett, 'Community Stewardship: The Foundation of Biocultural Rights' (2015) 6(1) *Journal of Human Rights and the Environment* 7–29.

105 RM Bratspies and RA Miller (eds), *Transboundary Harm in International Law: Lessons from the Trail Smelter Arbitration*, Cambridge University Press, 2006.

106 J Knox, 'The Myth and Reality of Transboundary Environmental Impact Assessment' (2002) 96(2) *American Journal of International Law* 291.

as 'transnational harm' – that is harm arising from foreign direct investment associated with the transfer of potentially hazardous industrial technologies, as found in Amnesty case studies 1–3, as well as to the actual transfer of the hazardous substances, as found in Amnesty case study 4, which can more easily be viewed as a type of transboundary movement.[107] While the ILC initially conceptualised transnational harm as falling within its plan of work, it was ultimately not explicitly included and has been described by Shinya Murase as having 'disappeared' over time.[108] Despite this, the Commentaries of the Loss Allocation Principles frequently reference the Bhopal disaster for support.[109]

Thus, fragmentation issues aside, a key question is whether the focus of the Prevention Articles and Loss Allocation Principles on *transboundary* harm should be understood as limited to situations of physical border-crossing of hazardous *substances* causing harm, or whether it should also include the border-crossing of foreign direct investment and related exports of potentially hazardous *technologies*.[110]

3.2. ILC PREVENTION ARTICLES AND LOSS ALLOCATION PRINCIPLES

The ILC Prevention Articles were designed to address the 'imperative for operators of hazardous activities to take all steps necessary to prevent harm'.[111] Article 1 provides that the Prevention Articles apply to 'activities not prohibited by international law which involve a risk of causing significant transboundary harm through their physical consequences'.[112] Transboundary harm is defined in Article 2(c) as 'harm caused in the territory of or in other places under the jurisdiction or control of a State other than the State of origin, whether or not the States concerned share a common border'.[113] State of origin is defined in Article 2(d) as 'the State in the territory or otherwise under the jurisdiction or control of which the activities referred to in draft Article 1 are planned or are carried out'.[114] Thus the scope of the Prevention Articles is dependent upon

107 Seck, above n 4, 180–81.
108 S Murase, 'Perspectives from International Economic Law on Transnational Environmental Issues' (1995) 253 *Recueil Des Cours* 287, 396–98.
109 SL Seck, *Home State Obligations for the Prevention and Remediation of Transnational Harm: Canada, Global Mining, and Local Communities* (DPhil thesis, York University 2008), p 295. See International Law Commission, above n 9, fnn 415, 468, 473 and 478.
110 This issue is explored at length in Seck, above n 109, pp 290–413.
111 International Law Commission, above n 8, p 377.
112 Ibid p 380.
113 Ibid p 386.
114 Ibid p 386.

understandings of 'territory', 'jurisdiction' and 'control', among other terms. As I have analysed in detail elsewhere, it is possible to argue that transnational harm associated with foreign direct investment in large-scale mining falls within the scope of the Prevention Articles, even if this was not the intention of the drafters.[115] One could then read the Prevention Articles with the understanding that the 'State of origin' could be the home state which serves as the base for foreign direct investment and thus transnational corporate conduct.

The ILC Prevention Articles have been described as a codification of 'pre-existing law on transboundary risk management'.[116] While not overly ambitious, they nevertheless provide useful lessons for a possible business and human rights treaty. Article 3 provides that the state of origin 'shall take all appropriate measures to prevent significant transboundary harm or at any rate to minimize the risk thereof'.[117] This includes an obligation to 'adopt and implement national legislation incorporating accepted international standards'.[118] It is understood as an obligation of 'due diligence' that is 'manifested in reasonable efforts by a State to inform itself of factual and legal components that relate foreseeably to a contemplated procedure and to take appropriate measures in a timely fashion, to address them. Thus States are under an obligation to take *unilateral* measures to prevent significant transboundary harm …' (emphasis added).[119] While the 'operator of an activity is expected to bear the costs of prevention', the state of origin is expected to put in place 'administrative, financial, and monitoring mechanisms' that meet a standard of 'good Government'.[120]

Article 4 addresses the importance of state cooperation in good faith, as the participation of the state likely to be affected is 'indispensable' to enhancing the effectiveness of preventative action.[121] This Article could be seen as promoting communication between home and host states. Articles 5–7 outline regulatory requirements that the state of origin must implement. These include requirements of prior authorisation[122] and prior assessment.[123] Article 8 provides for timely notification of risk of the state likely to be affected, including transmission of all available technical and other relevant information.[124] Articles 9–13 then provide procedures 'essential to balancing the interests of all States concerned',[125]

115 Seck, above, n 109, pp 296–303.
116 Boyle and Chinkin, above n 83, p 198.
117 International Law Commission, above n 8, p 390.
118 Ibid p 391.
119 Ibid p 393.
120 Ibid p 395.
121 Ibid p 396.
122 Ibid p 399 (Art 6).
123 Ibid p 402 (Art 7).
124 Ibid p 406.
125 Ibid p 406.

with factors to consider listed in Article 10, and a requirement in Article 12 that states exchange information concerning the proposed activity.[126]

Importantly, Article 13 contemplates that states shall provide the 'public likely to be affected' with the 'relevant information relating to [the] activity, the risk involved, and the harm which might result and ascertain their views'.[127] This obligation is applicable even if the public is beyond the borders of the state.[128] However, Article 14 provides a narrow exception with regard to national security and industrial secrets, including information protected by intellectual property.[129] Article 15 complements Article 13 by requiring that access to justice be provided in the courts of the state of origin, in keeping with the principle of non-discrimination.[130] However, the Prevention Articles do not impose a requirement that a judicial remedy or other procedure be in place for state nationals in the first place and so this Article must be distinguished from a true right of transnational access to justice.[131] Thus, a state would be in compliance with the Article 15 non-discrimination principle where access to justice is simply unavailable to anyone. The key is that the availability – or unavailability – of access to justice does not distinguish between citizens of the state of origin and the affected state. Additional articles contemplate the importance of emergency preparedness and notifications of emergencies.[132]

The 2006 Loss Allocation Principles were the result of a request that the ILC resume its work on liability 'largely at the behest of developing countries', despite the view of some ILC members and some governments that these were unnecessary due to the existence of the Articles on State Responsibility and the Prevention Articles.[133] The drafting process of the Loss Allocation Principles was politically charged, due in part to state rejection of the possibility of state liability, and the resulting 'pure soft law' text has been described as a 'collective failure of nerve' rather than a 'reasoned outcome'.[134] They are nevertheless – or perhaps for this reason – useful to consider. As noted above, access to justice is contemplated in the Prevention Articles. However, as will be seen, the Loss Allocation Principles consider the importance of remedy more expansively.

---

126 Ibid pp 413–20. See detailed analysis in Seck, above n 109, pp 308–10.

127 Ibid p 422.

128 Ibid p 424 (Commentary to Art 13, para (6)).

129 Ibid p 426. However, the state of origin 'shall cooperate in good faith with the State likely to be affected in providing as much information as possible in the circumstances'.

130 Ibid p 427.

131 See further analysis in Seck, above n 109, p 312.

132 International Law Commission, above n 8, p 429 (Art 16), p 431 (Art 17).

133 AE Boyle, 'Globalising Environmental Liability: the Interplay of National and International Law' (2005) 17 *Journal of Environmental Law* 3, 5; R Lefeber, *Transnational Environmental Interference and the Origin of State Liability*, Kluwer Law International, 1996, pp 190–91.

134 Boyle and Chinkin, above n 83, pp 199–200.

The scope of the Loss Allocation Principles is said to be the same as the scope of the Prevention Articles.[135] 'Victim' is defined as 'any natural or legal person or State that suffers damage',[136] while 'operator' is defined as 'any person in command or control of the activity at the time the incident causing transboundary damage occurs'.[137] According to Principle 3, the purpose of the Loss Allocation Principles is twofold: to 'ensure prompt and adequate compensation to victims of transboundary damage' and to 'preserve and protect the environment in the event of transboundary damage, especially with regard to mitigation of damage to the environment and its restoration and reinstatement'.[138] Accordingly, the Loss Allocation Principles contemplate the imposition of strict liability on the operator 'or, where appropriate, other person or entity', although liability may be limited.[139] Principle 4 contemplates that measures should require the operator or other entity to 'establish and maintain financial security such as insurance, bonds or other financial guarantees to cover claims of compensation' and, in appropriate cases, industry-wide funds should be established at the national level.[140]

Principle 6(1) is the only principle to be drafted using mandatory language and goes beyond the Prevention Articles by requiring states to 'provide their domestic judicial and administrative bodies with the necessary jurisdiction and competence and ensure that these bodies have prompt, adequate and effective remedies available in the event of transboundary damage … '.[141] Non-discrimination is then invoked more meaningfully here, and without prejudice to victims seeking remedies elsewhere, although states are also called upon to provide recourse to expeditious international claims settlement procedures.[142] Principle 7 encourages states to conclude 'specific global, regional or bilateral agreements' in respect of particular categories of hazardous activities, including with them arrangements for industry and/or State funds to provide supplementary compensation'.[143] Finally, Principle 9 provides that each state 'should adopt the necessary legislative, regulatory, and administrative measures to implement' the Principles, and should cooperate to do so.[144]

It is important to consider the relationship between the Prevention Articles, the Loss Allocation Principles and the DARS. According to the Preamble of

135 International Law Commission, above n 9, pp 111–12.
136 Ibid p 122 (Principle 2(f)).
137 Ibid p 122 (Principle 2(g)). Operator is not defined in the Prevention Articles.
138 Ibid p 140.
139 Ibid p 151 (Principle 4(2)).
140 Ibid p 151 (Principle 4(3) and (4)).
141 Ibid p 172.
142 Ibid pp 172–74.
143 Ibid p 180.
144 Ibid pp 181–82.

the Loss Allocation Principles, the Principles are without prejudice to the rules relating to state responsibility, and a claim may lie under those rules in the event of a breach of an obligation of prevention.[145] The 'basic understanding' of the Principles is described as the need to adopt a 'scheme of allocation of loss, spreading the loss among multiple actors, including as appropriate the State', with a 'central theme' being that each state has the freedom to choose 'one option or the other in accordance with its particular circumstances and conditions'.[146] As both the Prevention Articles and Loss Allocation Principles are understood as primary rules, state responsibility may also be invoked 'to implement not only the obligations of the State itself but also the civil responsibility or duty of the operator'.[147]

While the Loss Allocation Principles have been criticised by some as being too weak and not sufficiently reflective of existing international law obligations,[148] they nevertheless provide food for thought as a model for a business and human rights treaty. Several ideas are notable, perhaps especially that specific treaties, whether bilateral, regional or multilateral, be negotiated with regard to specific categories of hazardous activities; and that these treaties contemplate the need for strict civil liability, mandatory insurance and industry-wide supplementary funds.

4. CONCLUSIONS: LESSONS FOR THE TREATY PROCESS

The *Injustice Incorporated* case studies demonstrate that there is no single cause of transnational corporate impunity, but rather it is the result of many failings. The challenge, then, in the design of a business and human rights treaty is how to address these multiple failings in the design of a single treaty. For the purpose of this chapter, the question is whether the work of the ILC in the Prevention Articles and Loss Allocation Principles has anything to offer.

One key finding of the Amnesty case studies is that home and host states have failed to work cooperatively to meet their respective obligations to provide access to effective remedy for victims. Rather, state practice has been both sporadic

145 Ibid pp 111 and 114. This suggests that where a failure of prevention has occurred, recourse to state responsibility is in order; whereas where the obligations of prevention have been complied with yet damage occurs nonetheless, recourse to the Loss Allocation Principles is required. However, the relationship is not entirely clear.

146 Ibid p 112.

147 Ibid pp 118–19.

148 Boyle, above n 133; Boyle and Chinkin, above n 83, pp 198–200. See also the related yet distinct work of the International Law Association, 'Final Report of the Transnational Enforcement of Environmental Law Committee' in *Report of the 72nd Conference held in Toronto 4–8 June, 2006*, London, 2006, p 655. See comparative analysis of the ILA Report in Seck, above n 109, pp 326–29.

and inadequate. In addition, as noted above, the Amnesty report concludes that 'extraterritorial' legal issues such as separate legal personality, limited liability, and jurisdictional hurdles create obstacles to justice. The importance of cooperation between the state of origin and the state likely to be affected is stressed in both the Prevention Articles and the Loss Allocation Principles. This is in keeping with more recent statements by Professor John Knox on the obligations of states to cooperate in the protection of environmental rights, including rights affected by climate change.[149] Importantly, neither the Prevention Articles nor the Loss Allocation Principles conceptualise the solution to transboundary harm as requiring 'extraterritoriality', preferring instead to speak of a dual responsibility to regulate in keeping with duties of international cooperation. The Prevention Articles specifically contemplate that the state of origin shall regulate the industrial activity at issue, which, in a case of transboundary border-crossing pollution harm, would mean the state where the industrial activity is physically located is to regulate in a comprehensive manner.[150] Yet both the Prevention Articles and Loss Allocation Principles also contemplate a regulatory role for the affected state, whether the provision of information to those likely to be affected by environmental harm,[151] or more comprehensively that each state adopt legislative, administrative and regulatory measures necessary to implement the Loss Allocation Principles.[152] The relationship between a home and host state in a transnational foreign direct investment context is, of course, not identical to that of states in the transboundary pollution context, yet the idea that it is normal and essential for more than one state to play a role in addressing the problem at issue is surely an important lesson. The key is to move to a language of shared responsibility and away from the language of extraterritoriality, thereby opening the door to acceptance of the essential nature of the home state regulatory role as a demonstration of responsibility for existing transnational relationships.

A second lesson from the ILC and environmental law more generally is the focus upon the responsibility of 'operators' of hazardous activities, or, where appropriate, other persons or entities.[153] This language gets to the core of who is in control of the industrial activity, potentially overcoming issues of separate legal personality of parent and subsidiary companies in appropriate cases. Moreover, a focus on the operator of an activity moves away from questions surrounding the types of businesses that would be subject to a treaty obligation – for example,

149 International Law Commission, above n 8, Art 4; International Law Commission, above n 9, Principle 9; Knox, above n 78, 18.

150 International Law Commission, above n 8, Arts 5–7.

151 Ibid, Art 13.

152 International Law Commission, above n 9, Principle 9.

153 Ibid, Principle 2. The language of 'owner or operator' is found in some domestic environmental law statutes and has been interpreted to 'include individuals or corporations who exercise control even if title to the site is held by a distinct corporation'. Seck, above n 23, 182.

it would no longer appear relevant whether or not the business is a state-owned enterprise.[154] A related issue is the concern over limited liability being used to restrict the ability of victims to seek compensation for harm by insulating the parent company from liability. Lessons from the Loss Allocation Principles highlight the importance of insurance coverage for hazardous activities, as well as the need for supplementary industry funds.[155] Regulations mandating adequate insurance coverage could easily be incorporated into both home and host state regulation in line with the duty to cooperate to ensure no hazardous activity takes place without it; similarly, the importance of appropriate emergency preparedness and response is something that is contemplated by the ILC, and clearly of relevance to some of the Amnesty case studies, most notably Bhopal.

Another concern raised by the case studies is that of control over information with regard to the nature of hazardous materials being used and lack of access to information by victims in the event of harm. While the focus of the Amnesty report is upon the need for access to information in order to clean up and remedy environmental and health harms, the Prevention Articles stress the importance of participatory processes in environmental decision-making, loosely in line with the three pillars of participatory environmental rights.[156] The importance and content of these rights has been clarified recently by Professor Knox, including the need to respect freedom of expression and the right to protest of environmental human rights defenders, who face extraordinary risks.[157] Again, a key lesson from the ILC is the importance of both home and host states working cooperatively to ensure that procedural decision-making processes are inclusive before operations begin, with information shared at an early stage, and processes put in place to ensure ongoing communication, oversight and emergency preparedness throughout the lifecycle of a project.[158] In this way, problems will not fester (as in Ok Tedi), and if or when accidents happen (as in Bhopal, Cambior), processes and relationships will exist to address problems without the need for recourse to legal sanctions.

An additional lesson arises with regard to the nature of corporate–state relationships that impact the willingness and ability of states to uphold human rights, including the right to remedy. Both the Prevention Articles and

154 This has been an issue of concern with regard to the scope of the mandate of the treaty discussion at the UN Human Rights Council. See D Cassel and A Ramasastry, 'White Paper: Options for a Treaty on Business and Human Rights' (May 2015) 36–38.

155 International Law Commission, above n 9, Principle 4.

156 International Law Commission, above n 8, Arts 5–8, 13 and 15.

157 Knox, above n 78, 8–12.

158 Going beyond the environmental focus of the Prevention Articles, it would be necessary to incorporate free, prior and informed consent of indigenous peoples. This could lead to community/company agreements common in the extractive industries context for example. See J Gathii and IT Odumosu-Ayanu, 'The Turn to Contractual Responsibility in the Global Extractive Industry' (2015) 1 *Business and Human Rights Journal* 69–94.

Loss Allocation Principles emphasise the importance of access to remedy in accordance with the principle of non-discrimination – that is, access to home state courts should be available on equal terms to those within home or host states.[159] Of course, access to remedy must go beyond non-discrimination to mean access to effective remedy. Nevertheless, following the model of the ILC could place home state courts in a key residual role, overcoming challenges faced by host state capacity issues as well as host state reluctance to prosecute. Having said this, the Ok Tedi case study clearly demonstrates that while doctrines such as *forum non conveniens* are often blamed for access to remedy problems, even where it is not a barrier, effective remedy does not necessarily follow.

Notably, Principle 7 of the Loss Allocation Principles specifically contemplates the importance of treaties being developed to address specific issues. Here it is worth revisiting the fourth Amnesty case study, the Trafigura case, which raises distinct issues for it concerns transboundary movements of hazardous wastes rather than transnational movements of foreign direct investment and technologies. Curiously, and unlike the other three case studies, the problem that arose in Trafigura is already subject to multilateral environmental agreements. It is beyond the scope of this chapter to provide a history of the negotiations and controversy over the 1989 Basel Convention on the Control of Transboundary Movements of Hazardous Wastes and their Disposal.[160] This history has been well documented elsewhere, including the concerns expressed by countries of the Global South, which viewed the dumping of hazardous wastes in African countries as a crime and therefore something to be banned, rather than something that should be subject to a notification and consent procedure like the one established in the Basel Convention.[161] For the purpose of this chapter, what is of interest is that in addition to the Convention itself, a Protocol on Liability and Compensation was successfully negotiated and adopted in 1999.[162] However, beyond critiques of the substance of this Protocol is the fact that over 15 years since its negotiation, there are only 11 state parties – all of whom are from the Global South – and so the Protocol is not yet in force, as this requires a minimum of 20 state parties.[163]

---

159 International Law Commission, above n 8, Art 15; International Law Commission, above n 9, Principle 6.

160 Basel Convention on the Control of Transboundary Movements of Hazardous Wastes and their Disposal (adopted 22.03.1989, entered into force 05.05.1992) 1673 UNTS 126, 28 ILM 657.

161 Z Lipman, 'Trade in Hazardous Waste' in S Alam, S Atapattu, C Gonzalez, and J Razzaque (eds), *International Environmental Law and the Global South*, Cambridge University Press, 2015, pp 256, 262–65.

162 Basel Protocol on Liability and Compensation for Damage Resulting from Transboundary Movements of Hazardous Wastes and their Disposal, Basel, 10.12.1999, UN Doc UNEP/CHW.1/WG/1/9/2. See Lipman, above n 161, 268–69.

163 'List of Parties and Signatories', <http://www.basel.int/Countries/StatusofRatifications/TheProtocol/tabid/1345/Default.aspx#note1> accessed 26.05.2017.

This scenario is not uncommon. Principle 13 of the 1992 Rio Declaration calls for states to develop national laws on liability and compensation, and to 'more expeditiously' develop 'international law regarding liability and compensation for adverse effects of environmental damage caused by activities within their jurisdiction or control to areas beyond their jurisdiction'. Yet states have failed to do this in many contexts, and even where they have negotiated a treaty, a lack of widespread ratification, among other issues, has raised concerns that these treaties may not in fact be the best way to address the liability and compensation problem.[164] Ultimately, it is wise to remember that the adoption and negotiation of a text – whether a progressive codification of customary international law or a newly agreed treaty text – is only the first step.

Moreover, even well-ratified and implemented treaties will not solve problems if not appropriately designed. A different problem identified in the case studies that is not addressed by either the Prevention Articles or the Loss Allocation Principles is the problem of corruption at multiple levels, inhibiting both the awarding of compensation and its delivery once awarded. This may be surprising given the prevalence of anti-corruption conventions.[165] It is unclear, however, whether the explanation lies in the fact that implementation and enforcement of these state obligations has only recently begun to manifest in earnest, or whether the nature of the conventions misses the kinds of corruption experienced by human rights victims seeking access to remedy, as opposed to that facing business enterprises who seek a level playing field for commercial transactions. Whatever path is taken in the development of a business and human rights treaty, the work of the ILC on the prevention and loss allocation of transboundary harm and related treaty developments provides insights into what may be possible, and what may be required for an effective regime to prevent and remedy the kinds of harms highlighted in the Amnesty case studies.

---

164 J Brunnée, 'Of Sense and Sensibility: Reflections on International Liability Regimes as Tools for Environmental Protection' (2004) 53(2) *International and Comparative Law Quarterly* 351; A Daniel, 'Civil Liability Regimes as a Complement to Multilateral Environmental Agreements: Sound International Policy or False Comfort?' (2003) 12(3) *Review of European, Comparative & International Law* 225.

165 Convention on Combatting Bribery of Foreign Public Officials in International Business Transactions (adopted 21.11.1997, entered into force 15.02.1999); United Nations Convention Against Corruption (adopted 31.10.2003, entered into force 14.12.2005) 43 ILM 37. See also SL Seck, 'Unilateral Home State Regulation: Imperialism or Tool for Subaltern Resistance?' (2008) 46 *Osgoode Hall Law Journal* 565–603.

CONCLUSION

Jernej Letnar Černič and Nicolás Carrillo-Santarelli

What the future of business and human rights will be has been one of the most exciting debates in today's global arena. Victims from all parts of the world have been demanding greater corporate accountability for human rights and more effective and efficient access to justice. Rather than presenting one single conclusion reflecting an agreement of the authors of the different chapters on some ideas, we consider it appropriate to acknowledge that the different perspectives found therein reflect the ongoing diplomatic and academic discussions on central aspects, ranging from questions as to whether it is possible or necessary to adopt the proposed treaty on business and human rights, to those related to the content that such instrument or alternative sources of hard or soft law should include, which categories of corporations they ought to address, and which developments taking place in other normative regimes or regional systems can inspire normative processes. It is necessary to acknowledge and allow for a pluralistic debate on the future of business and human rights.

Nevertheless, such disagreements should not be construed as absolute, insofar as there is a public consensus that whatever normative development ends up occurring and succeeding – be it new negotiations or simply the concrete implementation of the UN Guiding Principles – the protection of individuals from corporate abuses should be at the centre of that dynamic and its underlying policies and aspirations.

Granted, some actors, including perhaps those representing corporate and economic interests from certain State delegations and other subjects, may have an interest in thwarting a treaty negotiation without openly expressing why, while publicly declaring that they deem a treaty inconvenient for a variety of fabricated reasons. Some have even argued that the treaty process has undermined the global 'consensus' reached at the time of the adoption of the Guiding Principles. But others legitimately and honestly consider that the adoption of a treaty could hinder or weaken existing guarantees and their natural evolution.

Conversely, some argue that the regulation of direct corporate obligations, or a clarification of State duties – extraterritorial and otherwise –, are necessary for the protection of individuals to be strengthened. This is so given the gaps and limitations of prevalent contemporary human rights assumptions, still largely based as they are on State obligations and voluntary corporate standards. After all, States may comply with the former by behaving diligently, but individuals may still be victimised and receive no protection, given both the problems of territorial jurisdiction and the influence of actors as transnational and other corporations. These actors may circumvent controls in the absence of an international harmonisation of regulations given their flexibility in operating, and capability of operating in multinational groups and of benefiting from doctrines such as the corporate veil.

In any case, whether because the purpose of effectively protecting individuals from corporate participation in abuses makes it necessary to fill gaps or simply to clarify existing norms, it is undeniable that the activities of businesses not only sometimes have a negative impact on the enjoyment of human rights through abusive conduct – which is legally relevant and requires a legal response – but are also embedded in dynamics that make it difficult for there to be an effective protection of certain victims, especially when compounded with questions of State jurisdiction, remedies, and their respective limits.

Granted, a treaty is not necessarily the only way in which those issues can be addressed, as some chapters reveal, it being possible to resort to Declarations or other alternatives, as customary law, if political machinations end up forestalling the treaty negotiations. However, the potential treaty would have the benefit of being hard law based and generating a 'common' binding instrument, and its existence need by no means imply that the Guiding Principles would be undermined and additional developments cannot take place in the future. Indeed, it could complement, rather than replace, the Guiding Principles, and could insist on States retaining their obligations. Thus, in no way does the adoption of a treaty necessarily presuppose that those stepping stones would be undermined. As mentioned at the outset of this conclusion, what is unquestionable is that individuals should be placed at the centre of a *human* rights analysis of protection from corporate conduct. Given the apparent limitations of existing standards – either because they actually have gaps, or because some authorities and participants in international and domestic legal processes misinterpret them, making them say things on corporate responsibility or other aspects not necessarily required by them – additional efforts must be made in order to address an undeniable contemporary problem of our societies. Those hurt when their labour or other rights are denied, who have so often failed to obtain justice as a result of arguments based on lack of responsibility in supply chain scenarios or an alleged lack of international legal obligations of businesses, deserve more and have a dignity that is above and beyond profit interests. The debate on the future of business and human rights should not automatically, without any arguments, exclude any proposal or initiative, including domestic ones, that may also have an ulterior positive impact on international developments.[1] All in all, corporations are obliged to respect, protect and fulfil human rights of individuals, minorities and indigenous peoples.[2] Simultaneously, States are obliged to establish genuine and effective access to judicial protections and guarantee that corporations will respect and, sometimes, protect human rights wherever they operate. Ultimately, a lot depends on international co-operation and mutual assistance between States to effectively address corporate violations. De Schutter argues that 'a reinforcement of inter-State co-operation, based on the mutual trust of States in their respective legal systems when they seek to address human rights violations by corporate actors, is the price to pay for ensuring effective access to remedies for victims of transnational corporate harms'.[3]

Corporations (and their legal counsel in the elite worldwide corporate law or consulting firms) are aware that the regulatory environment is still weak in the field of business and human rights. They know that they do not face any substantial risks from victims for their alleged involvement in corporate human rights violations. This is because (a) few effective judicial mechanisms for enforcing corporate accountability exist, and (b) where such judicial forums are available, victims often face almost insurmountable challenges in providing sufficient evidence that corporations have violated their human rights. This must stop.

1. ACTOR-RELATED SCOPE

The actor-related scope of the proposed treaty should not limit itself to transnational corporations, but must cover any kind of corporations, whether foreign, domestic, transnational, private or State owned. It is not entirely clear why the Ecuadorian proposal omits all corporations which are not transnational. Possible reasons may be found in the domestic problems with ensuring effective human rights protections in their domestic settings. Yet, since all businesses have the capacity to participate in abuses, the treaty on business and human rights should include and cover all corporations, not merely transnational

1 See J Letnar Černič, 'Business & Human Rights: How Should We Move Forward?' Business and Human Rights Resource Centre, 18.11.2015, <https://business-humanrights.org/en/business-human-rights-how-should-we-move-forward> accessed 20.05.2017. This chapter is a considerably extended and updated version of J Letnar Černič, 'Desarrollos internacionales recientes en el ámbito de los derechos humanos y las empresas' in H Cantú Rivera (ed) *Derechos Humanos y Empresas : Reflexiones desde América Latina* (San José, C.R.: Instituto Interamericano de Derechos Humanos, 2017), pp. 137–156.

2 See N Carrillo-Santarelli, 'Corporate Human Rights Obligations: Controversial but Necessary', Business and Human Rights Resource Centre, 24.08.2015, <https://business-humanrights.org/en/corporate-human-rights-obligations-controversial-but-necessary> accessed 20.05.2017.

3 O De Schutter, 'Towards a New Treaty on Business and Human Rights' (2016) 1(1) *Business and Human Rights Journal* 41–67, 67.

corporations. Several disadvantages have been identified against focusing only upon the activities of transnational corporations. Ruggie has argued that 'a growing number of local companies conduct business across borders, and thus may be said to have a transnational character'.[4] Ruggie has therefore rightly recognised that the approach of only addressing transnational corporations is erroneous.[5] One can concur with the previous ideas as the human rights of individuals are affected on a daily basis by the business operations of both local and transnational corporations. A UN treaty would nonetheless be welcomed as it would provide an incentive for States to improve the regulation of domestic, foreign and transnational corporations. Their regulation nonetheless depends upon – and goes hand in hand with – the quality of domestic protection of human rights, including domestic rules, the independence and impartiality of the judiciary, and the fight against corruption. However, it would be utopian to expect that the mere adoption of any international Convention would effectively address corporations if domestic systems are not capable of addressing their violations. That being said, such adoption could create common standards, increase the likelihood of legal action against corporations given the existence of an international norm, and complement voluntary standards.

2. SUBJECT-RELATED SCOPE

Which rights should the treaty cover? Business activities are often complex and affect all areas of human activity. It would seem logical, then, that the treaty can potentially also cover every aspect of human rights that corporations can infringe. Businesses can negatively affect all human rights, ranging from civil and political to economic, social and cultural rights; and from individual to collective rights. As corporations are artificial entities, some limitations may arise concerning certain rights, particularly when a corporate culture has been developed within large and complex corporate structures, in which no individual can be identified. If the interested groups proceed with the idea of the treaty, it would be preferable for it to cover a wide range of potential human rights abuses rather than focusing only on a limited set of rights, forbidding at the very least participation in abuses of rights enshrined in the so-called International Bill of Human Rights.

In addition to the previous questions, it can be discussed whether the treaty should include internationally recognised human rights stemming from recent UN human rights Conventions, such as the Convention on the Rights of All

---

4 JG Ruggie, 'Quo Vadis? Unsolicited Advice to Business and Human Rights Treaty Sponsors', 09.09.2014, <http://www.ihrb.org/commentary/quo-vadis-unsolicited-advice-business.html> accessed 20.05.2017. See also: JG Ruggie, 'Life in the Global Public Domain: Response to Commentaries on the UN Guiding Principles and the Proposed Treaty on Business and Human Rights', <http://business-humanrights.org/en/binding-treaty/latest-news-on-proposed-binding-treaty> accessed 20.05.2017.

5 Ruggie, above n 4.

Migrant Workers and Members of Their Families. The benefit of this would be that the treaty would address contemporary challenges recognised by those who drafted and endorsed those instruments. On the other hand, replicating the content of those treaties that lack wide participation and support, or that fail to reflect customary law, may discourage wide participation and mean that the future treaty is without wide support.

That being said, to select only a few rights may make the treaty redundant or open to arbitrary discretion. By concentrating only on the most heinous human rights abuses, which some consider are already implicitly forbidden, does not add much. Moreover, referring to them may make the treaty locate itself in a never-ending discussion about the hierarchy of rights in international law and the status of peremptory norms, which would get the treaty nowhere. At this stage of development, the potential contents of such a treaty are highly speculative as no comprehensive document to this effect is available.[6] International human rights treaties traditionally focus on protecting a certain right or rights, such as, for example, the Convention against Torture and Other Cruel, Inhuman or Degrading Treatment or Punishment,[7] or protecting certain vulnerable groups, such as the International Convention on the Protection of the Rights of All Migrant Workers and Members of Their Families.[8] It seems that any treaty on business and human rights would not be able to follow any of the traditional approaches as it would cover a highly complex subject area involving many different rights and fundamental freedoms. Any proposed treaty would therefore have to employ a wide range of strategies and would (as noted above) include many (but not necessarily all) human rights, and should benefit all individuals and vulnerable groups.

As such, it would be appropriate to employ a holistic approach with regard to the drafting of such a treaty, concentrating on rights, individuals and groups concurrently and identifying novel approaches. For these reasons, Mégret observes that 'an international treaty on multinational corporations would be an almost unprecedented treaty focused not on proclaiming certain rights or protecting certain groups (as has traditionally been the case), but on imposing obligations upon a certain category of actors'.[9] It is not clear whether this is

6 FIDH has formed an expert group on the treaty initiative, 30.01.2015, <https://www.fidh.org/International-Federation-for-Human-Rights/globalisation-human-rights/business-and-human-rights/16868-fidh-and-escr-net-new-joint-treaty-initiative> accessed 20.05.2017.

7 Convention against Torture and Other Cruel, Inhuman or Degrading Treatment or Punishment, GA Res. 39/46, [annex, 39 UN GAOR Supp. (No. 51) at 197, UN Doc. A/39/51 (1984)], entered into force 26.06.1987.

8 International Convention on the Protection of the Rights of All Migrant Workers and Members of Their Families, GA Res. 45/158, annex, 45 UN GAOR Supp. (No. 49A) at 262, UN Doc. A/45/49 (1990), entered into force 01.07.2003

9 F Mégret, 'Would a Treaty Be All It Is Made Up to Be?', 04.02.2015, <http://jamesgstewart.com/would-a-treaty-be-all-it-is-made-up-to-be/> accessed 20.05.2017.

the preferred strategy of proponents of a treaty, as obligations traditionally are correlated to and derived from the conferral of rights to their holders, namely individuals. At least at this stage, concentrating only on the obligations of corporations would be far fetched and therefore such proposals (if they indeed exist) have to be taken with pinch of salt. It seems unclear which duty-holders the proposed treaty would include. It is improbable (but by no means impossible or unnecessary) that the treaty will focus directly on corporations (although it should at least acknowledge core direct obligations of the latter), and may most likely impose obligations on States, in turn, to impose obligations on corporate actors in their domestic legal orders. If the treaty were to focus only on corporations, further difficulties would arise concerning the enforcement of the obligations of those duty-bearers. As the traditional method of enforcement is currently implemented through a solely State-based system, eliminating States from the equation would be very complicated. That being said, such a tradition must by no means always be followed, and this novel field requires imagination and efforts to better protect victims of corporations, the reason why stronger, even direct supervision mechanisms to govern their conduct are encouraged. On the other hand, State responsibilities, of an extraterritorial nature or regarding multinational groups, require clarification and development in the current context.

We can imagine what kind of problems could arise if the binding obligations of corporations existed without any enforcement mechanism at a national or international level. In any case, if direct obligations are regulated in the end, this would not be unheard of under international law, as the existence of non-State obligations in international humanitarian law demonstrates. In addition to imposing obligations on them, an alternative would be that of allowing businesses to commit to the treaty. It is not very common for actors other than States to become parties to international treaties and Conventions. Surely any proposed treaty could include various actors among its duty-bearers, as certain currently existing treaties already do. One example is the International Convention on the Protection and Promotion of the Rights and Dignity of Persons with Disabilities, which mentions several actors that are obliged to follow its obligations.[10] However, even this Convention employs a very traditional approach to a large extent, regulating other actors through States. For instance, its Article 4 provides in paragraph 1 that:

> States Parties undertake to ensure and promote the full realization of all human rights and fundamental freedoms for all persons with disabilities without discrimination of any kind on the basis of disability. To this end, States Parties undertake … (e) To take

[10] International Convention on the Protection and Promotion of the Rights and Dignity of Persons with Disabilities, GA Res. 61/106, Annex I, UN GAOR, 61st Sess., Supp. No. 49, at 65, UN Doc. A/61/49 (2006), entered into force 03.08.2008.

> all appropriate measures to eliminate discrimination on the basis of disability by any person, organization or private enterprise.[11]

Yet, the aforementioned Convention provides a clue, insofar as it permits certain international organisations to be directly bound by it, as Article 44 demonstrates. Thus, a Treaty on Business and Human Rights can likewise bind both States and corporations, if the drafters so decide. Mégret further observers that '[i]t would therefore be more a treaty on obligations than on rights, even though the implementation of the obligations would be presumed to lead to the fulfilment of the rights' and he proposes that there should be a 'regulatory division of labour between human rights treaties ... and implementing instruments'.[12] He therefore concludes that 'the move to a treaty is a move to "normalise" the regulation of corporations within the vernacular of public international law and away from the sort of "private ordering" that has become a hallmark of the regulation of corporations today'.[13] However, an alternative approach would be to move from a top-down State enforcement system to a bottom-up approach to enforcement involving civil society groups and other social movements. With such approaches, questions arise over how compatible they are with the rule of law, fair trial guarantees and the legal certainty principles of every State based on the respect of law. What is clear is that such bottom-up approaches should not cause new violations or drive foreign investment from already deprived States.

Why, then, do human rights advocates insist on opening discussion for the eventual adoption of the treaty? The answer does not lie exclusively in the added value (which could be statistically measured) that such a treaty would bring, but is also related to the symbolic meaning that its adoption would bring to local communities and individual victims of corporate human rights violations and to the expressive effects it can generate – including having an impact on corporate culture, which is crucial for the field.

Considering the advantages of the pluralistic debates, the Draft Treaty should therefore concentrate on the 10 essential points contained in the following checklist:

1. clarification of State obligations to respect, protect and fulfil human rights against negative corporate conduct;
2. extraterritorial obligations of States to control their own corporate nationals;
3. clear specification of corporate human rights obligations and obligations of States to implement them in domestic systems;

---

11 Mégret, above n 9.

12 ibid.

13 ibid.

4. the nature of corporate human rights obligations (corporate obligations to respect, protect and fulfil);
5. the draft proposal should address all human rights in the International Bill of Human Rights;
6. strict corporate exercise of due diligence and human rights impact assessment;
7. clear specification of corporate civil, criminal and administrative accountability, including through the control of supply chain;
8. effective and efficient victims' access to remedy;
9. independent, impartial and fair proceedings examining corporate accountability for human rights;
10. appropriate sanctions for corporations, their directors and employees and establishing system for victims' compensation.

All initiatives in business and human rights, however, should aim to improve victims' access to remedy. The debate on the Business and Human Rights Treaty can serve to propel the improvement of domestic regulation and generate a level playing field across countries, ensuring that certain conduct is forbidden everywhere. Moreover, previous research has shown that the human rights treaties can make a difference in State performance.[14]

3. FINAL REMARKS

In the end, corporations are undeniably participants on the world stage. They often have an economic leverage that challenges that of many States, and may defy local attempts at controlling them to prevent or respond to their abuses. While they can make a significant contribution to the enjoyment of human rights with breakthrough technologies, employment and in other ways, their profitability cannot be treated as an end in itself and it is important that law, which has a functional and constructed nature, ensures that the guarantees granted to businesses for legitimate reasons are not perverted, leading to an abuse of rights. After all, law must respect human beings at all times, and if the regulation of businesses is deficient in this regard due to excessive benefits given to them or gaps, it must be amended. Moreover, corporations are currently undeniably global actors, and even local ones can have a reach abroad through their operations. Given how domestic efforts have so often been non-existent or insufficient, it is important for international law to require them and to complement them in a multi-level and subsidiary way, for the sake of human beings, who ought to be treated as the protagonists in discourses on business and human rights.

---

[14] OA Hathaway, 'Do Human Rights Treaties Make a Difference?' (2002) 111(8) *Yale Law Journal* 1935–2042.

INDEX

www.ingramcontent.com/pod-product-compliance
Ingram Content Group UK Ltd.
Pitfield, Milton Keynes, MK11 3LW, UK
UKHW051920100926
8556IPUK00021B/1289